Contents

Preface

This book is about MIPS, the cult hit among the mid-80s crop of RISC CPU designs. MIPS is the best-selling RISC CPU, found everywhere from Sony and Nintendo games machines, through Cisco routers, up to Silicon Graphics supercomputers. With the RISC architectures now under furious assault from the ubiquitous and brilliantly developed x86, MIPS may be the only one of those original RISC CPU designs to end the century turning a healthy profit.

RISC is a useful acronym and not just marketing hype; it usefully encapsulates the many common features of a group of computer architectures invented in the 80s and designed for efficient pipelined implementation. The acronym CISC is much more troublesome, because it really refers to all that is not RISC. I'll use it in a narrower sense, to encapsulate the non-RISCness of the 68000, x86, and other pre-1982 architectures that were designed with microcoded implementations in mind.

This book is for programmers, and that's the test we've used to decide what gets included—if a programmer might see it, or is likely to be interested, it's here. That means we don't get to discuss, for example, the strange system interfaces with which MIPS has tortured two generations of hardware design engineers. And your operating system may hide many of the details we talk about here; there is many an excellent programmer who thinks that C is quite low level enough, portability a blessing, and detailed knowledge of the architecture irrelevant. But sometimes you do need to get down to the nuts and bolts—and human beings are born curious as to how bits of the world work.

A result of this orientation is that we'll tend to be rather informal when describing things that may not be familiar to a software engineer—particularly the inner workings of the CPU—but we'll get much more terse and technical when we're dealing with the stuff programmers have met before, such as registers, instructions, and how data is stored in memory.

We'll assume some familiarity and comfort with the C language. Much of the reference material in the book uses C fragments as a way of compressing operation descriptions, particularly in the chapters on the details of the instruction set and assembler language.

Some parts of the book are targeted at readers who've seen CISC (i.e., 680x0 or x86) assembly language, because the ingenuity and peculiarity of the MIPS architecture shows up best from that viewpoint. But if you are not familiar with CISC assembly language, it's not a disaster.

Mostly, the people who need to know a CPU at the level of detail described here are either operating system gurus or are working with embedded systems. The broadest definition of the term *embedded system* is every use of a computer that doesn't look like a computer. The unifying feature of such systems is that the operating system (if any) does not hide the workings of the CPU from the programmer. MIPS CPUs are used for a huge range of applications, from writing games through industrial control. But that doesn't mean that this book is just a reference manual: to keep an architecture in your head means coming to understand it in the round. I also hope the book will interest students of programming (at college or enrolled in the school of life) who want to understand a modern CPU architecture all the way through.

If you plan to read this book straight through from front to back, you will expect to find a progression from overview to detail, and you won't be disappointed. But you'll also find some progression through history; the first time we talk about a concept we'll usually focus on its first version. Hennessy and Patterson call this "learning through evolution" and what's good enough for them is certainly good enough for me.

So we start in Chapter 1 with some history and background, and set MIPS in context by discussing the technological concerns and ideas that were uppermost in the minds of its inventors. Then in Chapter 2 we discuss the characteristics of the MIPS machine language that follow from their approach.

To keep the instruction set simple, we leave out the details of processor control until Chapter 3, which introduces the ugly but eminently practical system that allows MIPS CPUs to deal with their caches, exceptions and startup, and memory management. Those last three topics, respectively, become the subjects of Chapters 4 through 6.

The MIPS architecture has been careful to separate out the part of the instruction set that deals with floating-point numbers. That separation allows MIPS CPUs to be built with various levels of floating-point support, from none at all through partial implementations to somewhere near the state of the art using four generations of hardware. So we have also separated out the floating-point functions, and we keep them back until Chapter 7.

Up to this point, the chapters follow a reasonable sequence for getting to know MIPS. The remaining chapters change gear and are more like reference manuals or example-based tutorials.

In Chapter 8 we go through the whole machine instruction set; the intention is to be precise but much more terse than the standard MIPS reference works—we cover in ten pages what takes a hundred in other sources. Chapter 9 describes assembly language programming and is more like a programming manual. This is a change of style from the rest of the book, but there has never been a proper assembly language manual for MIPS. Anyone programming at the assembler level will find the rest of the book relevant.

Chapter 10 is written for people who are already familiar with programming in C and focuses on aspects of C programming where the MIPS architecture shows through; examples include memory organization and parameter passing as implemented by MIPS compilers. Chapter 11 is a checklist with helpful hints for those of you who have to port software between another CPU and a MIPS CPU.

Chapter 12 is a collection of annotated pieces of real software, picked for their relevance to the themes of this book. Understanding real software can be hard going, but readers embarking on a challenging MIPS software project may find this chapter useful, both as a style guide and as a checklist.

Appendices A (on instruction timing), B (on assembler language syntax), and C (on object code) contain highly technical information that I felt shouldn't be completely omitted, although not many of you will need to refer to this material. Appendix D is the place where you can find late-breaking news about the MIPS architecture; you can read about MIPS16, MDMX, and the MIPS V extensions to the instruction set.

You will also find at the end of this book a glossary of terms—a good place to look for specialized or unfamiliar usage and acronyms—and a list of books, papers, and on-line references for further reading.

Style and Limits

Every book reflects its author, so we'd better make a virtue of it.

Since some of you will be students, I wondered whether I should distinguish general use from MIPS use. I decided not to; I am specific except where it costs the reader nothing to be general. I also try to be concrete rather than abstract. I don't worry about whatever meaning terms like TLB have in the wider industry but do explain them in a MIPS context. Human beings are great generalizers, and this is unlikely to damage your learning much.

This book has been at least seven years in gestation, though it didn't always have this form. The author has been working around the MIPS architecture since 1986. From 1988 onward I was giving training courses on the MIPS architecture to some customers, and the presentation slides began to take on some of the structure of this book. In 1993 I gathered them together to make a software manual for IDT to publish as a part of its MIPS documentation package, but the manual was specific to IDT's R3051 family components and left out all sorts of interesting details. Over 1995–96, this book grew to include 64-bit CPUs and to cover all the ground that seems relevant.

The MIPS story continues; if it did not, we'd only be writing this book for historians and Morgan Kaufmann wouldn't be very interested in publishing it.

Since the process of writing and reviewing books is lengthy, we have to define a suitable cut-off point. MIPS developments that were announced too late are not included in the main text of this book. But we have updated Appendix D at the last minute to reflect as many as possible of the more recent developments.

Conventions

A quick note on the typographical conventions used in this book:

- Type in this font (Minion) is running text.
- Type in this font (Futura) is a sidebar.
- **Type in this font (Courier bold) is used for assembler code and MIPS register names.**
- Type in this font (Courier) is used for C code and hexadecimals.
- *Type in this font (Minion italic, small) is used for hardware signal names.*
- Code in italics indicates variables.

Acknowledgments

The themes in this book have followed me through my computing career. Mike Cole got me excited about computing, and I've been trying to emulate his skill in picking out good ideas ever since. Many people at Whitechapel Workstations taught me something about computer architecture and about how to design hardware—Bob Newman and Rick Filipkiewicz probably the most. I also have to thank Whitechapel's salesperson Dave Gravell for originally turning me on to MIPS. My fellow engineers at Algorithmics (Chris Dearman, Rick Filipkiewicz, Gerald Onions, Nigel Stephens, and Chris Shaw) have to be doubly thanked, both for all I've learned through innumerable discussions, arguments, and designs and for putting up with the book's competition for my time.

I've worn out more than one editor at Morgan Kaufmann: Bruce Spatz originally encouraged me to start and Jennifer Mann took over; Denise Penrose has guided it through to publication. Many thanks are due to the reviewers who've read chapters over a long period of time: Phil Bourekas of Integrated Device Technology, Inc.; Thomas Daniel of the LSI Logic Corporation; Mike Murphy of Silicon Graphics, Inc.; and David Nagle of Carnegie Mellon University.

Nigel Stephens of Algorithmics wrote the original versions of parts of Chapter 9 and the appendices about assembler language syntax and object code. He is not responsible for any errors in this material that I may have inadvertently introduced.

1

RISCs and MIPS

MIPS is the most elegant among the effective RISC architectures; even the competition thinks so, as evidenced by the strong MIPS influence to be seen in later architectures like DEC's Alpha and HP's Precision. Elegance by itself doesn't get you far in a competitive marketplace, but MIPS microprocessors have usually managed to be among the fastest of each generation by remaining among the simplest.

Relative simplicity was a commercial necessity for MIPS, which spun off from an academic project as a small design group using multiple semiconductor partners to make and market the chips. As a result the architecture has the largest range of active manufacturers in the industry—working from ASIC cores (LSI Logic, Toshiba, Philips, NEC) through low-cost CPUs (IDT, LSI) and from low-end 64-bit (IDT, NKK, NEC) to the top (NEC, Toshiba, and IDT).

At the low end the CPU is 1.5 sq mm (rapidly disappearing from sight in the "system on a chip"); at the high end the R10000 is nearly an inch square and generates 30W of heat—and when first launched was probably the fastest CPU on the planet. And although MIPS looks like an outsider, sales volumes seem healthy enough: 44M MIPS CPUs were shipped in 1997, mostly into embedded applications.

The MIPS CPU is one of the RISC CPUs, born out of a particularly fertile period of academic research and development. RISC (reduced instruction set computer) is an attractive acronym that, like many such, probably obscures reality more than it reveals it. But it does serve as a useful tag for a number of new CPU architectures launched between 1986 and 1989, which owe their remarkable performance to ideas developed a few years earlier by a couple of seminal research projects. Someone commented that "a RISC is any computer architecture defined after 1984"; although meant as a jibe at the industry's use of the acronym, the comment is also true—no computer defined after 1984 can afford to ignore the RISC pioneers' work.

One of these pioneering projects was the MIPS project at Stanford. The project name MIPS (named for the key phrase microcomputer without interlocked pipeline stages) is also a pun on the familiar unit "millions of instructions per second." The Stanford group's work showed that pipelining, although a well-known technique, had been drastically underexploited by earlier architectures and could be much better used, particularly when combined with 1980 silicon design.

1.1 Pipelines

Once upon a time in a small town in the north of England, there was Evie's fish and chip shop. Inside, each customer got to the head of the queue and asked for his or her meal (usually fried cod, chips, mushy peas,[1] and a cup of tea). Then each customer waited for the plate to be filled before going to sit down.

Evie's chips were the best in town, and every market day the lunch queue stretched out of the shop. So when the clog shop next door shut down, Evie rented it and doubled the number of tables. But they couldn't fill them! The queue outside was as long as ever, and the busy townsfolk had no time to sit over their cooling tea.

They couldn't add another serving counter; Evie's cod and Bert's chips were what made the shop. But then they had a brilliant idea. They lengthened the counter and Evie, Bert, Dionysus, and Mary stood in a row. As customers came in, Evie gave them a plate with their fish, Bert added the chips, Dionysus spooned out the mushy peas, and Mary poured the tea and took the money. The customers kept walking; as one customer got his peas, the next was already getting chips and the one after that fish. Less hardy folk don't eat mushy peas— but that's no problem, those customers just got nothing but a vacant smile from Dionysus.

The queue shortened and soon they bought the shop on the other side as well for extra table space....

That's a pipeline. Divide any repetitive job into a number of sequential parts and arrange that the work moves past the workers, with each specialist doing his or her part for each unit of work in turn. Although the total time any customer spends being served has gone up, there are four customers being served at once and about three times as many customers being served in that market day lunch hour. Figure 1.1 shows Evie's organization, as drawn by her son Einstein in a rare visit to non-virtual reality.[2]

Seen as a collection of instructions in memory, a program ready to run doesn't look much like a queue of customers. But when you look at it from the CPU's point of view, things change. The CPU fetches each instruction from

---

1. Non-English readers should probably not inquire further into the nature of this delicacy.

2. It looks to me as if Einstein has been reading books on computer science.

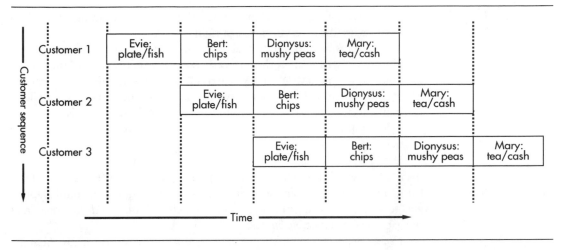

FIGURE 1.1   Evie's fish shop pipeline

memory, decodes it, finds any operands it needs, performs the appropriate action, and stores any results—and then it goes and does the same thing all over again. The program waiting to be run is a queue of instructions waiting to flow through the CPU one at a time.

The various different jobs required to deal with each instruction already require different specialized chunks of logic inside the CPU, so building a pipeline doesn't even make the CPU much more complicated; it just makes it work harder.

The use of pipelining is not new with RISC microprocessors. What makes the difference is the redesign of everything—starting with the instruction set—to make the pipeline more efficient.[1] So how do you make a pipeline efficient? Actually, that's probably the wrong question. The right one is, what makes a pipeline inefficient?

1.1.1   *What Makes a Pipeline Inefficient?*

It's not good if one stage takes much longer than the others. The organization of Evie's shop depends on Mary's ability to pour tea with one hand while giving change with the other—if Mary takes longer than the others, the whole queue will have to slow down to match her.

In a pipeline, you try to make sure that every stage takes roughly the same amount of time. A circuit design often gives you the opportunity to trade

---

1. The first RISC in this sense was probably the CDC6600, designed by Seymour Cray in the 70s, but the idea didn't catch on at that time. However, this is straying into the history of computer architecture, and if you like this subject you'll surely want to read (Hennessy and Patterson 1996).

the complexity of logic off against its speed, so designers can assign work to different stages until everything is just right.

The hard problem is not difficult actions, it's awkward customers. Back in the chip shop Cyril is often short of cash, so Evie won't serve him until Mary has counted his money. When Cyril arrives, he's stuck at Evie's position until Mary has finished with the three previous customers and can check his pile of old bent coins. Cyril is trouble because when he comes in he needs a resource (Mary's counting) that is being used by previous customers. He's a *resource conflict*.

Daphne and Lola always come in together (in that order) and share their meals. Lola won't have chips unless Daphne gets some tea (too salty without something to drink). Lola waits on tenterhooks in front of Bert until Daphne gets to Mary, and so a gap appears in the pipeline. This is a *dependency* (and the gap is called a *pipeline bubble*).

Not all dependencies are a problem. Frank always wants exactly the same meal as Fred, but he can follow him down the counter anyway—if Fred gets chips, Frank gets chips....

If you could get rid of awkward customers, you could make a more efficient pipeline. This is hardly an option for Evie, who has to make her living in a town of eccentrics. Intel is faced with much the same problem: The appeal of its CPUs relies on the customer being able to go on running all that old software. But with a new CPU you get to define the instruction set, and you can define many of the awkward customers out of existence. In Section 1.2 we'll show how MIPS did that, but first we'll come back to computer hardware in general with a discussion of caching.

1.1.2   *The Pipeline and Caching*

We said earlier that efficient pipeline operation requires every stage to take the same amount of time. But a 1996 CPU can add two 64-bit numbers about 10 times quicker than it can fetch a piece of data from memory.

So effective pipelining relies on another technique to speed most memory accesses by a factor of 10—the use of *caches*. A cache is a small, very fast, local memory that holds copies of memory data. Each piece of data is kept with a record of its main memory address (the *cache tag*) and when the CPU wants data the cache gets searched and, if the requisite data is available, it's sent back quickly. Since we've no way to guess what data the CPU might be about to use, the cache merely keeps copies of data the CPU has had to fetch from main memory in the recent past; data is discarded from the cache when its space is needed for more data arriving from memory.

Even a simple cache will provide the data the CPU wants more than 90% of the time, so the pipeline design need only allow enough time to fetch data from the cache: A cache miss is a relatively rare event and we can just stop the CPU when it happens.

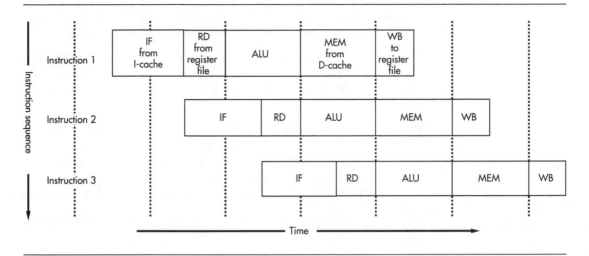

FIGURE 1.2   MIPS five-stage pipeline

The MIPS architecture was planned with separate instruction and data caches, so it can fetch an instruction and read or write a memory variable simultaneously.

CISC architectures have caches too, but they're most often afterthoughts, fitted in as a feature of the memory system. A RISC architecture makes more sense if you regard the caches as very much part of the CPU and tied firmly into the pipeline.

1.2   The MIPS Five-Stage Pipeline

The MIPS architecture is made for pipelining, and Figure 1.2 shows the pipeline of most MIPS CPUs. So long as the CPU runs from the cache, the execution of every MIPS instruction is divided into five phases (called *pipestages*), with each pipestage taking a fixed amount of time. The fixed amount of time is usually a processor clock cycle (though some actions take only half a clock, so the MIPS five-stage pipeline actually occupies only four clock cycles).

All instructions are rigidly defined so they can follow the same sequence of pipestages, even where the instruction does nothing at some stage. The net result is that, so long as it keeps hitting the cache, the CPU starts an instruction every clock cycle.

Let's look at Figure 1.2 and consider what happens in each pipestage.

IF   (instruction fetch) gets the next instruction from the instruction cache (*I-cache*).

RD   (read registers) fetches the contents of the CPU registers whose numbers are in the two possible source register fields of the instruction.

ALU   (arithmetic/logic unit) performs an arithmetical or logical operation in one clock cycle (floating-point math and integer multiply/divide can't be done in one clock cycle and are done differently, but that comes later).

MEM   is the stage where the instruction can read/write memory variables in the data cache (*D-cache*). On average about three out of four instructions do nothing in this stage, but allocating the stage for each instruction ensures that you never get two instructions wanting the data cache at the same time. (It's the same as the mushy peas served by Dionysus.)

WB   (write back) stores the value obtained from an operation back to the register file.

You may have seen other pictures of the MIPS pipeline that look slightly different; it has been common practice to simplify the picture by drawing each pipestage as if it takes exactly one clock cycle. Some later MIPS CPUs have longer or slightly different pipelines, but the pipeline with five stages in four cycles is where the architecture started, and implementations keep returning to something very close to it.

The tyranny of the rigid pipeline limits the kinds of things instructions can do. Firstly, it forces all instructions to be the same length (exactly one machine word of 32 bits), so that they can be fetched in a constant time. This itself discourages complexity; there are not enough bits in the instruction to encode really complicated addressing modes, for example.

This limitation has an immediate disadvantage; in a typical program built for an architecture like x86, the average size of instructions is only just over 3 bytes. MIPS code will use more memory space.

Secondly, the pipeline design rules out the implementation of instructions that do any operation on memory variables. Data from cache or memory is obtained only in phase 4, which is much too late to be available to the ALU. Memory accesses occur only as simple load or store instructions that move the data to or from registers (you will see this described as a *load/store architecture*).

The RISC CPUs launched around 1987 worked because these restrictions don't cause much trouble. An 87 or later RISC is characterized by an instruction set designed for efficient pipelining and the use of caches.

However, the MIPS project architects also attended to the best thinking of the time about what makes a CPU an easy target for efficient optimizing compilers. Many of those requirements are quite compatible with the pipeline requirements, so MIPS CPUs have 32 general-purpose registers and three-operand arithmetical/logical instructions. Happily, the complicated special-purpose instructions that particularly upset pipelines are often those that compilers are unwilling to generate.

1.3   RISC and CISC

We can now have a go at defining what we mean by these overused terms. For me, "RISC" is an adjective applied to machine architectures/instruction sets. In the mid-80s, it became attached to a group of relatively new architectures in which the instruction set had been cunningly and effectively specified to make pipelined implementations efficient and successful. It's a useful term because of the great similarity of approach apparent in SPARC, MIPS, PowerPC, HP Precision, and DEC Alpha.

By contrast to this rather finely aimed description, "CISC" (complex instruction set computer) is used negatively to describe architectures whose definition has not been shaped by a desire to fit pipelined implementations. The RISC revolution was so successful that no post-1985 architecture has abandoned the basic RISC principles; thus CISC architectures are inevitably those born before 1985. In this book you can reasonably assume that something said about CISC is being said to apply to both Intel's x86 family and Motorola's 680x0.

Both terms are corrupted when they are applied not to instruction sets but to implementations. It's certainly true that Intel accelerated the performance of its far-from-RISC x86 family by applying implementation tricks pioneered by RISC builders. But to describe these implementations as having a RISC core is misleading.

1.4   Great MIPS Chips of the Past and Present

We'll take a very fast and somewhat superficial tour. You'll get to know some of these names much better in the chapters that follow.

1.4.1   *R2000 to R3000*

MIPS Corporation was formed in 1984 to make a commercial version of the Stanford MIPS CPU. The Stanford project was one of several US academic projects that were bringing together chip design, compiler optimization, and computer architecture in novel ways with great success. The commercial CPU was enhanced with memory management hardware and first appeared late in 1985 as the R2000. An ambitious external math coprocessor (the R2010 floating-point accelerator, or FPA) first shipped in mid-87. The R3000, shipped in 1988–89, is a "midlife kicker": It's almost identical from the programmer's viewpoint, although small hardware enhancements combined to give a substantial boost to performance.

The R2000/R3000 chips include a cache controller—to get a cache, just add industry-standard static RAMs. The math coprocessor shares the cache buses to read instructions (in parallel with the integer CPU) and to transfer operands and results. The division of function was ingenious, practical, and workable, allowing the R2000/3000 generation to be built without extravagant ultra-high pin-count packages. As clock speeds increased, however, the very high speed signals in the cache interface caused design problems; between 1988 and 1991 R3000 systems took three years to grow from 25 to 40MHz.

1.4.2 *R6000: A Diversion*

You can speed up the caches two ways: either take them on chip or speed the interface to external memories. In the long run it was clear that as the amount of logic that could be put on a chip increased, this problem would be solved by bringing the caches on chip. In the short term, it looked as though it should be possible to push up the clock rate by changing the signalling technology between the CPU and cache chips from CMOS[1] (CMOS is the densest and cheapest process for complex chips) to ECL (as used in high-end minicomputer, mainframe, and supercomputer implementations throughout the 70s). ECL (emitter-coupled logic) uses a much smaller voltage change to signal "0" or "1" and is much less sensitive to noise than normal CMOS signalling, allowing much faster interfaces.

The prospect (back in 1988) was the possibility of making small computers that would redefine the performance of "super-minicomputers" in the same way as CMOS RISC microprocessors had redefined workstation performance.

There were problems: Although RISC CPUs were quite easy to implement in dense CMOS, they were large pieces of logic to build in the bipolar technology traditionally used for ECL computers. So most effort went into "BiCMOS" parts that could mix an internal CMOS core with bipolar circuits for interfacing.

The MIPS project was called the R6000. It didn't exactly fail, but it got delayed by one problem after another and got overtaken by the R4000–the first of a new generation of CMOS processors with on-chip caches.

Curiously, although the BiCMOS implementation strategy turned out to be a dead end, it turned out that the on-chip cache revolution that overwhelmed it was itself premature, at least in terms of making the fastest possible workstation. Hewlett Packard stuck with an external primary cache for its rather MIPS-like Precision architecture. HP eventually pushed its clock rate to around 120MHz—three times the fastest R3000 *without* using ECL signalling or BiCMOS chips. HP did careful development, as engineers are supposed to. This strategy put HP at the top of the performance stakes for a long, long time; the winner is not always the most ambitious architecture.

---

1. It would have been more precise to say TTL-compatible CMOS, but I wanted to leave "TTL" to the glossary.

1.4.3   *The R4000 Revolution*

The R4000, introduced in 1991, was a brave and ground-breaking development. Pioneering features included a complete 64-bit instruction set, the largest possible on-chip caches, extraordinarily fast clock rates (100MHz on launch), on-chip secondary cache controller, a system interface running at a fraction of the internal CPU clock, and on-chip support for a shared-memory multiprocessor system. With the benefit of hindsight we can see that the R4000 anticipated most of the engineering developments seen up to 1995 but avoided the (relatively complex and so far rather unsuccessful) superscalar route.

Not everything about the R4000 was perfect. It was an ambitious chip and took a while to get completely right. MIPS guessed that cache access times would lag behind the performance of the rest of the CPU, so it specified a longer pipeline to allow for two-clock-cycle cache accesses; and the long pipeline and relatively small primary caches made the chip much less efficient (in terms of performance/MHz) than the R3000. Moreover, MIPS Corporation fell victim to hubris, expecting to use the chip to become strong players in the systems market for workstations and servers; when this unrealistic ambition was dashed, some momentum was lost.

By 1992 the workstation company Silicon Graphics, Inc. (SGI) was the leading user of MIPS processors for computer systems. When MIPS Corporation's systems business collapsed in early 1993 SGI was willing to step in to rescue the company and the architecture. By the end of 1994 late-model R4400 CPUs (a stretched R4000 with bigger caches and performance tuning) were running at 200–250MHz and keeping SGI in touch with the RISC performance leaders.

R4000 itself never played well in embedded markets, but the compatible R4600 did. Reverting to the traditional five-stage pipeline and a product of the old MIPS design team (now trading as QED and designing for IDT), R4600 gave excellent performance at a reasonable price. Winning a place in Cisco routers and SGI Indy desktops led to another first: The R4600 was the first RISC CPU that plainly turned in a profit.

1.4.4   *R5000 and R10000*

The years 1995–96 saw a resurgence in the MIPS architecture; a design group called QED, spun out of MIPS at the time of the SGI takeover, is now established as an independent design group capable of developing state-of-the-art mid-range CPUs. With MIPS's own R10000 and the QED-designed R5000, both launched in early 1996, and low-end R4x00 chips making some very large volume embedded design gains, it's clear that the MIPS architecture will be around for a few more years.

The R10000 was a major departure for MIPS from the traditional simple pipeline; it was the first CPU to make truly heroic use of out-of-order execution. Although this was probably the right direction (Pentium II and HP's PA-8x00 series followed its lead and are now on top of their respective trees), the sheer difficulty of debugging R10000 may have set Silicon Graphics up to conclude that sponsoring its own high-end chips was a mistake.

R5000 is a stretched R4600 with tweaked floating point and a cost-effective secondary cache controller, built to keep the Indy going.

MIPS CPUs in use today come in four broad categories:

- *ASIC cores*: MIPS CPUs can be implemented in relatively little space and with low power consumption, and an architecture with mature software tools and support is an attractive alternative to architectures tailored for the low end. MIPS was the first "grown up" CPU to be available as an ASIC core—witness its presence in the Sony PlayStation games console. Companies that will provide a MIPS CPU in a corner of a silicon subsystem include LSI Logic, Toshiba, NEC, and Philips.

- *Integrated 32-bit CPUs*: From a few dollars upward, these chips contain CPU, caches, and a variable amount of system interface simplification. There's considerable variation in price, power consumption, and processing power. Most of them omit the memory management unit; hardware floating point is rare. IDT has the largest range, but LSI Logic, Toshiba, and NKK also have products. However, 32-bit CPUs are rapidly being squeezed out between ASIC cores at the bottom and high-end CPUs.

- *Integrated 64-bit CPUs*: Introduced late in 1993, these chips offer amazing speed, reasonable power consumption, and have become a cult hit in high-end embedded control. The range is now growing upward to higher performance and downward to low-cost CPUs that feature shrunken bus interfaces. Stars in this field are IDT and NEC, with NKK and Toshiba second-sourcing IDT's offerings. The second generation (1995) of these devices has featured cost-reduced CPUs and appears to be even more successful.

- *Ultimate power machines*: Silicon Graphics, the workstation company that is the adoptive parent of the MIPS architecture, develops high-end versions of the architecture in conjunction with some of the semiconductor vendors—in recent years, particularly with NEC. Some of the products of this work, such as the math-oriented "pocket supercomputer" R8000 chip set, are likely never to see application outside SGI's computers. But others, like the R5000 and top-end R10000, appeal to a select band of users with particular needs.

The major distinguishing features of some milestone products are summarized in Table 1.1. We haven't discussed the instruction set revision levels from MIPS I through MIPS IV, but there'll be more about them in Section 2.7, where you'll also find out what happened to MIPS II.

TABLE 1.1 Milestones in MIPS CPUs

Year	Designer/model/ clock rate (MHz)	Instruction set	Cache (I+D)	Notes
1987	MIPS R2000-16	MIPS I	External: 4K+4K to 32K+32K	External (R2010) FPA
1990	MIPS R3000-33		External, up to 64K+64K	The most efficient MIPS ever, in terms of speed per MHz. It turned out that MIPS abandoned external caches too early, leaving HP's similar Precision RISC driving the fastest systems.
1990	IDT R3051-20		4K+1K	The first embedded MIPS CPU with on-chip cache and progenitor of a family of pin-compatible parts.
1991	MIPS R4000-100	MIPS III	8K+8K	Integrates FPA and secondary cache controller with pinout option. Full 64-bit CPU (but completely compatible). Five years later few MIPS CPUs were exploiting their 64-bit instruction set. Long pipeline and half-speed interface help achieve high clock rates.
1993	IDT/QED R4600-100		16K+16K	QED's brilliantly tuned redesign is much faster than R4000 or R4400 at the same clock rate—partly because it returned to the classic MIPS five-stage pipeline. No secondary cache controller. Important to SGI's fast and affordable low-end Indy workstation and Cisco's routers.
1993	MIPS R4400-150		16K+16K	In SGI's workstations, careful development got late model R4400s running at 250MHz and performing very respectably.
1995	NEC/MIPS Vr4300-133		16K+8K	Very low cost, very low power but full-featured R4000 derivative. Initially aimed at Nintendo 64 games console, but embedded uses include HP's LJ4000 laser printers.
1996	MIPS R10000-200	MIPS IV	32K+32K	An astonishing tour de force using many implementation techniques new to MIPS and new to single-chip microprocessors even at more modest clock rates, particularly register renaming and out-of-order execution. It's not at all simple. The main MIPS tradition it upholds is that of taking a principle to extremes. The result is hot, unfriendly, and fast—three times the speed of an R4400, with a bigger margin on floating-point code.
1996	SGI/QED R5000-200		32K+32K	A derivative of the R4600, it's meant to be as fast a CPU as can be reasonably cheap, small, and cool running. Predestined for Indy use, it may also be quite widely used in high-end embedded applications.

1.5 MIPS Compared with CISC Architectures

Programmers who have some assembler-language-level knowledge of earlier architectures—particularly those brought up on x86 or 680x0 CISC instruction sets—may get some surprises from the MIPS instruction set and register model. We'll try to summarize them here, so you don't get sidetracked later into doomed searches for things that don't quite exist, like a stack with push/pop instructions!

We'll consider the following: constraints on MIPS operations imposed to make the pipeline efficient; the radically simple load/store operations; possible operations that have been deliberately omitted; unexpected features of the instruction set; and the points where the pipelined operation becomes visible to the programmer.

1.5.1 *Constraints on MIPS Instructions*

- *All instructions are 32 bits long*: That means that no instruction can fit into only 2 or 3 bytes of memory (so MIPS binaries are typically 20–30% bigger than for 680x0 or 80x86) and no instruction can be bigger.

  This means, for example, that it is impossible to incorporate a 32-bit constant into a single instruction (there would be no instruction bits left to encode the operation and the target register). The MIPS architects decided to make space for a 26-bit constant to encode the target address of a jump or jump-to-subroutine; however, most constant fields are 16 bits long. It follows that loading an arbitrary 32-bit value requires a two-instruction sequence, and conditional branches are limited to a range of 64K instructions.

- *Instruction actions must fit the pipeline*: Actions can only be carried out in the right pipeline phase and must be complete in one clock. For example, the register write-back phase provides for just one value to be stored in the register file, so instructions can only change one register.

- *Three-operand instructions*: Arithmetical/logical operations don't have to specify memory locations, so there are plenty of instruction bits to define two independent sources and one destination register. Compilers love three-operand instructions, which give optimizers much more scope to improve code that handles complex expressions.

- *The 32 registers*: The choice of the number of registers is largely a software issue, and a set of 32 general-purpose registers is by far the most popular in modern architectures. Using 16 would definitely not be as many as modern compilers like, but 32 is enough for a C compiler to keep frequently accessed data in registers in all but the largest and most intricate functions. Using 64 or more registers requires a bigger instruction field to encode registers and also increases context-switch overhead.

- *Register zero*: $0 always returns zero, to give a compact encoding of that useful constant.

- *No condition codes*: One feature of the MIPS instruction set that is radical even among the 1985 RISCs is the lack of any condition flags. Many architectures have multiple flags for "carry," "zero," and so on. CISC architectures typically set these flags according to the result written by any or a large subset of machine instructions, while some RISC architectures retain flags (though typically they are only set explicitly, by compare instructions).

  The MIPS architects decided to keep all this information in the register file: Compare instructions set general-purpose registers and conditional branch instructions test general-purpose registers. That does benefit a pipelined implementation, in that whatever clever mechanisms are built in to reduce the effect of dependencies on arithmetical/logical operations will also reduce dependencies in compare/branch pairs.

  We'll see later that efficient conditional branching means that the decision about whether to branch or not has to be squeezed into only half a pipeline stage; the architecture helps out by keeping the branch decision tests very simple. So conditional branches (in MIPS) test a single register for sign/zero or a pair of registers for equality.

1.5.2   *Addressing and Memory Accesses*

- *Memory references are always plain register loads and stores*: Arithmetic on memory variables upsets the pipeline, so it is not done. Every memory reference has an explicit load or store instruction. The large register file makes this much less of a problem than it sounds.

- *Only one data-addressing mode*: All loads and stores select the memory location with a single base register value modified by a 16-bit signed displacement.[1]

- *Byte-addressed*: Once data is in a register of a MIPS CPU, all operations always work on the whole register. But the semantics of languages such as C fit badly on a machine that can't address memory locations down to byte granularity, so MIPS gets a complete set of load/store operations for 8- and 16-bit variables (we will say *byte* and *halfword*). Once the data has arrived in a register it will be treated as data of full register length, so partial-word load instructions come in two flavors—sign-extend and zero-extend.

---

1. This is not quite true for MIPS CPUs from about 1996 on (MIPS IV), which have a special two-register addressing mode for floating-point loads and stores.

■ *Load/stores must be aligned*: Memory operations can only load or store data from addresses aligned to suit the data type being transferred. Bytes can be transferred at any address, but halfwords must be even-aligned and word transfers aligned to 4-byte boundaries. Many CISC microprocessors will load/store a 4-byte item from any byte address, but the penalty is extra clock cycles.

However, the MIPS instruction set architecture (ISA) does include a couple of peculiar instructions to simplify the job of loading or storing at improperly aligned addresses.

■ *Jump instructions*: The limited 32-bit instruction length is a particular problem for branches in an architecture that wants to support very large programs. The smallest op-code field in a MIPS instruction is 6 bits, leaving 26 bits to define the target of a jump. Since all instructions are 4 byte aligned in memory the two least-significant address bits need not be stored, allowing an address range of 2^{28} = 256MB. Rather than make this branch PC relative, this is interpreted as an absolute address within a 256MB segment. This imposes a limit on the size of a single program, although it hasn't been much of a problem yet!

Branches out of segment can be achieved by using a jump register instruction, which can go to any 32-bit address.

Conditional branches have only a 16-bit displacement field—giving a 2^{18}-byte range since instructions are 4 byte aligned—which is interpreted as a signed PC-relative displacement. Compilers can only code a simple conditional branch instruction if they know that the target will be within 128KB of the instruction following the branch.

1.5.3 *Features You Won't Find*

■ *No byte or halfword arithmetic*: All arithmetical and logical operations are performed on 32-bit quantities. Byte and/or halfword arithmetic requires significant extra resources, many more op-codes, and is rarely really useful. C programmers are exhorted to use the `int` data type for most arithmetic, and for MIPS an `int` is 32 bits and such arithmetic will be efficient. C's rules are to perform arithmetic in `int` whenever any source or destination variable is as long as `int`.

However, where a program explicitly does arithmetic as `short` or `char`, a MIPS compiler must insert extra code to make sure that the results wrap and overflow as they would on a native 16- or 8-bit machine.

■ *No special stack support*: Conventional MIPS assembler usage does define one of the registers as a stack pointer, but there's nothing special to the hardware about **sp**. There is a recommended format for the stack frame layout of subroutines, so that you can mix modules from different languages and compilers; you should almost certainly stick to these conventions, but they have no relationship to the hardware.

A stack pop wouldn't fit the pipeline, because it would have two register values to write (the data from the stack and the incremented pointer value).

■ *Minimal subroutine support*: There is one special feature: Jump instructions have a jump and link option, which stores the return address into a register. **$31** is the default, so for convenience and by convention **$31** becomes the return address register.

This is less sophisticated than storing the return address on a stack, but it has some significant advantages. Two examples will give you a feeling for the argument: Firstly, it preserves a pure separation between branch and memory-accessing instructions; and secondly, it can aid efficiency when calling small subroutines that don't need to save the return address on the stack at all.

■ *Minimal interrupt handling*: It is hard to see how the hardware could do less. It stashes away the restart location in a special register, modifies the machine state just enough to let you find out what happened and to disallow further interrupts, then it jumps to a single predefined location in low memory. Everything else is up to the software.

■ *Minimal exception handling*: Interrupts are just one sort of exception (the MIPS word *exception* covers all sorts of events where the CPU may want to interrupt normal sequential processing and invoke a software handler). An exception may result from an interrupt, an attempt to access virtual memory that isn't physically present, or many other things. You go through an exception, too, on a deliberately planted trap instruction like a system call that is used to get into the kernel in a protected OS. All exceptions result in control passing to the same fixed entry point.[1]

On any exception, a MIPS CPU *does not* store anything on a stack, write memory, or preserve any registers for you.

By convention, two general-purpose registers are reserved so that exception routines can bootstrap themselves (it is impossible to do anything on a MIPS CPU without using some registers). For a program running in any system that takes interrupts or traps, the values of these registers may change at any time, so you'd better not use them.

---

1. I exaggerate slightly; one particular kind of exception (a TLB miss from a user program, if you really want to know now) has a different dedicated entry point. Details will be given in Section 5.3.

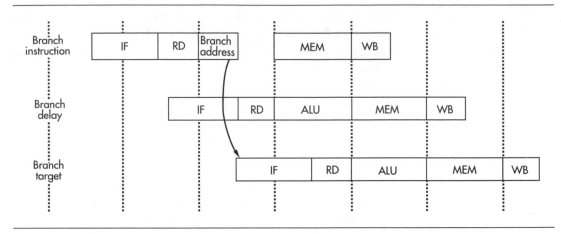

FIGURE 1.3 The pipeline and branch delays

1.5.4 *A Feature You Might Not Expect*

The MIPS CPU does have an integer multiply/divide unit; this is worth mentioning because many RISC machines don't have multiply hardware. The multiply unit is relatively independent of the rest of the CPU, with its own special output registers. In many MIPS implementations it is tuned for small size rather than speed, and integer multiplication is relatively slow. Later CPUs, particularly those aimed at the embedded market, typically used bigger, faster designs.

1.5.5 *Programmer-Visible Pipeline Effects*

So far, this has all been what you might expect from a simplified CPU. However, the pipeline tuning has some stranger effects as well, and to understand them we're going to draw some pictures.

- *Delayed branches*: The pipeline structure of the MIPS CPU (Figure 1.3) means that when a jump instruction reaches the execute phase and a new program counter is generated, the instruction after the jump will already have been started. Rather than discard this potentially useful work, the architecture dictates that the instruction after a branch must always be executed before the instruction at the target of the branch. The instruction position following any branch is called the *branch delay slot*.

  If nothing special was done by the hardware, the decision to branch or not, together with the branch target address, would emerge at the end of the ALU pipestage—in time to fetch the branch target instruction instead of the next instruction but two. But branches are important enough to justify special treatment, and you can see from Figure 1.3 that

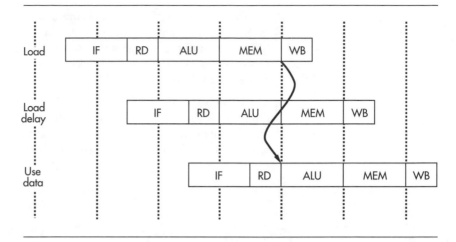

FIGURE 1.4   The pipeline and load delays

a special path is provided through the ALU to make the branch address available half a clock cycle early. Together with the odd half-clock-cycle shift of the instruction fetch stage, that means that the branch target can be fetched in time to become the next but one, so the hardware runs the branch instruction, then the branch delay slot instruction, and then the branch target—with no other delays.

It is the responsibility of the compiler system or the assembler programming wizard to allow for and even to exploit the branch delay; it turns out that it is usually possible to arrange that the instruction in the branch delay slot does useful work. Quite often, the instruction that would otherwise have been placed before the branch can be moved into the delay slot.

This can be a bit tricky on a conditional branch, where the branch delay instruction must be (at least) harmless on both paths. Where nothing useful can be done, the delay slot is filled with a **nop** instruction.

Many MIPS assemblers will hide this odd feature from you unless you explicitly ask them not to.

■ *Late data from load (load delay slot)*: Another consequence of the pipeline is that a load instruction's data arrives from the cache/memory system *after* the next instruction's ALU phase starts—so it is not possible to use the data from a load in the following instruction. (See Figure 1.4 for how this works.)

The instruction position immediately after the load is called the *load delay slot*, and an optimizing compiler will try to do something useful with it. The assembler will hide this from you but may end up putting in a **nop**.

Usually, and certainly on all CPUs implementing MIPS III or higher, the load result is interlocked: If you try to use the result too early, the CPU stops until the data arrives. But on early MIPS CPUs there were no interlocks, and the attempt to use data in the load delay slot led to unpredictable results.

■ *Bizarre multiply/divide effects*: The MIPS integer multiply/divide unit runs outside the main pipeline and continues to run even when operations in the main pipeline are abandoned, as happens during exception processing. There's a note on the trouble this can cause in Section 2.3.

Chapter

2 MIPS Architecture

The rather grandiose word *architecture* is used in computing to describe the abstract machine you program, rather than the actual implementation of that machine. That's a useful distinction—and one worth defending from the widespread misuse of the term in marketing hype. The abstract description may be unfamiliar, but the concept isn't. If you drive a stick-shift car you'll find the gas pedal on the right and the clutch on the left, regardless of whether the car is front-wheel drive or rear-wheel drive. The architecture (which pedal is where) is deliberately kept the same although the implementation is different.

Of course, if you're a rally driver concerned with going very fast along slippery roads, it's suddenly going to matter a whole lot which wheels are driven. Computers are like that too—once your performance needs are extreme or unusual, the details of the implementation may become important to you.

In general, a CPU architecture consists of an instruction set and some knowledge about registers. The terms "instruction set" and "architecture" are pretty close to synonymous, so you'll often see the acronym ISA (instruction set architecture).

The MIPS architecture has racked up a number of generations, and some of those have different implementations:

MIPS I: The instruction set used by the original 32-bit processors; it is still common.

MIPS II: A minor upgrade defined for a machine called the R6000, which didn't get beyond preproduction. But it's made a comeback in 1995's new implementations of 32-bit MIPS.

MIPS III: The 64-bit instruction set used by CPUs called R4xxx.

MIPS IV: A minor upgrade from MIPS III, appearing in two different implementations (R10000 and R5000).

The architecture levels define everything the original company documentation chose to define; that has typically been rather more than enough to ensure the ability to run the same UNIX application and less than enough to ensure complete portability of code that uses OS or low-level features. Other essential software-visible characteristics of a MIPS CPU are specific to the CPU implementation.

In this book, I will be rather more generous; I'll sometimes ascribe a feature to MIPS III that does not appear in the architecture manual, so long as that feature is to be found in all the implementations of the MIPS III architecture that you're likely to meet.

Moreover, even outside the ISA levels and in their implementation-specific areas the great majority of MIPS CPUs have generally fallen into two families: The first was led off by the early MIPS R3000 CPU and including pretty much all 32-bit CPUs, and the second was founded by the 64-bit pioneer, the R4000.

Quite a few other implementations add some of their own new instructions and interesting features. It's not always easy to get software or tools (particularly compilers) that take advantage of implementation-specific features.

There are two levels of detail at which we can describe the MIPS architecture. The first (this chapter) is the kind of view you'd get if you were writing a user program for a workstation but chose to look at your code at the assembler level. That means that the whole normal working of the CPU would be visible.

In the next chapters we'll take on everything, including all the gory details that a high-level operating system hides—CPU control registers, interrupts, traps, cache manipulation, and memory management. But at least we can cut the task into smaller pieces.

CPUs are often much more compatible at the user level than when everything is exposed. MIPS III (R4xxx) CPUs are 100% compatible with their predecessors at the user level.

2.1 A Flavor of MIPS Assembly Language

Assembly language is the human-writable (and readable) version of the CPU's raw binary instructions, and there's a whole chapter devoted to it later. Readers who have never seen any assembly language will find some parts of this book mystifying.

Most MIPS assembler programs interpret a rather stark language, full of register numbers. But toolchains often make it easy to use a macroprocessor language, at least to allow the programmer to write names where the strict assembler language requires numbers. Most use the C preprocessor because of its familiarity. The C preprocessor strips out C-style comments, which therefore become usable in assembler code.

With the help of the C preprocessor, MIPS assembler code almost invariably uses names for the registers. The names reflect each register's conventional use (which we'll talk about in Section 2.2).

For readers familiar with assembly language, but not the MIPS version, here are some examples of what you might see:

```
/* this is a comment */
    # so is this

entrypoint:                 # that's a label
    addu $1, $2, $3         # (registers) $1 = $2 + $3
```

Like most assembler languages, it is line oriented. The end of a line delimits instructions, and the assembler's native comment convention is that it ignores any text on a line beyond a "**#**" character. But it is possible to put more than one instruction on a line, separated by semicolons.

A label is a word followed by a colon ":"—*word* is interpreted loosely, and labels can contain all sorts of strange characters. Labels are used to define entry points in code and to name storage locations in data sections.

A lot of instructions are three-operand, as shown. The destination register is on the left (watch out, that's opposite to the Intel x86 convention). In general, the register result and operands are shown in the same order you'd use to write the operation in C or any other algebraic language, so

```
subu $1, $2, $3
```

means exactly

```
$1 = $2 - $3;
```

That should be enough for now.

2.2 Registers

There are 32 general-purpose registers for your program to use: **$0** to **$31**. Two, and only two, behave differently from the others:

$0 always returns zero, no matter what you store in it.

$31 is always used by the normal subroutine-calling instruction (**jal**) for the return address. Note that the call-by-register version (**jalr**) can use *any* register for the return address, though use of anything except **$31** would be eccentric.

In all other respects all these registers are identical and can be used in any instruction (you can even use **$0** as the destination of instructions, though the resulting data will disappear without a trace).

In the MIPS architecture the program counter is not a register, and it is probably better for you not to think of it that way—in a pipelined CPU there are multiple candidates for its value, which gets confusing. The return address of a **jal** is the next instruction *but one* in sequence:

```
...
jal printf
move $4, $6
xxx # return here after call
```

That makes sense because the instruction immediately after the call is the call's delay slot—remember, the rules say it must be executed before the branch target. The delay slot instruction of the call is rarely wasted, because it is typically used to set up a parameter.

There are no condition codes; nothing in the status register or other CPU internals is of any consequence to the user-level programmer.

There are two register-sized result ports (called **hi** and **lo**) associated with the integer multiplier. They are not general-purpose registers, nor are they useful for anything except multiply and divide operations. However, there are instructions defined that insert an arbitrary value back into these ports—after some reflection, you may be able to see that this is required when restoring the state for a program that has been interrupted.

The floating-point math coprocessor (floating-point accelerator, or FPA), if available, adds 32 floating-point registers; in simple assembler language they are called **$f0** to **$f31**.

Actually, for MIPS I and MIPS II machines only the 16 even-numbered registers are usable for math. However, they can be used for either single-precision (32-bit) or double-precision (64-bit) numbers; when you do double-precision arithmetic, register **$f1** holds the remaining bits of the register identified as **$f0**. Only moves between integer and FPA, or FPA load/store instructions, ever refer to odd-numbered registers (and even then the assembler helps you forget).

MIPS III CPUs have 32 genuine FP registers, but even then software might not use the odd-numbered ones, preferring to maintain software compatibility with the old family.

2.2.1 *Conventional Names and Uses of General-Purpose Registers*

We're a couple of pages into an architecture description and here we are talking about software. But I think you need to know this now.

TABLE 2.1   Conventional names of registers with usage mnemonics

Register number	Name	Used for
0	**zero**	Always returns 0
1	**at**	(assembler temporary) Reserved for use by assembler
2–3	**v0, v1**	Value returned by subroutine
4–7	**a0–a3**	(arguments) First few parameters for a subroutine
8–15	**t0–t7**	(temporaries) Subroutines can use without saving
24, 25	**t8, t9**	
16–23	**s0–s7**	Subroutine register variables; a subroutine that writes one of these must save the old value and restore it before it exits, so the *calling* routine sees the values preserved
26, 27	**k0, k1**	Reserved for use by interrupt/trap handler; may change under your feet
28	**gp**	Global pointer; some run-time systems maintain this to give easy access to (some) "static" or "extern" variables
29	**sp**	Stack pointer
30	**s8/fp**	Ninth register variable; subroutines that need one can use this as a frame pointer
31	**ra**	Return address for subroutine

Although the hardware makes few rules about the use of registers, their practical use is governed by a forest of conventions. The hardware cares nothing for these conventions, but if you want to be able to use other people's subroutines, compilers, or operating systems, then you had better fit in.

With the conventional uses of the registers go a set of conventional names. Given the need to fit in with the conventions, use of the conventional names is pretty much mandatory. The common names are listed in Table 2.1.

Somewhere about 1996 Silicon Graphics began to introduce compilers that use new conventions. The new conventions can be used to build programs that use 32-bit addresses or that use 64-bit addressing, and in those two cases they are called respectively "n32" and "n64." We'll ignore them for now, but we describe them in detail in Chapter 10.

Conventional Assembler Names and Usages for Registers

- **at**: This register is reserved for the synthetic instructions generated by the assembler. Where you must use it explicitly (such as when saving or restoring registers in an exception handler) there's an assembler directive to stop the assembler from using it behind your back (but then some of the assembler's macro instructions won't be available).

■ **v0, v1**: Used when returning non-floating-point values from a subroutine. If you need to return anything too big to fit in two registers, the compiler will arrange to do it in memory. See Section 10.1 for details.

■ **a0–a3**: Used to pass the first four non-FP parameters to a subroutine. That's an occasionally false oversimplification—see Section 10.1 for the grisly details.

■ **t0–t9**: By convention, subroutines may use these values without preserving them. This makes them a good choice for "temporaries" when evaluating expressions—but the compiler/programmer must remember that values stored in them may be destroyed by a subroutine call.

■ **s0–s8**: By convention, subroutines must guarantee that the values of these registers on exit are the same as they were on entry, either by not using them or by saving them on the stack and restoring them before exit. This makes them eminently suitable for use as register variables or for storing any value that must be preserved over a subroutine call.

■ **k0, k1**: Reserved for use by an OS's trap/interrupt handlers, which will use them and not restore their original value; so they are of little use to anyone else.

■ **gp**: If a global pointer is present, it will point to a load-time-determined location in the midst of your static data. This means that loads and stores to data lying within 32KB of either side of the **gp** value can be performed in a single instruction using **gp** as the base register.

Without the global pointer, loading data from a static memory area takes two instructions: one to load the most significant bits of the 32-bit constant address computed by the compiler and loader and one to do the data load.

To use **gp** a compiler must know at compile time that a datum will end up linked within a 64KB range of memory locations. In practice it can't know; it can only guess. The usual practice is to put small global data items (8 bytes and less in size) in the **gp** area and to get the linker to complain if it still gets too big.

Not all compilation systems and not all run-time systems support **gp**.

■ **sp**: It takes explicit instructions to raise and lower the stack pointer, so MIPS code usually adjusts the stack only on subroutine entry and exit; it is the responsibility of the subroutine being called to do this. **sp** is normally adjusted, on entry, to the lowest point that the stack will need to reach at any point in the subroutine. Now the compiler can access stack variables by a constant offset from **sp**. Once again, see Section 10.1 for conventions about stack usage.

- **fp**: Also known as **s8**, a frame pointer will be used by a subroutine to keep track of the stack if it wants to do things that involve extending the stack by an amount that is determined at run time. Some languages may do this explicitly; assembler programmers are always welcome to experiment; and C programs that use the `alloca()` library routine will find themselves doing so.

  If the stack bottom can't be computed at compile time, you can't access stack variables from **sp**, so **fp** is initialized by the function prologue to a constant position relative to the function's stack frame. Cunning use of register conventions means that this behavior is local to the function and doesn't affect either the calling code or any nested function calls.

- **ra**: On entry to any subroutine, return address holds the address to which control should be returned—so a subroutine typically ends with the instruction **jr ra**.

  Subroutines that themselves call subroutines must first save **ra**, usually on the stack.

There is a corresponding set of standard uses for floating-point registers too, which we'll summarize in Section 7.5. We've described here the original conventions promulgated by MIPS; some evolution has occurred in recent times, but we'll keep that back until Section 10.8, which discusses the details of some newer standards for calling conventions.

2.3   Integer Multiply Unit and Registers

The MIPS architects decided that integer multiplication was important enough to deserve a hardwired instruction. This is not so common in RISCs. One alternative would be to implement a multiply step that fits in the standard integer execution pipeline and to require software routines for every multiplication; early SPARC CPUs did just that.

Another way of avoiding the complexity of the integer multiplier would be to perform integer multiplication in the floating-point unit—a good solution used in Motorola's short-lived 88000 family—but that would compromise the optional nature of the MIPS floating-point coprocessor.

The multiply unit in early MIPS CPUs is not spectacularly fast. Its basic operation is to multiply two register-sized values together to produce a twice-register-sized result, which is stored inside the multiply unit. The instructions **mfhi**, **mflo** retrieve the result in two halves into specified general registers.

Unlike results for integer operations, the multiply result registers are *interlocked*. An attempt to read out the results before the multiplication is complete results in the CPU being stopped until the operation completes.

The integer multiply unit will also perform an integer division between values in two general-purpose registers; in this case the **lo** register stores the result (quotient) and the **hi** register stores the remainder.

In MIPS CPUs the integer multiply unit operations are relatively lengthy: Multiply takes 5–12 clock cycles and division 35–80 clock cycles (it depends on the implementation, and for some implementations it depends on the size of the operands). These are significantly slower than the same operations on double-precision floating-point values and not internally pipelined—signs that the hardware implementation traded performance for simplicity and economy in chip space.

The assembler has a synthetic multiply operation that starts the multiply and then retrieves the result into an ordinary register. The MIPS Corporation's assembler will replace a multiply instruction with a series of shifts and adds if it thinks it will go faster; in my opinion compilers should be allowed to make such transformations but assemblers should not!

The multiply unit is not itself pipelined but runs one instruction at a time. Old results will be lost soon after the start of a new multiply instruction, without that change being deferred to the write-back pipeline stage. This leads to a hard-to-understand problem, which can cause your program to generate garbage as a result of an interrupt if you don't follow the rules.

If an **mfhi** or **mflo** instruction is interrupted by some kind of exception before it reaches the write-back stage of the pipeline, it will be aborted with the intention of restarting it. However, a subsequent multiply instruction that has passed the ALU stage would continue (in parallel with exception processing) and would overwrite the **hi** and **lo** register values, so that the re-execution of the **mfhi** would get wrong (i.e., new) data. For this reason it is recommended that a multiply should not be started within two instructions of an **mfhi/mflo**. Some assemblers (definitely SGI and Algorithmics) will put in **nop** padding if you write this in sequential code, but they probably won't notice if there's an intervening branch. See Section 2.9 for a list of potential pipeline-visibility problems.

Integer multiply and divide operations never produce an exception, though divide by zero produces an undefined result. Compilers will often generate code to trap on errors, particularly on divide by zero.

Instructions **mthi**, **mtlo** are defined to set up the internal registers from general-purpose registers. They are essential to restore the values of **hi** and **lo** when returning from an exception, but probably not for anything else.

2.4 Loading and Storing: Addressing Modes

As mentioned above, there is only one addressing mode. Any load or store machine instruction can be written

```
lw       $1, offset($2)
```

You can use any registers for the destination and source. The offset is a signed, 16-bit number (and so can be anywhere between -32768 and 32767); the program address used for the load is the sum of **rd** and the offset. This address mode is normally enough to pick out a particular member of a C structure (offset being the distance between the start of the structure and the member required). It implements an array indexed by a constant; it is enough to reference function variables from the stack or frame pointer and to provide a reasonable-sized global area around the **gp** value for static and extern variables.

The assembler provides the semblance of a simple direct addressing mode, to load the values of memory variables whose address can be computed at link time.

More complex modes such as double-register or scaled index must be implemented with sequences of instructions.

2.5   Data Types in Memory and Registers

MIPS CPUs can load or store between 1 and 8 bytes in a single operation. Naming conventions used in the documentation and to build instruction mnemonics are as follows:

C name	MIPS name	Size (bytes)	Assembler mnemonic
long long	dword	8	"d" as in **ld**
int	word	4	"w" as in **lw**
long[1]			
short	halfword	2	"h" as in **lh**
char	byte	1	"b" as in **lb**

2.5.1   *Integer Data Types*

Byte and halfword loads come in two flavors. Sign-extending instructions **lb** and **lh** load the value into the least-significant bits of the 32-bit register but fill the high-order bits by copying the sign bit (bit 7 of a byte, bit 15 of a halfword). This correctly converts a signed integer value to a 32-bit signed integer.

---

1. Nothing is simple. Recent MIPS compilers offering 64-bit pointers interpret the long data type as 64 bits (it's good practice for a C compiler that a long should be big enough to hold a pointer).

The unsigned instructions **lbu** and **lhu** zero-extend the data; they load the value into the least-significant bits of a 32-bit register and fill the high-order bits with zeros.

For example, if the byte-wide memory location whose address is in **t1** contains the value 0xFE (−2, or 254 if interpreted as unsigned), then

```
lb      t2, 0(t1)
lbu     t3, 0(t1)
```

will leave **t2** holding the value 0xFFFF FFFE (−2 as signed 32-bit value) and **t3** holding the value 0x0000 00FE (254 as signed or unsigned 32-bit value).

The above description relates to MIPS machines considered as 32-bit CPUs, but those implementing MIPS III and above have 64-bit registers. It turns out that *all* partial-word loads (even unsigned ones) *sign-extend* into the top 32 bits; this behavior looks bizarre but is helpful, as is explained in Section 2.7.3.

Subtle differences in the way shorter integers are extended to longer ones are a historical cause of C portability problems, and the modern C standards have very definite rules to remove possible ambiguity. On machines like the MIPS, which cannot do 8- or 16-bit precision arithmetic directly, expressions involving short or char variables require the compiler to insert extra instructions to make sure things overflow when they should: This is nearly always undesirable and rather inefficient. When porting code that uses small integer variables to a MIPS CPU, you should consider identifying which variables can be safely changed to int.

2.5.2 *Unaligned Loads and Stores*

Normal loads and stores in the MIPS architecture must be aligned; halfwords may be loaded only from 2-byte boundaries and words only from 4-byte boundaries. A load instruction with an unaligned address will produce a trap. Because CISC architectures such as the MC680x0 and Intel x86 do handle unaligned loads and stores, you may come across this as a problem when porting software; in extremity, you may even decide to install a trap handler that will emulate the desired load operation and hide this feature from the application—but that's going to be horribly slow unless the references are very rare.

All data items declared by C code will be correctly aligned.

Where you know in advance that you want to code a transfer from an address whose alignment is unknown and that may turn out to be unaligned, the architecture does allow for a two-instruction sequence (much more efficient than a series of byte loads, shifts, and adds). The operation of the constituent instructions is obscure and hard to grasp, but they are normally generated by the macro-instruction **ulw** (unaligned load word). They're described fully in Section 8.4.1.

A macro-instruction **ulh** (unaligned load half) is also provided and is synthesized by two loads, a shift, and a bitwise "or" operation.

By default, a C compiler takes trouble to align all data correctly, but there are occasions (when importing data from a file or sharing data with a different CPU) when being able to handle unaligned integer data efficiently is a requirement. Some compilers permit you to flag a data type as potentially unaligned and will generate special code to cope; ANSI has #pragma align nn and GNU C has the less ugly (but even more non-ANSI) packed structure field attribute type.

Even if your compiler implements packed data types, there's no guarantee that the compiler will use the special MIPS instructions to implement unaligned accesses.

2.5.3 *Floating-Point Data in Memory*

Loads into floating-point registers from memory move data without any interpretation—you can load an invalid floating-point number (in fact, an arbitrary bit pattern) and no FP error will result until you try to do arithmetic with it.

On 32-bit processors, this allows you to load single-precision values by a load into an even-numbered floating-point register, but you can also load a double-precision value by a macro-instruction, so that on a 32-bit CPU the assembler instruction

```
l.d      $f2, 24(t1)
```

is expanded on a 32-bit CPU to two loads to consecutive registers:

```
lwc1     $f2, 24(t1)
lwc1     $f3, 28(t1)
```

On a 64-bit CPU, **l.d** is an alias for the machine instruction **ldc1**, which does the whole job.

Any C compiler that complies with the MIPS/SGI rules aligns 8-byte-long double-precision floating-point variables to 8-byte boundaries. The 32-bit hardware does not require this alignment, but it's done for forward compatibility: 64-bit CPUs will trap if asked to load a double from a location that is not 8 byte aligned.

2.6 Synthesized Instructions in Assembly Language

MIPS machine code might be rather dreary to write; although there are excellent architectural reasons why you can't load a 32-bit constant value into a register with a single instruction, assembler programmers don't want to think about it every time. So MIPS Corporation's assembler (and other good MIPS assemblers) will synthesize instructions for you. You just write a load immediate instruction and the assembler will figure out when it needs to generate two machine instructions.

This is obviously useful but having been invented is bound to be abused. Many MIPS assemblers end up hiding the architecture to an extent that is not really necessary. In this manual we will try to use synthetic instructions sparingly, and we will tell you when it happens. Moreover, in the instruction tables below, we will consistently distinguish between synthetic and machine instructions.

It is my feeling that these features are there to help human programmers and that serious compilers should generate instructions that are one-for-one with machine code. But in an imperfect world many compilers will in fact generate synthetic instructions.

Helpful things the assembler does include the following:

- *A 32-bit load immediate*: You can code a load with any value (including a memory location that will be computed at link time), and the assembler will break it down into two instructions to load the high and low half of the value.

- *Load from memory location*: You can code a load from a memory-resident variable. The assembler will normally replace this by loading a temporary register with the high-order half of the variable's address, followed by a load whose displacement is the low-order half of the address. Of course, this does not apply to variables defined inside C functions, which are implemented either in registers or on the stack.

- *Efficient access to memory variables*: Some C programs contain many references to `static` or `extern` variables, and a two-instruction sequence to load/store any of them is expensive. Some compilation systems, with run-time support, get around this. Certain variables are selected at compile/assemble time (by default MIPS Corporation's assembler selects variables that occupy 8 or less bytes of storage) and are kept together in a single section of memory that must end up smaller than 64KB. The run-time system then initializes one register—**$28** or **gp** by convention—to point to the middle of this section.

    Loads and stores to these variables can now be coded as a single **gp**-relative load or store.

- *More types of branch conditions*: The assembler synthesizes a full set of branches conditional on an arithmetic test between two registers.

- *Simple or different forms of instructions*: Unary operations such as **not** and **neg** are produced as a **nor** or **sub** with the zero-valued register **$0**. You can write two-operand forms of three-operand instructions and the assembler will put the result back into the first-specified register.

- *Hiding the branch delay slot*: In normal coding the assembler will not let you access the branch delay slot. The SGI assembler, in particular, is exceptionally ingenious and may reorganize the instruction sequence substantially in search of something useful to do in the delay slot. An assembler directive `.set noreorder` is available where this must not happen.

- *Hiding the load delay*: The assembler will detect an attempt to use the result of a load in the next instruction and will move code around. In early MIPS CPUs (with no load data interlock) it will insert a `nop` if required.

- *Unaligned transfers*: The unaligned load/store instructions will fetch half-word and word quantities correctly, even if the target address turns out to be unaligned.

- *Other pipeline corrections*: Some instructions (such as those that use the integer multiply unit) have additional constraints—e.g., the multiply unit's input registers must not be reset until the third instruction after a previous result is delivered. You probably don't want to think about those details, and the assembler will patch them up for you.

- *Other optimizations*: Some MIPS instructions (particularly floating point) take quite a few clock cycles to produce results but the hardware is interlocked, so you do not need to take account of these delays to write correct programs. But the SGI assembler is particularly heroic in these circumstances and will move code all over the place to try to make it run faster. You may or may not welcome this.

In general, if you really want to correlate assembler source language (not enclosed by a `.set noreorder`) with instructions stored in memory, you need help. Use a disassembler utility.

2.7   MIPS I to MIPS IV: 64-Bit (and Other) Extensions

The MIPS architecture has grown since its invention—notably, it's grown from 32 to 64 bits. That growth has been done so neatly that it would be quite possible to describe contemporary MIPS as a 64-bit architecture with a well-defined 32-bit subset for lower-cost implementations. We haven't quite done that, for several reasons. Firstly, that is not how it happened, so such a description is in danger of mystifying you. Secondly, one of the lessons that MIPS has to offer the world is the art of extending an architecture nicely. And thirdly, the material in this book was in fact written about 32-bit MIPS before it was extended to encompass 64 bits.

So the approach is a hybrid one. We will usually introduce the 32-bit version first, but once we get down to the details we'll handle both versions together. We'll use the acronym ISA for the long-winded term instruction set.

Once the MIPS ISA started to evolve, the ISA of the original 32-bit MIPS CPUs (the R2000, R3000, and descendants) was retrospectively called MIPS I.[1] The next variant to be widely used is a substantial enhancement that leads to a complete 64-bit ISA for the R4000 CPU and its successors; this is called MIPS III.

One of the blessings of MIPS is that at user level (all the code that you can see when writing applications on a workstation) each MIPS ISA has been a superset of the previous one. Nothing gets left out, only added.

There was a MIPS II, but it came to nothing because its first implementation (the R6000) ended up being overtaken by the MIPS III R4000. However, MIPS II was very close to being the same as the subset of MIPS III that you get by leaving out the 64-bit integer operations. The MIPS II ISA is making a comeback now as the ISA of choice for new implementations of 32-bit MIPS CPUs.

As we mentioned above, the different ISA levels define whatever they define; at a minimum they define all the instructions usable by a user-level program in a protected operating system—which includes the floating-point operations.[2] To go with the instructions, the ISA defines and describes the integer, floating-point data, and floating-point control register.

But each ISA definition carefully excludes the CPU control (coprocessor 0) registers and more recently the whole CPU control instruction set. I don't know how much this helps, though it does create employment for MIPS consultants by concealing information; a book called "MIPS IV Instruction Set" is no good if you want to know how to program the cache on an R5000.

In practice, coprocessor 0 has evolved in step with the formal ISA and like the formal ISA there are two major variants: one associated with the R3000 (the MIPS I CPU that is the ancestor of the biggest family of MIPS CPUs) and the other deriving from the very first MIPS III CPU, the R4000. I'll refer to these family groups as "R3000-style" and "R4000-style," respectively. Later MIPS CPUs such as R5000 and R10000 have remained R4000-style in this sense.

2.7.1 *To 64 Bits*

With the introduction of the R4000 CPU in 1990, MIPS became the first 64-bit RISC architecture to reach production. The MIPS III version of the instruction set has 64-bit integer registers; all the general-purpose registers are 64 bits long,

---

1. This is similar to a film fan asking whether you've seen "Terminator 1," even though there never was a film called that. Even Beethoven's Symphony no. 1 was once called "Beethoven's Symphony."

2. But it's always been possible to make a CPU that doesn't implement floating point.

and some of the CPU control registers are too. Moreover, all operations produce 64-bit results, though some of the instructions carried forward from the 32-bit instruction set do not do anything useful on 64-bit data. New instructions are added where the 32-bit operation can't be compatibly extended to do the right thing for 64-bit operands.

With MIPS III the FPA gets individual FP registers that are 64 bits long, so you don't need a pair of them to hold a double-precision value any more. This extension is incompatible, so a mode switch in a CPU control register can be set to make the registers behave like a MIPS I CPU and allow the use of old software.

2.7.2 *Who Needs 64 Bits?*

By 1996 32 bits was no longer a big enough address space for the very largest applications. Pundits seem to agree that programs have been growing bigger exponentially, doubling every 18 months or so. So long as this goes on, demand for address space is expanding at about $\frac{3}{4}$ of a bit per year. Genuine 32-bit CPUs (68020, i386) appeared to replace 16/20-bit machines somewhere around 1984—so 32 bits will seem small around 2002. If this makes MIPS's 1991 move seem premature, that's probably true—big-MIPS proponent Silicon Graphics did not introduce its first 64-bit-capable OS into general use until 1995.

MIPS's early move was spurred by research interest in operating systems using large sparse virtual address spaces, which permit objects to be named by their virtual address over a long period of time. MIPS was by no means the most prestigious organization to be deceived about the rate at which operating systems would evolve; Intel's world-dominating 32-bit CPU range had to wait *11 years* before Windows 95 brought 32-bit operation to the mass market.

A side effect of the 64-bit architecture is that such a computer can handle more bits at once, which can speed up some data-intensive applications in graphics and imaging. It's not clear, though, whether this is really preferable to the multimedia instruction set extensions exemplified by Intel's MMX, which not only features wide data paths but some way of operating simultaneously on 1-byte or 16-bit chunks of that wide data.

By 1996 any architecture with pretensions to longevity needed a 64-bit implementation. Maybe getting there early was not a bad thing.

The nature of the MIPS architecture—committed to a flat address space and the use of general-purpose registers as pointers—means that 64-bit addressing and 64-bit registers go together. Even where the long addresses are irrelevant, the increased bandwidth of the wide registers and ALU may be useful for routines that shovel a lot of data, which are often found in graphics or high-speed communication applications.

It's one of the signs of hope for the MIPS architecture (and certain other simpler RISC architectures) that the move to 64 bits makes segmentation (featured in x86 and PowerPC architectures) totally pointless.

2.7.3 *Regarding 64 Bits and No Mode Switch: Data in Registers*

The "standard" way to extend a CPU to new areas is to do what DEC did long ago when taking the PDP-11 up to the VAX and Intel did when going from the 8086 to the i286 and i386: they defined a mode switch in the new processor that, when turned on, makes the processor behave exactly like its smaller ancestor.

But mode switches are kludges and in any case are difficult to implement in a non-microcoded machine. So the R4000 uses a different approach:

- All MIPS II instructions are preserved.

- So long as you only run MIPS II instructions you get 100% compatibility, in the sense that the low 32 bits of each MIPS III 64-bit register hold the same values as would have filled the corresponding MIPS II register.

- As many as possible of the MIPS II instructions are defined so as to be both compatible and still to be useful 64-bit instructions.

The crucial decision (and an easy one, once you identify the question) is: What shall be in the high-order 32 bits of a register when we're being 32 bit compatible? There are a number of choices, but only a few of them are simple.

We could simply decide that the high bits should be undefined; when you're being 32 bit compatible the high bits of registers can contain any old garbage. This is easy to achieve but fails the third test above: We will now need separate 32- and 64-bit versions of test instructions and conditional branches (they test registers for equality, or for being negative, by looking at the top bit).

A second and more promising option would be to decide that the high-register bits should remain zero while we're running 32-bit instructions; but again, this means we'll have to double up tests for negatives and for comparisons of negative numbers. Also, a 64-bit "nor" instruction between two top-half-zero values doesn't naturally produce a top-half-zero value.

The third, and best, solution is to maintain the top half of the register full of copies of bit 31. If (when running only 32-bit instructions) we ensure that each register contains the correct low 32 bits and the top half flooded with copies of bit 31, then all 64-bit comparisons and tests are compatible with their 32-bit versions. All bitwise logical instructions must work too (anything that works on bit 31 works the same on bits 32–63).

The successful candidate can be described by saying that you keep 32-bit values in registers by sign-extending them to 64 bits; this is done without regard to whether the value is being interpreted as signed or unsigned.

With that decided, MIPS III needs new 64-bit versions of simple arithmetic (the 32-bit **addu** instruction, when confronted by 32-bit overflow, has to produce the overflow value in the low half of the register and bit 31 copies in the top half—not the same as a 64-bit add!). It also needs a load-64-bits and new shift instructions, but it's a modest enough set. Where new instructions are needed for 64-bit data they get a "d" for double in the instruction mnemonic, generating names like **daddu**, **dsub**, **dmult**, and **ld**.

Slightly less obvious is that the existing 32-bit load instruction **lw** is now more precisely described as load word signed, so a new zero-extending **lwu** appears. The number of instructions added is fattened by the need to support existing variants and (in the case of shift-by-a-constant) the need to use a different op-code to escape the limits of a fixed 5-bit shift amount field.

All MIPS instructions are listed in horrible detail in Chapter 8.

2.7.4   *Other Innovations in MIPS III*

The widespread extensions required in going to 64 bits provide an opportunity to add some useful instructions (unrelated to 64-bit operation).

Multiprocessor Synchronization Operations

There's a special pair of instructions—a load linked and a store conditional—whose job is to allow the implementation of software semaphores in a way that works with shared memory multiprocessor systems. They do the same job as the atomic read-modify-write (RMW) or locked instructions offered by more recent CISC architectures—but RMW and locking get very inefficient in large multiprocessor systems. We'll account for their operation in Section 5.8.4 below. Meanwhile, here's what they do.

ll is a regular load-word instruction, but it keeps a record of the address you used in a special internal register; **sc** is a store-word instruction, but it only does the store if

- The CPU has not taken any interrupt or exception since a preceding **ll** at the same address, and
- (For multiprocessor systems) no other CPU has signalled a write to (or intention to write to) a region of memory including the address used by the **ll**

And then **sc** returns a value telling the program whether or not the store succeeded.

Although designed for multiprocessor systems, **ll** and **sc** allow you to implement a semaphore in a uniprocessor without having to disable all interrupts.

Loop-Closing Branches (Branch Likely)

Efficient MIPS code requires that the compiler be able to find useful work to do in most branch delay slots. In many cases, the instruction that would logically have preceded the branch is a good choice. This can't be done, of course, when the branch is a conditional one and the instruction sequence before it is devoted to computing the condition.

This happens most often for the branch back that closes a loop; the smaller the loop, the more likely it is that the compiler won't be able to find an earlier instruction to put in the delay slot.

With a loop, the compiler's second possible choice to fill the delay slot is to use a copy of the instruction at the branch target (back at the start of the loop) and to bump the branch target up one. This doesn't make the program smaller but does make it run faster. But this is often not possible; when the loop exits, the delay slot instruction will be spuriously executed, and it's hard for the compiler to make sure that it won't do any damage.

What the compiler needs here is a branch instruction where the delay slot instruction is executed only if the branch is taken.[1] And that's what it gets in MIPS II. The instructions are called *branch likely*—one of those awful bits of nomenclature that confuse more than they enlighten. Their mnemonics add a trailing **l** to the existing instruction: so **beq** begets **beql** and so on.

Conditional Traps

With MIPS II come a whole bundle of instructions that take an exception based on a condition: The conditions tested for are the same as the "set if..." instructions. They have no role in C code but could be useful in implementing languages that call for run-time array bounds checking.

Extended Floating Point

The R6000 implementation extended the floating-point registers to 64-bit width, but I'm going to pretend that's part of the general move to 64 bits that comes with MIPS III. If the new MIPS II CPUs ever get floating-point units (unlikely), they will probably be 32-bit ones!

2.8   Basic Address Space

The way in which MIPS processors use and handle addresses is subtly different from that of traditional CISC CPUs, and we know that it causes confusion. Read the first part of this section carefully. We'll start off with the original 32-bit picture and then describe the 64-bit version—if you'll bear with me you'll see why.

Here are some guidelines. With a MIPS CPU the addresses you put in your programs are *never* the same as the physical addresses that come out of the chip

---

1. In the MIPS pipeline, of course, the delay slot instruction is always started—but it can be *nullified*, turning it into a **nop** by suppressing any effects.

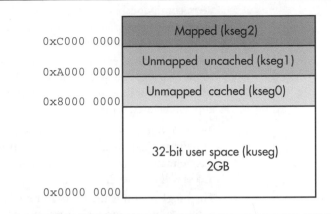

FIGURE 2.1 MIPS memory map: the 32-bit view

(sometimes they're close, but not the same). We'll refer to them as *program addresses*[1] and *physical addresses*, respectively.

A MIPS CPU runs at one of two privilege levels: user and kernel.[2] We'll often talk about "user mode" and "kernel mode" for brevity, but it's a feature of the MIPS architecture that the change from kernel to user never makes anything work differently, it just sometimes makes it illegal. At the user level, any program address with the most-significant bit of the address set is illegal and causes a trap. Also, some instructions cause a trap in user mode.

In the 32-bit view (Figure 2.1), the program address space is divided into four big areas with traditional (and thoroughly meaningless) names; different things happen according to the area an address lies in, as follows:

kuseg   0x0000 0000–7FFF FFFF (low 2GB): These are the addresses permitted in user mode. In machines with an MMU, they will always be translated (see Chapter 6). You should not attempt to use these addresses unless the MMU is set up.

For machines without an MMU, what happens is implementation defined; your particular CPU's manual may tell you about something useful you could do with them. But if you want your code to be portable to and between MMU-less MIPS processors, avoid this area.

kseg0   0x8000 0000–9FFF FFFF (512MB): These addresses are translated into physical addresses by merely stripping off the top bit and mapping

---

1. I had worked with operating systems before I met up with MIPS, so it's natural for me to call the program addresses "virtual addresses"—but for many people "virtual address" suggests a lot of operating system complications that aren't relevant here.

2. MIPS CPUs after R4000 have a third "supervisor" mode; however, since all MIPS OSs so far have ignored it, we will mostly do so too.

them contiguously into the low 512MB of physical memory. Since this is a trivial translation, these addresses are often called "untranslated," but now you know better!

Addresses in this region are almost always accessed through the cache, so they may not be used until the caches are properly initialized. They will be used for most programs and data in systems not using the MMU and will be used for the OS kernel for systems that do use the MMU.

kseg1   0xA000 0000 -- BFFF FFFF (512MB): These addresses are mapped into physical addresses by stripping off the leading 3 bits, giving a duplicate mapping of the low 512MB of physical memory. But this time, access will not use the cache.

The kseg1 region is the only chunk of the memory map that is guaranteed to behave properly from system reset; that's why the after-reset starting point (0xBFC0 0000) lies within it. The *physical* address of the starting point is 0x1FC0 0000—tell your hardware engineer.[1]

You will therefore use this region to access your initial program ROM, and most people use it for I/O registers. If your hardware designer proposes to map such things outside the low 512MB of physical memory, apply persuasion.

kseg2   0xC000 0000 -- FFFF FFFF (1GB): This area is only accessible in kernel mode but is once again translated through the MMU. Don't access it before the MMU is set up. Unless you are writing a serious operating system, you will probably never have cause to use kseg2.

2.8.1 *Addressing in Simple Systems*

MIPS program addresses are never simply the same as physical addresses, but simple embedded software will probably use addresses in kseg0 and kseg1, where the program address is related in an obvious way to physical addresses.

Physical memory locations from 0x2000 0000 (512MB) upward are not mapped anywhere in that simple picture; you can reach them by putting translation entries in the memory management unit (translation lookaside buffer) or by using some of the extra spaces available in 64-bit CPUs.

2.8.2 *Kernel vs. User Privilege Level*

With kernel privileges (where the CPU starts up) it can do anything. In user mode, program addresses above 2GB (top bit set) are illegal and will cause a trap. Note that if the CPU has an MMU, this means that all user addresses must be translated by the MMU before reaching physical memory, giving an OS the

---

1. The engineer wouldn't be the first to have put the ROM at physical address 0xBFC0 0000 and found that the system wouldn't bootstrap.

chance to prevent a user program from running amok. That means, though, that the user privilege level is redundant for a MIPS CPU running without a memory-mapped OS.

Also, in user mode some instructions—particularly the CPU control instructions an OS needs—become illegal.

Note that when you change the kernel/user privilege mode bit, it does not change the interpretation of anything—it just means that some things cease to be allowed in user mode. At kernel level the CPU can access low addresses just as if it were in user mode, and they will be translated in the same way.

Note also that, though it can sound as if kernel mode is for operating systems writers and user mode is the simple everyday mode, the reverse is the truth. Simple systems (including many real-time operating systems) never leave MIPS kernel mode.

2.8.3   *The Full Picture: The 64-Bit View of the Memory Map*

MIPS addresses are always formed by adding a 16-bit offset to a value in a register. In MIPS III+ CPUs, the register always holds a 64-bit value, so there are 64 bits of program address. Such a huge space permits a rather cavalier attitude to chopping up the address space, and you can see how it's done in Figure 2.2.

The first thing to notice is that the 64-bit memory map is packed inside of the 32-bit map. That's an odd trick—like Dr. Who's "Tardis," the inside is much bigger than the outside—and it depends upon the rule we described in Section 2.7.3: When emulating the 32-bit instruction set, registers always contain the 64-bit sign extension of the 32-bit value. As a result, a 32-bit program gets access to the lowest and highest 2GB of the 64-bit program space. So the extended map assigns those lowest and highest regions to the same purpose as in the 32-bit version, and extension spaces are defined in between.

In practice, the vastly extended user space and supervisor-accessible spaces are not likely to be of much significance unless you're implementing a virtual memory operating system; hence many MIPS III users will continue to define pointers as 32-bit objects. The large unmapped windows onto physical memory might be useful to overcome the 512MB limit of kseg0 and kseg1, but you can achieve the same effect by programming the memory manager unit (translation lookaside buffer).

2.9   Pipeline Hazards

Any pipelined CPU hardware is always subject to timing delays for those operations that inevitably can't fit into a strict one-clock-cycle regime. The designers of the architecture, though, get to choose which (if any) of these delays become visible to the programmer. Hiding timing foibles simplifies the programmer's

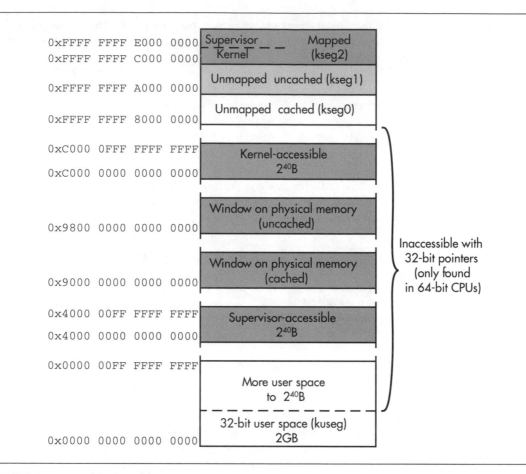

FIGURE 2.2 A 64-bit view of the memory map

model of what the CPU is doing, but it also loads complexity onto the hardware implementor. Leaving the scheduling problem to programmers and their software tools simplifies the hardware but can create development and porting problems.

As we've said several times already, the MIPS architecture leaves some pipeline artifacts visible and makes the programmer or compiler responsible for making the system work. The following points summarize where the pipeline shows up:

■ *Branch delay*: In all MIPS CPUs the instruction following any branch instruction (in the branch delay slot) is executed even though the branch is taken. In the odd-looking branch likely instructions, introduced with the MIPS II instruction set, the delay slot instruction is executed *only* if the branch is taken; see Section 8.4.4 for a rationale.

The programmer or compiler should find a useful, or at worst harmless, instruction for the branch delay slot. But even the assembler will hide the branch delay from you unless you specify otherwise.

■ *Load delay*: In MIPS I CPUs the instruction following a load instruction (in the load delay slot) must not use the data that was loaded. A useful or harmless instruction needs to separate load and usage. Again, the assembler will hide this from you unless you specify otherwise.

MIPS II and subsequent CPUs don't suffer from this hazard; CPU hardware stalls the second instruction until the data arrives. But optimizing compilers and programmers should always be aware of how much time a particular CPU needs to get data ready to use.

■ *Integer multiply/divide trouble*: The integer multiplier hardware is separately pipelined from the regular ALU and does not properly implement "precise exceptions" (see Section 5.1 for what that means). The fix is simple and usually implemented by the assembler—you just have to avoid starting one multiply/divide operation too quickly after retrieving the results of the last one. The explanation of why this fix is both necessary and sufficient is rather more complicated (see Section 5.1).

■ *Floating-point (coprocessor 1) foibles*: Floating-point computations nearly always take multiple clock cycles to complete, and typical MIPS FPA hardware has several somewhat independent pipelined units. Under these circumstances the hardware has just got to hide the pipeline; FP computations are allowed to proceed in parallel with the execution of later instructions, and the CPU is stalled if an instruction reads a result register before the computation finishes. Really heavyweight optimization requires the compiler to have tables of instruction repeat rates and latencies for each target CPU type, but you won't want to depend on those for the program to work at all.

If computation presents no pipeline hazards, the same is not true of the interaction between the floating-point coprocessor and the integer execution unit. There are two effects.

Firstly, the instruction that moves data from floating-point to integer registers, which is called `mfc1`, delivers data a clock cycle late—in fact, with the same timing as loads from memory. Just as with loads, this is a hazard in MIPS I CPUs but interlocked with later hardware; optimizing compilers will try to do something useful in the delay slot.

Secondly, the branch instructions that test the floating-point condition code(s) cannot run in the instruction slot immediately following the floating-point compare operation that generates the condition. A one-instruction delay is specified and is required by most MIPS implementations.

■ *CPU control instruction problems*: This is where life gets tricky. When you change fields like those in the CPU status register, you are potentially affecting things that happen at all pipeline stages. Since the architecture descriptions regard the whole CPU control system as implementation dependent, there are no ISA-version-fixed rules about what is needed. And an unfortunate consequence is that CPU vendors have not even had a template for how such hazards should be documented.

Look in Chapter 3 for a summary of the CPU control instructions used on MIPS CPUs to date, and then refer to Appendix A for a summary of the timing issues as they affect at least the key R4000 CPU.

Chapter

3

Coprocessor 0: MIPS Processor Control

In addition to its normal computational functions, any CPU needs units to handle interrupts, configuration options, and some way of observing or controlling on-chip functions like caches and timers. But it's difficult to do this in the neat implementation-independent way that the ISA does for the computational instruction set.

It would be desirable, and be easier for you to follow, if we could introduce this through some chapters that separate out the different functions, and we're going to do that. But we have to describe the common mechanisms used to implement these features first. You should read the first part of this chapter before tackling the next three chapters of this book; take particular note of the use of the word *coprocessor* as explained on page 44.

So what jobs does CP0 on a MIPS CPU do?

- *Configuration*: MIPS hardware is often very flexible, and you may be able to select quite major features of the CPU (such as its endianness; see Chapter 11) or alter the way the system interface works. One or more internal registers provide control and visibility of these options.

- *Cache control*: MIPS CPUs have always integrated cache controllers, and all but the oldest integrate caches too. Even the very first MIPS CPUs had cache control fields in status registers, and from the R4000 onward, there's a specific CP0 instruction to manipulate cache entries. We'll talk about caches in Chapter 4.

- *Exception/interrupt control*: What happens on an interrupt or any exception, and what you do to handle it, are defined and controlled by CP0 registers and a few special instructions. This is described in Chapter 5.

- *Memory management unit control*: This is discussed in Chapter 6.

- *Miscellaneous*: There's always more: timers, event counters, parity error detection. Whenever additional functions are built into the CPU and

43

Special MIPS Use of the Word *Coprocessor*

The word *coprocessor* is normally used to mean an optional part of a processor that takes responsibility for some extension to the instruction set. The MIPS standard instruction set omits many features needed in any real CPU, but op-codes are reserved and instruction fields defined for up to four coprocessors.

One of these (coprocessor 1) is the floating-point co-processor, which really is a coprocessor in anyone's language.

Another (coprocessor 0 or CP0) is described by MIPS as the system control coprocessor, and these instructions are essential to handle all those functions outside the responsibility of the standard ISA; they are the subject of this chapter.

Coprocessor 0 has no independent existence and is certainly not optional—you can't possibly make a

MIPS CPU without a CPU status register, for example. But it does provide a standard way of encoding the instructions that access the status register, so that, although the definition of the status register changes between the R3000 and R4000 families, you can use the same assembler program for both CPUs.

The coprocessor 0 functions are deliberately corralled off from the MIPS ISA and are in principle implementation dependent. In practice, these functions have evolved in partnership with the regular instruction set; for example, the CP0 features of all MIPS III CPUs built to date have been similar enough to allow the same OS binaries to run over the whole family (with some care).

Of the four coprocessors, CP3 has been invaded by "standard" instructions from MIPS III and (particularly) MIPS IV and is now unusable. CP2 may yet be used by some system-on-a-chip applications.

built in too tightly to be conveniently accessed as I/O devices, this is where they get attached.

We'll summarize everything found in "standard" CPUs in the second half of this chapter. But first, we'll leave aside what we're trying to do and look at the mechanisms we use to do it. There are relatively few CP0 instructions—wherever possible, low-level control over the CPU involves reading and writing bitfields within special CP0 registers.

Table 3.1 introduces the functions of those CPU control registers that have become de facto standards. The first group of functions in the table has been implemented in every MIPS CPU to date; the second has been in every MIPS CPU since the R4000 (which marked an attempt to improve the organization of the CP0 units).

This is not a complete list; we'll see some more control registers in the sections on memory management and cache control. In addition, some MIPS CPUs have gained implementation-specific registers—this is a preferred way to add features to the MIPS architecture. Refer to your particular CPU's manuals.

To avoid burying you in detail at this stage, we've banished the bit-by-bit description of the CP0 registers to separate sections: Section 3.3 for those registers common to every MIPS CPU to date and Section 3.4 for those common to most implementations following the R4000. You can skip over those sections for now if you're interested in going on to the following chapters.

While we're listing registers, **k0** and **k1** are worth a mention. These are two general-purpose registers reserved (by software convention) for use in exception-

TABLE 3.1 Common MIPS CPU control registers (not MMU)

Register mnemonic	CP0 register no.	Description
PRId	15	An identifier identifying this CPU's generic type, with a revision level. The type IDs are supposedly policed by MIPS Corporation and should (at least) change whenever the architecture or coprocessor 0 register set changes. There's a list of values issued up to mid-97 in Table 3.2 below.
SR	12	The *status register*, which, perversely, consists mostly of writable control fields. Fields determine the CPU privilege level, which interrupt pins are enabled, and other CPU modes.
Cause	13	What caused that exception or interrupt?
EPC	14	*Exception Program Counter*: where to restart after exception/interrupt.
BadVaddr	8	The program address that caused the last address-related exception. Set by address errors of all kinds, even if there is no MMU.
Index	0	All these are MMU manipulation registers, described in Chapter 6.
Random	1	**EntryLo1** and **Wired** got introduced with the R4000.
EntryLo0	2	
EntryLo1	3	
Context	4	
EntryHi	10	
PageMask	5	
Wired	6	

Registers introduced with the R4000

Count	9	Together, these form a simple but useful high-resolution interval timer, ticking at half the CPU pipeline clock rate.
Compare	11	
Config	16	CPU setup parameters, usually system determined; some writable here, some read-only.
LLAddr	17	Address from last **ll** (load-linked) instruction. For diagnostics only.
WatchLo	18	Data watchpoint facility. Can cause an exception when the CPU attempts to load or store at this address—potentially useful for debugging.
WatchHi	19	
CacheERR	27	Fields for analyzing (and possibly recovering from) a memory error, for CPUs using error-correcting code on the data path. See Figure 4.4 and the explanation around it for details.
ECC	26	
ErrorEPC	30	
TagLo	28	Registers for cache manipulation, described in Section 4.10.
TagHi	29	

processing routines. It's pretty much essential to reserve at least one register; the choice of which register is arbitrary but it must be one that is embedded in all extant MIPS toolkits and binaries.

3.1 CPU Control Instructions

There are several special CPU control instructions used in the memory management implementation, but we'll leave those until Chapter 6. MIPS III CPUs have a polymorphic **cache** instruction that contrives to do everything required to caches, described below in Chapter 4.

But those aside, MIPS CPU control requires very few instructions. Let's start with the ones that give you access to all the registers we just listed off:

```
mtc0    rs, <nn> # Move to coprocessor 0
dmtc0   rs, <nn> # Move doubleword to control register
```

These instructions load coprocessor 0 register number **nn** from CPU general register **rs**, with either 32 or 64 bits of data (even in 64-bit CPUs many of the CP0 registers are only 32 bits long). This is the only way of setting bits in a CPU control register.

It is not good practice to refer to CPU control registers by their number in assembler programs; normally you use the mnemonic names shown in Table 3.1. Most toolchains define these names in a C-style *include* file and arrange for the C preprocessor to be run as a front end to the assembler; see your toolkit documentation for guidance on how to do this. Although there's a fair amount of influence from original MIPS standards, there is some variation in the names used for these registers. We'll stick to the mnemonics shown in Table 3.1.

Getting data out of CP0 registers is the opposite:

```
mfc0    rd, <nn>  # Move from coprocessor 0
dmfc0   rd, <nn>  # Move doubleword from coprocessor 0
```

In either case **rd** is loaded with the values from CPU control register number **nn**. This is the only way of inspecting bits in a control register. So if you want to update a single field inside, say, the status register **SR** you're going to have to code something like

```
mfc0    t0, SR
and     t0, <complement of bits to clear>
or      t0, <bits to set>
mtc0    SR, t0
```

The last crucial component of the control instruction set is a way of undoing the effect of an exception. We'll discuss exceptions in detail in Chapter 5, but the basic problem is shared by any CPU that can implement any kind of secure OS; the problem is that an exception can occur while running user (low-privilege) code but that the exception handler runs at high privilege.[1] So when returning from the exception back to the user program, the CPU needs to steer between two dangers: On the one hand, if the privilege level is lowered before control returns to the user program, you'll get an instant and fatal second exception caused by the privilege violation; on the other hand, if you return to user code before lowering the privilege level, a malicious program might get the chance to run an instruction with kernel privileges. The return to user mode and the change of privilege level must be indivisible from the programming viewpoint (or *atomic*, in architecture jargon).

On R3000 and similar CPUs this job is done by a jump instruction with an **rfe** in its delay slot, but from the R4000 onward **eret** does the whole job. We'll go into the details in Chapter 5.

3.2 What Registers Are Relevant When?

These are the registers you will need to consult in the following circumstances:

- *After power-up*: You'll need to set up **SR** to get the CPU into the right state to bootstrap itself.

  Most MIPS CPUs other than the earliest have a configuration register **Config** where some options may need to be set up before very much will work. Consult your hardware engineer about making sure that the CPU and system agree enough about configuration to get to the point of writing these registers!

- *Handling any exception*: Any MIPS exception (apart from one particular MMU event) invokes a single common "general exception handler" routine at a fixed address.

  On entry no program registers have been saved, only the return address in **EPC**. The MIPS hardware knows nothing about stacks. In any case, in a secure OS the privileged exception handler can't assume anything about the integrity of the user-level code—in particular, it can't assume that the stack pointer is valid or that stack space is available.

  You need to use at least one of **k0** and **k1** to point to some memory space reserved to the exception handler. Now you can save things, using

---

1. Almost universally, CPUs use a software-triggered exception—a *system call*—as the only mechanism that user code can employ to invoke a service from the OS kernel (which runs at a higher privilege level).

Encoding of Control Registers

A note about reserved fields is in order here. Many unused control register fields are marked "0." Bits in such fields are guaranteed to read zero, and it is harmless to write them (though the value written is ignored). Other reserved fields are marked "reserved" or "×"; you should take care to always write them as zero, and you should not assume that you will get back zero or any other particular value.

---

the other **k0** or **k1** register to stage data from control registers where necessary.

Consult the **Cause** register to find out what kind of exception it was and dispatch accordingly.

- *Returning from exception*: Control must eventually be returned to the value stored in **EPC** on entry. Whatever kind of exception it was, you will have to adjust **SR** back when you return, restoring the user-privilege state, enabling interrupts, and generally unwinding the exception effect.

  On the R3000 the special instruction **rfe** does the job, but note that it does not transfer control. To make the jump back you will load the original **EPC** value back into a general-purpose register and use a **jr** operation.

  On the R4000 and all 64-bit CPUs to date, the return-from-exception instruction **eret** combines the return to user space and resetting of **SR**.

  Strictly speaking, the CP0 instruction set, including **rfe** and **eret**, is implementation dependent. But no MIPS CPU has ever invented a third way of doing the job, and it's fairly safe to suppose that none ever will. However, what you might well see one day is a 32-bit CPU that bases its CP0 design on the R4000.

- *Interrupts*: **SR** is used to adjust the interrupt masks, to determine which (if any) interrupts will be allowed higher priority than the current one. The hardware offers no interrupt prioritization, but the software can do whatever it likes.

- *Instructions that always cause exceptions*: These are often used (for system calls, breakpoints, and to emulate some kinds of instruction). All MIPS CPUs have implemented instructions called **break** and **syscall**; some implementations have added extra ones.

3.3 Encodings of Standard CPU Control Registers

This section tells you about the format of the control registers, with a sketch of the function of each field. In most cases, more information about how things work is to be found in separate sections below. However, we've left the registers that are specific to the memory management system to Chapter 6.

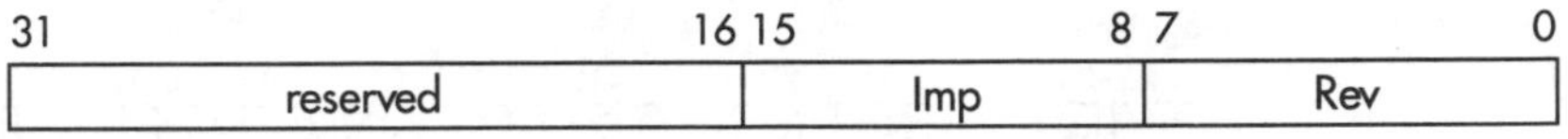

31	16 15	8 7	0
reserved	Imp	Rev	

FIGURE 3.1 **PRId** register fields

TABLE 3.2 MIPS CPU implementation numbers in **PRId(Imp)**

CPU type	Imp value
R2000	1
R3000, IDT R3051, R3052, R3071, R3081. Most early 32-bit MIPS CPUs	2
R6000	3
R4000, R4400	4
Some LSI Logic 32-bit CPUs	5
R6000A	6
IDT R3041	7
R10000	9
NEC Vr4200	10
NEC Vr4300	11
R8000	16
R4600	32
R4700	33
R3900 and derivatives	34
R5000	35
QED RM5230, RM5260	40

3.3.1 *Processor ID (PRId) Register*

Figure 3.1 shows the layout of the **PRId** register, a read-only register to be consulted to identify your CPU type. "Imp" will change whenever there's a change in either the instruction set or the CPU control register definitions. "Rev" is strictly manufacturer dependent and wholly unreliable for any purpose other than helping a CPU vendor to keep track of silicon revisions. Some settings we know about are listed in Table 3.2.

If you want to print out the values, it is conventional to print them out as "x.y" where x and y are the decimal values of Imp and Rev, respectively. Try not to use the contents of this register to establish parameters (like cache size, speed, and so on) or to establish the presence or absence of particular features;

R3000 (MIPS I) status register

31	30	29	28 27 26 25 24 23	22	21	20	19	18	17	16 15	8 7	6	5	4	3	2	1	0
0	CU1	CU0	0	RE	0	BEV	TS	PE	CM	PZ	SwC IsC IM	0	KUo	IEo	KUp	IEp	KUc	IEc

R4000 (MIPS III) status register

31	30	29	28	27	26	25 24	23	22	21	20	19 18	17	16	15						
0	CU1	CU0	RP	FR	RE	0	BEV	TS	SR	0	CH	CE	DE	IM	KX	SX	UX	KSU	ERL	EXL	IE

FIGURE 3.2 Fields in status register (**SR**)

your software will be more portable and robust if you design code sequences to probe for the existence of individual features. In many cases you will find examples or suggestions throughout this book.

3.3.2 *Status Register (SR)*

The MIPS CPU has remarkably few mode bits; those that exist are defined by fields in the CPU status register **SR**, as shown in Figure 3.2. We've shown fields for the "standard" R3000 and R4000 CPUs; other CPUs occasionally use other fields, sometimes alter the interpretation of fields, and commonly don't implement all of the fields.

We emphasize again that there are no nontranslated or noncached modes in MIPS CPUs; all translation and caching decisions are made on the basis of the program address.

The fields that are shared by the R3000 and R4000 CPUs are provided by most MIPS CPUs.

Key Fields Common to R3000 and R4000 CPUs

Here are the critical shared fields; it would be very bad form for a new implementation to recycle any of them for any purpose, and they are probably now nailed down for the foreseeable future.

CU1   Coprocessor 1 usable: 1 to use FPA if you have it, 0 to disable. When 0, all FPA instructions cause an exception. While it's obviously a bad idea to enable FPA instructions if your CPU lacks FPA hardware, it can be useful to turn off an FPA even when you have one.[1]

---

1. Why turn off a perfectly good FPA? Some operating systems disable FP instructions for every new task; if the task attempts some floating point it will trap and the FPA will be enabled for that task. But now we can distinguish tasks that never use floating-point instructions, and when such a task is suspended and restored we don't need to save or restore the FP registers; that may save some time in crucial context-saving code.

Bits 31 and 30 control the usability of coprocessors 3 and 2, respectively, and might be used by some MIPS CPUs that want to define more instructions. CP2 instructions may appear in some core implementations.

BEV   Boot exception vectors: When BEV == 1, the CPU uses the ROM (kseg1) space exception entry point (described in Section 5.3). BEV is usually set to 0 in running systems.

IM   Interrupt mask: An 8-bit field defining which interrupt sources, when active, will be allowed to cause an exception. Six of the interrupt sources are generated by signals from outside the CPU core (one may be used by the FPA, which although it lives on the same chip is logically external); the other two are the software-writable interrupt bits in the **Cause** register.

The 32-bit CPUs with floating-point hardware use one of the CPU interrupts to signal floating-point exceptions; MIPS III and subsequent CPUs usually have an interval timer as part of the co-processor 0 features, and timer events are signalled on the highest interrupt bit. Otherwise, interrupts are signalled from outside the CPU chip.

No interrupt prioritization is provided for you: The hardware treats all interrupt bits the same. See Section 5.8 for details.

Less Obvious Shared Fields

These fields are obscure, generally unused, but scary to change and therefore universal to date.

CU0   Coprocessor 0 usable: Set 1 to be able to use some nominally privileged instructions in user mode. You don't want to do this. The CPU control instructions encoded as coprocessor 0 type are always usable in kernel mode, regardless of the setting of this bit.

RE   Reverse endianness in user mode: The MIPS processors can be configured, at reset time, with either endianness (see Section 11.6 if you don't know what that means). Since human beings are perverse, there are now two universes of MIPS implementation: DEC and Windows NT are little-endian; SGI and their UNIX world are big-endian. Embedded applications originally showed a strong big-endian bias but are now thoroughly mixed.

It could be a useful feature in an operating system to be able to run software from the opposite universe; the RE bit makes it possible. When RE is active, user-privilege software runs as if the CPU had been configured with the opposite endianness.

However, achieving cross-universe running would require a large software effort as well, and to date nobody has done it.

TS   TLB shutdown: See Chapter 6 for details. TS gets set if a program address simultaneously matches two TLB entries, which is certainly a sign of something horribly wrong in the OS software. Prolonged operation in this state, in some implementations, could cause internal contention and damage to some chips, so the TLB ceases to match anything. TLB shutdown is terminal and can be cleared only by a hardware reset.

Some MIPS CPUs have foolproof TLB hardware and may not implement this bit.

On IDT R3051 family CPUs you can inspect this bit following hardware reset, and it will be set if and only if the CPU lacks a TLB (the memory management hardware). This test is not reliable across all implementations.

R3000-Specific Fields in the Status Register: Everyday Use

SwC, IsC   Swap caches and isolate (data) cache: These are cache mode bits for cache management and diagnostics; see Section 4.9 for details. In simple terms, when **SR(IsC)** is set, all loads and stores access only the data cache and never memory; in this mode a partial-word store invalidates the cache entry.

When **SR(SwC)** is set, the roles of the I-cache and the D-cache are reversed so that you can access and invalidate I-cache entries.

KUc, IEc   These are the two basic CPU protection bits.

KUc is set 1 when running with kernel privileges, 0 for user mode. In kernel mode you can get at the whole program address space and use privileged (coprocessor 0) instructions. In user mode you are restricted to program addresses between zero and 0x7FFF FFFF and can't run privileged instructions; attempts to break the rules result in an exception.

IEc is set 0 to prevent the CPU taking an interrupt, 1 to enable.

KUp, IEp   KU previous, IE previous: On an exception, the hardware takes the values of KUc and IEc and saves them here at the same time as changing the values of KUc, IEc to [1, 0] (kernel mode, interrupts disabled). The instruction **rfe** can be used to copy KUp, IEp back into KUc, IEc.

KUo, IEo   KU old, IE old: On an exception the KUp, IEp bits are saved here. Effectively, the six KU/IE bits are operated as a three-deep, 2-bit-wide stack that is pushed on an exception and popped by an **rfe**. The process is described in Chapter 5 and illustrated in Figure 5.1.

This provides a chance to recover cleanly from an exception occurring so early in an exception-handling routine that the first
exception has not yet saved **SR**. The circumstances in which this
can be done are limited, and it is probably only really of use in
allowing the user TLB refill code to be made a little shorter; see
Section 6.7 for more information.

Obscure R3000-only Bits

PE   Set if a cache parity error has occurred. No exception is generated by this condition, which is really only useful for diagnostics. The MIPS architecture has cache diagnostic facilities
because earlier versions of the CPU used external caches, and
signal timing on the cache buses was at the limits of technology. For those implementations the cache parity error bit was an
essential design debug tool.

For CPUs with on-chip caches, this feature is probably obsolete.

CM   This shows the result of the last load operation performed with
the D-cache isolated (see bit IsC of this register or Section 4.9.1
to know more about what "isolated" means). CM is set if the
cache really contained data for the addressed memory location
(i.e., if the load would have hit in the cache even if the cache had
not been isolated).

PZ   When set, cache parity bits are written as zero and not checked.
This is a fossil from CPUs with external caches, where it allowed
confident designers to dispense with the external memory that
held the cache parity bits, saving a little money. You won't use
this if the CPU has on-chip caches.

Common SR Fields in R4x00 CPUs

Remember, these fields are in principle entirely CPU dependent; however, there's
been a lot of commonality in CPUs from MIPS III upward.

FR   A mode switch: Set 1 to expose all 32 double-sized floating-point
registers to software; set 0 to make them behave as they do on the
R3000.

SR   Soft reset occurred: MIPS CPUs offer several different grades of
reset, distinguished by hardware signals. The field **SR(SR)** is
clear following a hard reset (one where all operating parameters
are reloaded from scratch) but set following a soft reset or NMI.
In particular, the configuration register **Config** retains its values
across a soft reset but must be reprogrammed after a hard reset.

Why Is There a Supervisor Mode?

The R3000 CPU offered only two privilege levels, which are all that is required by most UNIX implementations and all that has ever been used in any MIPS OS. So why did the R4000's designers go to considerable trouble to add a feature that has never been used?

In 1989–90 one of the biggest successes for MIPS was the use of the R3000 CPU in DEC's DECstation product line, and MIPS wanted the R4000 to be selected as DEC's future workstation CPU. The competition was an in-house development that evolved into DEC's Alpha architecture, but they were coming from behind; R4000 was usable about 18 months before Alpha. Whichever CPU was chosen had to run not only UNIX but DEC's minicomputer operating system VMS; apparently VMS architects claimed that it wasn't possible to implement VMS on a system with only two privilege levels.

Alpha's basic instruction set is almost identical to MIPS's; its biggest difference was the attempt to do without any partial-word loads or stores, and newer Alpha instruction sets have regained those.

In the end, it appears that the VMS software team was decisive in choosing Alpha over the R4000 because of its insistence that certain differences in the instruction set and CPU control architectures would make a VMS port to R4000 crucially slower. I am very skeptical about this and put the choice down to NIH (not invented here). DEC was probably right to believe that control over its microprocessor development was essential, but it's interesting to speculate how things might have turned out differently if DEC had stayed on board with the R4000.

I also suspect that sales of VMS on Alpha have been negligible, but that's another story.

DE	Disable cache and system interface data checking: You may need to set this for some hardware systems that don't provide parity on cache refills (though the hardware designer has the option of flagging data returning to the CPU as having no parity, which is probably a better approach). You should also set it for CPUs that don't implement cache parity.
UX, SX, KX	These support a mix of R3000-compatible and expanded address spaces: There are separate bits for the three different privilege levels; when the appropriate one is set, the most common memory translation exceptions (TLB misses) are redirected to a different entry point where the software will expect to deal with 64-bit addresses. Also, when **SR(UX)** is zero the CPU won't run 64-bit instructions from the MIPS-III ISA in user mode.
KSU	CPU privilege level: 0 for kernel, 1 for supervisor, 2 for user. Regardless of this setting, the CPU is in kernel mode whenever the EXL or ERL bits are set following an exception. The supervisor privilege level was introduced with the R4x00 but has never been used; see the sidebar for an explanation (or speculation) why.
ERL	Error level: This gets set when the CPU takes a parity/ECC mischeck exception. This uses a separate bit because a correctable ECC error can happen anywhere—even in the most sensitive part of an ordinary exception routine—and if the system is aim-

31	30	29	28	27	16	15	8	7	6	2	1	0
BD	0	CE		0		IP		0	ExcCode		0	

FIGURE 3.3 Fields in the **Cause** register

ing to patch up ECC errors and keep running, it must be able to fix them regardless of when they occur. That's challenging, since the exception routine has no registers it can safely use; and with no registers to use as pointers, it can't start saving register values.

To get us out of this hole, **SR(ERL)** has drastic effects; all access to normal user-space-translated addresses disappears, and program addresses from 0 through `0x7FFF.FFFF` become uncached windows onto the same physical addresses. The intention is that the cache error exception handler can use base+offset addressing off the **zero** register to get itself some memory space to save registers.

EXL   Exception level: Set by any exception, this forces kernel mode and disables interrupts; the intention is to keep EXL on for long enough for software to decide what the new CPU privilege level and interrupt mask is to be.

IE   Global interrupt enable: Note that either ERL or EXL inhibit all interrupts, regardless.

CPU-Dependent Fields in R4x00 CPUs

RP   Reduced power: Lowers the CPU's operating frequency, usually by dividing it by 16. In many R4x00 CPUs this doesn't work; even where it does, it requires that the CPU system interface be built to cope with it. Read the CPU manual, and talk to the system designer.

CH   Cache hit indicator: Used for diagnostics only.

CE   Cache error: This is only useful for diagnostics and recovery routines, and those should rely on information in the **ECC** register instead.

3.3.3   Cause Register

Figure 3.3 shows the fields in the **Cause** register, which you consult to find out what kind of exception happened and which you will use to decide what exception routine to call. **Cause** is a key register in exception handling and is defined the same way in all the MIPS CPUs I know of, though the list of exception types has grown.

BD   Branch delay: **EPC** is committed to being the address where control should go back to after an exception. Normally, this also points at the exception victim instruction.

But when the exception victim is an instruction that is in the delay slot following a branch, **EPC** has to point to the branch instruction; it is harmless to re-execute the branch, but if you returned from the exception to the branch delay instruction itself the branch would not be taken and the exception would have broken the interrupted program.

Cause(BD) is set only if the exception victim instruction was in a branch delay slot. You need only look at **Cause(BD)** if you want to analyze the exception victim instruction (if **Cause(BD)** == 1 then the instruction is at **EPC** + 4).

CE   Coprocessor error: If the exception is taken because a coprocessor format instruction was not enabled by the corresponding **SR(CUx)** field, then **Cause(CE)** has the coprocessor number from that instruction.

IP   Interrupt pending: Shows you the interrupts that want to happen. These bits follow the CPU inputs for the six hardware levels. Bits 9 and 8 are readable/writable and contain whatever value you last wrote to them. However, any of the 8 bits active when enabled by the appropriate **SR(IM)** bit and the global interrupt enable flag **SR(IEc)** will cause an interrupt.

Cause(IP) is subtly different from the rest of the **Cause** register fields: It doesn't tell you what happened when the exception took place; instead, it tells you what is happening now.

ExcCode   This is a 5-bit code that tells you what kind of exception happened, as detailed in Table 3.3.

3.3.4   *Exception Return Address (EPC) Register*

This is just a register that holds the address of the return point for this exception. The instruction causing (or suffering) the exception is at EPC, unless BD is set in **Cause**, in which case EPC points to the previous (branch) instruction. **EPC** is 64 bits wide if the CPU is.

3.3.5   *Bad Virtual Address (BadVaddr) Register*

This register holds the address whose use led to an exception; it is set on any MMU-related exception, on an attempt by a user program to access addresses outside kuseg, or if an address is wrongly aligned. After any other exception it is undefined. Note in particular that it is not set after a bus error. **BadVaddr** is 64 bits wide if the CPU is.

TABLE 3.3 ExcCode values: different kinds of exceptions

ExcCode value	Mnemonic	Description
0	Int	Interrupt
1	Mod	TLB modification: This is an attempt to store to a program address in a mapped region but where the MMU entry is marked as write only.
2	TLBL	TLB load/TLB store: No valid entry in the TLB matches a program address used for a read or write, respectively. This exception gets a special entry point for handling most translations (exactly which exceptions get special treatment changes between R3000- and R4000-like CPUs).
3	TLBS	
4	AdEL	Address error (on load/I-fetch or store, respectively): This is either an attempt to get outside kuseg when in user mode or an attempt to read a doubleword, word, or halfword at a misaligned address.
5	AdES	
6	IBE	Bus error (instruction fetch or data read, respectively): External hardware has signalled an error of some kind; what you have to do about it is system dependent. A bus error on a store can only come about indirectly, as a result of a cache read to obtain the cache line to be written.
7	DBE	
8	Syscall	Generated unconditionally by a **syscall** instruction.
9	Bp	Breakpoint: This is a **break** instruction.
10	RI	Reserved instruction: This is an instruction code undefined in this CPU.
11	CpU	Coprocessor unusable: This is a special kind of undefined instruction exception, where the instruction is in a coprocessor or load/store coprocessor format. In particular, this is the exception you get from a floating-point operation if the FPA usable bit, **SR(CU1)**, is not set; hence it is where floating-point emulation starts.
12	Ov	Arithmetic overflow: Note that unsigned versions of instructions (e.g., **addu**) never cause the exception.
13	TRAP	This comes from one of the conditional trap instructions added with MIPS II.
14	VCEI	Virtual coherency error in the I-cache: This is only relevant to R4000 and above CPUs that have a secondary cache and that use the secondary cache tag bits to check for cache aliases. Explained in Section 4.14.2.
15	FPE	Floating-point exception: This occurs only in MIPS II and higher CPUs. In MIPS I CPUs, floating-point exceptions are signalled as interrupts.

continued

TABLE 3.3 *continued*

ExcCode value	Mnemonic	Description
16	C2E	Exception from coprocessor 2: No R4x00 CPU (yet) has had a coprocessor 2, so this needn't worry you.
17–22	–	Reserved for future expansion.
23	Watch	Physical address of load/store matched enabled value in **WatchLo/WatchHi** registers.
24–30	–	Reserved for future expansion.
31	VCED	Virtual coherency error on data: This is the same as for VCEI.

3.4 Control Registers for the R4000 CPU and Followers

The R4000 (the first CPU implementing the 64-bit MIPS III ISA) was a brave attempt to regularize some features of CPU implementations that were showing signs of getting out of control and an attempt to provide a regular structure for some irresistible features.

The most obvious change is that the caches now come under the control of a new instruction (really a set of instructions) called **cache**; additional features include an on-CPU timer, some debug facilities, and mechanisms for handling recoverable bit errors in the extensive cache. Also there's a **Config** register that allows parameterization of some key features (cache size, cache line size, etc.) by communicating those parameters to the software that needs to know it.

We'll introduce the registers that are just for cache management in Chapter 4 where we're dealing with caches in general and the MMU/TLB registers in Chapter 6.

3.4.1 *Count/Compare Registers: The R4000 Timer*

These registers provide a simple general-purpose interval timer that runs continuously and that can be programmed to interrupt. In most CPUs, it's a reset-time configuration option whether the timer is wired to an interrupt. The timer is always the interrupt input found at **Cause(IP7)** (usually making the hardware input *Int5** redundant).

Count is a 32-bit counter that counts up continually, at exactly half the CPU's pipeline clock rate. When it reaches the maximum 32-bit value it overflows quietly back to zero. You can read **Count** to find the current time. You can also write **Count** at any time—but it's normal practice not to do so.

31	30 28	27 24	23 22	21	20	19 18	17	16	15	14	13	12 11	9 8	6 5	4	3 2	0
CM	EC	EP	SB	SS	SW	EW	SC	SM	BE	EM	EB	0	IC	DC	IB	DB	CU	K0

FIGURE 3.4 Fields in the R4000's **Config** register

Compare is a 32-bit read/write register. When **Count** increments to a value equal to **Compare**, the interrupt is raised. The interrupt remains asserted until cleared by a subsequent write to **Compare**.

To produce a periodic interrupt, the interrupt handler should always increment **Compare** by a fixed amount (not an increment to **Count**, because the period would then get slightly increased by interrupt latency). The software needs to check for the possibility that a late interrupt response might lead it to set **Compare** to a value that **Count** has already passed; typically, it rereads **Count** after writing **Compare**.

3.4.2   *Config Register: R4x00 Configuration*

CPU configuration is firmly CPU dependent, but all members of the R4x00 family have the **Config** register and share many of its fields. Figure 3.4 shows the set of flags provided by the original R4000 CPU.

The fields in Figure 3.4 are as follows:

CM   Set 1 for master/checker mode—applicable to fault-tolerant systems only. Set at reset time and read only.

EC   This 3-bit field encodes the clock divider: the ratio between the internal pipeline clock and the clock used to run the system interface. In some CPUs, the system interface clock is the same as the input clock, and this acts as a multiplier for the internal clock; in older CPUs, the pipeline always runs at twice the input clock rate, and this acts as a programmable divider for the system interface clock.

For the R4000, when the field holds the number n, the ratio is (n+ 2). But the introduction of such clock ratios as 1.5 and 2.5 in later CPUs has forced a change of encoding. Refer to the individual CPU manual.

This field is (so far) set at reset time and read-only.

EP   This 4-bit field encodes the transmit data pattern. The R4000 CPU and many of its successors have a system interface that has no external handshake signal on the multiple data of a cache line write-back cycle. The CPU is capable of sending the data at one bus-width quantity per clock cycle. Because this is sometimes too fast for the interface to cope with, the rate and rhythm with which data is sent can be programmed here.

The following table shows the data pattern as a pattern of "D", meaning a clock cycle where a word of data is sent, or "×", where the system interface rests for a clock:

EP field	Data pattern	EP field	Data pattern
0	D	8	D×× ×
1	DD×	9	DD× × × × ×
2	DD× ×	10	D× × × ×
3	D×	11	DD× × × × × ×
4	DD× × ×	12	D× × × × ×
5	DD× × × ×	13	DD× × × × × × ×
6	D× ×	14	D× × × × × ×
7	DD× × × ×	15	DD× × × × × × × ×

Short patterns are repeated as necessary, so a write back of an 8-word (4-doubleword) cache line programmed with **Config(EP)** == 5 would be "DD× × × ×DD". (Or would it be correctly written "DD× × × ×DD× × × ×", implying a three-cycle quiet period on the bus?) Our experience is that many CPUs do not implement dead time at the end of a write but that some do. Ask your CPU supplier if this is important to you.

Most CPUs support only a subset of these values. Some use different encodings. The EP field is sometimes set at reset time and read-only and sometimes programmable here.

SB

Off-chip secondary cache block size (or line size). This field is usually hardware configured and read-only here. R4000 encodings are

SB value	Block size (32-bit words)
0	4
1	8
2	16
3	32

SS
On the R4000 CPU, the off-chip secondary cache can either be operated as split (separate cache locations used for instructions and data, regardless of their addresses) or unified (all treated the same according to their address). It is set 1 for split, 0 for unified.

SW
On the R4000 (and maybe some others), it is set 1 if the secondary cache is 128 bits wide like the original R4000SC, 0 for 64 bits wide.

EW
System interface width: 0 for 64 bit, 1 for 32 bit.

SC
In R4000 and R5000 CPUs and their immediate descendants, this field is writable and acts as a software-controlled enable for the secondary cache; it is very useful for diagnostic purposes. It is set 1 if there is an on-chip controlled secondary cache, 0 otherwise.

Some later uniprocessor CPUs with provision for secondary caches report the secondary cache size in another field, recycling some bitfields that are used for multiprocessor purposes in R4000. However, typically those size fields are just blindly passing on information received at power-on configuration time and have no hardware impact.

SM
Multiprocessor cache coherency protocol configuration.

BE
CPU endianness (see Section 11.6): 1 for big-endian, 0 for little-endian. On the NEC Vr4300 (at least) this field is software writeable, but on most MIPS CPUs it's part of the hardware configuration.

EM
Data checking mode: 1 for ECC checking, 0 for per-byte parity.

EB
Must be 0. There was once going to be a hardware interface option to do all cache refills/write backs in sequential order, rather than in sub-block order; this option has never been implemented.

IC/DC
Size of primary I- and D-cache: A binary value n codes for a cache size of 2^{12+n} bytes.

IB/DB
Line (block) size of primary I- and D-cache: 0 for 4×32-bit words, 1 for 8×32-bit words.

CU
Another multiprocessor cache coherency protocol configuration bit.

K0
This is a writable field that allows you to configure cache behavior for accesses in kseg0. The codes here are just the same as those that can be entered into the MMU tables to control caching on a page-by-page basis and appear to you as the **EntryLo(C)** field. Outside of cache-coherent multiprocessors, the only interesting standard values are 3 = cached and 2 = uncached.

Post-R4000 CPUs not offering multiprocessor cache facilities have used other values to configure different cache behaviors

```
 31                        3  2  1  0
  MatchAddr(31..3)   0   R   W
```

FIGURE 3.5 Layout of the **WatchLo** register

such as write through and write allocate—see Section 4.3 for what those mean.

3.4.3 *Load-Linked Address (LLAddr) Register*

This register holds the physical address of the last-run load-linked operation, which is kept to monitor accesses that may cause a future store conditional to fail; see Section 5.8.4. Software access to **LLAddr** is for diagnostic use only.

3.4.4 *Debugger Watchpoint (WatchLo/WatchHi) Registers*

These registers implement a *watchpoint*: They hold a physical address that is checked against each load or store operation and that causes a trap if the load/store address matches. They are intended for use by debug software.

WatchLo is shown in Figure 3.5. Watchpoint addresses are maintained only to the nearest doubleword (8 bytes), so only address bits down to 3 need be kept. **WatchHi** holds high-order address bits. The other **WatchLo** bits enable the watchpoint check on reads if **WatchLo(R)** = 1 or writes if **WatchLo(W)** = 1. There's nothing to stop you from enabling both read and write watchpoint.

Some debuggers make use of the hardware watchpoint and some don't. Debuggers that do have a watchpoint facility (sometimes also called *data breakpoint*) normally allow you to set an arbitrary number of them and are likely to use **WatchLo/WatchHi** only when you've specified exactly one debugger watchpoint.

4 Caches for MIPS

A MIPS CPU without a cache isn't really a RISC. Perhaps that's not fair; for special purposes you might be able to build a MIPS CPU with a small, tightly coupled memory that can be accessed in a fixed number of pipeline stages (preferably one). But MIPS CPUs have pretty much always had cache hardware built in.

This chapter will describe the way in which MIPS caches work and what the software has to do to make them useful and reliable. From reset almost everything about the cache state is undefined, so the software must build carefully. You might also benefit from some hints and tips for use when sizing the caches (it would be bad software practice to assume you know how big the cache is). For the diagnostics programmer, we discuss how to test the cache memory and probe for particular entries.

Some real-time applications writers may want to control exactly what will get cached at run time. We discuss how to do it, even though I am skeptical about the wisdom of using such tricks.

There's also some evolution to contend with. In early 32-bit MIPS processors, cache management functions relied upon putting the cache into a special state and then using ordinary reads and writes whose side effects could initialize or invalidate cache locations. For later CPUs, special instructions are defined to do the relevant operations.

4.1 Caches and Cache Management

The cache's job is to keep a copy of memory data that has been recently read or written, so it can be returned to the CPU quickly and in a fixed period of time to keep the pipeline running.

MIPS CPUs always have separate caches for instructions and data (I-cache and D-cache, respectively) so that an instruction can be read and a load or store done simultaneously.

Older CPU families (such as the x86) have to be compatible with code that was written for CPUs that didn't have any caches. Modern x86 chips contain ingeniously designed hardware to make sure that software doesn't have to know about the caches at all (if you're building a machine to run MS/DOS this is essential to provide backward compatibility).

But because MIPS machines have always had caches, there's no need for the cache to be so clever. The caches must be transparent to application software, apart from the increased speed. But in a MIPS CPU, which has always had cache hardware, there is no attempt to make the caches invisible to system software or device drivers—cache hardware is installed to make the CPU go fast, not to help the system programmer. In a unix-like OS the operating system hides the cache from applications, of course, but while a more lightweight OS might well hide the details of cache manipulation from you, you will still probably have to know when to invoke the appropriate subroutine.

4.2   How Caches Work

Conceptually, a cache is an associative memory, a chunk of storage where data is written marked with an arbitrary data pattern as a key. In a cache, the key is the full memory address. Produce the same key back to an associative memory and you'll get the same data back again. A real associative memory will store items using any set of keys at all, at least until it's full; however, since a presented key has to be compared with every stored key simultaneously, a genuine associative memory of any size is either hopelessly resource hungry, slow, or both.

So how can we make a useful cache that is fast and efficient? Figure 4.1 shows the basic layout of the simplest kind of cache, the direct-mapped cache used in most MIPS CPUs up to the 1992 generation.

The direct-mapped arrangement uses a simple chunk of high-speed memory (the *cache store*) indexed by enough low address bits to span its size. Each *line* inside the cache store contains one or more words of data and a *cache tag* field that records the memory address where this data belongs.

On a read, the cache line is accessed and the tag field is compared with the higher addresses of the memory address; if the tag matches, we know we've got the right data and have "hit" in the cache. Where there's more than one word in the line, the appropriate word will be selected based on the very lowest address bits.

If the tag doesn't match, we've missed and the data will be read from memory and copied into the cache. The data that was previously held in the cache is simply discarded and will need to be fetched from memory again if the CPU references it.

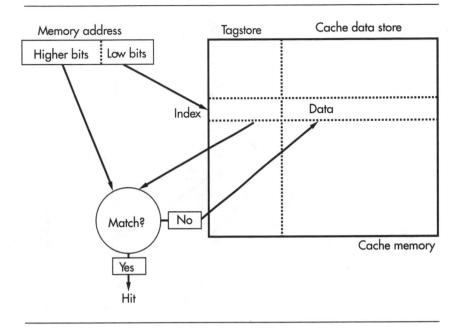

FIGURE 4.1   Direct-mapped cache

A direct-mapped cache like this one has the property that, for any given memory address, there is only *one* line in the cache store where that data can be kept.[1] That might be good or bad; it's good because such a simple structure will be fast and will allow us to run the whole CPU faster. But simplicity has its bad side too: If your program makes repeated reference to two data items that happen to share the same cache location (presumably because the low bits of their addresses happen to be close together), then the two data items will keep pushing each other out of the cache and efficiency will fall drastically.

A real associative memory wouldn't suffer from this kind of thrashing but would be impossibly complex, expensive, and slow for any reasonable size.

A common compromise is to use a two-way set-associative cache—which is really just a matter of running two direct-mapped caches in parallel and looking up memory locations in both of them, as shown in Figure 4.2.

Now we've got two chances of getting a hit on any address. Four-way set-associative caches (where there are effectively four direct-mapped subcaches) are also fairly common in on-chip caches.

There are penalties, however. A set-associative cache requires many more bus connections than a direct-mapped cache, so caches too big to integrate

---

1. In a fully associative memory, data associated with any given memory address (key) can be stored anywhere; a direct-mapped cache is as far from being content addressable as a cache store can be.

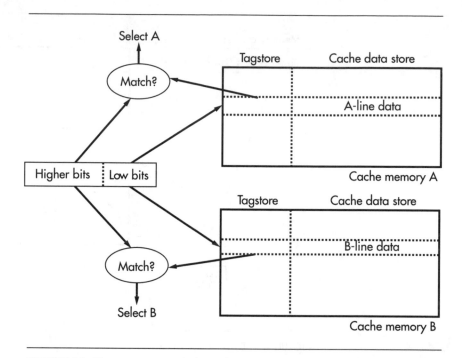

FIGURE 4.2 Two-way set-associative cache

onto a single chip are much easier to build direct mapped. More subtly, because the direct-mapped cache has only one possible candidate for the data you need, it's possible to keep the CPU running ahead of the tag check (just so long as the CPU does not do anything irrevocable based on the data). Simplicity and running ahead can translate to a faster clock rate.

Once the cache has been running for a while it will be full, so storing the incoming memory data usually means discarding some previously cached data. If you know that the data in the cache is already safely in memory, you can just discard the cached copy; if the data in the cache is more up to date than memory, you need to write it back first.

That brings us to how the cache handles writes.

4.3   Write-Through Caches in Early MIPS CPUs

CPUs don't just read data (as the above discussion seems to be assuming)— they write it too. Since a cache is intended to be a local copy of some data from main memory, one obvious way of handling the CPU's writes is the use of what is called a *write-through* cache.

In a write-through cache the CPU's data is always written to main memory; if a copy of that memory location is resident in the cache, the cached copy is updated too. If we always do this, then any data in the cache is known to be in memory too, so we can discard the contents of a cache line any time we need a cache location and we lose nothing but time.

There's a danger that we will slow the processor down drastically if we make it wait for the memory write to finish, but we can fix that. Writes (address and data together) destined for main memory can always be kept on one side while the memory controller gets itself ready and completes the write. The place where writes are kept temporarily is organized as a first in, first out (FIFO) store and is called a *write buffer*.

Early MIPS CPUs had a direct-mapped write-through cache and a write buffer, a setup motivated by the R3000 chip, which found space for an on-chip cache controller but needed external high-speed memory chips to store the cache tags and data. So long as the memory system can happily absorb writes at the average rate produced by a CPU, running a particular program this way works very well.

But CPU speeds have grown much faster than memory speeds; and somewhere around the time that the 32-bit MIPS generation was giving way to the 64-bit R4000, MIPS speeds passed the point where a memory system could reasonably hope to absorb every write.[1]

4.4   Write-Back Caches in Recent MIPS CPUs

While early MIPS CPUs use simple write-through data caches, later CPUs are too fast for this approach—they would swamp their memory systems with writes and slow to a (relative) crawl.

The solution is to retain write data in the cache. Write data goes into the cache only, and the cache line is marked to make sure we don't forget to write it back to memory sometime (a line that needs writing back is called *dirty*).[2]

There's a subvariant here: If the addressed data is not currently in the cache, we can either write it to main memory and ignore the cache, or we can bring the data in specially just so we can write it—this is called *write allocate*. Seen from the selfish point of view of one program running on one CPU, write allocate looks like a waste of time; however, it makes the system design simpler because it means that a running program only ever reads/writes memory in whole-cache-line-sized blocks.

---

1. A very rough rule of thumb for programs suggests one store per 10 instructions, so a write-through solution may work until the memory cycle time reaches about 5–7 instruction times. With DRAM cycle times around 180ns, the simple solution ran out of steam at about 30–40MHz.

2. You might ask: Since we're going to have to write it back sometime, surely we might as well do it now? But actually programs often write many times in quick succession to the same small patch of memory, and the write-back cache allows many individual write operations to be achieved with just one write to memory.

From the MIPS R4000 on, MIPS CPUs have on-chip caches that are write through, write allocate, and have line sizes of 16 or 32 bytes.

The design choices in MIPS caches as applied to the R4000 and other large CPUs used in Silicon Graphics and other computers are influenced by the needs of multiprocessor systems (not discussed in this book).

4.5 Other Choices in Cache Design

The 80s and 90s have seen much work and exploration of how to build caches. So there are yet more choices:

- *Physically addressed/virtually addressed*: While the CPU is running a grown-up OS, data and instruction addresses in your program (the *program address* or *virtual address*) are translated before appearing as physical addresses in the system memory.

    A cache that works purely on physical addresses is easier to manage (we'll explain why below), but raw program (virtual) addresses are available to start the cache lookup earlier, letting the system run that little bit faster.

    So what's wrong with program addresses? They're not unique; many different programs running in different address spaces on a CPU may share the same program address for different data. We could reinitialize the entire cache every time we switch contexts between different address spaces; that used to be done some years ago and may be a reasonable solution for very small caches. But for big caches it's ridiculously inefficient, and we'll need to include a field identifying the address space in the cache tag to make sure we don't mix them up.

    There's another, more subtle problem with program addresses: The same physical location may be described by different addresses in different tasks. In turn, that might lead to the same memory location cached in two different cache entries (because they were referred to by different virtual addresses that selected different cache indexes). These *cache aliases* must be avoided by the OS's memory manager; see Section 4.14.2 for details.

    From the R4000 on, MIPS primary caches have used the program address to provide a fast index to start the cache lookup. But rather than using the program address plus an address space identifier to tag the cache line, they use the physical address. The physical address is unique to the cache line and is efficient because the scheme allows the CPU to translate program addresses to physical addresses at the same time it is looking up the cache.

- *Choice of line size*: The line size is the number of words of data stored with each tag. Early MIPS caches had one word per tag, but it's usually advantageous to store multiple words per tag, particularly when your memory system will support fast burst reads (most do). Modern MIPS caches tend to use four- or eight-word line sizes, but large secondary and tertiary caches often have bigger line sizes.

  When a cache miss occurs, the whole line must be filled from memory. But it is quite possible to fetch several lines of data; MIPS CPUs with one word/line caches often fetch more than one word at a time.

- *Split/unified*: MIPS primary caches are always separated into an I- and a D-cache; the selection is done purely by function, in that instruction fetches look in the I-cache and data loads/stores in the D-cache. (This means, by the way, that if you try to execute code which the CPU just copied into memory you must both flush those instructions out of the D-cache and ensure they get loaded into the I-cache.)

  However, off-chip secondary caches are rarely divided up this way—there's no real advantage unless you can afford to provide separate data buses to the two caches, and that would cost far too many pins.

4.6 Managing Caches

The cache system, with the help of system software, must be able to ensure that any application gets the same data as it would have in an uncached system and that any direct memory access (DMA) I/O controller (getting data directly from memory) obtains the data that the program thinks it has written.

We've said before that in CISC CPUs the assistance of system software is often not required; it's worth spending the money, silicon area, and extra cycles to get the hardware to make the cache genuinely transparent.

The MIPS CPU is responsible for initializing its caches at system boot-up; this can be quite an intricate process and there's some advice about it below. But once the system is up and running there are only three circumstances in which the CPU must intervene:

- *Before DMA out of memory*: If a device is taking data out of memory, it's vital that it gets the right data. If the data cache is write back and a program has recently written some data, some of the correct data may still be held in the D-cache but not yet be written back to main memory. The CPU can't see this problem, of course; if it looks at the memory locations it will get the correct data back from its cache.

  So before the DMA device starts reading data from memory, any data for that range of locations that is currently held in the D-cache must be written back to memory if necessary.

Why Not Manage Caches in Hardware?

Caches managed with hardware are often called "snoopy." When another CPU or some DMA device accesses memory, the addresses concerned are made visible to the cache. With a CPU attached to a shared bus, this is pretty straightforward; the address bus contains most of the information you need. The hardware watches (snoops) the address bus even when the CPU is not using it and picks out relevant cycles. It does that by looking up its own cache to see whether it holds a copy of the location being accessed.

If someone is *writing* data that is inside the cache, the controller can pick up the data and update the cache line but is more likely to just invalidate its own, now stale, copy. If someone is *reading* data for which updated information is held in the cache, the controller may be able to intervene on the bus, telling the memory controller that it has a more up-to-date version.

One major problem with doing this is that it works only within a system designed to operate that way. Not all systems have a single bus where all transactions appear; bought-in I/O controllers are unlikely to conform to the right protocols.

Also, it's very complicated. Most of the locations that CPUs work with are the CPU's private areas; they will never be read or written by any other CPU or device. We'd like not to build hardware ingenuity into the cache, loading every cache location and bus cycle with complexity that will only sometimes be used.

It's easy to suppose that a hardware cache control mechanism must be faster than software, but that's not necessarily so. A snoopy cache controller must look at the cache tags on every external cycle, which could shut the CPU out of its cache and slow it down; complex cache controllers usually hold two copies of the cache tags for this reason. Software management can operate on blocks of cache locations in a single fast loop; hardware management will interleave invalidations or write backs with CPU accesses at I/O speed, and that usually implies more arbitration overhead.

So MIPS took the radical RISC position: MIPS CPUs either have no cache management hardware or, where designed for multiprocessors, they have everything—like the R4400MC or R10000.

- *DMA into memory*: If a device is loading data into memory, it's important to invalidate any cache entries purporting to hold copies of the memory locations concerned; otherwise, the CPU reading these locations will obtain stale cached data. The cache entries should be invalidated before the CPU uses any data from the DMA input stream.

- *Writing instructions*: When the CPU itself is storing instructions into memory for subsequent execution, you must first ensure that the instructions are written back to memory and then make sure that the corresponding I-cache locations are invalidated: The MIPS CPU has no connection between the D-cache and the I-cache.

If your software is going to fix these problems, it needs to be able to do two distinct operations on a cache entry.

The first operation is called *write back*. The CPU must be able to look in the cache for data for a particular location. If it is present in the cache and is dirty (marked as having been written by the CPU since it was last obtained from memory or written back to memory), then the CPU copies the data from the cache into main memory.

The second is *invalidate*. The CPU should look in the cache for data for a particular location; if it is there, the CPU marks it invalid so that any subsequent access will fetch the data from memory again.

It's tempting to use the more colorful and evocative word "flush" in this context, but it has been ambiguously used to mean write back, invalidate, or the combination of the two—so we'll avoid it.

There are some much more complicated issues involved when two or more processors share memory. Most shared-memory systems are too complex for one CPU to know what locations the other will read or write, so invalidation and write back are not effective. CPUs must either share uncached memory (very slow unless the amount of interaction is very limited), or the caches must have special hardware that keeps the caches (and memory) coherent. Multi-CPU cache coherency got less scary after it was systematized by a group of engineers working on the ambitious FutureBus standard in the mid-80s; locations inside caches are modeled as simple state machines with inter-CPU and CPU/memory interactions causing well-defined state transitions.

There's a very brief discussion of multiprocessor mechanisms in Section 4.14.1, but this book is mostly about single-CPU systems.

4.7   Secondary and Tertiary Caches

In larger systems, there's often a nested hierarchy of caches. A small and fast *primary* cache is close to the CPU. Accesses that miss in the primary cache are looked up not just in memory but in a *secondary cache*, which is intermediate in speed and size between the primary cache and the memory system. The number of levels of hierarchy that might be useful depends on how slow main memory is compared to the CPU's fastest access; with CPU cycle times falling much faster than memory access times, desktop systems have gone from no cache to two-level caches in the past 12 years. The fastest CPUs of the late 90s, running at 500MHz or so, will have three-level caches.

4.8   Cache Configurations for MIPS CPUs

We can now classify some landmark MIPS CPUs, ancient and modern, by their cache implementations and see how the cache hierarchy has evolved (Table 4.1).

As clock speeds get higher, we see more variety in cache configurations as designers try to cope with a CPU that is running increasingly ahead of its memory system. To earn its keep, a cache must improve performance by supplying data significantly faster than the next outer memory and must usually succeed in supplying the data (*hitting*).

TABLE 4.1 Cache evolution in MIPS CPUs

CPU (MHz)	Primary				Secondary			Tertiary		
	Size I-cache	Size D-cache	direct/ n-way	on-chip?	Size	direct/ n-way	on-chip?	Size	direct/ n-way	on-chip?
R3000-33	32K	32K	Direct	Off						
R3052-33	8K	2K	Direct	On						
R4000-100	8K	8K	Direct	On	1M	Direct	Off			
R4600-100	16K	16K	Two-way	On						
R10000-250	32K	32K	Two-way	On	4M	Two-way	Off			
R5000-200	32K	32K	Two-way	On	1M	Direct	Off			
RM7000-xxx	16K	16K	Four-way	On	256K	Four-way	On	8M	Direct	Off

CPUs that add another level of hierarchy reduce the miss penalty for the next cache inward, so the designers may be able to simplify the inner cache in search of higher clock rates, most obviously by making the next inner cache smaller. It seems likely that as many high-end CPUs gain on-chip secondary caches (from 1998 on), primary cache sizes will fall slightly, with dual 16KB primary caches a favored "sweet spot."[1]

An off-chip cache is generally direct mapped because a set-associative cache system needs multiple buses and therefore an awful lot of pins to connect it. This is still an area for experimentation; the MIPS R10000 implements an external two-way set-associative cache with one data bus by delaying the returned data when the hit is not in the expected set.

Amidst all this evolution, there have been two main generations of the software interface to the cache. From a software point of view there is one style founded by the R3000 and followed by practically all 32-bit MIPS CPUs; there is another starting with the R4000 and used by all 64-bit CPUs to date.[2] R3000-type MIPS CPUs have caches that are write through, direct mapped, and physically addressed. Cache locations are accessible only as whole words, so an operation that writes a byte (or anything less than a whole word) has to be managed specially. Cache management is done using special modes in which regular loads and stores do magic things to the cache.

---

1. At least this is true of architectures where the primary cache access is mostly fitted into one clock cycle—always true of MIPS so far. It's intuitively plausible that there should be a more or less fixed cache size whose access takes about the same time as the other activities traditionally fitted into one pipeline stage. However, early versions of the RISC HP-8x00 CPU family accept a two-clock-cycle primary cache latency in return for a huge external primary cache, and they seem to work well.

2. One day (perhaps by the time you read this) there will probably be 32-bit MIPS CPUs with R4000-type caches.

By contrast the R4000-type CPUs have primary caches that are write back with write allocate, virtually indexed, physically tagged, and sometimes two- or four-way set associative. Cache management is done using a special `cache` instruction.

Many R4x00 and successor CPUs have on-chip secondary cache controllers, and 1998 should see the first MIPS CPU with an on-chip secondary cache.

Since the two generations are so different, we'll split the detailed description into two sections.

CAUTION!   Some system implementations have secondary caches that are not controlled by hardware inside the MIPS CPU but built on to the memory bus. The software interface to caches like that is going to be system specific and may be quite different from the CPU-implemented or CPU-controlled caches described in this chapter.

4.9   Programming R3000-Style Caches

The MIPS R2000 broke new ground in its on-chip cache controller for an external split I- and D-cache. It's not surprising, in hindsight, that such a pioneering venture should lead to some flaws. The cache had one particular software-visible defect.

To save package pins, the cache didn't have separate write strobes to implement byte, halfword, and other partial-word write cycles. So in the R2000 an attempt to perform a partial-word write at a cached location wrote main memory and invalidated the word in the cache. That also gave you a way of invalidating cache entries, which is required for cache management: just write a byte.

You can see the arguments for this simplification. The R2000 architects reasoned that partial-word operations are most often used for strings, that strings are almost always manipulated by library routines, and that these routines can be recoded to use mostly word writes. These assumptions were respectively mostly right, wrong, and right—and there are no prizes for being partly right.

It didn't take long before MIPS realized that not all systems used the same library functions and that a cache entry that disappeared on every byte write wasn't such a good idea. Such a large change in the CPU pin-out was not tolerable, so the R3000 implements cached partial-word writes with a read-modify-write (RMW) sequence. The RMW appears in all the 32-bit MIPS CPUs you'll meet outside of a museum and adds an extra clock cycle of delay every time the CPU writes a partial word.

The cache invalidation mechanism was caught in the crossfire; the R2000 had made a virtue of its strange behavior by using byte writes to invalidate cache locations. However, the R3000 could be rescued using a mode called *cache isolation*, which was originally intended for cache diagnostics only. The RMW sequence is suppressed with the cache isolated and in that state a partial-word write still invalidates the line. It's unfortunate, but not catastrophic, that isolating the cache has rather undesirable side effects for something to be done in a running system; notably, with the cache isolated *no* load/store operation, even one that would normally be uncached, gets to memory.

4.9.1 *Using Cache Isolation and Swapping*

All R3000-style CPUs have write-through caches, which means they never hold data that is more up to date than main memory. That means that they never need a write back, so we only need the ability to invalidate a location in either the D-cache or the I-cache.

You need a way of distinguishing operations for cache management from regular memory references, and cache management is not seen as important enough to get a special address region. So there's a status register bit **SR(IsC)** that will *isolate* the D-cache; in this mode, loads and stores affect only the cache and loads also hit regardless of whether the tag matches. With the D-cache isolated, a partial-word write will invalidate the appropriate cache line.

CAUTION! When the D-cache is isolated, not even loads/stores marked by their address or TLB entry as uncached will operate normally. One consequence of this is that the cache management routines must not make any data accesses; you can only write them in a high-level language if you have very good control over your compiler and can ensure that all the variables you use are maintained in registers. It's also essential to run that routine with interrupts disabled!

The I-cache is completely inaccessible in normal running. So the CPU provides a mode where the caches are *swapped*, by setting the status register bit **SR(SwC)**; then the D-cache acts as an I-cache and the I-cache acts as the D-cache. Once the caches are swapped, isolated I-cache entries may be read, written, and invalidated.

The D-cache behaves perfectly as an I-cache (provided it was sufficiently initialized to work as a D-cache) but the I-cache does not behave properly as a D-cache. It is unlikely that it will ever be useful to have the caches swapped but not isolated.

If you should use a swapped I-cache for word stores (a partial-word store invalidates the line, as before) you must make sure those locations are invalidated before returning to normal operation.

4.9.2   *Initializing and Sizing*

At machine startup the caches are in a random state, so the result of a cached read is unpredictable. You should also remember that following a reset the status register **SR(SwC)** and **SR(IsC)** bits are also in a random state, so startup software had better set them to a known state before attempting any load or store (even uncached).

Different MIPS CPUs have different cache sizes. It makes your software more portable if you work out the size of the I-cache and D-cache at initialization time, rather than hardwiring a particular value.

To size the cache, do the following:

- Isolate the caches, and swap the cache for the I-cache.

- For each *n* that is a plausible size for the cache (starting with the largest value), set the word at physical address *n* to the value *n*. The easiest way to generate the physical address is to use the kseg0 address *n*+0x8000 0000.

   On R3000 CPUs, plausible cache sizes are 256K, 128K, 64K, 32K, 16K, 8K, 4K, 2K, 1K, and 0.5K (where K = 1024, of course).

   The cache addresses wrap around, so if *n* is a multiple of the cache size it will set the lowest word in the cache.

- Read the word at physical address zero (i.e., 0x8000 0000) to obtain the size of the cache in bytes.

To initialize the cache, you should ensure that every cache entry is either invalid or correctly corresponds to a memory location and that it also contains correct parity:

- Check that **SR(PZ)** is set 0 (1 disables parity, which is never a good idea with an on-chip cache).

- Isolate the D-cache and swap to access the I-cache.

- For each word of the cache, first write a word value (which will put correct tag, data, and parity in the line), then write a byte (invalidating the line).

   Note that for an I-cache with four words per line this is inefficient; it would be enough to write just 1 byte in each line to invalidate the entry. Unless you are going to use the invalidate routine often it doesn't seem worth the trouble; however, if you do want to optimize it do so conditionally, identifying the cache organization at boot time.

4.9.3   *Invalidation*

To invalidate the cache, do the following:

- Figure out the address range you want to invalidate. Invalidating a region larger than the cache size is a waste of time.

- Isolate the D-cache. Once it is isolated you can't read or write memory, so you must at all costs prevent any exception. Disable interrupts and ensure that subsequent software cannot cause a memory access exception.

- Swap the caches if you want to work on the I-cache.

- Write a byte value to each cache line in the range.

- Unswap and unisolate.

You should normally run the invalidate routine with its instructions cacheable. This sounds confusing and dangerous, but in fact you don't normally have to take any extra steps to run cached. An invalidation routine in uncached space will run 4–10 times slower.

It's essential to disable interrupts while your CPU is running with **SR(IsC)** set, because it isn't able to access memory at all.

4.9.4   *Testing and Probing*

During testing, debugging, or when profiling, it may be useful to build up a picture of the cache contents. You cannot read the tag value directly, but for a valid line you can find it by exhaustive search:

- Isolate the cache.

- Load from the cache line at each possible line start address (low-order bits fixed, high-order bits ranging over the physical memory that exists in your system). After each load consult the status register bit **SR(CM)**, which will be 0 only when you guess the tag value right.

This takes a long time by computer terms, but to fully search a 1K D-cache with 4MB of cacheable physical memory on a 20MHz processor will take only a couple of seconds.

4.10   Programming R4000-Style Caches

The R4000 fixed the unseemly cache maintenance of the earlier CPUs. But the R4000 and its successors have much more sophisticated caches—write back, write allocate, and with longer lines. Because it's a write-back cache, each line needs a status bit that marks it as dirty when it gets written by the CPU (and hence becomes different from the main memory copy of the data).

`TagLo` **register**

31		8	7	6	5		1	0
	PTagLo		PState			0		P

`TagHi` **register**

PTagHi

FIGURE 4.3 Layout of the R4000's **TagLo/TagHi** register

With these caches, we need both an invalidate and a write-back operation: The latter ensures that any CPU-written data in a cache line is sent back to main memory.

For diagnostic and maintenance purposes it's good to be able to read and write the cache tags; the R4000 adds a pair of registers **TagLo** and **TagHi** to stage data between the tag part of the cache and management software. There's no direct way of reading the data in an R4000-style cache line, though you can of course access the data by hitting on it. The CPU implements **cache** instructions that either load the 32-bit **TagLo**, **TagHi** registers from the cache tag or copy the contents of the registers into the cache line. Figure 4.3 shows what the registers look like.

A cache address tag holds all the address bits that have not been used up for the cache index; hence the primary cache tag's length is the difference between the biggest physical address (36 bits on R4x00) and the number of bits used to index the primary cache—13 bits for the 8KB primary caches of the original R4000 and never less since. That's 23 bits, and **TagLo(PTagLo)** has room for 24 bits; so **TagHi** is always zero in current CPUs. It becomes necessary with either smaller cache set sizes (unlikely to happen) or to support a larger physical address. For the R4000 **TagHi** is a placeholder for now; set it zero and forget it.

So **TagLo(PTagLo)** holds all the address tag bits for this cache line. **TagLo (PState)** contains the state bits. In the most general (multiprocessor) case this can be pretty complicated, but for all cache management and initialization it suffices to know that a zero value of **PState** is always a legitimate code representing an invalid cache entry.

The field shown as zero here is colonized by later CPUs to store recently used state information in secondary caches, but it's a convention that the value zero is safe and appropriate for initialization.

Lastly, **TagLo(P)** is a parity bit, set to give the entire cache tag even parity. An all-zero value for **TagLo** has correct even parity. Some CPUs ignore this bit and don't check it, but it does no harm to get it right.

4.10.1 *CacheERR, ERR, and ErrorEPC Registers: Cache Error Handling*

The CPU's caches form a vital part of the memory system, and high-availability or trustworthy systems may find it worthwhile to use some extra bits to monitor the integrity of the data stored there.

Memory system checks should ideally be implemented end to end; check bits should be computed as soon as data is generated or introduced to the system, stored with the data, and checked just before it's used. That way the check catches faults not just in the memory array but in the complex buses and gizmos that data passes through on its way to the CPU and back.

For this reason, R4x00 CPUs (designed to support large computers) provide error checking in the caches. Like a main memory system, you can use either simple parity or an error-correcting code (ECC).

Parity is simple to implement as an extra bit for each byte of memory. A parity error tells the system that data is unreliable and allows a somewhat-controlled shutdown instead of creeping random failure. A crucial role of parity is that it can be an enormous help during system development, because it unambiguously identifies problems as being due to memory data integrity.

But a byte of complete garbage has a 50% chance of having correct parity, and random rubbish on the 72-bit data bus will still escape detection one time in 256. Some systems want something better.

An error-correcting code is more complex to calculate, because it involves the whole 64-bit word with eight check bits used together. It's more thorough: A 1-bit error can be uniquely identified and corrected, and no 2-bit error can escape detection. ECC is seen as essential to weed out random errors in very large memory arrays.

Because the ECC bits check the whole 64-bit word at once, ECC memories can't perform a partial-word write by just selecting which part of the word to operate on but must always merge the new data and recompute the ECC. MIPS CPUs running uncached require their memory system to implement partial-word writes, making things complicated. Memory system hardware must transform partial-word writes into a read-merge-recalculate-write sequence.

For simpler systems the choice is usually parity or nothing. It can be valuable to make parity optional, to get the diagnostic benefits during design development without paying the price in production.

Whatever check mechanism is implemented in the memory system, inside the R4x00 caches the CPU may offer per-byte parity, a per-doubleword 8-bit ECC field, or possibly no protection.

Where checking is supported, the data check bits are usually carried straight from the system interface into the cache store and not checked at cache-refill time. The data is checked when it's used, which ensures that any cache parity exception is delivered to the instruction that causes it, not just to one that happens to share the same cache line. As a degenerate case, an error on an uncached fetch is flagged as a cache parity error—which can confuse you.

31	30	29	28	27	26	25	24	0
ER	0	ED	ET	0	EE	EB	PIdX	

FIGURE 4.4 CacheERR register fields

Note that it's possible for the system interface to mark incoming data as having no valid check bits. In this case the CPU will regenerate check bits for its internal cache.

If an error occurs, the CPU takes the special error trap. This vectors through a location in uncached space (if the cache contains bad data, it would be foolish to execute code from it). If a system uses ECC the hardware generates the check bits on a write and checks them for an error. The hardware doesn't know how to correct errors; that's left to software.

The fields in the ERR register (Figure 4.4) are as follows:

- *ER/ED/ET/EE/EB*: These distinguish which cache (primary/secondary, instruction/data) had the error or whether it was out on the system interface.

- *PIdX*: This field gives the cache index of the failing location. You can grab this field and use it in an index-type cache operation; it should get you the right line, regardless of whether the cache is direct mapped or set associative.

After an error **ErrorEPC** points to the offending load instruction. **ERR** holds the ECC bits you need to fix up correctable errors, but we're not going to tell you how that's done—it's pretty heavy stuff, and you'll need to commune with the processor manual for a while. You may be able to get some sample code from MIPS or Algorithmics.

4.10.2 *The Cache Instruction*

The **cache** instruction has the general form of a MIPS load or store instruction (with the usual register plus 16-bit signed displacement address), but where the data register would have been encoded is an option field. There are no standard names for the operations; I've arbitrarily used those from the Algorithmics SDE-MIPS package, which in turn were based on one of the SGI/MIPS include files. The option field is not quite bit coded, but nearly; see Table 4.2.

The **cache** options allow you to choose the following:

- *Which cache*: Selects I- or D-cache and primary or secondary cache. There's no provision yet for tertiary caches and not many bits left. But I remind you that this stuff is all CPU dependent, and all the post-R4000

TABLE 4.2 Operation codes for the cache instruction

Conventional name	Code (hex)	Conventional name	Code (hex)
Index_Invalidate_I	0x0	Hit_Invalidate_I	0x10
Index_Writeback_Inv_D	0x1	Hit_Invalidate_D	0x11
Index_Invalidate_SI	0x2	Hit_Invalidate_SI	0x12
Index_Writeback_Inv_SD	0x3	Hit_Invalidate_SD	0x13
Index_Load_Tag_I	0x4	Fill_I	0x14
Index_Load_Tag_D	0x5	Hit_Writeback_Inv_D	0x15
Index_Load_Tag_SI	0x6		
Index_Load_Tag_SD	0x7	Hit_Writeback_Inv_SD	0x17
Index_Store_Tag_I	0x8	Hit_Writeback_I	0x18
Index_Store_Tag_D	0x9	Hit_Writeback_D	0x19
Index_Store_Tag_SI	0xA		
Index_Store_Tag_SD	0xB	Hit_Writeback_SD	0x1B
Create_Dirty_Exc_D	0xD		
		Hit_Set_Virtual_SI	0x1E
Create_Dirty_Exc_SD	0xF	Hit_Set_Virtual_SD	0x1F

64-bit CPUs that provide compatibility with the R4000 are just being helpful.

- *How cache is addressed*: Two different styles are used. In hit-type operations you provide a regular program address (virtual address), which is translated as necessary. If that location is currently cached, the operation is carried out on the relevant cache line; if the location is not in the cache, nothing happens.

  Alternatively, there are index operations where the low bits of the address are used directly to select a cache line, without regard to the line's present contents. This exposes the cache's internal organization in a nonportable way.

  Running cache maintenance is done almost entirely with hit operations, while initialization requires index types.

- *Write back*: Causes the cache line to be written back to memory if it is marked dirty—for clean lines this is a **nop**.

- *Invalidate*: Marks the line as invalid so that its data won't be used again.

Commands are available that do both write back and invalidate; this is not automatic, and you can invalidate a dirty line if you want to. Some applications are likely to lose data, though.

- *Load/store tags*: These operations move the cache tag fields of the specified line into and out of the **TagLo** and **TagHi** CPU registers.

  Store tags are used in a degenerate case (where **TagLo** and **TagHi** are preset to zero) as part of cache initialization. Load tags and more ambitious use of store tags are solely for diagnostics.

- *Fill*: Only defined for the I-cache, this operation fills a cache line from the specified memory address. There's no need for a Fill_D because you can achieve the same result by a cacheable load that misses.

- *Create data*: The Create dirty exclusive operation is intended to allow a user to write a memory array at very high speed by avoiding any cache refills. This will generate garbage unless you can be sure that you will overwrite all the data in the cache line before the data gets used or flushed.

  This feature can be useful for initialization and diagnostics (you'll see it used in the secondary cache initialization code examples below to set up known clean data in the secondary cache). It could be used to tune a heavily used OS facility when zeroing or copying a whole page of data, but most often that's a bad idea.

4.10.3 *Cache Sizing and Figuring Out Configuration*

In R4x00 CPUs (and most likely in future CPUs too) the primary cache sizes and line size are reliably reported to you as part of the CP0 **Config** register.

It's really quite hard to find out whether your cache is direct mapped or set associative. It isn't too hard to concoct a test for a running cache, where you can reference two locations that can't both be present in a direct-mapped cache and then use index operations to find out whether both are present; however, that doesn't work until you've initialized the cache. Fortunately, you can write a routine that will initialize either a direct-mapped or a set-associative cache.

4.10.4 *Initialization Routines*

Here's one good way to do it:

1. Set up some memory to arbitrary data, but correct the parity/ECC if your system uses it, ready to use for filling the cache. (In the Algorithmics routines we reserve the bottom 32K of system memory up to initialization time; once it's been written [uncached] it should return correct parity.)

A buffer that size isn't big enough to initialize a secondary cache; we'll use a devious trick to manage without.

2. Set **TagLo** to zero, which makes sure that the valid bit is unset and the tag parity is consistent.

   The **TagLo** register will be used by the **cache Store_Tag** cache instructions to forcibly invalidate a line and clear the tag parity.

3. Disable interrupts if they might otherwise happen.

4. Initialize the I-cache first, then the D-cache. Following is C code for I-cache initialization. (You have to believe in the functions or macros like Index_Store_Tag_I() which do low-level functions; they're either trivial assembler code subroutines that run the appropriate machine instructions or—for the brave GNU C user—macros invoking a C asm statement.)

```
for (addr = KSEG0; addr < KSEG0 + size; addr += lnsize) {
    /* clear tag to invalidate */
    Index_Store_Tag_I (addr);
    /* fill so data field parity is correct */
    Fill_I (addr);
    /* invalidate again - prudent but not strictly necessary */
    Index_Store_Tag_I (addr);
}
```

5. D-cache initialization is slightly more awkward because there is no **cache Index_Fill_D** operation; we have to load through the cache and rely on normal miss processing. In turn, while the **Fill** instruction operates on a cache index, load processing always relates to memory addresses and hits in the cache based on the tags. You have to be careful about the tags; with a two-way cache the I-cache-style loop would initialize half the D-cache twice, since clearing **PTagLo** will reset the bit used to decide which set of the cache line is to be used on the next cache miss. Here's how it's done:

```
/* clear all tags */
for (addr = KSEG0; addr < KSEG0 + size; addr += lnsize)
    Index_Store_Tag_D (addr);
/* load from each line (in cached space) */
for (addr = KSEG0; addr < KSEG0 + size; addr += lnsize)
    junk = *addr;
/* clear all tags */
for (addr = KSEG0; addr < KSEG0 + size; addr += lnsize)
    Index_Store_Tag_D (addr);
```

4.10.5   *Invalidating or Writing Back a Region of Memory in the Cache*

The parameters for an invalidate or write back will invariably be a range of program or physical addresses corresponding to some I/O buffer.

You will nearly always do this using the hit-style operations, which invalidate or write back only locations that need it. If you needed to invalidate or write back a huge area of memory, it might be faster to use index operations to invalidate or write back the entire cache, but this is an optimization you may well choose to ignore.

It's sufficient to do this:

```
PI_cache_invalidate (void *buf, int nbytes)
{
    char *s;

    for (s = (char *)buf; s < buf+nbytes; s += lnsize)
            Hit_Invalidate_I (s);
}
```

Note that there's no need to generate a special address so long as buf is a program address, but if p is a physical address you would just add a constant to generate the corresponding kseg0 region address:

```
PI_cache_invalidate (p + 0x80000000, nbytes);
```

4.11   Cache Efficiency

Ever since the move to on-chip caches in the early 90s the performance of high-end CPUs has been to a large extent determined by the efficiency of their cache systems. In many current systems (particularly embedded systems, where there's a need to economize on cache sizes and memory performance) the CPU is waiting for a cache refill for 50–65% of its time. At this point doubling the performance of the CPU core will deliver only a 15–25% increase in application performance.

Cache efficiency depends on the amount of time the system is waiting for a cache refill. You can define it as the product of two numbers:

- *Cache miss rate*: The proportion of CPU references (I-fetches or data loads/stores) that miss in the cache and need an external memory reference.

- *Cache miss/refill penalty*: The time it takes for the memory system to refill the cache and restart the CPU.

These are not necessarily the best measures. For example, x86 CPUs are rather short of registers, so a program compiled for x86 will generate many more data load and store events than the same program compiled for MIPS. But the extra loads and stores will be of the stack locations that the x86 compiler uses as surrogates for registers; this is a very heavily used area of memory and will be very effectively cached. To some extent the number of cache misses is likely to be characteristic of tracing through a chunk of a particular program.

However, the above comments are useful in pointing out the following obvious ways of making a system go faster.

- *Reduce the cache miss rate*:
  - Make the cache bigger. Always effective, but expensive. In 1996, 64KB of cache occupied something over half the silicon area of a top-end embedded CPU, so doubling the cache size is economically feasible only if you wait for Moore's Law to give you the extra transistors in the same space.
  - Increase the set associativity of the cache. It's worth going up to four-way but after that the gains are too small to notice.
  - Add another level of cache. That makes the calculation much more complicated, of course. Apart from the complication of yet another subsystem, the miss rate in a secondary cache will be depressingly high; the primary cache has already skimmed the cream of the repetitive data access behavior of the CPU. To make it worthwhile, the secondary cache must be much larger (typically eight times or greater) than the primary cache, and a secondary cache hit must be much faster (two times or better) than a memory reference.
  - Reorganize your software to reduce the miss rate. It's not clear if this works in practice: it's easy to reorganize a small or trivial program to great effect, but so far nobody has succeeded in building a general tool that has any useful effect on an arbitrary program. See Section 4.12.

- *Decrease the cache refill penalty*:
  - Get the first word back to the CPU faster. DRAM memory systems have to do a lot of work to start up, then tend to provide data quite fast. The closer the memory is to the CPU and the shorter the data path between them, the sooner the data will arrive back.
    Note that this is the only entry in this list where better performance goes with a cheaper system. Paradoxically, it's had the least attention, probably because it requires more integration between the CPU interface and memory system design. CPU designers are loath to deal with system issues when they decide the interface of their chips, perhaps because their job is too complicated already!

- Increase the memory burst bandwidth. This is traditionally approached by the expensive technique of *bank interleaving*, where two or more memories are used to store alternate words; after the startup delay, you can take words from each memory bank alternately, doubling the available bandwidth. The first large-scale use of a memory technology, synchronous DRAM (or SDRAM) emerged in 1996. SDRAM changes the DRAM interface to deliver much more bandwidth from a single bank making bank interleaving an obsolete technique.

■ *Restart the CPU earlier*: The simplest method is to arrange that the cache refill bursts start with the word that the CPU missed on and to restart the CPU as soon as that data arrives. The rest of the cache refill continues in parallel with CPU activity. MIPS CPUs since R4x00 have allowed for this technique by using *sub-block order* for cache refill burst data, which can deliver any word of the block first. But only R4600 and its descendants have taken advantage of this for data misses.

More radically, you can just let execution continue through a load; the load operation is handed off to a bus interface unit and the CPU runs on until such time as it actually refers to the register data that was loaded. This is called a nonblocking load and is implemented on the R10000 and slated for the RM7000.

Most drastically, you can just keep running any code that isn't dependent on unfetched data as is done by the out-of-order execution R10000. This kind of CPU uses this technique quite generally, not just for loads but for computational instructions and branches.

Intel's Pentium Pro (progenitor of the Pentium II), MIPS's R10000, and HP's PA-8000 are out-of-order implementations; these 200+ MHz multiple-issue CPUs are reasonably happy being served by a large (and thus relatively slow) external cache.

4.12   Reorganizing Software to Influence Cache Efficiency

Most of the time, we work on the assumption that program accesses show locality of access, and we operate within fairly constrained *working sets*. For most purposes we also assume that, within the working set, its accesses are pretty randomly distributed. For a workstation that must perform adequately on many different applications, this is a fair assumption, but where an embedded system runs a single application the pattern of misses is likely to be very characteristic of a particular build of a particular piece of software. It's tempting to wonder whether we can massage the application code in a systematic manner to improve caching efficiency. To see how this might work, you can classify cache misses by their cause:

- *First-time accesses*: Everything has to be read from memory once.

- *Replacement*: The cache has a finite size, and soon after your program starts every cache miss and refill will be displacing some other valid data. As the program runs it will repeatedly lose data and have to load it again. You can minimize replacement misses by using a bigger cache or a smaller program (it's the ratio of program size to cache size that matters).

- *Thrashing*: Practical caches are usually no more than four-way set associative, so for any given program location there are at best four positions in the cache that can keep it; in a direct-mapped cache there's just one and for a two-way set-associative cache there are two. (Thrashing losses diminish rapidly with set associativity; most research suggests that a four-way set-associative cache loses little performance this way.)

  If your program happens to make heavy use of a number of pieces of data whose low-order addresses are close enough that they use the same cache line, then once the number of pieces is higher than the set associativity of the cache you can get periods of very high cache misses as the different chunks of data keep pushing each other out of the cache.

With this background, what kind of changes to a program will make it behave better in a cache?

- *Make it smaller*: A good idea if you can do it. You can use modest compiler optimization (exotic optimization often makes programs larger).

- *Make the heavily used portion of the program smaller*: Access density in programs is not at all uniformly distributed. There's often a significant amount of code that is almost never used (error handling, obscure system management), or used only once (initialization code). If you can separate off the rarely used code, you might be able to get better cache hit rates for the remainder.

  An approach that has been tried with qualified success is to use a profiler to establish the most heavily used functions in a program while running a representative workload, then to arrange the functions in memory in decreasing order of execution time. That means at least that the very most frequently used functions won't fight each other for cache locations.

- *Force some important code/data to be cache resident*: Some vendors provide a mechanism to allow part of the cache to be loaded and then those contents to be protected from replacement. This has been marketed to people who are concerned about having deterministic performance in interrupt handlers or other crucial pieces of software. This is usually implemented by consuming a set from a two-way set-associative cache (so that the cache acts as direct mapped for the rest of the system).

I am very skeptical about the viability of this approach, and I don't know of any research that backs up its usefulness. The loss in performance to the rest of the system is likely to outweigh the performance gain of the critical code. Cache locking has been used as a rather dubious marketing tool to tackle customer anxiety about the heuristic nature of caches. The anxiety is understandable, but the problem comes with faster, more complex, larger systems—caches are only one part of this issue.

- *Lay out the program to avoid thrashing*: Beyond making the active part of the program smaller (see above) this seems to me to be too unmaintainable to be a good idea. And a set-associative cache (even just two-way) makes it quite pointless.

- *Make some rarely used data or code uncacheable*: It seems appealing to just reserve the cache for important code, leaving used-once or used-rarely code out.

  This is almost always a mistake. If the data is really rarely used, it will never get into the cache in the first place. And because caches usually read data in lines of 4–16 words, they often produce a huge speedup even when traversing data or code that is used only once; the burst refill from memory takes little longer than a single-word access and gives you the next 3–15 words free.

In short, we warmly recommend the following approach as a starting point (to be abandoned only after much measurement and deep thought). To start with, allow everything to be cacheable except I/O registers and lightly used remote memory. See what the cache heuristics do for your application before you try to second-guess them. Secondly, fix hardware problems in hardware. There's no software band-aid that will regain performance lost to excessive cache refill latency or low memory bandwidth. The attempt to lower cache miss rates by reorganizing software is bound to be lengthy and complicated, but be aware at the start that the gains will be small and hard-won. Try to get the hardware fixed too!

4.13   Write Buffers and When You Need to Worry

The write-through cache common to all 32-bit MIPS CPUs demands that all CPU stores be immediately sent to main memory, which would be a big performance bottleneck if the CPU waited for each write to finish.

In an average C program compiled for MIPS, about 10% of instructions executed are stores, but these accesses tend to come in bursts, for example when a function prologue saves a few registers.

DRAM memory frequently has the characteristic that the first write of a group takes quite a long time (5–10 clock cycles is typical on these CPUs), and subsequent ones are relatively fast so long as they follow quickly.

If the CPU simply waits while a write completes, the performance hit will be huge. So it is common to provide a *write buffer*, a FIFO store in which each entry contains both data to be written and the address at which to write it. MIPS CPUs have used FIFOs with between one and eight entries.

The 32-bit MIPS CPUs with write-through caches depend heavily on write buffers. In these CPUs, a four-entry queue has proved efficient for well-tuned local DRAM with CPU clock rates up to 40MHz.

Later MIPS CPUs (with write-back caches) retain the write buffer as a holding area for cache line write backs and as a time saver on uncached writes.

Most of the time the operation of the write buffer is completely transparent to software. But sometimes the programmer needs to be aware of what is happening:

- *Timing relations for I/O register accesses*: This affects *all* MIPS CPUs. When you perform a store to an I/O register, the store reaches memory after a small, but indeterminate, delay. Other communication with the I/O system (e.g., interrupts) may happen more quickly—for example, you may see an active interrupt from a device "after" you have told it to generate no interrupts. In a different case, if an I/O device needs some time to recover after a write you must ensure that the write buffer FIFO is empty before you start counting out that time period. Here, you must ensure that the CPU waits while the write buffer empties. It is good practice to define a subroutine that does this job; it is traditionally called `wbflush()`. See Section 4.13.1 below for hints on implementing it.

The above describes what can happen on any MIPS R4x00 (MIPS III ISA) or subsequent CPU implemented to date. It's also enough for the whole IDT R3051 family, the most popular embedded component CPUs. But on some earlier 32-bit systems, even stranger things can happen:

- *Reads overtaking writes*: When a load instruction (uncached or missing in the cache) executes while the write buffer FIFO is not empty, the CPU has a choice: Should it finish off the write or use the memory interface to fetch data for the load? It's more efficient to do the read first—the CPU is certainly stopped until the read data arrives, but there's a good chance that the write can be deferred and still performed in parallel with later CPU activity.[1]

---

1. You may observe that there is some danger that the overtaking read may be trying to fetch locations for which there is still a write pending, which would be disastrous; however, CPUs

The original R3000 hardware left this decision in the hands of the system hardware implementation. The most popular integrated MIPS I CPUs from IDT don't permit reads to overtake writes—they have unconditional *write priority*. Most MIPS III CPUs have not permitted read overtaking, but robust software doesn't have to assume this any more. See the description of the **sync** instruction in Section 8.4.9.

If you believe that your MIPS I CPU might not have unconditional write priority, then when you are dealing with I/O registers the necessary address check may not save you; a load may misbehave because an earlier store to a *different* address is still pending. In this case you need to call wbflush().

- *Byte gathering*: Some write buffers watch for partial-word writes within the same memory word and will combine those partial writes into a single operation. This is not done by any current R3051-family CPU, but it can wreak havoc with I/O register writes.

  It is not a bad idea to map your I/O registers such that each register is in a separate word location (i.e., 8-bit registers should be at least 4 bytes apart). You can't always do it.

4.13.1   *Implementing wbflush*

Unless your CPU is one of the peculiar type above, you can ensure that the write buffer is empty by performing an uncached load from anywhere (which will stall the CPU until the writes have finished and the load has finished too). This is inefficient; you can minimize the overhead by loading from the fastest memory available to you.

For those who never want to think about it again, a write to memory followed by an uncached read from the same address (with a **sync** in between the two if you're running on a MIPS III or later CPU) will flush out the write FIFO on any MIPS CPU built to date (and it's difficult to see how a CPU without this behavior could be a correct implementation).

Some systems use a hardware signal that indicates whether the FIFO is empty, wired to an input that the CPU can sense directly. But this isn't done on any MIPS CPU to date.

CAUTION!   Systems often have write buffers outside the CPU. Any bus or memory interface that boasts of having *write posting* as a feature is behaving similarly. Write buffers outside the CPU can give you just the same sort of trouble as those inside it. Take care with your programming.

---

allowing read overtaking will compare read and write addresses and give the write priority if the addresses overlap.

4.14   More about MIPS Caches

Although you may never need to know about these subjects, we mention them for the sake of completeness.

4.14.1   *Multiprocessor Cache Features*

Our discussion in this book will stick to single-CPU systems. Interested parties should read the classic paper (Sweazey and Smith 1986).

4.14.2   *Cache Aliases*

This problem only afflicts caches where the address used to generate the *cache index* is different from the address stored in the *cache tag*. In the primary caches of R4000-style CPUs, the index is taken from the program (virtual) address and the tag from the physical address. This is good for performance, because cache lookup can parallel address translation, but it can lead to *aliases*.

Most of these CPUs can translate addresses in 4KB pages and have caches of 8KB or larger. It's therefore possible that a single physical page is mapped to two different program addresses, which are sequential pages—let's say those starting at 0 and 4KB. If the program accesses data at 0, it will be loaded into the cache at index 0. If it accesses the same data at the alternate address of 4KB, it will be fetched again from memory into the cache at the different index of 4KB. Now there are two copies of the same cache line, and modifications made at one address will not find their way to the other one. This is a cache alias.

MIPS secondary caches are always physically indexed and tagged, so they don't suffer from aliases.[1]

However, it's easier to avoid this problem than to fix it. Aliases can't arise between any pair of translations where the two alternative program addresses will produce the same cache index. With 4KB pages, the low 12 bits of the cache index are guaranteed to be equal; it's only necessary to ensure that any two alternative program addresses for any physical page are equal modulo the largest likely primary cache set size. If you only issue multiple program addresses that are a multiple of 64KB apart, it's hard to imagine that you'll ever have any trouble.[2]

---

1. CPUs with on-chip secondary cache controllers can use some bits in the secondary cache to keep track of cache fetches into the primary cache; R4000 and R4400 CPUs use this to detect cache aliases and take a special exception to allow system software to resolve the problem. But this doesn't seem to be a tradition being carried on in later MIPS CPUs.

2. Although CPUs get relentlessly bigger and faster with every year that passes, it's likely that primary cache set sizes will peak not far beyond the current 16KB record. Primary caches run at the full CPU clock rate, and smaller is faster; future, more highly integrated CPUs will probably go for on-chip secondary caches instead.

Chapter

5

Exceptions, Interrupts, and Initialization

In the MIPS architecture interrupts, traps, system calls, and everything else that disrupts the normal flow of execution are called *exceptions* and are handled by a single mechanism. What sort of events are they?

- *External events*: These are interrupts, or bus errors on a read. Interrupts are used to direct the attention of the CPU to some external event, which can be faster or more efficient than insisting that the CPU regularly poll for that event.

  Interrupts are the only exception conditions that arise from something independent of the CPU's normal instruction stream. Since you can't avoid interrupts just by being careful, there have to be software mechanisms to inhibit the effect of interrupts when necessary.

- *Memory translation exceptions*: These are caused by an address that should be translated, but for which no valid translation currently exists, or a write to a write-protected page. The OS checks these exceptions, some of which are symptomatic of an application program stepping outside its permitted address space and will be fixed by terminating the application to protect the rest of the system. The more common benign memory translation exceptions can be used to initiate operating system functions as complex as a complete demand-paged virtual memory system or as simple as extending the space available for a stack.

- *Other unusual program conditions for the kernel to fix*: Notable among these are conditions resulting from floating-point instructions, where the hardware is unable to cope with some difficult and rare combination of operation and operands and is seeking the services of a software emulator.

This category is fuzzy, since different kernels have different ideas about what they're willing to fix. An unaligned load may be an error on one system and something to be handled in software on another.

■ *Program or hardware-detected errors*: This includes nonexistent instructions, instructions that are illegal at user privilege level, coprocessor instructions executed with the appropriate **SR** flag disabled, integer overflow, address alignment errors, and accesses outside kuseg in user mode.

■ *Data integrity problems*: Many MIPS CPUs continually check data on the bus or data coming from the cache for a per-byte parity or for word-wide error-correcting code. Cache or parity errors generate a (special) exception in R4000 and subsequent CPUs.

■ *System calls and traps*: These are instructions whose whole purpose is to generate recognizable exceptions; they are used to build software facilities in a secure way (system calls, conditional traps planted by careful code, and breakpoints).

Some things do not cause exceptions, though you'd expect them to. For example, you will have to use other mechanisms to detect bus errors on write cycles, because the CPU places data and address in its write buffer and the external write cycle happens sometime later, so an exception would be hard to relate to the instruction that caused it. Some systems may use external mechanisms, perhaps signalled with an interrupt.

Even stranger, parity errors detected in the cache of most 32-bit CPUs don't cause an exception; the fault shows up in the status register bit **SR(PE)**, but you have to look for it. R3000 cache parity was added late and for diagnostic purposes only.

In this chapter, we'll look at how MIPS CPUs decide to take exceptions and what the software has to do to handle them cleanly. We'll explain why MIPS exceptions are called "precise," discuss exception entry points, and discuss some software conventions.

Hardware interrupts from outside the CPU are the most common exceptions for embedded applications, the most time critical, and the ones most likely to cause subtle bugs. Special problems can arise with *nested exceptions*, those exceptions occurring while you are still handling an earlier exception.

The way that a MIPS CPU starts up after system reset is implemented as a kind of exception and borrows functions from exceptions—so that's described in this chapter too. At the end of the chapter, we'll look at a couple of related subjects: how to emulate an instruction (as needed by an instruction set extension mechanism) and how to build semaphores to provide robust task-to-task communication in the face of interrupts. Chapter 12 contains the annotated source code of an interrupt/exception handler taken from a real MIPS system.

5.1   Precise Exceptions

You will see the phrase *precise exceptions* used in the MIPS documentation. It is a useful feature, but to understand why, you need to meet its alternative.

In a CPU tuned for the best performance by pipelining (or by more complicated tricks for overlapping instruction execution), the architecture's sequential model of execution is an illusion maintained by clever hardware. Unless the hardware is designed cleverly, exceptions can cause this illusion to unravel.

When an exception suspends its thread of execution, a pipelined CPU has several instructions in different phases of completion. Since we want to be able to return from the exception and carry on without disruption to the interrupted flow of execution, each instruction in the pipeline must be either completed, made as though we never saw it, or its half-completed state stored. Moreover, we need to be able to remember which instruction falls in each of those categories.

A CPU architecture features precise exceptions when it prescribes a solution to this problem that makes life as easy as possible for the software. In a precise-exception CPU, on any exception we get pointed at one instruction (the *exception victim*). All instructions preceding the exception victim in execution sequence are complete; any work done on the victim and on any subsequent instructions has no side effects that the software need worry about.[1] The software that handles exceptions can ignore all the timing effects of the CPU's implementation.

The MIPS architecture comes close to prescribing that all exceptions are precise. Here are the ingredients:

■ *Unambiguous proof of guilt*: After any exception the CPU control register **EPC** points to the correct place to restart execution after the exception is dealt with. In most cases, it points to the exception victim, but if the victim was in a branch delay slot **EPC** points to the preceding branch instruction: Returning to the branch instruction will re-execute the victim instruction, but returning to the victim would cause the branch to be ignored. When the victim is in a branch delay slot, the cause register bit **Cause(BD)** is set, because some exception handlers need to inspect the victim instruction—in this case found at location **EPC + 4**.

It may seem obvious that it should be easy to find the victim, but on some heavily pipelined CPUs it may not be possible.

---

1. This is not quite the same as saying that the exception victim and subsequent instructions haven't done anything. But it does require that, when re-executed after the exception, those instructions will behave exactly as they would have done if the exception hadn't happened. Computer architects say that any side effect must be idempotent—doing it twice is the same as doing it once.

- *Exceptions appear in instruction sequence*: This would be obvious for a nonpipelined CPU, but exceptions can arise at several different stages of execution, creating a potential hazard. For example, if a load instruction suffers an address exception this won't happen until the MEM pipestage; if the next instruction hits an address problem on an instruction fetch (at the IF pipestage) the exception event affecting the second-in-sequence instruction will actually happen first.

  To avoid this problem, an exception that is detected early is not activated until it is known that all previous instructions will complete successfully; the event is just noted and passed along the pipeline until a fixed pipeline stage. If an earlier instruction's later-detected event reaches the finish line while our exception note is making its way down the pipeline, the exception note just gets discarded. In the case above the instruction-fetch address problem is suppressed—it will likely happen again when we finish handling the victim instruction's problem and re-execute the victim and subsequent instructions.

- *Subsequent instructions nullified*: Because of the pipelining, instructions lying in sequence after the victim at **EPC** have been started. But you are guaranteed that no effects produced by these instructions will be visible in the registers or CPU state, and no effect at all will occur that will prevent execution, properly restarted at **EPC**, from continuing just as if the exception had not happened.

MIPS implementations fall short of precise exception heaven in a few respects. For example, the integer multiply unit doesn't respond to exceptions—see the sidebar. This problem can be avoided by some instruction-ordering rules, which are normally enforced by the assembler program.

The MIPS implementation of precise exceptions is quite costly, because it limits the scope for pipelining. That's particularly painful in the FPA, because floating-point operations often take many pipeline stages to run. A MIPS FP instruction cannot be allowed to progress past the ALU pipeline stage until it is known that it won't produce an exception.

5.2 When Exceptions Happen

Since exceptions are precise, the programmer's view of when an exception happens is unambiguous: The last instruction executed before the exception was the one before the exception victim. And, if the exception wasn't an interrupt, the victim is the instruction that caused it.

On an interrupt in a typical MIPS CPU, the last instruction to be completed before interrupt processing starts will be the one that has just finished its MEM stage when the interrupt is detected. The exception victim will be the one that has just finished its ALU stage. However, take care: MIPS architects don't make

Nonprecise Exception Handling in the Integer Multiplier

The integer multiplier has its own separate pipeline. Operations are started by instructions like **mult** or **div**, which take two register operands and feed them into the multiplier machine. The program then issues an **mflo** instruction (and sometimes also **mfhi**, for a 64-bit result or to obtain the remainder) to get the results back into a general-purpose register. The CPU stalls on **mflo** if the computation is not finished; so a programmer concerned with maximizing performance will put as much useful work as possible between the two. In most MIPS implementations a multiply takes 10 or more clock cycles, with divide even slower.

The multiply machine is separately pipelined from the regular integer unit. Once launched, a multiply/divide operation is unstoppable even by an exception. That's not normally a problem, but suppose we have a code sequence like the following

where we're retrieving one multiply unit result and then immediately firing off another operation:

```
mflo    $8
mult    $9, $10
```

If we take an exception whose restart address is the **mflo** instruction, then the first execution of **mflo** will be nullified under the precise-exception rules and the register **$8** will be left as though the **mflo** had never happened. Unfortunately, the **mult** will have been started too and since the multiply unit knows nothing of the exception will continue to run. Before the exception returns, the computation will most likely have finished and the **mflo** will now deliver the result of the **mult** that should have followed it.

We can avoid this problem, on all MIPS CPUs, by interposing at least two harmless instructions between the **mflo/mfhi** on the one hand and the **mult** (or any other instruction that starts a multiply unit computation) on the other.

---

promises about exact interrupt latencies and signals may be resynchronized through one or more clock stages before reaching the CPU core.

5.3   Exception Vectors: Where Exception Handling Starts

Most CISC processors have hardware (or concealed microcode) that analyzes an exception, dispatching the CPU to different entry points according to what kind of exception happened. A MIPS CPU does very little of this. If that seems a serious omission, consider the following.

Firstly, vectored interrupts are not as useful in practice as we might hope. In most operating systems, interrupt handlers share code (for saving registers and such like) and it is common for CISC microcode to spend time dispatching to different interrupt entry points, where OS software loads a code number and jumps back to a common handler.

Secondly, it's difficult to envision much exception analysis being done by pure hardware rather than microcode; on a RISC CPU ordinary code is fast enough to be used in preference.

Here and elsewhere, you should bear in mind just how fast CPUs of the RISC generation are compared with their peripherals. A useful interrupt routine is going to have to read/write some external registers, and on a mid-90s CPU that external bus cycle is likely to take 20–50 internal clock cycles. It's easy to write interrupt dispatch code on a MIPS CPU that will be faster than a single peripheral access—so this is unlikely to be a performance bottleneck.[1]

However, even in MIPS not all exceptions were ever equal, and differences have grown as the architecture has developed. So we can make some distinctions:

- *TLB refill of user-privilege address*: There is one particularly frequent exception in a protected OS, related to the address translation system (see Chapter 6). The TLB hardware only holds a modest number of address translations, and in a heavily used system running a virtual memory OS it's common for the application program to run on to an address whose translation is not recorded in the TLB—an event called a *TLB miss* (because the TLB is used as a software-managed cache).

  The use of software to handle this condition was controversial when RISC CPUs were introduced, and MIPS CPUs provide significant support for a preferred scheme for TLB refill. The hardware helps out enough that the exception handler for the preferred refill scheme usually runs in about 13 clock cycles.

  As part of this, common classes of TLB refill are given an entry point different from all other exceptions so that the finely tuned refill code doesn't have to waste time figuring out what kind of exception has happened.

- *TLB refill for 64-bit address spaces*: Memory translation for tasks wanting to take advantage of the larger program address space available on 64-bit CPUs uses a slightly different register layout and a different TLB refill routine; MIPS calls this XTLB refill ("X" for extended, I guess). Again, a desire to keep this very efficient makes a separate entry point useful.

- *Uncached alternative entry points*: For good performance on exceptions the interrupt entry point must be in cached memory, but this is highly undesirable during system bootstrap; from reset or power-up, the caches are unusable until initialized. If you want a robust and self-diagnosing startup sequence, you have to use uncached read-only memory entry points for exceptions detected in early bootstrap. In MIPS CPUs there is no uncached "mode"—there are uncached program memory regions instead—so there's a mode bit **SR(BEV)** that reallocates the exception entry points into the uncached, startup-safe kseg1 region.

- *Parity/ECC error*: R4000 and later CPUs detect a data error (usually in data arriving from main memory, but often not noticed until it's used from cache) and take a trap. It would be silly to vector through a cached

---

1. We labor this point because the lack of vectored interrupt hardware has been cited by some of the MIPS competitors as a problem for embedded systems.

TABLE 5.1 Hardwired reset and exception entry points for MIPS CPU

Exception type	Entry point			
	SR(BEV)==0		SR(BEV)==1	
	Program	*Physical*	*Program*	*Physical*
Reset, NMI			0xBFC0 0000	0x1FC0 0000
TLB refill, 32-bit task	0x8000 0000	0x0	0xBFC0 0200	0x1FC0 0200
XTLB refill, 64-bit task	0x8000 0080	0x80	0xBFC0 0280	0x1FC0 0280
Cache error (R4x00 and later)	0xA000 0100	0x100	0xBFC0 0300	0x1FC0 0300
Interrupt (some QED CPUs only)	0x8000 0200	0x200	0xBFC0 0400	0x1FC0 0400
All other exceptions	0x8000 0180	0x180	0xBFC0 0380	0x1FC0 0380

location to handle a cache error, so regardless of the state of **SR(BEV)** the *cache error exception* entry point is in uncached space.

- *Reset*: For many purposes it makes sense to see reset as another exception, particularly when the R4x00 and later CPUs use the same entry point for *cold reset* (where the CPU gets completely reconfigured; indistinguishable from power-up) and *warm reset* (where the software gets completely reinitialized). In fact, *nonmaskable interrupt* (NMI) turns out to be a slightly weaker version of warm reset, differing only in that it waits for an instruction to finish before taking effect.

All exception entry points lie in untranslated regions of the MIPS memory map, in kseg1 for uncached entry points and kseg0 for cached ones. In these areas the nominal 32-bit addresses given in Table 5.1 extend to a 64-bit memory map by sign extension: The program address 0x8000 0000 in the 32-bit view is the same as 0xFFFF FFFF 8000 0000 in the 64-bit view. Table 5.1 describes the entry points with just 32-bit addresses.

Presumably the 128-byte (0x80) gap between the exception vectors occurs because the MIPS architects felt that 32 instructions would be enough to code the basic exception routine, saving a branch instruction without wasting too much memory!

Here's what a MIPS CPU does when it decides to take an exception:

1. It sets up **EPC** to point to the restart location.

2. The CPU changes into kernel (high-privilege) mode and disables interrupts. The way this is done is different in 32-bit (pre-R4x00) and 64-bit MIPS CPUs—see the following for details.

3. **Cause** is set up so that software can see the reason for the exception. On address exceptions **BadVaddr** is also set. Memory management system

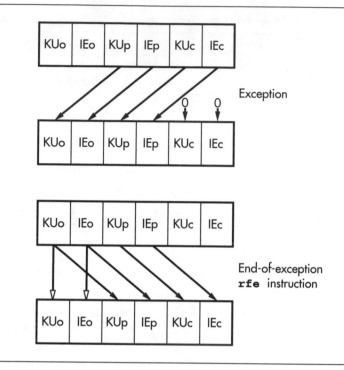

FIGURE 5.1 Privilege state mini-stack for pre-R4x00 MIPS CPUs

exceptions set up some of the MMU registers too; more details are given in Chapter 6.

4. The CPU then starts fetching instructions from the exception entry point, and everything else is up to software.

We said that the mechanism used to change into the high-privilege/ interrupts-disabled state changed between early and later MIPS CPUs. This is one of the few examples where the CPU actually got simpler.

Pre-R4x00 32-bit CPUs have a kernel/user privilege bit and an interrupt enable/disable bit. Inside the **SR** register there is a three-entry stack whose operation is illustrated by Figure 5.1; on an exception the existing 2-bit state is pushed and replaced by kernel mode with interrupts off. The end-of-exception instruction **rfe** (restore from exception) pops the stack and restores the CPU to its pre-exception condition.

System software can use this (under very limited circumstances) to handle a nested exception within a primitive exception routine that makes no software provision for saving and restoring **SR**; this allows simplification of the frequently called TLB miss exception (see Section 6.7).

On the R4000 and subsequent CPUs, the normal privilege field is 2 bits long, due to the introduction of the intermediate supervisor privilege level. An exception doesn't change this field; it just sets the **SR(EXL)** (exception level) bit, which has the side effects of forcing kernel mode and disabling interrupts. Very short exception routines can run entirely at this exception level (in exception mode, as we'll sometimes say) and need never touch the rest of **SR**. For more conventional exception handlers, which save state and pass control over to more complex software, exception level provides a cover under which system software can save the old **SR** value in safety.

It turns out that the R4x00 model can also be used to allow an exception within the primitive TLB miss handler, but we'll talk more about how that's done when we get to it.

5.4   Exception Handling: Basics

Any MIPS exception handler has to go through the same stages:

- *Bootstrapping*: On entry to the exception handler very little of the state of the interrupted program has been saved, so the first job is to make yourself enough room to do whatever it is you want without overwriting something vital to the software that has just been interrupted.

  Almost inevitably, this is done by using the **k0** and **k1** registers (which are conventionally reserved for kernel mode use) to reference a piece of memory that can be used for other register saves.

- *Dispatching different exceptions*: Consult the Cause register field **Cause (ExcCode)**. This 5-bit code distinguishes all exceptions on MIPS CPUs (so far).

- *Constructing the exception processing environment*: Complex exception-handling routines will probably be written in a high-level language, and you will want to be able to use standard library routines. You will have to provide a piece of stack memory that isn't being used by any other piece of software and save the values of any CPU registers that both might be important to the interrupted program and that called subroutines are allowed to change.

- *Processing the exception*: You can do whatever you like now.

- *Preparing to return*: The high-level function is usually called as a subroutine and therefore returns into the low-level dispatch code. Here, saved registers are restored, and the CPU is returned to its safe (kernel mode, exceptions off) state by changing **SR** back to its post-exception value.

■ *Returning from an exception*: The end-of-exception processing is another area where the CPU has changed, and its description follows in Section 5.5.

5.5 Returning from an Exception

The return of control to the exception victim and the change (if required) back from kernel to a lower privilege level must be done at the same time ("atomically," in the jargon of computer science). It would be a security hole if you ran even one instruction of application code at kernel privilege level; on the other hand, the attempt to run a kernel instruction with user privileges would lead to a fatal exception.

On 32-bit CPUs modeled on the R3000 we use the instruction **rfe** (restore from exception), which is *not* the same as "return from exception." This instruction patches up the status register to make it ready to go back to the state you were in before a trap happened; but it doesn't do the return itself. The only secure way of returning to user mode from an exception is to return with a **jr** instruction that has the **rfe** in its delay slot—a rather nice exploitation of an architectural foible.

With MIPS III and subsequent CPUs there's an instruction **eret** that does the whole job; it both clears the **SR(EXL)** bit and returns control to the address stored in **EPC**.

5.6 Nesting Exceptions

In many cases you will want to permit (or will not be able to avoid) further exceptions occurring within your exception processing routine; these are called *nested* exceptions.

Naively done, this would cause chaos; vital state from the interrupted program is held in **EPC** and **SR**, and another exception would immediately overwrite them. Before you permit nested exceptions you must save these values. Moreover, once exceptions are re-enabled you can no longer rely on the values of **k0** and **k1**.

An exception handler that is going to survive a nested exception must use some memory locations to save register values. The data structure used is often called an *exception frame*; multiple exception frames from nested exceptions are usually arranged on a stack.

Stack resources are consumed by each exception, so arbitrarily deep nesting of exceptions cannot be tolerated. Most systems award each kind of exception a priority level and arrange that while an exception is being processed only higher-priority exceptions are permitted. Such systems need have only as many exception frames as there are priority levels.

You can avoid all exceptions; interrupts can be individually masked by software to conform to your priority rules, masked all at once with the **SR(IE)** bit, or implicitly masked (for later CPUs) by the exception level bit. Other kinds of exceptions can be avoided by appropriate software discipline. For example, privilege violations can't happen in kernel mode (used by most exception processing software); and programs can avoid the possibility of addressing errors and TLB misses. It's essential to do so when processing higher-priority exceptions.

Typical priorities from lowest to highest are as follows: nonexception code, TLB miss on kuseg address, TLB miss on kseg2 address, interrupt (lowest), ..., interrupt (highest), illegal instructions and traps, and bus errors.

5.7   An Exception Routine

The following MIPS I code fragment is as simple as an exception routine can be. It does nothing except increment a counter on each exception:

```
        .set noreorder
        .set noat
xcptgen:
        la      k0,xcptcount    # get address of counter
        lw      k1,0(k0)        # load counter
        nop                     # (load delay)
        addu    k1,1            # increment counter
        sw      k1,0(k0)        # store counter
        mfc0    k0,C0_EPC       # get EPC
        nop                     # (load delay, mfc0 slow)
        j       k0              # return to program
        rfe                     # branch delay slot
        .set at
        .set reorder
```

Note that this routine cannot survive a nested exception (the original return address in **EPC** would be lost, for example). It doesn't re-enable interrupts (and thus is safe that way) but the counter xcptcount must be at an address that can't possibly cause any kind of address exception.

5.8   Interrupts

The MIPS exception mechanism is general purpose, but democratically speaking there are two exception types that happen far more often than all the rest put together. One is the TLB miss when an application running under a memory-mapped OS like unix steps outside the (limited) boundaries of the on-chip translation table; we mentioned that before and will come back to it in Chapter 6. The other popular exceptions are interrupts, occurring when a device outside the CPU wants attention. Since we're dealing with an outside world that won't wait for us, interrupt service time is often critical.

Embedded-system MIPS users are going to be most concerned about interrupts, which is why they get a special section. We'll talk about the following:

- *Interrupt resources in MIPS CPUs*: This describes what you've got to work with.

- *Implementing interrupt priority*: All interrupts are equal to MIPS CPUs, but in your system you probably want to attend to some of them before the others.

- *Critical regions, disabling interrupts, and semaphores*: It's often necessary to prevent an interrupt from occurring during critical operations, but there are particular difficulties about doing so on MIPS CPUs. We look at solutions.

5.8.1 *Interrupt Resources in MIPS CPUs*

Almost all MIPS CPUs have a set of eight independent interrupt bits in their **Cause** register. On most general-purpose CPUs you'll find five or six of these driven by CPU input pins, and two of them are purely software accessible. If you have a pre-R4000 CPU with floating-point hardware one interrupt pin will be required for floating-point exception signalling; on R4000 and subsequent CPUs there's a counter/timer on-chip that uses up one pin.

An active level on any pin is sensed in each cycle and will cause an exception if enabled.

The CPU's willingness to respond to an interrupt is affected by bits in **SR**. There are three relevant fields:

- The global interrupt enable bit—**SR(IEc)** for R3000 CPUs and **SR(IE)** for later ones. This bit must be set 1 or no interrupt will be serviced. On R3000 CPUs, the **SR(IEc)** bit is automatically cleared when any exception is taken.

- In R4000 and subsequent CPUs, the **SR(EXL)** (exception level) and **SR(ERL)** (error level) bits will inhibit interrupts if set (as one of them will be after any exception).

- The status register also has individual interrupt mask bits **SR(IM)**, one for each interrupt bit in **Cause**. Each **SR(IM)** bit should be set to 1 to enable the corresponding interrupt so that programs can determine exactly which interrupts can happen and which cannot. Changes to the individual bits are made under cover, with interrupts disabled globally.

What Are the Software Interrupt Bits For?

Why on earth should the CPU provide two bits in the **Cause** register that, when set, immediately cause an interrupt unless masked?

The clue is in the expression "unless masked." Typically this is used as a mechanism for high-priority interrupt routines to flag actions that will be performed by lower-priority interrupt routines once the system has dealt with all high-priority business. As the high-priority processing completes, the software will open up the interrupt mask, and the pending software interrupt will occur.

There is no absolute reason why the same effect should not be simulated by system software (using flags in memory, for example) but the soft interrupt bits are convenient because they fit in with an interrupt handling mechanism that has to be provided.

To discover what interrupt inputs are currently active, you look inside the **Cause** register. Note that these are exactly that—current levels—and do not necessarily correspond to the signal pattern that caused the interrupt exception in the first place. The active input levels in **Cause(IP)** and the masks in **SR(IM)** are helpfully aligned to the same bit positions, in case you want to "and" them together. The software interrupts are at the lowest positions, and the hardware interrupts are arranged in increasing order.

In architectural terms, all interrupts are equal. But to help you avoid trouble with some CPU implementations there are one or two special uses of interrupt signals we ought to mention here.

In R4000 and descendant CPUs, interrupt number 7 is used for the internal timer. This interrupt corresponds to the hardware pin *Int5**, and some of these CPUs don't provide an input at all. But where the pin exists, you can only use the pin by eschewing the timer—and the timer is too useful to do that.

When R3000 and other MIPS I CPUs have floating-point hardware, FP exceptions are communicated through an interrupt pin. The MIPS convention was to use *Int3** for this purpose, but DECstations used *Int5**. Although 32-bit CPUs with integrated floating point are fairly rare, those that do exist have usually offered some software-controlled selection of which interrupt gets tied to the FPA.

Interrupt processing proper begins after you have received an exception and discovered from **Cause(ExcCode)** that it was a hardware interrupt. Consulting **Cause(IP)** we can find what interrupt is active and thus what device is signalling us. Here is the usual sequence:

- Consult the **Cause** register IP field and logically "and" it with the current interrupt masks in **SR(IM)** to obtain a bitmap of active, enabled interrupt requests. There may be more than one, any of which would have caused the interrupt.

- Select one active, enabled interrupt for attention. The selection is normally done using fixed priorities, but it is all decided by the software.

- You need to save the old interrupt mask bits in **SR(IM)**, but you probably already saved the whole **SR** register in the main exception routine.

- Change **SR(IM)** to ensure that the current interrupt and all interrupts your software regards as being of equal or lesser priority are inhibited.

- If you haven't already done it in the main exception routine, save the state (user registers, etc.) required for nested exception processing.

- Now change your CPU state to that appropriate to the higher-level part of the interrupt handler, where typically some nested interrupts and exceptions are permitted.

  In all cases, set the global interrupt enable bit, **SR(IE)** (for R3000-style CPUs) or **SR(IEc)** (for R4000-style CPUs), to allow higher-priority interrupts to be processed. On an R4000 you'll also change the CPU privilege level field **SR(KSU)** to kernel mode and clear **SR(EXL)** to leave exception mode and expose the changes made in the status register.

- Call your interrupt routine.

- On return you'll need to disable interrupts again so you can restore the pre-interrupt values of registers and resume execution of the interrupted task. On an R3000 or similar CPU you will do this by clearing **SR(IEc)**; on an R4000 or later CPU you will set **SR(EXL)**. That sounds different, but in both cases you'll probably do this implicitly by restoring the just-after-exception value of the whole **SR** register before getting into your end-of-exception sequence.

When making changes to **SR**, you need to be careful about changes whose effect is delayed due to the operation of the pipeline. At worst, different **SR** fields can take effect at slightly different times, so an alteration of **SR** that simultaneously changes two fields may produce an unexpected window of opportunity for an interrupt, as the interrupt-enabling change to one field works its way through faster than the interrupt-disabling effect of another. There's some information on how to read your CPU manual to avoid this sort of event in Appendix A, Section A.4.

5.8.2 *Implementing Interrupt Priority*

The MIPS CPU has a simple-minded approach to interrupt priority; all interrupts are equal.

If your system implements an interrupt priority scheme, then:

- At all times the software maintains a well-defined *interrupt priority level* (IPL) at which the CPU is running. Every interrupt source is allocated to one of these levels.

- If the CPU is at the lowest IPL, any interrupt is permitted. This is the state in which normal applications run.

- If the CPU is at the highest IPL, then all interrupts are barred.

Not only are interrupt handlers run with the IPL set to the level appropriate to their particular interrupt cause, but there's provision for programmers to raise and lower the IPL. Those parts of the application side of a device driver that communicate with the hardware or the interrupt handler will often need to prevent device interrupts in their critical regions, so the programmer will temporarily raise the IPL to match that of the device's interrupt input.

In such a system, high-IPL interrupts can continue to be enabled without affecting the lower-IPL code, so we've got the chance to offer better interrupt response time to some interrupts, usually in exchange for a promise that their interrupt handlers will run to completion in a short time.

Most unix systems have between four and six IPLs.

While there are other ways of doing it, the simplest schemes have the following characteristics:[1]

- *Fixed priorities*: At any IPL interrupts assigned to that and lower IPLs are barred but interrupts of higher IPLs are enabled. Different interrupts at the same IPL are typically scheduled first come, first served.

- *IPL relates to code being run*: Any given piece of code always executes at the same IPL.

- *Simple nested scheduling (above IPL 0)*: Except at the lowest level, any interrupted code will be returned to as soon as there are no more active interrupts at a higher level. At the lowest level there's quite likely a scheduler that shares the CPU out among various tasks, and it's common to take the opportunity to reschedule after a period of interrupt activity.

On a MIPS CPU a transition between interrupt levels must (at least) be accompanied by a change in the status register **SR**, since that register contains all the interrupt control bits. On some systems interrupt level transitions will require doing something to external interrupt control hardware, and most OSs have some global variables to change, but we don't care about that here; for now we'll characterize an IPL by a particular setting of the **SR** interrupt fields.

In the MIPS architecture **SR** (like all coprocessor registers) is not directly accessible for bit setting and clearing. Any change in the IPL, therefore, requires a piece of code that reads, modifies, and writes back the **SR** in separate operations:

```
    mfc0    t0, SR
1:
    nop     # all MIPS CPUs need at least one, maybe more
    or      t0, things_to_set
    and     t0, ~(things_to_clear)
```

1. Since unix kernels are built like this, the scheme can't be too restrictive.

```
2:
    mtc0    t0, SR
    nop         # waiting for change to take effect
    nop
```

In general, this piece of code may itself be interrupted, and a problem arises: Suppose we take an interrupt somewhere between label **1** and **2** and that interrupt routine itself causes any change in **SR**? Then when we write our own altered value of **SR** at label **2**, we'll lose the change made by the interrupt routine.

It turns out that we can only get away with the code fragment above—which is pretty much universal in MIPS implementations of OSs—in systems where we can rely on the IPL being constant in any particular piece of code. If that's true, then it follows that even if we get interrupted in the middle of our read-modify-write sequence, it will do no harm; when the interrupt returns it will do so with the same IPL, and therefore the same **SR** value, as before.

Where this assumption breaks down, we need the following discussion.

5.8.3 *Atomicity and Atomic Changes to SR*

In systems with more than one thread of control—including a single application with interrupt handlers—you will quite often find yourself doing something at which you don't want to be caught halfway. In more formal language, you may want a set of changes to be made *atomically*, so that some cooperating task or interrupt routine in the system will see either none of them made or all of them, but never in between.[1] The code implementing the atomic change is sometimes called a *critical region*.

In an embedded system interrupt routines represent a change in the control thread; and the rescheduling that runs one task instead of another (without the running task's knowledge) can only be the eventual consequence of an interrupt. So any critical region can be simply protected by disabling all interrupts around it; this is crude but effective.

But as we saw above, there's a problem: The interrupt-disabling sequence (requiring a read-modify-write sequence on **SR**) is itself not guaranteed to be atomic. I know of two ways of fixing this impasse and one way to avoid it.

The first fix is to insist that no interrupt may change the value of **SR** held by any interruptible code; this requires that interrupt routines always restore **SR** before returning, just as they're expected to restore the state of all the user-level registers. If so, the non-atomic RMW sequence above doesn't matter; even if an interrupt gets in, the old value of **SR** you're using will still be correct. This first approach is generally used in unix-like OS kernels for MIPS and goes well with

---

1. An old saying goes: "Never show fools and children things half done."

the interrupt priority system in which every piece of code is associated with a fixed IPL.

But sometimes this restriction is too much. For example, when you've sent the last waiting byte on a byte-at-a-time output port, you'd like to disable the ready-to-send interrupt (to avoid eternal interrupts) until you have some more data to send. And again, some systems like to rotate priorities between different interrupts to ensure a fair distribution of interrupt service attention.

The second solution is to use a system call to disable interrupts (probably you'd define the system call as taking separate bit-set and bit-clear parameters and get it to update the status register accordingly). Since a **syscall** instruction works by causing an exception, it disables interrupts atomically; on an R3000-type CPU that's because it cleared **SR(IEc)**, and on an R4000-type CPU it will have set **SR(EXL)**. Under this protection your bit-set and bit-clear can proceed cheerfully. It won't work with **SR(EXL)** itself, but it makes no sense to fiddle with **SR(EXL)** in ordinary code on an R4000 and I hope you wouldn't want to. When the system call exception handler returns, the global interrupt enable status is restored (once again atomically).

A system call sounds pretty heavyweight, but it actually doesn't need to take long to run; however, you will have to untangle this system call from the rest of the system's exception-dispatching code.

The third solution is available only with the MIPS III instruction set. This is to use the load-linked and store-conditional instructions to build critical regions without disabling interrupts at all, as described in Section 5.8.4.

5.8.4   *Critical Regions with Interrupts Enabled: Semaphores the MIPS Way*

A semaphore is a coding convention for multitasking programs. The semaphore is a shared memory location used by concurrently running processes to arrange that some resource is only accessed by one of them at once.

Each atomic chunk of code has the following structure:[1]

```
wait(sem);
/* do your atomic thing */
signal(sem);
```

Think of the semaphore as having two values: 1 meaning "in use" and 0 meaning "available." The signal() is simple; it just sets the semaphore to 0. wait() checks for the variable to have the value 0 and won't continue until it

---

1. Two gurus formulated these ideas. Hoare calls the functions wait() and signal()—and that's what we've used. Dijkstra calls equivalent functions (but with a slightly more general concept of semaphore) p() and v(), respectively. You can understand why he called them "p" and "v" quite easily if you speak Dutch.

does. It then sets the variable to 1 and returns. That should be easy, but you can see that it's essential that the process of checking the value of sem and setting it again is itself atomic. High-level atomicity (at the task level) is dependent on being able to build low-level atomicity, where a test-and-set operation can operate correctly in the face of interrupts (or, on a multiprocessor, in the face of access by other CPUs).

Most mature CPU families have some special instruction set features for this: 680x0 CPUs have an atomic test-and-set instruction; x86 CPUs have an "exchange register with memory" operation that can be made atomic with a prefix "lock" instruction.

For large multiprocessor systems this kind of test-and-set process becomes expensive; essentially, all shared memory access must be stopped while the semaphore user obtains the value, completes the test-and-set operation, and the set operation percolates through to every cached copy in the system. This doesn't scale well to large multiprocessors.

It's much more efficient to allow the test-and-set operation to run without any guarantee of atomicity and then to make the set take effect only if we got away with it. There also needs to be some way to find out whether it was OK; now unsuccessful test-and-set sequences can be hidden inside the wait() function and retried as necessary.[1]

This is what MIPS has, using the **ll** (load-linked) and **sc** (store-conditional) instructions in sequence. **sc** will only write the addressed location if there has been no competing access since the last **ll** and will leave a 1/0 value in a register to indicate success or failure.[2]

Here's wait() for the binary semaphore sem:

```
wait:
    la      t0, sem
TryAgain:
    ll      t1, 0(t0)
    bne     t1, zero, WaitForSem
    li      t1, 1
    sc      t1, 0(t0)
    beq     t1, zero, TryAgain
    /* got the semaphore...  */
    jr      ra
```

---

1. Of course, you'd better make sure that there are no circumstances where it ends up retrying forever!

2. Note that we say "if" and not "if and only if." Sometimes **sc** will fail even though the location has not been touched; most uniprocessors will fail the **sc** when there's been any exception serviced since the **ll**. It's only important that the **sc** should usually succeed when there's been no competing access and that it *always* fails when there has been one such.

Even in a uniprocessor system this can be useful, because it does not involve shutting out interrupts. It avoids the interrupt-disabling problem described above and can be an important part of a coordinated effort to reduce worst-case interrupt latency, which is often important in embedded systems.

5.9   Starting Up

In terms of its effect on the CPU, reset is almost the same as an exception, though one from which we're not going to return. In the original MIPS architecture this is mostly a matter of economy of implementation effort and documentation, but the R4000 offers several different levels of reset from a cold reset through to a nonmaskable interrupt—so reset and exception conditions do shade imperceptibly into each other.

Since we're recycling mechanisms from regular exceptions, following reset **EPC** points to the instruction that was being executed when reset was detected, and most register values are preserved. However, reset disrupts normal operation and a register being loaded or a cache location being stored to or refilled at the moment reset occurred may be trashed.

It is quite possible to use the preservation of state through reset to implement some useful postmortem debugging, but your hardware engineer needs to help; the CPU cannot tell you whether reset occurred to a running system or from power-up. But postmortem debugging is an exercise for the talented reader; we will focus on starting up the system from scratch.

The CPU responds to reset by starting to fetch instructions from 0xBFC0 0000. This is physical address 0x1FC0 0000 in the uncached kseg1 region.

Following reset, enough of the CPU's control register state is defined so that the CPU can execute uncached instructions. "Enough state" is interpreted minimally; note the following points:

- Only three things are guaranteed in **SR**: the CPU is in kernel mode; interrupts are disabled; and exceptions will vector through the uncached entry points—that is, **SR(BEV)** = 1.[1]

  Some implementations may guarantee more: For example, IDT documentation states that the **SR(TS)** bit is initialized on R3051-family CPUs; it will be set 0 if the CPU has MMU hardware, 1 otherwise. You should not rely on this promise for MIPS CPUs outside the R3051 family.

- In a CPU with R3000-type caches the D-cache may be isolated if **SR(IsC)** happens to have come upset, so until you've set that bit explicitly you

---

1. In R4000-style CPUs, the first two conditions (and more besides) are typically guaranteed by setting the exception-mode bit **SR(EXL)**, and this is implied by treating reset as an exception.

can't rely on data loads and stores working, even to uncached space. It's probably best to be pessimistic and assume the same about any MIPS CPU.

■ The caches will be in a random, nonsensical state, so a cached load might return rubbish without reading memory.

■ The TLB will be in a random state and *must not be accessed* until initialized (the hardware has only minimal protection against the possibility that there are duplicate matches in the TLB, and the result could be a TLB shutdown which can be amended only by a further reset).

The traditional startup sequence is as follows:

1. Branch to the main ROM code. Why do a branch now?

   ■ The uncached exception entry points start at 0xBFC0 0100, which wouldn't leave enough space for startup code to get to a "natural break."

   ■ The branch represents a very simple test to see if the CPU is functioning and is successfully reading instructions. If something terrible goes wrong with the hardware, the MIPS CPU is most likely to keep fetching instructions in sequence (and next most likely to get permanent exceptions).

   If you use test equipment that can track the addresses of CPU reads and writes, it will show the CPU's uncached instruction fetches from reset; if the CPU starts up and branches to the right place, you have strong evidence that the CPU is getting mostly correct data from the ROM.

   By contrast, if your ROM program plows straight in and fiddles with **SR**, strange and undiagnosable consequences may result from simple faults.

2. Set the status register to some known and sensible state. Now you can load and store reliably in uncached space.

3. You will probably have to run using registers only until you have initialized and (most likely) run a quick check on the integrity of some RAM memory. This will be slow (we're still running uncached from ROM) so you will probably confine your initialization and check to a chunk of memory big enough for the ROM program's data.

4. You will probably have to make some contact with the outside world (a console port or diagnostic register) so you can report any problem with the initialization process.

5. You can now assign yourself some stack and set up enough registers to be able to call a standard C routine.

6. Now you can initialize the caches and run in comfort. Some systems can run code from ROM cached and some can't; on most MIPS CPUs a memory supplying the cache must be able to provide four-word bursts, and your ROM subsystem may or may not oblige.

5.9.1   *Probing and Recognizing Your CPU*

You can identify your CPU implementation number and a manufacturer-defined revision level from the **PRId(Imp)** and **PRId(Rev)** fields. However, it's best to rely on this information as little as possible; changes to the CPU may or may not be reflected in **PRId**. In principle, a particular value of the **PRId(Imp)** field should characterize your CPU—the ISA version it runs and its CP0 registers.[1] But whenever you can probe for a feature directly, do so.

Nonetheless, diagnostic software should certainly make **PRId(Rev)** visible. And should you ever need to include a truly unpleasant software workaround for a hardware bug you may be able to test **PRId(Rev)** to find out when you can leave it out.

It's much more robust, though, to probe for individual features. Here are some examples:

- *Have we got FP hardware?* The "official" technique is to set **SR(CU1)** to enable coprocessor 1 operations and to use a **cfc1** instruction from coprocessor 1 register 0, which is defined to hold the revision ID. A nonzero value in bits 8–15 indicates the presence of FPA hardware; good values you might see are listed in Table 7.3. A skeptical programmer[2] will probably follow this up by checking that it is possible to store and retrieve data from the FPA registers. Unless your system supports unconditional use of the floating-point unit, don't forget to reset **SR(CU1)** afterward.

- *Cache size*: You can determine the cache size for an R3xxx CPU by probing it (see Section 4.9 for one way of doing so). Don't use **PRId**, because there are already many implementations using the same **PRId** value but with different cache sizes.

  R4x00 and subsequent CPUs have the primary cache size encoded in the **Config** register; however, if a secondary cache is fitted the size field is pure convention, and you'd be better building a secondary cache sizing routine to check anything reported.

---

1. Product politics gets in the way of the use of ID registers. Big companies require the parts they use to be requalified if there's a change of specification. A documented change to a register, even the **PRId** register, is a change of specification; a new mask version of the chip that leaves **PRId** alone probably isn't. Once a product is in the field, silicon vendors therefore are under pressure not to change **PRId** so long as they are producing a compatible part.

2. I assume, Gentle Reader, that this is you.

- *Have we got a TLB?* That's memory translation hardware. In IDT's R3051 family you can look at **SR(TS)** following a hardware reset; it will be set for no TLB, 0 otherwise. But this is specific to the R3051 family.

  Alternatively, you can read and write values to **Index** or look for evidence of a continuously counting **Random** register. If it looks promising, you may want to check that you can store and retrieve data in TLB entries.

- *CPU clock rate*: It is often useful to work out your clock rate. You can do this by running a loop of known length, cached, that will take a fixed large number of CPU cycles and then comparing with before and after values of a counter that increments at known speed. Do make sure that you are really running cached, or you will get strange results—remember that some hardware can't run cached out of ROM.

Some maintenance engineer will bless you one day if you make the CPU type, clock rate, and cache sizes available, perhaps as part of a sign-on message.

5.9.2 *Bootstrap Sequences*

Startup code suffers from the clash of two opposing but desirable goals. On the one hand, it's robust to make minimal assumptions about the integrity of the hardware and to attempt to check each subsystem before using it (think of climbing a ladder and trying to check each rung before putting your weight on it). On the other hand, it's desirable to minimize the amount of tricky assembler code. Bootstrap sequences are almost never performance sensitive, so an early change to a high-level language is desirable. But high-level language code tends to require more subsystems to be operational.

After you have dealt with the MIPS-specific hurdles (like setting up **SR** so that you can at least perform loads and stores), the major question is how soon you can make some read/write memory available to the program, which is essential for calling functions written in C.

You have an option here. Most MIPS CPUs now have some data cache on chip, and it is reasonable to regard on-chip resources as the lowest rungs on your ladder.[1] You could rely on the data cache to provide enough storage for your C functions during bootstrap; memory might be read or written, but provided you use less than a cache-size chunk of memory space you will not depend on being able to read memory and get good data back.

The trouble is that some data caches are small, and programs seem to need more and more data space; so Algorithmics doesn't do that.

---

1. Sometimes diagnostic suites include bizarre things like the code in the original PC BIOS, which tests each 8086 instruction in turn. This seems to me like chaining your bicycle to itself to foil thieves.... However, the more positive side of this is that if a subsystem is implemented inside the CPU chip, you don't lose much by trusting it.

5.9.3   *Starting Up an Application*

To be able to start a C application (presumably with its instructions coming safely from ROM) you need three chunks of writable memory.

Firstly, you need stack space. Assign a large enough piece of writable memory and initialize the **sp** register to its upper limit (aligned to an 8-byte boundary). Working out how large the stack should be can be difficult, so a large guess helps.

Then you may need some initialized data. Normally the C data area is initialized by the program loader to set up any variables that have been allocated values. Most compilation systems that purport to be usable for embedded applications permit read-only data (implicit strings and data items declared const) to be managed in a separate segment of object code and put into ROM memory.

Initialized writable data can be used only if your compilation system and run-time system cooperate to arrange to copy writable data initializations from ROM into RAM before calling main().[1]

Lastly, C programs use a different segment of memory for all static and extern data items that are not explicitly initialized—an area sometimes called the "bss" for reasons long lost. Such variables should be cleared to zero, which is readily achieved by zeroing the whole data section before starting the program.

If your program is built carefully, that's enough. However, it can get more complicated: Take care that your MIPS program is not built to use the global pointer register **gp** to speed access to nonstack variables, or you'll need to do more initialization.

You'll find an example (taken from the Algorithmics toolkit) in Section 12.1.

5.10   Emulating Instructions

Sometimes an exception is used to invoke a software handler that will stand in for the exception victim instruction, as when you are using software to implement a floating-point operation on a CPU that doesn't support FP in hardware. Debuggers and other system tools may sometimes want to do this too.

To emulate an instruction, you need to find it, decode it, and find its operands (which by now will be copies of the data in the appropriate registers when the exception triggered, stored in some exception frame). Armed with these you do the operation in software and patch the results back into the exception frame copy of the appropriate result register. You then need to fiddle with the

---

1. We can't resist a small advertisement: The GNU C–based SDE-MIPS cross-compiler (available from Algorithmics and known to your IDT distributor) has this feature.

stored exception return address so as to step over the emulated instruction, and then return. We'll go through these step by step.

Finding the exception-causing instruction is easy; it's usually pointed to by **EPC**, unless it was in a branch delay slot, in which case **Cause(BD)** is set and the exception victim is at the address **EPC** + 4.

To decode the instruction, you need some kind of reverse-assembler table. A big decode-oriented table of MIPS instructions is part of the widely available GNU debugger gdb, where it's used to generate disassembly listings. So long as the GNU license conditions aren't a problem for you, that will save you time and effort.

To find the operands you'll need to know the location and layout of the exception frame, which is dependent on your particular OS (or exception-handling software, if it's too humble to call an OS).

You'll have to figure out for yourself how to do the operation, and once again you need to be able to get at the exception frame, to put the results back in the saved copy of the right register.

There's a trap for the unwary in incrementing the stored **EPC** value to step over the instruction you've emulated.[1] If your emulated instruction was in a branch delay slot, the next instruction in program sequence is not simply the following instruction. In this case you first have to emulate the branch instruction, testing for whether the branch should be taken or not. If the branch should be taken you need to compute its target and return straight there from the exception.

Fortunately, all MIPS branch instructions are side effect free, so this shouldn't be too difficult.

---

1. In early MIPS CPUs **EPC** itself is read-only, so don't try to write it. But in these CPUs the actual return from exception is always accomplished by loading the return address into a general register and executing a **jr**.

Chapter

Memory Management and the TLB

We've tended to introduce most topics in this book from the bottom, which is perhaps natural in a book about low-level computer architecture. But to describe the memory management hardware we're instead going to start off with a description of the unix-style virtual memory system that the MIPS R2000 sought to implement. Later in the chapter we'll come around and look at how the same hardware can be made to work in other contexts.

Early MIPS CPUs sought applications in UNIX workstations and servers, so the MIPS memory management hardware was conceived as the minimum hardware that could hope to provide memory management for BSD UNIX— used here as a well-documented exemplar of the needs of any adequate virtual memory OS. It's clear that the designers were familiar with the DEC VAX minicomputer and recycled many ideas from that architecture, while omitting many complications. In particular, many problems that the VAX solves with microcode are left to software by the MIPS system.

In this chapter we'll start where MIPS started, with the requirements of a basic unix-like OS and its virtual memory system. We'll show how the MIPS hardware is a response to that requirement. At the end, we'll say something about the kinds of use you might make of the memory translation hardware in embedded systems that don't make generic use of that hardware.

Memory translation hardware (we'll call it MMU for *memory management unit*) serves several distinct purposes:

- *Relocation*: The addresses of program entry points and predeclared data are fixed at program compile/build time. The MMU allows the program to be run anywhere in physical memory.

- *Allocating memory to programs*: The MMU can build contiguous program space out of physically scattered pages of memory, allowing us to allocate memory from a pool of fixed-size pages. If we are continually allocating and freeing variable-size chunks of memory, we will suffer fragmentation problems: We'll end up with lots of small islands of memory space and unable to respond to requests for a larger chunk, even though the total free space is quite adequate.

- *Hiding and protection*: User-privilege programs can only access data whose program address is in the kuseg memory region (lower program addresses). Such a program can only get at the memory regions that the OS allows.

  Moreover, each page can be individually specified as writable or write protected; the OS can even stop a program from accidentally overwriting its code.

- *Extending the address range*: Some CPUs can't directly access their full potential physical memory range. MIPS I CPUs, despite their genuine 32-bit architecture, arrange their address map so that the unmapped address space windows kseg0 and kseg1 (which don't depend on the MMU tables to translate addresses) are windows onto the first 512MB of physical memory. If you need to access higher locations, you must go through the MMU.

- *Making the memory map suit your program*: With the MMU, your program can use the addresses that suit it. In a big OS there may be many copies of the same program running, and it's much easier for them all to be using the same program addresses.

- *Demand paging*: Programs can run as if all the memory resources they needed were already allocated, but the OS can actually give them out only as needed. A program accessing an unallocated memory region will get an exception that the OS can process; the OS then loads appropriate data into memory and lets the program continue.

The essence of the UNIX memory manager's job is to run many different processes (multitasking), each in its own memory space.[1] If the job is done properly, the fate of each process is independent of the others (the OS protects itself too): A process can crash or misbehave without bringing down the whole system. This is obviously a useful attribute for a university departmental computer running student programs; but even the most rigorous commercial environment needs to support experimental or prototype software alongside the tried and tested.

The MMU is not just for big, full virtual memory systems; even small embedded programs benefit from relocation and more efficient memory alloca-

---

1. In this section we're going to commit the unix-style confusion that identifies "process" (thread of control) with a separate address space. Modern OSs have separate concepts: Threads are what is scheduled, and address spaces are the protection units. Many threads can share one address space. The memory translation system is obviously interested in address spaces and not in threads. But for now we'll stick with the unix oversimplification, so we can use the familiar word process.

tion. Any system where you may want to run different programs at different times will find it easier if it can map the program's idea of addresses onto whatever physical address space is readily available.

Multitasking and separation between various tasks' address spaces have steadily migrated downward into smaller computers and are now commonplace in personal computers and Internet servers.

Embedded applications frequently use explicit multitasking, but few embedded OSs use separate address spaces. This is probably not so much because this would not be useful but due to the lack of consistent features on embedded CPUs and their available operating systems.

The MIPS minimalism that was so necessary to make the workstation CPU cheap in 1986 may prove relevant to embedded systems in the late 90s. Even small applications, beset by rapidly expanding code size, need to use all known tricks to manage software complexity; and the flexible software-based approach pioneered by MIPS is likely to deliver whatever is needed. A few years ago it was hard to convince CPU vendors addressing the embedded market that the MMU was worth including; by 1997, however, Microsoft's Windows/CE, which cannot be supported without memory management hardware, was being proposed as a solution for a wide range of embedded problems.

6.1   Memory Management in Big Computers

It's probably easiest to start with the whole job of the memory management system in a unix-like system (selected for study because, despite its big-system capabilities, it's much simpler than PC operating systems). The typical view is illustrated as Figure 6.1.

6.1.1   *Basic Process Layout and Protection*

The biggest split in Figure 6.1 is between the low part, labeled "accessible to user programs," and the rest. The user-accessible part of the application map is what we called kuseg in the generic MIPS memory maps described in Section 2.8. All higher memory is reserved to the OS. From the OS's point of view, the low part of memory is a safe "sandbox" in which the user program can play all it wants. If the program goes wild and trashes all its own data, that's no worry to anyone else.

From the application's point of view, this area is free for use in building arbitrarily complicated private data structures and to get on with the job.

Inside the user area, within the program's sandbox, the OS provides more stack to the program on demand (implicitly, as the stack grows down). It will also provide a system call to make more data available starting from the highest predeclared data addresses and growing up—systems people call this a

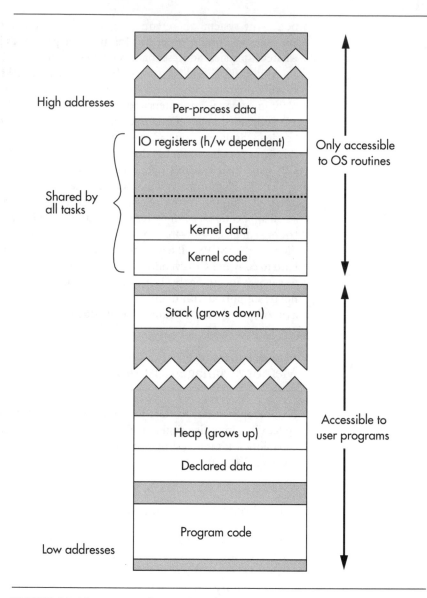

FIGURE 6.1 Memory map for a protected process

heap. The heap feeds library functions such as `malloc()`, which provide your program with chunks of extra memory.

Stack and heap are supplied in chunks small enough to be reasonably thrifty with system memory but big enough to avoid too many system calls or exceptions. However, on every system call or exception the OS has a chance to police the application's memory consumption. An OS can enforce limits that make sure the application doesn't get so large a share of memory as to threaten other vital activities.

In unix-like systems the process keeps its identity inside the OS kernel; most kernel facilities are provided effectively as special subroutines (system calls) invoked by the application under special rules to make sure they only do what the application is entitled to do.

The operating system's own code and data are of course not accessible to user space programs. On some systems this is done by putting them in a completely separate address space; on MIPS the OS shares the same address space, and when the CPU is running at the user-program privilege level, access to these addresses is illegal and will trigger an exception.

Note that while each process's user space maps to its own private real storage, the OS space is mostly shared. Much of the OS code and resources are seen at the same address by all processes—an OS kernel is a multithreaded but single-address-space system inside—but each process's user space addresses access its own separate space. Kernel routines running application system calls are trusted to cooperate safely, but the application need not be trusted at all.

The active parts of the user space are spread out, with stack at the top and code and compiled-in data at the bottom. This allows the stack to grow downward (implicitly, as the program runs and references data deeper) and the data to grow upward (explicitly, as the program calls library functions that allocate memory). The OS can allocate more memory for stack or data and can arrange to map it into the appropriate address.

Note that, in order to allow for programs that use vast quantities of data space, it's usual to have the stack grow down from the highest permissible user addresses. The wide spread of addresses in use (with a huge hole in between) is one characteristic of this address map with which any translation scheme must cope.

Real-life systems make things more complicated in search of efficiency and more functions. Most systems map application code as read-only to the application, meaning that it can safely be shared by many processes—it's common to have many processes running the same application.

Many systems share not just whole applications but chunks of applications accessed through library calls (shared libraries). That opens a whole other can of worms that we will keep sealed up for now.

6.1.2   *Mapping Process Addresses to Real Memory*

What mechanisms are needed to support this model?

The MIPS architecture more or less dictates that the addresses used by programs (whether application or kernel routines) are fixed when the program is compiled and linked.[1] That means that applications can't possibly all be built to use explicit different addresses—and in any case we want to be able to run multiple copies of the same application. So during program execution application addresses are mapped to physical addresses according to a scheme fixed by the OS when the program is loaded.

Although it would be possible for the software to rush around patching all the address translation information whenever we switched contexts from one process to another, it would be very inefficient. Instead, we award each active process a number (in UNIX it's called the process ID but these days is more wisely called the *address space ID* or ASID). Any address from a process is implicitly extended by that process's ASID to produce a unique address to submit for translation. The ASID needs to be loaded into a CPU register whenever a new process is scheduled so that the hardware can use it.

The mapping facility also allows the OS to discriminate between different parts of the user address space: Some parts of the application space (typically code) can be mapped read-only and some parts can be left unmapped and accesses trapped, meaning that a program that runs amok is likely to be stopped earlier.

The kernel part of the process's address space is generally shared by all processes and most of it maps permanently resident OS code and data. Since this code can be linked to run at this address, it doesn't need a flexible mapping scheme, and most MIPS kernels are happy to put most of their code and data in areas whose mapping is fixed by the architecture.

6.1.3 *Paged Mapping Preferred*

Many exotic schemes have been tried for mapping addresses, commonly using base/bound pairs to police correct accesses. But mapping memory in whatever size chunks the programs ask for, while apparently providing the best service for applications, rapidly leads to available memory being fragmented into awkward-sized pieces. All practical systems map memory in *pages*—fixed-size chunks of memory. Pages are always a power of 2 bytes big, with 4KB being overwhelmingly popular.

With 4KB pages, a CPU address can be simply partitioned thus:

nn	12 11	0
Virtual page number (VPN)		Address within page

The address-within-page bits don't need to be translated, so the memory management hardware only has to cope with translating the high-order addresses, traditionally called virtual page number (VPN), into the high-order bits of a

---

1. It is possible to generate position-independent code (PIC) for MIPS CPUs but pure PIC is somewhat awkward on MIPS. (See Section 10.11.2 for an account of the compromises made to provide enough position independence for shared libraries in the MIPS/ABI standard.)

physical address (a physical frame number, or PFN—nobody can remember why it's not PPN).

6.1.4   *What We Really Want*

The mapping mechanism must allow a program to assert a particular address within its own process/address space and translate that efficiently into a real physical address to access memory.

A good way to do this would be to have a table (the *page table*) containing an entry for each page in the whole address space, with that entry containing the correct physical address. This is clearly a fairly large data structure and is going to have to be stored in main memory. But there are two big problems.

The first is that we now need two references to memory to do any load or store, and that's obviously hopeless for performance. You may foresee the answer to this: We can use a high-speed cache memory to store translation entries and go to the memory-resident table only when we miss in the cache. Since each cache entry covers 4KB of memory space, it's plausible that we can get a satisfactorily low miss rate out of a reasonably small cache. (At the time this scheme was invented, memory caches were rare and were sometimes also called "lookaside buffers," so the memory translation cache became a translation lookaside buffer or TLB; the acronym survives.)

The second problem is the size of the page table; for a 32-bit application address space split into 4KB pages, there are a million entries, which will take at least 4MB of memory. We really need to find some way to make the table smaller, or there'll be no memory left to run the programs.

We'll defer any discussion of the solution for this, beyond observing that real running programs have huge holes in their program address space, and if we can invent some scheme that avoids using physical memory for the corresponding holes in the table, things are likely to get better.

We've now arrived, in essence, at the memory translation system DEC figured out for its VAX minicomputer, which has been extremely influential in most subsequent architectures. It's summarized in Figure 6.2.

The sequence in which the hardware works is something like this:

- A virtual address is split into two, with the least-significant bits (usually 12 bits) passing through untranslated—so translation is always done in pages (usually 4KB).

- The more-significant bits, or VPN, are concatenated with the currently running process's ASID to form a unique page address.

- We look in the TLB (translation cache) to see if we have a translation entry for the page. If we do, it gives us the high-order physical address bits and we've got the address to use.

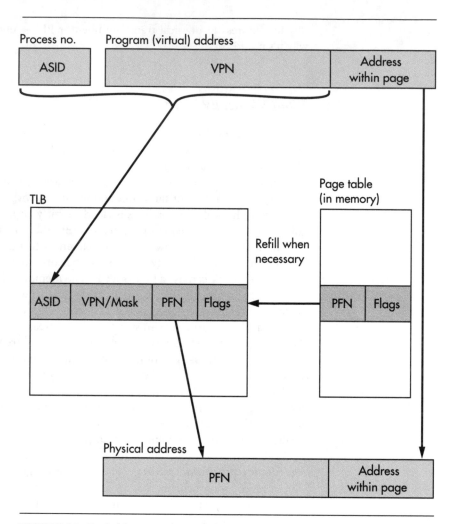

FIGURE 6.2 Desirable memory translation system

The TLB is a special-purpose store and can match addresses in various useful ways. It may have a global flag bit that tells it to ignore the value of ASID for some entries, so that these TLB entries map some range of virtual addresses for *every* process.

Similarly, the VPN may be stored with some Mask bits that cause some parts of the VPN to be excluded from the match, allowing the TLB entry to map a larger range of virtual addresses.

Both of these special cases are available in some MIPS MMUs.

■ There are usually extra bits (flags) stored with the PFN that are used to control what kind of access is allowed—most obviously, to permit reads but not writes. We'll discuss the MIPS architecture's flags in Section 6.2.

- If there's no matching entry in the TLB, the system must locate or build an appropriate entry (using main-memory-resident page table information) and load it into the TLB and then run the translation process again.

In the VAX minicomputer, this process was controlled by microcode and seemed to the programmer to be completely automatic.

6.1.5   *Origins of the MIPS Design*

The MIPS designers wanted to figure out a way to offer the same facilities as the VAX with as little hardware as possible. The microcoded TLB refill was not acceptable, so they took the brave step of consigning this part of the job to software.

That means that apart from a register to hold the current ASID, the MMU hardware is just a TLB, which is simply a high-speed, fixed-size table of translations. System software can (and usually does) use the TLB as a cache to front a memory-resident page table, but there's nothing in the TLB hardware to make it a cache, except this: When presented with an address it can't translate, the TLB triggers a special exception (*TLB refill*) to invoke the software routine. However, considerable care is taken with the details of the TLB design and associated control registers to help the software to be efficient.

6.2   MIPS TLB Facts and Figures

The MIPS TLB has always been implemented on chip: The memory translation step is required even for cached references, so it's very much on the critical path of the machine. That meant it had to be small, particularly in the early days, so it makes up for its small size by being clever.

It's basically a genuine *associative memory*. Each entry in an associative memory consists of a key field and a data field; you present the key and the hardware gives you the data of any entry where the key matches. Associative memories are wonderful, but they are expensive in hardware. MIPS TLBs have had between 32 and 64 entries; a store of this size is manageable as a silicon design.

R4000-style CPUs so far have used a TLB where each entry is doubled up to map two consecutive VPNs to independently specified physical pages. The paired entries double the amount of memory that can be mapped by the TLB with only a little extra logic, without requiring any large-scale rethinking of TLB management.

TLB entry (R3000-style MIPS CPU)   Output

VPN	ASID	G	PFN	Flags N D V

TLB entry (R4000-style MIPS CPU)   Output

VPN2	PageMask	ASID	G	PFN	Flags C D V	PFN	Flags C D V

FIGURE 6.3 TLB entry fields

You will see the TLB referred to as being fully associative; this emphasizes that all keys are really compared with the input value in parallel.[1]

The TLB entry is shown schematically in Figure 6.3 (you'll find detailed programming information later in Section 6.5). The TLB's key consists of the following:

- *VPN*: The high order bits of the virtual address (*the virtual address of the page less low bits*). It becomes VPN2 with the double entry, to emphasize that if each physical page is 4KB, the virtual address selecting a pair of entries loses its least-significant bit (which now selects the left or right output field).

- *PageMask*: This is only found on later CPUs. It controls how much of the virtual address is compared with the VPN and how much is passed through to the physical address; a match on fewer bits maps a larger region. MIPS CPUs can be set up to map up to 16MB with a single entry. With a page size larger than 4KB, the second output-side entry is ignored.

- *ASID*: Marks the translation as belonging to a particular address space, so it won't be matched unless the CPU's current ASID value matches too. The **G** bit, if set, disables the ASID match, making the translation entry apply to all address spaces (so this part of the address map is shared between all spaces). The ASID is 6 bits long on early CPUs, 8 bits on later ones.[2]

---

1. The R4000's TLB would be correctly, if pedantically, described as a 48-way set-associative store, with two entries per set.

2. The OS-aware reader will appreciate that even 256 is too small an upper limit for the number of simultaneously active processes on a big unix system. However, it's a reasonable limit so long as "active" in this context is given the special meaning of "may have translation entries in the TLB." Software has to recycle ASIDs where necessary, which will involve purging the TLB of translation entries for the process that is being downgraded. It's a dirty business, but so is quite a lot of what OSs have to do; and 256 entries should be enough to make sure it doesn't have to be done so often as to constitute a performance problem. For programming purposes, the **G** bit is stored with the output side's flags.

The TLB's output side gives you the physical frame number and a small but sufficient bunch of flags:

- *Physical frame number (PFN)*: This is the physical address with the low 12 bits cut off.

- *Cache control (N/C)*: The 32-bit CPUs have just the **N** (noncacheable) bit—0 for cacheable, 1 for noncacheable.

  The 64-bit CPUs provide a 3-bit field **C** that can contain a larger range of values that tell multiprocessor hardware what protocols to use when data in this page is shared with other processors. Those 64-bit CPUs that don't have hardware cache coherency features have maintained this TLB entry layout; only the two code values that mean cacheable with all R4000 cache features (3) and uncached (2) are standard over all R4000-style CPUs. Modern embedded CPUs can select different cache management strategies with different values: write through vs. write back or write allocate vs. uncached write on miss. See your CPU manual.

- *Write control bit (D)*: Set 1 to allow stores to this page to happen. The "D" comes from this being called the "dirty bit"; see Section 6.8 for why.

- *Valid bit (V)*: If this is 0, the entry is unusable. This seems pretty pointless: Why have a record loaded into the TLB if you don't want the translation to work? It's because the software routine that refills the TLB is optimized for speed and doesn't want to check for special cases. When some further processing is needed before a program can use a page referred to by the memory-held table, the memory-held entry can be left marked invalid. After TLB refill, this will cause a different kind of trap, invoking special processing without having to put a test in every software refill event.

Translating an address is now simple, and we can amplify the description above:

- *CPU generates a program address*: This is accomplished either for an instruction fetch, a load, or for a store that doesn't lie in the special unmapped regions of the MIPS address space.

  The low 12 bits are separated off, and the resulting VPN together with the current value of the ASID field in **EntryHi** is used as the key to the TLB, as modified in effect by the **PageMask** and **G** fields in TLB entries.

- *TLB matches key*: The matching entry is selected. The PFN is glued to the low-order bits of the program address to form a complete physical address.

- *Valid?* The V and D bits are consulted. If it isn't valid or a store is being attempted with D unset, the CPU takes a trap. As with all translation traps, the **BadVaddr** register will be filled with the offending program address; as with any TLB exception, the TLB **EntryHi** register will be preloaded with the VPN of the offending address.

Don't use the convenience registers **Context** (and **XContext** on 64-bit CPUs) other than in TLB miss processing. At other times they might track things like **BadVaddr** or they might not; either would be a legitimate implementation.

- *Cached?* If the C bit is set the CPU looks in the cache for a copy of the physical location's data; if it isn't there it will be fetched from memory and a copy left in the cache. Where the C bit is clear the CPU neither looks in nor refills the cache.

Of course, the number of entries in the TLB permits you to translate only a relatively small number of program addresses—a few hundred KB worth. This is far from enough for most systems. The TLB is almost always going to be used as a software-maintained cache for a much larger set of translations.

When a program address lookup in the TLB fails, a *TLB refill* trap is taken.[1] System software has the following job:

- It figures out whether there is a correct translation; if not, the trap will be dispatched to the software that handles address errors.

- If there is a correct translation, it constructs a TLB entry that will implement it.

- If the TLB is already full (and it almost always is full in running systems), the software selects an entry that can be discarded.

- The software writes the new entry into the TLB.

See Section 6.7 for how this can be tackled, but note here that although special CPU features help out with one particular class of implementations, the software can refill the TLB any way it likes.

6.3   MMU Registers Described

We'll now put aside our top-down approach and get down to the details of the MIPS implementation. I hope you've got enough background to set the bits in context; once we've set out the details, we can show how the facilities are used.

Like everything else in a MIPS CPU, MMU control is effected by a rather small number of extra instructions and a set of registers taken from the copro-

---

1. Should this be called a "TLB miss" (which is what just happened) or a "TLB refill" (which is what we're going to do to sort it out)? I'm afraid we probably use both terms in MIPS documentation.

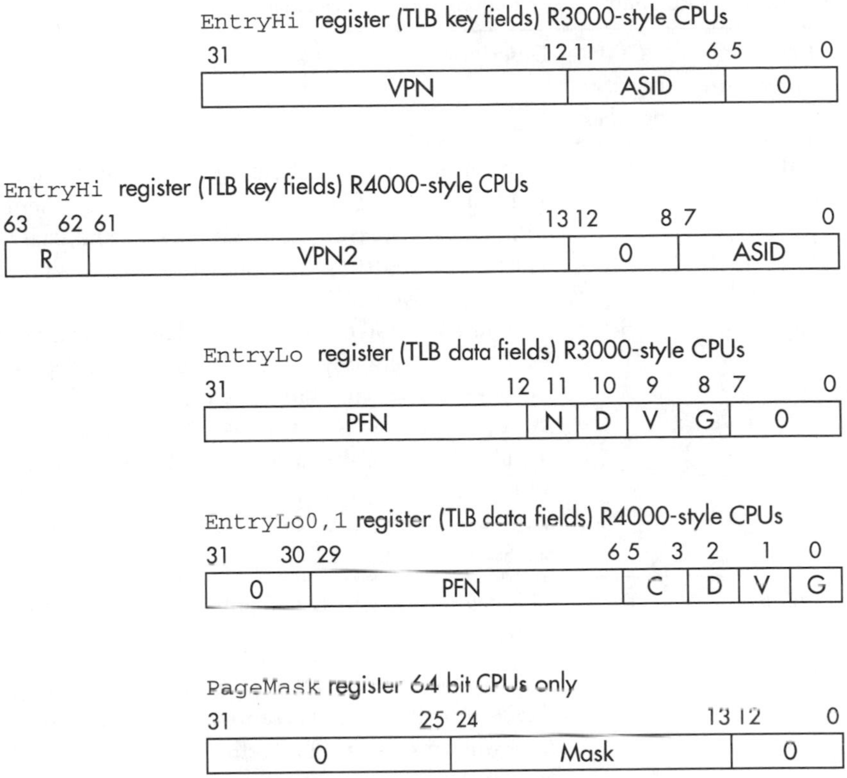

EntryHi register (TLB key fields) R3000-style CPUs

31	12 11 6 5	0
VPN	ASID	0

EntryHi register (TLB key fields) R4000-style CPUs

63 62 61	13 12 8 7		0
R	VPN2	0	ASID

EntryLo register (TLB data fields) R3000-style CPUs

31	12 11 10 9 8 7				0
PFN	N	D	V	G	0

EntryLo0,1 register (TLB data fields) R4000-style CPUs

31 30 29	6 5 3 2 1				0
0	PFN	C	D	V	G

PageMask register 64 bit CPUs only

31 25 24	13 12	0
0	Mask	0

FIGURE 6.4 **EntryHi**, **EntryLo**, and **PageMask** register fields

cessor 0 set. Table 6.1 lists the control registers, and we'll get around to the instructions in Section 6.4.

6.3.1 *EntryHi, EntryLo, and PageMask*

Figure 6.4 shows these registers, which are the programmer's only view of a TLB entry and are best considered together.

The fields in **EntryHi** are as follows:

- *VPN, VPN2 (virtual page number)*: These are the high-order bits of a program address (with bits 0–12 omitted). VPN2 omits bit 13 too, because it's used where each TLB entry will map a pair of 4KB virtual pages. Following a refill exception this field is set up automatically to match the program address that could not be translated. When you want to write a different TLB entry, or attempt a TLB probe, you have to set it up by hand.

TABLE 6.1 CPU control registers for memory management

Register mnemonic	CP0 register number	Description
EntryHi	10	Together these registers hold everything needed for a TLB entry. All reads and writes to the TLB must be staged through them. **EntryHi** holds the VPN and ASID; **EntryLo** holds the PFN and flags.
EntryLo/ EntryLo0	2	The field **EntryHi(ASID)** does double duty, since it remembers the currently active ASID.
EntryLo1	3	
PageMask	5	In some CPUs (all 64-bit CPUs to date) each entry maps two consecutive VPNs to different physical pages, specified independently by two registers called **EntryLo0** and **EntryLo1**.
		EntryHi grows to 64 bits in 64-bit CPUs but in such a way as to preserve the illusion of a 32-bit layout for software that doesn't need long addresses.
		PageMask can be used to create entries that map pages bigger than 4KB; see Section 6.3.1.
Index	0	This determines which TLB entry will be read/written by appropriate instructions.
Random	1	This pseudo-random value (actually a free-running counter) is used by a **tlbwr** to write a new TLB entry into a randomly selected location. Saves time when processing TLB refill traps, for software that likes the idea of random replacement (there is probably no viable alternative).
Context Xcontext	4 20	These are convenience registers, provided to speed up the processing of TLB refill traps. The high-order bits are read/write; the low-order bits are taken from the VPN of the address that couldn't be translated.
		The register fields are laid out so that, if you use the favored arrangement of memory-held copies of memory translation records, then following a TLB refill trap **Context** will contain a pointer to the page table record needed to map the offending address. See Section 6.3.5.
		Xcontext does the same job for traps from processes using more than 32-bits of effective address space; a straightforward extension of the **Context** layout to larger spaces would be unworkable because of the size of the resulting data structures. Some 64-bit CPU software is happy with 32-bit virtual address spaces, but for when that's not enough 64-bit CPUs are equipped with "mode bits" **SR(UX), SR(KX)** which can be set to cause an alternative TLB refill handler to be invoked; in turn that handler can use **Xcontext** to support a huge but manageable page table format.

The 64-bit systems (so far) don't actually support virtual address spaces as huge as is implied by the above. VPN2 is actually a 27-bit field in R4x00 CPUs, corresponding to a 40-bit program address space. Higher bits of VPN2 *must* be written as all ones or all zeros, matching the most-significant bit of the **EntryLo** register; equivalently, the higher bits are all 1 when accessing kernel-only address spaces and all 0 otherwise.

If you are only using the 32-bit instruction set this will happen automatically, because when you work this way all register values contain the 64-bit sign extension of a 32-bit number.

- *ASID (address space identifier)*: This is normally left holding the operating system's idea of the current address space. This is not changed by exceptions, so after a refill exception, this will still have the right value in it for the currently running process.

  Most software systems will deliberately write this field only to set up the current address space. However, you have to be careful when using **tlbr** to inspect TLB entries; that operation overwrites the whole of **EntryHi**, so you will have to restore the correct current ASID value afterward.

- *R*: This is an address region. You can consistently regard this field as just more bits of **EntryHi(VPN2)**; it's just the highest-order bits of the 64-bit MIPS virtual address. However, if you remember the 64-bit extended-memory map (see Figure 2.2 in Section 2.8), you can see that these high-order bits select memory areas with different access privileges. Also, they're unlike the high bits of VPN2 because they can indeed take on different values—an implementation-defined number of high-order bits of **EntryHi(VPN2)** must be all ones or all zeros.

Fields in **EntryLo** are as follows:

- *PFN*: These are the high-order bits of the physical address to which values matching **EntryHi**'s VPN will be translated.

- *N (noncacheable)*: Set 0 to make the access cacheable, 1 for uncacheable.

- *C*: For R4000 and later CPUs there's a much richer choice of cache algorithm to use for this access, encoded into a 3-bit field. But values other than uncached (2) and cached without multiprocessor signalling (3) are used differently by cache-coherent multiprocessors and later embedded CPUs.

- *D (dirty)*: This functions as a write-enable bit. Set 1 to allow writes, 0 to cause any store using this translation to be trapped. See Section 6.8 for an explanation of the term "dirty."

- *V (valid)*: If set 0, any use of an address matching this entry will cause an exception. Used either to mark a page that is not available for access (in a true virtual memory system), or to mark one **EntryLo** part of a paired translation as not available.

■ *G (global)*: When the G bit in a TLB entry is set, that TLB entry will match solely on the VPN field, regardless of whether the TLB entry's ASID field matches the value in **EntryHi**. This allows us to implement parts of the address space that are shared between all processes without adding additional page tables.

■ *Fields called 0*: These fields always return zero, but unlike many re-served fields, they do not need to be written as zero (nothing happens regardless of the data written). This is important; it means that the memory-resident data that is used to generate **EntryLo** when refill-ing the TLB can contain some software-interpreted data in these fields, which the TLB hardware will ignore without the need to spend precious CPU cycles masking it out.

The **PageMask** register has been implemented in all 64-bit CPUs to date. The current mask field is copied into a TLB entry as it's made, and 1 bits have the effect of causing the corresponding bit of the virtual address to be ignored when matching the TLB entry (and causing that bit to be carried unchanged to the resulting physical address), effectively matching a larger page size. Masked bits in the address are copied directly to the physical address, too.

No MIPS CPU permits arbitrary bit patterns in Mask. Most allow page sizes between 4KB and 16MB in ×4 steps:

PageMask bits	*Page size*		
24–21	*20–17*	*16–13*	
0000	0000	0000	4KB
0000	0000	0011	16KB
0000	0000	1111	64KB
0000	0011	1111	256KB
0000	1111	1111	1MB
0011	1111	1111	4MB
1111	1111	1111	16MB

NEC's Vr4200 CPU supports only 4KB and 16MB pages but uses the standard encodings for those sizes.

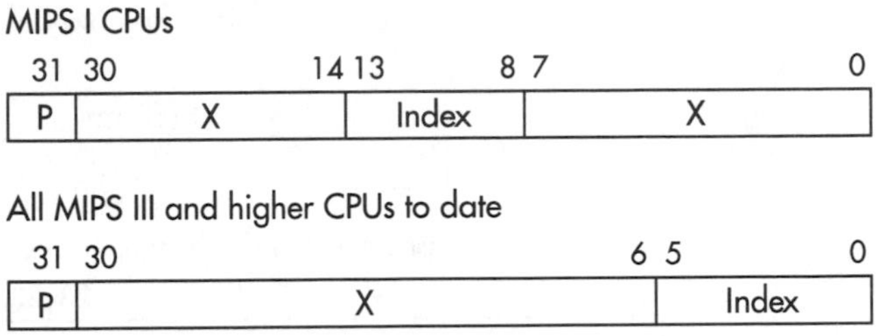

MIPS I CPUs

```
 31  30              14 13      8 7              0
┌───┬──────────────┬──────────┬────────────────┐
│ P │      X       │  Index   │       X        │
└───┴──────────────┴──────────┴────────────────┘
```

All MIPS III and higher CPUs to date

```
 31  30                        6 5              0
┌───┬──────────────────────────┬────────────────┐
│ P │           X              │     Index      │
└───┴──────────────────────────┴────────────────┘
```

FIGURE 6.5 Fields in the **Index** register

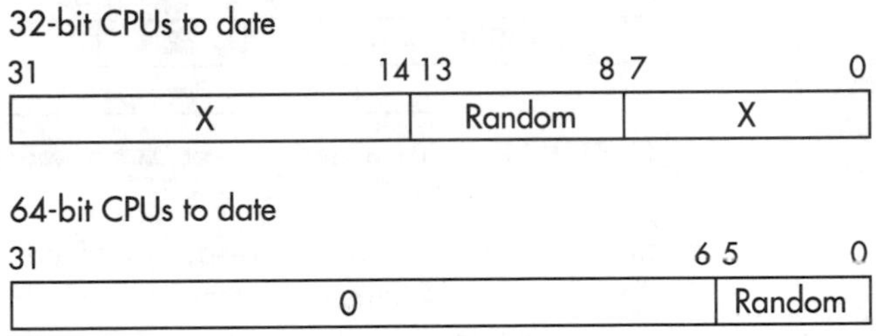

32-bit CPUs to date

```
 31                 14 13      8 7              0
┌──────────────────┬──────────┬────────────────┐
│        X         │  Random  │       X        │
└──────────────────┴──────────┴────────────────┘
```

64-bit CPUs to date

```
 31                            6 5              0
┌──────────────────────────────┬────────────────┐
│              0               │    Random      │
└──────────────────────────────┴────────────────┘
```

FIGURE 6.6 Fields in the **Random** register

6.3.2   *Index*

The **Index** register is used to specify a TLB index when you deliberately want to write a particular entry and is used to return a TLB index after you look up a translation with **tlbp**.

Figure 6.5 shows that **Index** is not quite just a number. The P field is set when a **tlbp** instruction fails to find a valid translation; since it is the top bit it appears to make the 32-bit value negative, which is easy to test for.

Note the different position of the field in early MIPS CPUs and that there are only 6 significant bits (addressing a maximum of 64 TLB entries).

6.3.3   *Random*

Random holds an index into the TLB that counts (downward, if that's important to you) with each instruction the CPU executes. It acts as an index into the TLB for the write-entry instruction **tlbwr**, supporting a random replacement strategy when you need to write a TLB entry.

You never have to read or write the **Random** register (shown as Figure 6.6) in normal use, but it may be useful for diagnostics. The hardware is supposed to set the **Random** field to its maximum value—matching the highest-

Context register for R3x00 CPUs

	31		21 20		2 1	0
	PTEBase		Bad VPN		0	

Context register for R4x00 and subsequent CPUs

63		23 22		4 3	0
PTEBase		Bad VPN2		0	

XContext register for R4x00 and subsequent CPUs only

63		33 32	31 30		4 3	0
PTEBase		R	Bad VPN2		0	

FIGURE 6.7 Fields in the `Context/XContext` registers

numbered entry in the TLB—on reset, and it decrements every clock period until it reaches a floor value, when it wraps back to 63 and starts again.

TLB entries from 0 and whose index is less than the floor value are therefore immune from random replacement, and an OS can use those slots for permanent translation entries—they are referred to as "wired" in MIPS OS documentation.

In early CPUs the floor value is fixed to 8, but there were complaints about the arbitrary nature of this constant and 64-bit CPUs introduced the `Wired` register, which allows you to change the floor and thus the range of `Random`.

6.3.4 *Wired*

This is just a number, but the effect of writing numbers larger than the highest index in your TLB is unlikely to be helpful. When you write `Wired` the `Random` register is automatically reset to point to the top of the TLB.

6.3.5 *Context and XContext*

When the CPU takes an exception because a translation isn't in the TLB, the virtual address whose translation wasn't available is already in `BadVaddr`, and the VPN (which is all that matters) is already in `EntryHi`. This is clearly sufficient; however, in order to speed the processing of this exception, the `Context` or `XContext` register repackages the same information in a format that can be a ready-made pointer to a memory-based page table.

Figure 6.7 shows these registers, and the fields are described in the notes following:

- *PTEBase*: This is a location that just stores what you put in it. To implement the "standard" refill handler, this will be the high-order bits of the (appropriately aligned) starting address of a memory-resident page table. The starting address must be picked to have zeros in bits 20 and downward, since **Context** is an "or" of its fields, not their sum. That constrains the memory-held page table to start on a 1MB boundary in kernel virtual address—probably not much of a problem.

- *Bad VPN/Bad VPN2*: Following an addressing exception this holds the high-order bits of the address, which are exactly the same as the high-order bits of **BadVaddr**. Why is it VPN2? If your CPU's TLB stores pairs of entry, then bit 12 of the address is not part of the TLB key field.

  The VPN or VPN2 value is shifted left, so as to precalculate a pointer into a structure whose entries are bigger than bytes. The 2-bit shift for 32-bit CPUs allows a 4-byte entry, which is large enough to hold information to fill the **EntryLo** register which forms the other half of the TLB entry. The 64-bit CPUs not only have 64-bit **EntryLo0** and **EntryLo1** registers, but they have two of them because each TLB entry maps two pages; hence the page table is expected to have entries 16 bytes in size, and the VPN is shifted left by four.

- *Fields marked 0*: These will always read zero.

6.4 MMU Control Instructions

The instructions

```
tlbr     # read TLB entry at index
tlbwi    # write TLB entry at index
```

move MMU data between the TLB entry selected by the **index** register and the **EntryHi** and **EntryLo** registers.

You won't often read a TLB entry; when you do, remember that you'll have overwritten the **EntryHi(ASID)** field, which is supposed to relate to the address map of the currently running process. So put it back again.

The instruction

```
tlbwr    # write TLB entry selected by Random
```

copies the contents of **EntryHi** (including the included ASID field), **EntryLo**, and **PageMask** into the TLB entry indexed by the **random** register—this saves time if you are adopting a random replacement policy. In practice, **tlbwr** will be used to write a new TLB entry in a TLB refill exception handler; **tlbwi** will be used anywhere else.

The instruction

```
tlbp    # TLB lookup
```

searches the TLB for an entry whose virtual page number and ASID matches those currently in **EntryHi** and stores the index of that entry in the **Index** register. **Index(P)** is set if nothing matches—this makes the value look negative, which is easy to test.

If more than one entry matches, anything might happen. This is a horrible error and is never supposed to happen.

Note that **tlbp** does not fetch data from the TLB; you have to run a subsequent **tlbr** (TLB read indexed) instruction to do that.

The TLB is internally pipelined, and these management/diagnostic instructions cheat. Many implementations require that the instruction following a **tlbp** not be a load or store.

6.5   Programming the TLB

TLB entries are set up by writing the required fields into **EntryHi** and **EntryLo** and by using a **tlbwr** or **tlbwi** instruction to copy that entry into the TLB proper.

When you are handling a TLB refill exception, you will find that **EntryHi** has been set up for you already.

Be very careful not to create two entries that will match the same program address/ASID pair. If the TLB contains duplicate entries an attempt to translate such an address, or probe for it, has the potential to damage the CPU chip. Some CPUs protect themselves in these circumstances by a TLB shutdown, which shows up as the **SR(TS)** bit being set. The TLB will now match nothing until a hardware reset.

System software often won't need to read TLB entries at all. But if you need to read them, you can find the TLB entry matching some particular program address using **tlbp** to set up the **Index** register. Don't forget to save **EntryHi** and restore it afterward because its ASID field is likely to be important.

Use a **tlbr** to read the TLB entry into **EntryHi** and **EntryLo**.

You'll see references in the CPU documentation to separate ITLB and DTLB structures that perform translation for instruction and data addresses, respectively; these are tiny hardware-managed caches whose operation is completely transparent to software.

6.5.1   *How Refill Happens*

When a program makes an access in any of the translated address regions (normally kuseg for application programs under a protected OS and kseg2 for kernel-privilege mappings), and no translation record is present, the CPU takes a TLB refill exception.

The TLB can only map a fraction of the physical memory range of a modern server or workstation. Large OSs maintain some kind of memory-held page table that holds a large number of page translations and uses the TLB as a cache of recently used translations. Most often the page table will be an array of ready-to-use TLB entries, set out so that you can use the **Context** register as a pointer into it.

Since MIPS systems usually put their OS kernel into the untranslated kseg0 memory region, the common situation will be a user-privilege program that wants to translate a kuseg address. Several hardware features are provided with the aim of speeding up the exception handler in this common case. Firstly, these refill exceptions are vectored through a low-memory address used for no other exception.[1] Secondly, a series of cunning tricks allow the memory-held page table to be located in kernel virtual memory (the kseg2 region or its 64-bit alternative) so that physical memory space is not needed for the parts of the page table that map "holes" in the process's address map.

And to top it off, the **Context** or **XContext** register can be used to give immediate access to the right entry from a memory-held page table.

We'll work through this process in Section 6.7. But before we get too far into it, we should note that use of all these features is *not compulsory*. In a smaller system the TLB can be used to produce a fixed or rarely changing translation from program (virtual) to physical addresses; in these cases it won't even need to be a cache.

Even some big virtual memory OSs implemented for MIPS have not used the "standard" page table. Early versions of the portable NetBSD kernel organized a relatively large software-managed second-level cache of translations that was searched by the regular refill code; access to pages whose translations aren't present in the second-level cache are rare and can be handed off to a relatively heavyweight handler written in C and drawing on a machine-independent page table.

6.5.2   *Using ASIDs*

By setting up TLB entries with a particular ASID setting and with the **EntryLo** G bit set 0, those entries will only ever match a program address when the CPU's **EntryHi(ASID)** register field matches the TLB entry's value. This allows you to map up to 64 or 256 different address spaces simultaneously, with-

---

1. On the original MIPS architecture this is the *only* event deemed worthy of its own entry point. The exact criteria for use of the special entry point changed between the R3000 and R4000 generations of the CPU, but the aim is the same.

out requiring that you clear out the TLB on a context change.[1] If you do run out of ASIDs you will have to go through the TLB and discard mappings for the address space(s) whose ASID you want to revoke.

6.5.3 *The Random Register and Wired Entries*

The hardware offers you no way of finding out which TLB entries have been used most recently. When you are using the TLB as a cache and you need to install a new mapping, the only practicable strategy is to replace an entry at random. The CPU makes this easy for you by maintaining the **Random** register, which counts (down, actually) with every processor cycle.

Random replacement sounds horribly inefficient; you may end up discarding the translation entry that has been in heaviest use recently and that will almost certainly be needed again very soon. But in fact this doesn't happen so often as to be a real problem when you have a reasonable number of possible victims to choose from, and most MIPS OSs leave themselves at least 40.

However, it is often useful to have some TLB entries that are guaranteed to stay there until you choose to remove them. These may be useful to map pages that you know will be required very often, but they are really important because they allow you to map pages and *guarantee* that no refill exception will be generated on them.

The stable TLB entries are described as "wired": On R3000 CPUs they consist of TLB entries 0 through 7 and on R4x00 and subsequent CPUs they are between 0 and whatever value you programmed into the **Wired** register. The TLB itself does nothing special about these entries; the magic is in the **Random** register, which never takes values 0 through "wired-1"; it cycles directly from "wired-1" to its maximum value. So conventional random replacement leaves TLB entries 0 through "wired-1" unaffected, and entries written there will stay until explicitly removed.

6.6 Memory Translation: Setup

The following code fragments initialize the TLB to ensure that there is no match on any kuseg or kseg2 address. We've done the usual R3000- and R4000-style TLB arrangements separately. Here is a simple TLB initialization for an R3000 or similar CPU:

---

1. The exact number depends on the width of the ASID field, which has grown from 6 bits to 8 bits during the evolution of MIPS.

```
#include <mips/r3kc0.h>

LEAF(mips_init_tlb)
    mfc0    t0,C0_ENTRYHI            # save ASID
    mtc0    zero,C0_ENTRYLO         # tlblo = !valid
    li      a1,NTLBID<<TLBIDX_SHIFT # index
    li      a0,KSEG1_BASE           # tlbhi = impossible VPN


    .set noreorder
1:  subu    a1,1<<TLBIDX_SHIFT
    mtc0    a0,C0_ENTRYHI
    mtc0    a1,C0_INDEX
    addu    a0,0x1000               # increment VPN, so all entries differ
    bnez    a1,1b
    tlbwi                           # in branch delay slot
    .set    reorder


    mtc0    t0,C0_ENTRYHI           # restore ASID
    j       ra
END(mips_init_tlb)
```

Here is a simple TLB initialization for an R4000 or similar CPU:

```
#include <mips/r4kc0.h>

LEAF(mips_init_tlb)
    dmfc0   t0,C0_ENTRYHI           # save for ASID field
    li      a1,NTLBID               # start one above top of TLB
    li      a0,KSEG1_BASE           # impossible VPN
    mtc0    zero,C0_ENTRYLO0        # zero is invalid
    mtc0    zero,C0_ENTRYLO1


1:  subu    a1,1
    dmtc0   a0,C0_ENTRYHI
    dmtc0   a1,C0_INDEX
    addu    a0,0x2000               # increment VPN, so all entries differ
    tlbwi                           # in branch delay slot
    bnez    a1,1b


    .set noreorder
    nop                             # tlbwi uses entryhi late
    dmtc0   t0,C0_ENTRYHI           # restore ASID
    .set reorder


    j       ra
END(mips_init_tlb)
```

Let's look at the TLB initialization process.

- Both routines start at the top of the TLB (constant NTLBID is found in the include file, which Algorithmics calls r3kc0.h or r4kc0.h).

- The zero value of **EntryLo0** and **EntryLo1** means that any translation is not valid, but that may not on its own be enough to prevent trouble with duplicated entries.

- Note that the R3000 version of **Index** has the field shifted up the register, so we can't just add one to it.

- The VPN stored in each entry is that of a page in the kseg0 area, which by definition is a nontranslated address and can therefore never be looked up. But even so, we make sure that all the VPNs are different.

6.7   TLB Exception Sample Code

This routine implements the translation mechanism that the MIPS architects undoubtedly had in mind for user addresses in a unix-like OS. It relies upon building a page table in memory for each address space. The page table consists of a linear array of entries, indexed by the VPN, whose format is matched to the bitfields of the **EntryLo** register. R3000-type single-entry TLBs need one word per entry, while R4000-type paired TLBs need four (each entry having grown to accommodate the bigger address space).

Such a scheme is simple but opens up other problems. Since each 4KB of user address space takes 4 bytes of table space, the entire 2GB of user space needs a 2MB table, which is an embarrassingly large chunk of data.[1] Of course, most user address spaces are only filled at the bottom (for code and data) and at the top (for a downward growing stack) with a huge gap in between. The solution MIPS adopted is inspired by DEC's VAX architecture and is to locate the page table itself in virtual memory in the kseg2 region. This neatly solves two problems at once:

- It saves physical memory; since the unused gap in the middle of the page table will never be referenced, no physical memory need actually be allocated for those entries.

- It provides an easy mechanism for remapping a new user page table when changing context, without having to find enough virtual addresses in the OS to map all the page tables at once. Instead, you just change the **ASID** value, and the kseg2 pointer to the page table is now automatically remapped onto the correct page table. It's nearly magic.

---

1. On an R4000-type 64-bit CPU each 8KB of address space takes 16 bytes of table space, needing a 4MB table for a 2GB "compatibility mode" task and much more for an application that is taking advantage of R4000's potential 0.5TB user space.

Of course, it also seems to lead to a fatal vicious circle, where a TLB refill (to load the kseg2 mapping for the page table) is required to process a TLB refill. We can solve that problem too:

- The superfast TLB refill routine is not used for all refill exceptions; a nested TLB miss on the page table address is dispatched to the general exception entry point.

- A limited mechanism is provided that allows us to handle a nested exception (the kernel TLB miss) from within the user TLB miss exception handler. We'll discuss it under the individual examples, because the R4x00 and subsequent 64-bit CPUs use a trick different from the R2000 and 32-bit CPUs.

The MIPS architecture supports this kind of linear page table in the form of the **Context** register (or **XContext** for extended addressing in 64-bit CPUs).

If you make your page table start at a 1MB boundary (since it is in virtual memory any gap created won't use up physical memory space) and set up the **Context** PTEBase field with the high-order bits of the page table starting the address, then following a user refill exception the **Context** register will contain the address of the entry you need for the refill with no further calculation needed.

6.7.1   *The 32-Bit R3000-Style User TLB Miss Exception Handler*

The 32-bit CPUs have one special TLB miss exception entry point that is used for TLB misses resulting from a user-accessible address. TLB misses caused by privileged-access addresses (in the top half of the memory map) are sent through the standard exception entry point. Here's a typical refill routine for a TLB miss handler for a 32-bit CPU:

```
        .set    noreorder
        .set    noat
TLBmissR3K:
        mfc0    k1,C0_CONTEXT    # (1)
        mfc0    k0,C0_EPC        # (2)
        lw      k1,0(k1)         # (3)
        nop                      # (4)
        mtc0    k1,C0_ENTRYLO    # (5)
        nop                      # (6)
        tlbwr                    # (7)
        jr      k0               # (8)
        rfe                      # (9)
        .set    at
        .set    reorder
```

The UTLB miss exception is a very low level piece of code, so the `.set noreorder` tells the assembler that we're taking responsibility for making sure this code sequence runs OK on the CPU's pipeline, and we don't want the assembler worrying about it. The `.set noat` tells the assembler that it is not allowed to use the **at** register to synthesize instructions—this is essential, because we've arrived from an arbitrary exception and **at** has unsaved user state in it.

k0 and **k1** are by convention ours to play with, so we can use them without worrying about what previous value we're overwriting.

Following is a line-by-line analysis of this code:

(1) The **Context** register is a pointer to the page table. The **mfc0** instruction does not take immediate effect in the MIPS five-stage pipeline, so we won't be able to use the pointer value until line (3).

(2) We need to get the return address sometime; do it now in the load delay slot. This is also required in case the load from the page table entry itself suffers a TLB miss exception.

(3) At this point the address of the page table entry may itself not have a valid translation entry in the TLB, in which case we'll take another exception here. We'll deal with that case below.

(4) The load takes two clock cycles, so we need to wait before we can use the value from the page table.

(5) Store the new value in **EntryLo**. **EntryHi(VPN)** was set up automatically by the hardware for the TLB miss exception to refer to the missing translation. **EntryHi** still contains the **EntryHi(ASID)** value we stored there, presumably the last time the OS did a process context switch.

(6) Wait while the new value reaches **EntryLo**.

(7) Write it to wherever in the TLB the **Random** register happens to be pointing, discarding... who knows what. Never mind, that's the fun of random replacement.

(8) We go back to the user program, but in every branch the delay slot instruction is executed before we get there....

(9) The **rfe** instruction restores the CPU state held in **SR** back to how it was before the exception.

So we've taken nine instructions and are off back to the program that suffered the translation miss. In practice, the biggest overhead is likely to be felt when the load from the page table misses in the data cache.[1]

But we promised to tell you what happens if you are unlucky and the page table entry address does not have a translation entry.

One thing isn't a problem: Double translation faults like this are not very common, so we don't have to worry too much about efficiency. It's OK to implement the TLB miss on the page table (in the privileged address space) with a heavyweight general-purpose exception handler.

MIPS exceptions really only do three things:

- Then modify **SR** to disable interrupts and put the CPU in kernel mode.
- Then store the restart location in **EPC**.
- Then vector to the exception handler.

In order to survive a second exception and still get back to the original program correctly, we need to avoid losing the original return address and to be able to restore **SR** to its pre-exception value.

There's no hardware support for saving the return address, but as you can see above, the exception handler has already saved it in **k0**; we just need to make sure that the general-purpose exception handler treats **k0** like most other registers and preserves its value.[2]

The status register is more complicated, but here the hardware does help. The 2 bits that do the work are the interrupt enable bit **SR(IEc)** and the kernel-mode flag **SR(KUc)**. The status register is in fact provided with a three-entry stack for this pair of bits, which is pushed on exceptions and popped by the end-of-exception **rfe** instruction, as shown in Figure 6.8.

Because the **SR(KUx,IEx)** forms a three-deep stack, even after the second exception the user program values are still safe in **SR(KUo,IEo)** and ready to be popped back into place.

6.7.2   *TLB Miss Exception Handler for R4x00 CPU*

The R4000 and subsequent CPUs use a TLB with pairs of entries and handle the double-exception condition differently, leading to this different handler code.

Also, the R4000 has two special entry points. The handler at the same location as the R3000's is used to handle translations for processes using only 32 bits of address space; an additional entry point is provided and invoked

---

1. That highlights an unexpected virtue of the MIPS do-it-in-software approach: By using software and not microcode to refill the TLB, the TLB refill job gets the benefit of working through the CPU's cache hierarchy and not always having to go out to memory.

2. This is why the register conventions reserve *two* general-purpose registers for the use of exception handlers.

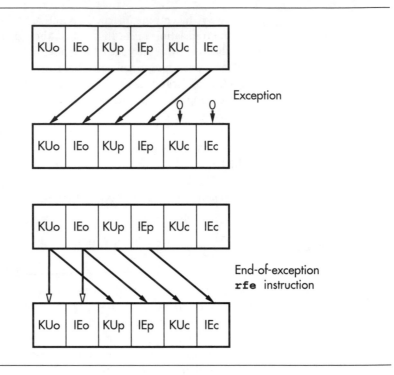

FIGURE 6.8 Status register fields in exceptions (32-bit MIPS)

for programs marked as using the bigger address spaces available with 64-bit pointers.

The R4000 status register has three fields, **SR(UX)**, **SR(SX)**, and **SR(KX)**, that select which exception handler to use, based on the CPU privilege level at the time of the failed translation.[1]

The R4000 has a different criteria for deciding when a TLB miss can use the special entry point and when it should be sent to the general exception handler. The R4000 always uses the special entry point unless it's already handling an exception—that is, unless **SR(EXL)** is set. This deals with the double-exception condition as above; but since misses on kernel addresses normally go through the same TLB handler as user address misses, the R4000's page table must be big enough to span kernel virtual addresses too (but with yet more big holes).

Here is the code for a TLB miss handler for an R4000-type CPU with a 32-bit address space:

---

1. **SR(UX)** is something of a 64-bit mode bit for user programs; when it's zero, 64-bit instructions are not available to a user program. But the other two bits are only used to select the TLB refill routine.

```
        .set    noreorder
        .set    noat
TLBmissR4K:
        dmfc0   k1,C0_CONTEXT    # (1)
        nop                      # (2)
        lw      k0,0(k1)         # (3)
        lw      k1,8(k1)         # (4)
        mtc0    k0,C0_ENTRYLO0   # (5)
        mtc0    k1,C0_ENTRYLO1   # (6)
        nop                      # (7)
        tlbwr                    # (8)
        eret                     # (9)
        .set    at
        .set    reorder
```

Following is a line-by-line analysis of the code:

(1)   Oddly enough, the 64-bit move here is probably unnecessary: If the page table is located in kseg2 as usual, the page table base part of **Context** is guaranteed to be all ones in its high bits, so the **k1** register will end up with the same value if you used a 32-bit-wide **mfc0** instruction.

(2, 7) Some CPUs (typically those with pipelines longer than five stages, such as the R4000) will need an extra **nop** in these positions.

(3–6)   The entries are paired here, but **EntryLo0** and **EntryLo1** are still only 32-bit registers. However, the **Context** register is set up for 16-byte page table entries; **EntryLo0** and **EntryLo1** on these CPUs have no don't-care bits, and software routines need some page table space to keep software-only information.

        No **nop** is required because we interleave the second load so there's always at least one instruction between the load and **mtc0**.

        As before, we may get another exception here if the page table entry's address does not have a valid translation in the TLB. Again, we'll deal with that later.

(7)   The sequence may need an extra **nop** on some CPUs; you need one on the long-pipeline R4000.

(8)   This is random replacement of a translation pair as discussed.

(9)   MIPS III and subsequent CPUs have the **eret** instruction to return from exception and undo the exception-caused changes to **SR**. (For MIPS III CPUs all an exception does to **SR** is to set the **SR(EXL)** bit.)

What happens on one of these later CPUs when you get another TLB miss? As before, the second miss is sent through the general-purpose exception entry point, but this time that happens because **SR(EXL)** is set (we're already handling an exception).

The outcome is quite different too. With **SR(EXL)** set a second exception is allowed to happen, but this doesn't alter the exception return register **EPC**.

In effect, the kernel TLB miss exception causes control to transfer into the general exception handler with the **Cause** register and with all the address registers set up to show a TLB miss on the page table entry address, *but* with **EPC** pointing back at the offending user-space instruction. The kernel page table miss will be fixed up (if it can be) and the general exception handler will return into the user program. Of course, we haven't done anything about the user address that originally caused the user-space TLB miss, so it will immediately miss again. But this time, the required kernel translation will be available and the user miss handler will complete successfully.

6.7.3   *XTLB Miss Handler*

With the appropriate status bit set (usually just **SR(UX)**), a TLB miss is sent to a different vector, where we should have a routine that will reload translations for a huge address space. The handler code (of an XTLB miss handler for a CPU with 64-bit address space) looks identical, except for the use of the **XContext** register in place of **Context**:

```
        .set    noreorder
        .set    noat
TLBmissR4K:
        dmfc0   k1,C0_XCONTEXT
        nop
        lw      k0,0(k1)
        lw      k1,8(k1)
        mtc0    k0,C0_ENTRYLO0
        mtc0    k1,C0_ENTRYLO1
        nop
        tlbwr
        eret
        .set    at
        .set    reorder
```

Note, though, that the resulting page table structure in kernel virtual memory is far bigger and we'll need to make significant changes in the kernel memory map and translation code to accommodate it.

6.8   Keeping Track of Modified Pages (Simulating "Dirty" Bits)

An operating system that provides a page for an application program to use often wants to keep track of whether that page has been modified since the OS last obtained it (perhaps from disc or network) or saved a copy of it. Nonmodified ("clean") pages may be quietly discarded, since they can easily be recovered from a file system if they're ever needed again.

In OS parlance the modified pages are called "dirty" and the OS must take care of them until the application program exits or the dirty page is cleaned by being saved away to backing store. To help out with this process it is common for CISC CPUs to maintain a bit in the memory-resident page table indicating that a write operation to the page has occurred. The MIPS CPU does not support this feature, even in the TLB entries. The D bit of the page table (found in the **EntryLo** register) is a write-enable and is of course used to flag read-only pages.

So here's the trick:

- When a writable page is first loaded into memory you mark its page table entry with D clear (leaving it read-only).

- When any write is attempted to the page a trap will result; system software will recognize this as a legitimate write but will use the event to set a modified bit in the memory resident tables—which, since it's in the **EntryLo(D)** position, permits future writes to be done without an exception.

- You will also want to set the D bit in the TLB entry so that the write can proceed, but since TLB entries are randomly and unpredictably replaced this would be useless as a way of remembering the modified state.

6.9   Memory Translation and 64-Bit Pointers

When the MIPS architecture was invented, 32-bit CPUs had been around for a while and the largest programs' data sets were already moving up toward 100MB—the address space had only 4 bits or so to spare.[1] There was therefore every reason to be reasonably careful with the 32-bit space and not to reduce it by profligate fragmentation; this is why application programs (running with user privilege) keep 31 bits' worth of addressing for themselves.

When the MIPS III instruction set introduced 64-bit registers in 1991 it was leading the industry, and as we discussed in Section 2.7 MIPS was probably 4–6 years ahead of real pressure on a 32-bit address boundary. The doubling of

---

1. Historically, application program demand for memory space seems to have grown at about $\frac{3}{4}$ bit per year, and this rate appears to be currently sustained.

register size only had to yield a few bits of extra address space to be remarkably future-proof; it's been more important to be cautious about the potentially exploding size of OS data structures than to make efficient use of all address space.

The limitations to the practical address space resulting from the basic 64-bit memory map are not going to be reached for a while; they permit the mapped user and other spaces to grow to 61 bits without any reorganization. However, the **XContext(VPN2)** field is "only" 27 bits, limiting the mappable user virtual address to 40 bits. So how do we go about implementing a 40-bit user space?

A page table compatible with the layout of **XContext** has 2^{29} entries (one for each value of **R/VPN2**, each 16 bytes long). That's 8GB of space, which is larger than the whole of kseg0, kseg1, and kseg2 combined. Fortunately, the R4x00 CPU and its successors have another 2^{40}-byte, kernel-privilege, mapped region starting at 0xC000.0000.0000.0000 that can be used. Most of this page table is likely to be empty, since the 40-bit user program address space (for which **R** == 0) has an immense gap between stack and data segments, and there'll be even less in the privileged areas. The part of the page table corresponding to the gap will never be accessed and need not be mapped to physical memory at all. Clearly it's going to be useful to have some relatively compact data structure to map the kernel-privilege addresses, but that's straying into the design of operating systems and is beyond the scope of this book.

6.10   Everyday Use of the MIPS TLB

If you're using a big OS, then it will use the TLB and you'll hardly see it. If not, you may wonder whether it's useful. Because the MIPS TLB provides a rather general address translation service, there are a number of ways you might take advantage of it.

The TLB mechanism permits you to translate addresses (at page granularity) from any mapped address to any physical address and therefore to relocate regions of program space to any location in your machine's address map. There's no need to support a TLB refill exception or a separate memory-held page table if your mapping requirements are modest enough that you can accommodate all the translations you need in the TLB.

The TLB also allows you to define some address as temporarily or permanently unavailable, so that accesses to those locations will cause an exception that can be used to run some operating system service routine. By using user-privilege programs you can give some software access only to those addresses you want it to have, and by using address space IDs in the translation entries you can efficiently manage multiple mutually inaccessible user programs. You can write-protect some parts of memory.

The applications for this are endless, but here's a list to indicate the range:

- *Accessing inconvenient physical address ranges*: Hardware registers for a MIPS system are most conveniently located in the physical address range 0–512MB, where you can access them with a corresponding pointer from the kseg1 region. But where the hardware can't stay within this desirable area, you can map an arbitrary page of higher physical memory into a convenient mapped area such as kseg2. The TLB flags for this translation should be set to ensure uncached access, but then the program can be written exactly as though the address was in the convenient place.

- *Memory resources for an exception routine*: Suppose you'd like to run an exception handler without using the reserved **k0/k1** registers to save context. If so, you'd have trouble because a MIPS CPU normally has nowhere to save any registers without overwriting at least one of these.

   You can do loads or stores using the **zero** register as a base address, but with a positive offset these addresses are located in the first 32KB of kuseg, and with a negative offset they are located in the last 32KB of kseg2. Without the TLB, these go nowhere. With the TLB, you could map one or more pages in this region into read/write memory and then use zero-based stores to save context and rescue your exception handler.

- *Extendable stacks and heaps in a non-VM system*: Even when you don't have a disk and have no intention of supporting full demand paging, it can still be useful to grow an application's stack and heap on demand while monitoring its growth. In this case you'll need the TLB to map the stack/heap addresses, and you'll use TLB miss events to decide whether to allocate more memory or whether the application is out of control.

- *Emulating hardware*: If you have hardware that is sometimes present and sometimes not, then accessing registers through a mapped region can connect directly to the hardware in properly equipped systems and invoke a software handler on others.

The main idea is that the TLB, with all the ingenuity of a specification that fits so well into a big OS, is a useful, straightforward general resource for programmers.

6.11   Memory Management in a Non-unix OS

OSs designed for use off the desktop are generally called real-time OSs (RTOSs), hijacking a term that once meant something about real time. The unix-style system outlined in the first part of this chapter has all the elements you're likely to find in a smaller OS, but many RTOSs are much simpler.

This field is new enough that there are no real standards. The likely pioneer in this area is Microsoft's Windows/CE, and internal descriptions of that OS may not yet be freely available. So we'll limit ourselves to a few general points.

Off-desktop systems are likely to be providing a single fairly tightly integrated function; without the need to support a diverse range of programs, including third-party and customer-written software, process protection is much less of an issue. We expect smaller OSs to be more permissive, since the applications writers have more influence. It's not clear that this is actually a good thing, but older RTOSs had no protection at all.

Demand paging makes a lot of sense as a way of loading a program, since you don't have to do the work of loading parts of the program that aren't used. Systems without a disk probably won't page out dirty data; however, demand paging remains useful without it.

When you're trying to understand a new memory management system, the first thing is to figure out the memory maps, both the virtual map presented to application software and the physical map of the system. It's the simple-minded virtual address map that makes unix memory management relatively straightforward to describe. But operating systems targeted at embedded applications do not usually have their roots in hardware with memory management, and the process memory map often has the fossils of unmapped memory maps hidden inside it. The use of a pencil, paper, and patience will sort it out.

7 Floating-Point Support

You are increasingly unlikely to meet a MIPS floating-point coprocessor—always known as floating-point accelerator, or FPA—in the flesh. In newer MIPS CPUs the FPA is either part of the CPU or isn't there at all.

In 1987 the MIPS FPA set a new benchmark for performance for microprocessor math performance in affordable workstations. Unlike the CPU, which was mostly a rather straightforward implementation relying on its basic architecture for its performance, the FPA was a heroic silicon design bristling with innovation and ingenuity. Of course, now everyone has learned how to do it!

Since then the MIPS FPA has been pulled onward by Silicon Graphics's need for math performance that would once have been the preserve of supercomputers. I expect to see a lot more embedded applications that need very high floating-point performance in the next few years, so even the most abstruse and high-end features may move rapidly down the MIPS family.

7.1   A Basic Description of Floating Point

Floating-point math retains a great deal of mystery. You probably have a very clear idea of what it is for, but you may be hazy about the details. This section describes the various components of the data and what they mean. In so doing we are bound to tell most of you things you already know; please skip ahead but keep an eye on the text!

People who deal with numbers that may be very large or very small are used to using exponential (scientific) notation; for example, the distance from the earth to the sun is

$$93 \times 10^6 \text{ miles}$$

The number is defined by 93, the *mantissa*, and 6, the *exponent*.

The same distance can be written

$$9.3 \times 10^7 \text{ miles}$$

Numerical analysts like to use the second form; a decimal exponent with a mantissa between 1.0 and 9.999... is called *normalized*.[1] The normalized form is useful for computer representation, since we don't have to keep separate information about the position of the decimal point.

Computer-held floating-point numbers are an exponential form, but in base 2 instead of base 10. Both mantissa and exponent are held as binary fields. Just changing the exponent into a power of two, the distance quoted above is

$$1.38580799102783203125 \times 2^{26} \text{ miles}$$

The mantissa can be expressed as a binary "decimal," which is just like a real decimal; for example,

$$1.38580799102783203125 = 1 + 3 \times \frac{1}{10} + 8 \times \frac{1}{100} + 5 \times \frac{1}{1000} + \cdots$$

is the same value as binary

$$1.01100010110001000101 = 1 + 0 \times \frac{1}{2} + 1 \times \frac{1}{4} + 1 \times \frac{1}{8} + \cdots$$

However, neither the mantissa nor the exponent are stored just like this in standard formats—and to understand why, we need to review a little history.

7.2   The IEEE754 Standard and Its Background

Because floating point deals with the approximate representations of numbers (in the same way as decimals do), computer implementations used to differ in the details of their behavior with regard to very small or large numbers. This meant that numerical routines, identically coded, might behave differently. In some sense these differences shouldn't have mattered: You only got different answers in circumstances where no implementation could really produce a "correct" answer.

The use of calculators shows the irritating consequences of this: If you take the square root of a whole number and square it, you will rarely get back the whole number you put in, but rather something with lots of nines.

Numerical routines are intrinsically hard to write and hard to prove correct. Many heavily used functions (common trigonometric operations, for example) are calculated by repeated approximation. Such a routine might reliably converge to the correct result on one CPU and loop forever on another when fed a difficult value.

---

1. In this form the mantissa may also be called "the fractional part" or "fraction"—it's certainly easier to remember.

The ANSI/IEEE Std 754—1985 IEEE Standard for Binary Floating-Point Arithmetic (usually referred to simply as the IEEE 754 standard) was introduced to bring order to this situation. The standard defines exactly what result will be produced by a small class of basic operations, even under extreme situations, ensuring that programmers can obtain identical results from identical inputs regardless of what machine they are using. Its approach is to require as much precision as is possible within each supported data format.

Perhaps IEEE754 has too many options, but it is a huge improvement on the chaos that motivated it; since it became a real international standard in 1985, it has become the basis for all new implementations.

The operations regulated by IEEE754 include every operation that MIPS FPAs can do in hardware, plus some that must be emulated by software. IEEE754 legislates the following:

■ *Rounding and precision of results*: Even results of the simplest operations may not be representable as finite fractions; for example, in decimals

$$\frac{1}{3} = 0.33333\ldots$$

is infinitely recurring and can't be written precisely. IEEE754 allows the user to choose between four options: round up, round down, round toward zero, or round to nearest. The rounded result is what would have been achieved by computing with infinite precision and then rounding. This would leave an ambiguity in round to nearest when the infinite-precision result is exactly halfway between two representable forms; the rules provide that in this case you should round toward zero.

■ *When is a result exceptional?* IEEE754 has its own meaning for the word "exception." A computation can produce a result that is

  – Nonsense, such as the square root of -1 ("invalid")

  – "Infinite," resulting from an explicit or implicit division by zero

  – Too big to represent ("overflow")

  – So small that its representation becomes problematic and precision is lost ("underflow")

  – Not perfectly represented, like 1/3 ("inexact")—needless to say, for most purposes the nearest approximation is acceptable

All of these are bundled together and described as exceptional results.

■ *Action taken when an operation produces an exception result*: For each class of exceptional result listed above the user can choose between the following:

  – The user can have the computation interrupted and the user program signalled in some OS- and language-dependent manner. Partly because the standard doesn't actually define a language binding for user exceptions, they're pretty much never used. Some Fortran compiler systems are wired to cause a fatal error invalid or infinite results.

– Most often, the user program doesn't want to know about the IEEE exception. In this case, the standard specifies what value should then be produced. Overflows and division by zero generate infinity (with a positive and negative type); invalid operations generate NaN (not a number) in two flavors called "quiet" and "signalling." Very small numbers get a "denormalized" representation that loses precision and fades gradually into zero.

The standard also defines the result when operations are carried out on exceptional values. Infinities and NaNs necessarily produce further NaNs and infinities, but while a quiet NaN as operand will not trigger the exception-reporting mechanism, a signalling NaN causes a new exception whenever it is used.

Most programs leave the IEEE exception reporting off but do rely on the system producing the correct exceptional values.

7.3 How IEEE Floating-Point Numbers Are Stored

IEEE recommends a number of different binary formats for encoding floating-point numbers, at several different sizes. But all of them have some common ingenious features, which are built on the experience of implementors in the early chaotic years.[1]

The first thing is that the exponent is not stored as a signed binary number, but *biased* so that the exponent field is always positive: The exponent value 1 represents the tiniest (most negative) legitimate exponent value; for the 64-bit IEEE format the exponent field is 11 bits long and can hold numbers from 0 to 2047. The values 0 and 2047 (all ones, in binary) are kept back for special purposes we'll come to in a moment, so we can represent a range of exponents from -1022 to $+1023$.

For a number

$$\text{mantissa} \times 2^{\text{exponent}}$$

we actually store the binary representation of

$$\text{exponent} + 1023$$

in the exponent field.

---

1. IEEE754 is a model of how good standardization should be done; a fair period of chaotic experimentation allowed identifiably good practice to evolve, and it was then standardized by a small committee of strong-minded users (numerical programmers in this case), who well understood the technology. However, the ecology of standards committees, while a fascinating study, is a bit off the point.

The biased exponent (together with careful ordering of the fields) has the useful effect of ensuring that FP comparisons (equality, greater than, less than, etc.) have the same result as is obtained from comparing two signed integers composed of the same bits. FP compare operations can therefore be provided by cheap, fast, and familiar logic.

7.3.1   *IEEE Mantissa and Normalization*

The IEEE format uses a single sign bit separate from the mantissa (0 for positive, 1 for negative). So the stored mantissa only has to represent positive numbers. All properly represented numbers in IEEE format are normalized, so

$$1 \leq \text{mantissa} < 2$$

This means that the most significant bit of the mantissa (the single binary digit before the point) is always a 1, so we don't actually need to store it. The IEEE standard calls this the *hidden bit*.

So now the number 93,000,000, whose normalized representation has a binary mantissa of 1.01100010110001000101 and a binary exponent of 26, is represented in IEEE 64-bit format by setting the fields

$$\text{mantissafield} = 0110001011000100010101000\ldots$$
$$\text{exponentfield} = 1049 = 10000011001$$

Looking at it the other way, a 64-bit IEEE number with an exponent field of E and a mantissa field of m represents the number *num* where

$$num = 1.m \times 2^{E-1023}$$

(provided that you accept that 1.*m* represents the binary fraction with 1 before the point and the mantissa field contents after it).

7.3.2   *Reserved Exponent Values for Use with Strange Values*

The smallest and biggest exponent field values are used to represent otherwise-illegal quantities.

$E == 0$ is used to represent zero (with a zero mantissa) and denormalized forms, for numbers too small to represent in the standard form. The denormalized number with E zero and mantissa m represents *num* where

$$num = 0.m \times 2^{-1022}$$

As denormalized numbers get smaller, precision is progressively lost. No R3000-series MIPS FPA is able to cope with either generating denormalized numbers or computing with them, and operations creating or involving them will be punted to the software exception handler. The R4000 and its successors can be configured to replace denormalized results by zero and keep going.

Single

| | 31 | 30   23 | 22   0 |
	Sign	Exponent	Mantissa
93000000	0	0001 1010	101 1000 1011 0001 0001
0	0	0000 0000	000 0000 0000 0000 0000
+Infinity	0	1111 1111	000 0000 0000 0000 0000
−Infinity	1	1111 1111	000 0000 0000 0000 0000
Quiet NaN	x	1111 1111	0xx xxxx xxxx xxxx xxxx
Signalling NaN	x	1111 1111	1xx xxxx xxxx xxxx xxxx

High-order word   Low-order word

Double

| | 31 | 30   20 | 19   0\|31 | 0 |
	Sign	Exponent	Mantissa	
93000000	0	000 0001 1010	1011 0001 0110 0010 0010 1000 0000	
0	0	000 0000 0000	0000 0000 0000 0000 0000 0000	
+Infinity	0	111 1111 1111	0000 0000 0000 0000 0000 0000	
−Infinity	1	111 1111 1111	0000 0000 0000 0000 0000 0000	
Quiet NaN	x	111 1111 1111	0xxx xxxx xxxx xxxx xxxx xxxx	
Signalling NaN	x	111 1111 1111	1xxx xxxx xxxx xxxx xxxx	

FIGURE 7.1 Floating-point data formats

$E == 111\ldots 1$ (i.e., the binary representation of 2047 in the 11-bit field used for an IEEE double) is used to represent the following:

- With the mantissa zero, it is the illegal values +inf, −inf (distinguished by the usual sign bit).

- With the mantissa nonzero, it is a NaN. For MIPS, the most significant bit of the mantissa determines whether the NaN is quiet (MS bit 0) or signalling (MS bit 1).

7.3.3 *MIPS FP Data Formats*

The MIPS architecture uses two FP formats recommended by IEEE754:

- *Single precision*: These are fitted into 32 bits of storage. Compilers for MIPS use single precision for `float` variables.

- *Double precision*: These use 64 bits of storage. C compilers use double precision for C `double` types.

The memory and register layout is shown in Figure 7.1, with some examples of how the data works out. Note that the `float` representation can't hold a number as big as 93,000,000 exactly.

The way that the two words making up a double are ordered in memory (most-significant bits first, or least-significant bits first) is a configuration option on a MIPS CPU. It needs to be done consistently with the choice of how integers are stored in memory, a matter that is also configurable. This endianness is discussed to the point of exhaustion in Section 11.6.

The C structure definition following defines the fields of the two FP types for a MIPS CPU (this works on most MIPS CPUs, but note that, in general, C structure layout is dependent on a particular compiler and not just on the target CPU):

```
#if BYTE_ORDER == BIG_ENDIAN

struct ieee754dp_konst {
    unsigned sign:1;
    unsigned bcxp:11;
    unsigned manthi:20;  /* cannot get 52 bits into   */
    unsigned mantlo:32;  /*     a regular C bitfield   */
};

struct ieee754sp_konst {
    unsigned sign:1;
    unsigned bexp:8;
    unsigned mant:23;
};

#else /* little-endian */

struct ieee754dp_konst {
    unsigned mantlo:32;
    unsigned manthi:20;
    unsigned bexp:11;
    unsigned sign:1;
};

struct ieee754sp_konst {
    unsigned mant:23;
    unsigned bexp:8;
    unsigned sign:1;
};

#endif
```

7.4   MIPS Implementation of IEEE754

IEEE754 is quite demanding and sets two major problems. Firstly, building in the ability to detect exceptional results makes pipelining harder. You might want to do this to implement the IEEE exception signalling mechanism, but the deeper reason is to be able to detect certain cases where the hardware cannot produce the correct result and needs help.

If the user opts to be told when an IEEE exceptional result is produced, then to be useful this should happen synchronously;[1] after the trap, the user will want to see all previous instructions complete and all FP registers still in the pre-instruction state and will want to be sure that no subsequent instruction has had any effect.

In the MIPS architecture hardware traps (as noted in Section 5.1 above) were traditionally like this. This does limit the opportunities for pipelining FP operations, because you cannot commit the following instruction until the hardware can be sure that the FP operation will not produce a trap. To avoid adding to the execution time, an FP operation must decide to trap or not in the first clock phase after the operands are fetched. For most kinds of exceptional result, the FPA can guess reliably and stop the pipeline for any calculation that might trap;[2] however, if you configure the FPA to signal IEEE inexact exceptional results, all FP pipelining is inhibited and everything slows down. You probably won't do that.

The MIPS IV instruction set version introduces (as an implementation option) a mode switch that relaxes the synchronous trap requirement. The resulting computational model may not be truly IEEE754 compliant but may go faster.

The second big problem regarding IEEE754 is the use of exceptional results, particularly with denormalized numbers—which are legitimate operands. Chip designs like the MIPS FPA are highly structured pieces of logic, and the exceptional results don't fit in well. Where correct operation is beyond the hardware, it traps with an unimplemented operation code in the **Cause(ExcCode)** field. This immediately make an exception handler compulsory for FP applications.

---

1. Elsewhere in this manual and in the MIPS documentation you will see exactly this condition referred to as a "precise exception." But since both "precise" and "exception" are used to mean different things by the IEEE standard, we will instead talk about a "synchronous trap." (Sorry for any confusion.)

2. Some CPUs may use heuristics for this that sometimes stop the pipeline for an operation that in the end does not trap; that's only a performance issue and is not important if they don't do it often.

7.4.1   *Need for FP Trap Handler and Emulator in All MIPS CPUs*

The MIPS architecture does not prescribe exactly what calculations will be performed without software intervention. A complete software floating-point emulator is mandatory for serious FP code.

In practice, the FPA traps only on a very small proportion of the calculations that your program is likely to produce. Simple uses of floating point are quite likely never to produce anything that the hardware can't handle.

A good rule of thumb, which seems to cover the right cases, follows:

- MIPS FPAs take the unimplemented trap whenever an operation should produce *any* IEEE exception or exceptional result other than inexact and overflow. For overflow, the hardware will generate an infinity or a largest-possible value (depending on the current rounding mode). The FPA hardware will not accept or produce denormalized numbers or NaNs.

- MIPS FPAs from the R4000 onward (i.e., those using instruction set MIPS III and after) offer you a non-IEEE optional mode for underflow, where a denormalized (tiny) result can be automatically written as zero.

The unimplemented trap is a MIPS architecture implementation trick and is quite different from the IEEE exceptions, which are standardized conditions. You can run a program and ignore IEEE exceptions, and offending instructions will produce well-defined exceptional values; but you can't ignore the unimplemented trap without producing results that are nonsense.

7.5   Floating-Point Registers

MIPS CPUs have 32 floating-point registers, usually referred to as **$f0–$f31**. However, even 32-bit MIPS CPUs support the 64-bit IEEE double-precision format, hence 32-bit CPUs only do arithmetic in the 16 even-numbered registers **$f0–$f30**. In those early CPUs the 16 odd-numbered registers are used to take care of the high-order bits of a 64-bit double value stored in the preceding even-numbered register.[1] The odd-numbered registers can be accessed by move and load/store instructions; however, the assembler provides synthetic macro instructions for move and load/store double, so you will probably never see the odd-numbered registers when writing 32-bit-compatible code.

The 64-bit CPUs (MIPS III and above) give you the option of either emulating the MIPS I register organization or of exposing 32 genuine full 64-bit registers. Bear in mind that this is not a free personal choice; you need to check

---

1. It may be worth stressing that the role of the odd-numbered registers is not affected by the CPU's endianness.

TABLE 7.1 FP register usage conventions (16 FP registers)

Register numbers	Name	Use
$f0,$f2	fv0–fv1	Value returned by function. **fv1** is used only for "complex" data type; it is not available in C.
$f4,$f6, $f8,$f10	ft0–ft3	Temporaries—subroutines can use without saving.
$f12,$f14	fa0–fa1	Function arguments.
$f16,$f18	ft4–ft5	Temporaries.
$f20,$f22, $f24,$f26, $f28,$f30	fs0–fs5	Register variables: A function that will write one of these must save the old value and restore it before it exits. The calling routine can rely on the value being preserved.

what your compiler will support, and the entire system (including all libraries and other imported code) needs to be consistent in its register usage.

It's worth pointing out that MIPS FP registers sometimes get used for storing and manipulating signed integer data (32 or 64 bits); all integer/FP conversion operations operate entirely within the FPA and don't touch the general-purpose registers.

7.5.1 Conventional Names and Uses of Floating-Point Registers

Like the general-purpose registers, the MIPS calling conventions add a whole bunch of rules about register use that have nothing to do with the hardware; they tell you which FP registers are used for passing arguments, which register values are expected to be preserved over function calls, and so on. Table 7.1 shows these for a program compiled to run on MIPS I CPUs or later CPUs with the compatibility bit set. For that reason, there are no odd-numbered registers in the table. Standards for using all 32 registers were first defined with SGI's n32/n64 compiler options and are described in Section 10.8.

The division of functions is much the same as for the integer registers, without the special cases.

7.6 Floating-Point Exceptions/Interrupts

Floating-point exceptions (for reporting IEEE exceptional results, where they're enabled, or for the unimplemented operation trap) are reported by a MIPS exception, as described in Chapter 5. In MIPS I CPUs, where early implementations had the FPA as a separate chip, the floating-point exception is signalled

31	25	24	23	22	18	17	16	12	11	7	6	2	1	0
FCC7-1		FS	C	0		Unlmp	Cause		Enable		Flag		RM	

FIGURE 7.2 FPA control/status register fields

using one of the CPU's interrupt lines. The choice of which interrupt input to use was a board layout decision, though most programmers followed MIPS Corporation's systems and used *Int3**.

In later MIPS I CPUs with on-chip floating-point units (such as IDT's R3081), the interrupt bit was either chosen arbitrarily by the hardware manufacturer or configured through a programmable register. The second was preferred, because despite MIPS Corporation's lead and the fact that the choice of interrupt was wholly arbitrary, DEC systems seem to mostly use the seventh interrupt bit (corresponding to hardware input *Int5**).

One drawback of using the general interrupt mechanism is that the interrupt signal can be masked. Failure to accept an FPA emulation request interrupt will leave the destination register of the unemulated operation containing whatever was in it before, which is incorrect and erratic behavior. You can't even escape the consequences of this by leaving all IEEE signalling disabled: The hardware will still attempt to trap on some operation/operand combinations that fall outside its limits.

So long as the appropriate interrupt is not disabled, a floating-point exception will happen (on a MIPS I CPU) immediately: No FP or integer operation following the FP instruction that caused the exception will have had any effect. At this point **EPC** will point to the correct place to restart the instruction. As described in Chapter 5 above, **EPC** will either point to the offending instruction or to a branch instruction immediately preceding it. If it is the branch instruction, the BD bit will be set in the CPU status register **SR**.

In MIPS III CPUs, the FPA gets a dedicated exception cause and there's much less trouble.

7.7   Floating-Point Control: The Control/Status Register

The floating-point control/status register (Figure 7.2) is coprocessor 1, control register 31 (mnemonic **FCR31**) and is accessed by **mtc1**, **mfc1** instructions. In accordance with MIPS coprocessor rules, those transfer data between **FCR31** and general-purpose registers.

The following are notes regarding Figure 7.2. The field marked 0 will read, and should be written, as zero.

TABLE 7.2 Rounding modes encoded in FP control/status register

RM value	Description
0	RN (round to nearest): Round a result to the nearest representable value; if the result is exactly halfway between two representable values, round to zero.
1	RZ (round toward zero): Round a result to the closest representable value whose absolute value is less than or equal to the infinitely accurate result.
2	RP (round up, or toward +infinity): Round a result to the next representable value up.
3	RN (round down, or toward −infinity): Round a result to the next representable value down.

- *FCC7-1, C*: These are condition bits, set by FP compare instructions and tested by conditional branches. The 7 additional bits called FCC7-1 are a 1995 invention, present only in ISA version MIPS IV and higher.

  Note that here, as elsewhere, the floating-point implementation cuts across the RISC principles we talked about in Chapter 1. There are a number of reasons for this:

  - The original FPA was a separate chip. The conditional branches that tested FP conditions had to execute inside the integer unit (it was responsible for finding the address of the branch target), so they were remote from the FP registers. A single condition bit corresponds to a single hardware signal.

  - FP operations are just too computationally demanding to be carried out in one clock cycle, so a pure and simple pipeline didn't deliver the best performance.

  MIPS IV branch or set instructions have an additional 3-bit field that specifies which of 8 possible condition bits they will set or test. That field was reserved in previous ISA versions, and all good assemblers made sure it was zero—so this should still be backward compatible.

- *FS (flush to zero)*: This causes a result that is too small for the standard representation (a denormalized result) to be quietly replaced with zero. This is not IEEE compatible, but it makes it much more plausible that you can run code without depending on an FP trap handler and emulator.

- *RM (rounding mode)*: This is required by IEEE754. The values are as shown in Table 7.2.

  Most systems define RN as the default behavior. You'll probably never use anything else.

- *UnImp*: Following an FPA trap, this bit will be set to mark an unimplemented instruction exception.[1]

  This bit will be set and an interrupt raised whenever there really is no instruction like this that the FPA will perform (but the instruction is a coprocessor 1 encoding) *or* the FPA is not confident that it can produce an IEEE754-correct result and/or exception signalling on this operation, using these operands.

  For whatever reason, when UnImp is set you should arrange for the offending instruction to be re-executed by a software emulator.

  If you run FP operations without the interrupt enabled, then any FPA operation that wants to take an exception will leave the destination register unaffected and the FP Cause bits undefined.

- *Causes/Enables/Flags*: Each of these is a 5-bit field, one bit for each IEEE exception type:

  Bit 4   Invalid operation

  Bit 3   Division by zero

  Bit 2   Overflow

  Bit 1   Underflow

  Bit 0   Inexact

  The three different fields work as follows:

  - *Cause*: Bits are set (by hardware or emulation software) according to the result of the last completed FP instruction.
  - *Flag*: Bits are "sticky" versions of the **FCR31(Cause)** bits and are the logical "or" of the exceptional results that have occurred since the register was last cleared. The Flag bits can only be zeroed again by writing **FCR31**.
  - *Enable*: If one of these bits is set when an operation produces an exceptional result that would have set the corresponding **FCR31 (Cause)** bit, then the CPU will trap so that software can do whatever is necessary to report the exceptional result.

The architecture promises you that if an operation doesn't set the **FCR31 (UnImp)** bit but does set one of the **FCR31(Cause)** bits, then both the Cause bit setting and the result produced (if the corresponding **FCR31(Enable)** bit is off) are in accordance with the IEEE754 standard.

MIPS FPAs rely on software emulation (i.e., use the unimplemented trap) for several purposes:

- Any operation that is given a denormalized operand or underflows (produces a denormalized result) will trap to the emulator. The emulator

---

1. The MIPS documentation looks slightly different because it treats this as part of the Cause field.

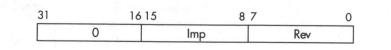

31		16	15		8	7		0
	0			Imp			Rev	

FIGURE 7.3 FPA implementation/revision register

itself must test whether the enable underflow bit is set and either cause an IEEE-compliant exception or produce the correct result.

- Operations that should produce the invalid trap are correctly identified, so if the IEEE exception is enabled the emulator need do nothing. But if the IEEE invalid exception is disabled, the software emulator is invoked because the hardware is unable to generate the appropriate result (usually a quiet NaN).

  Exactly the same is done with a signalling NaN operand.

- FP hardware can handle overflow on regular arithmetic (producing either the extreme finite value or a signed infinity, depending on the rounding mode). But the software emulator is needed to implement a convert-to-integer operation that overflows.

The Cause bits are undefined after an unimplemented operation traps to the emulator.

It is normal practice to provide a full emulator (capable of delivering IEEE-compatible arithmetic on a CPU with no FPA fitted) to back up the FPA hardware. If your system provides less than this, it is hard to figure out where it's safe to leave functions out.

7.8 Floating-Point Implementation/Revision Register

This read-only register's fields are shown in Figure 7.3

This register is coprocessor 1, control register 0 (mnemonic **FCR0**) and is accessed by **mtc1** and **mfc1** instructions.

The **FCR0(Imp)** field is probably more useful than the corresponding one for the main CPU. It will return one of the values listed in Table 7.3 (unless your CPU is newer than those discussed in this book), but note that zero means there's no FPA. The entries called "CPU" in Table 7.3 are for integrated CPUs and mostly have the same ID value as the CPU has in its **PRId(Imp)** field—but that's a helpful convention rather than a guarantee.

Reading this register is the recommended way of sensing the presence of an FPA. You have to enable coprocessor 1 instructions before you try it. A skeptical programmer will be ready to get an exception, or garbage returned, and will probe further.

TABLE 7.3 MIPS FP accelerator ID codes from **FCR0**

Hardware type	Imp value
No FPA hardware	0
R2360 (R2000 accelerator board)	1
R2010 (R2000 FPA chip)	2
R3010 (R3000 FPA chip)	3
R6010 (R6000 FPA chip)	4
R4000 CPU	5
LSI LR3xxxx CPU	6
R10000 CPU	9
Vr4200 CPU	10
R8000 chip set	16
R4600	32
Sony R3xxx CPU	33
Toshiba R3xxx CPU	34
R5000 CPU	35
QED RM5230/5260 CPU	40

The Rev field is for use at the whim of implementors; it is probably useful to make this field visible to commissioning or test engineers, and it may have some meaning defined by your component supplier.

7.9   Guide to FP Instructions

This section gives a summary of FP instructions by function. FP instructions are listed in mnemonic order in Table 8.4.

We've divided the instructions up into the following categories:

- *Load/store*: Moving data directly between FP registers and memory.
- *Move between registers*: Data movement between FP and general-purpose registers.
- *Three-operand arithmetic operations*: The regular add, multiply, etc.
- *Multiply-add operations*: Fancy (and distinctly non-RISC) high-performance instructions, introduced with the MIPS IV ISA. (If you think this is complicated, just wait for MIPS V....)

- *Sign changing*: Simple operations, separated out because their dumb implementation means no IEEE exceptions.

- *Conversion operations*: Conversion between single, double, and integer values.

- *Conditional branch and test instructions*: Where the FP unit meets the integer pipeline again.

7.9.1 *Load/Store*

These operations load or store 32 or 64 bits of memory in or out of an FP register.[1] On loads and stores, note the following points:

- The data is unconverted and uninspected, so no exception will occur even if it does not represent a valid FP value.

- These operations can specify the odd-numbered FP registers; on the 32-bit CPUs this is required to load the second half of 64-bit (double-precision) floating-point values. For the 32-bit CPUs, these data movements are the only instructions that ever access odd-numbered registers.

- The load operation has a delay of one clock cycle, and (like loading to an integer register) this is not interlocked before MIPS III. The compiler and/or assembler will usually take care of this for you, but it is invalid for an FP load to be immediately followed by an instruction using the loaded value.

- When writing assembler, the synthetic instructions are preferred; they can be used for all CPUs, and the assembler will use multiple instructions for CPUs that don't implement the machine instruction. You can feed them any addressing mode that the assembler can understand (as described in Section 9.4 below).

- The address for an FP load/store operation must be aligned to the size of the object being loaded—on a 4-byte boundary for single-precision or word values or an 8-byte boundary for double-precision or 64-bit integer type.

Machine instructions (disp is signed 16 bit):

```
lwc1 fd, disp(rs)    fd = *(rs + disp);
swc1 fs, disp(rs)    *(rs + disp) = fd;
```

From MIPS III ISA onward we get 64-bit loads/stores:

---

1. The 64-bit loads appear only from the MIPS III ISA and R4000 CPU forward.

```
ldc1 fd, disp(rs)      fd = (double)*(rs + disp);
sdc1 fd, disp(rs)      *(rs + disp) = (double)fd;
```

From MIPS IV ISA onward we get indexed addressing, with two registers:

```
lwxc1 fd, ri(rs)       fd = *(rs + ri);
swxc1 fs, ri(rs)       *(rs + ri) = fd;
ldxc1 fd, ri(rs)       fd = (double)*(rs + ri);
sdxc1 fd, ri(rs)       *(rs + ri) = (double)fd;
```

But in fact you don't have to remember any of these when you're writing assembler. Instead, "addr" can be any address mode the assembler understands:

```
l.d fd, addr           fd = (double)*addr;
l.s fd, addr           fd = (float)*addr;
s.d fs, addr           (double)*addr = fs;
s.s fs, addr           (float)*addr = fs;
```

The assembler will generate the appropriate instructions, including allowing a choice of valid address modes. Double-precision loads on a 32-bit CPU will assemble to two load instructions.

7.9.2   *Move between Registers*

No data conversion is done here (bit patterns are copied as is) and no exception results from any value. These instructions can specify the odd-numbered FP registers:

Between integer and FP registers:

```
mtc1 rs, fd            fd = rs;  /* 32b uninterpreted */
mfc1 rd, fs            rs = fd;
dmtc1 rs, fd           fd = (long long) rs; /* 64 bits */
dmfc1 rs, fd           rs = (long long) fd;
```

Between FP registers:

```
mov.d fd,fs            fd = fs;
                        /* move 64b between register pairs */
mov.s fd,fs            fd = fs;  /* 32b between registers */
```

Conditional moves (added in MIPS IV)—the .s versions are omitted to save space:

```
movt.d fd,fs,cc        if (fpcondition(cc)) fd = fs;
```

```
movf.d fd,fs,cc          if (!fpcondition(cc)) fd = fs;
movz.d fd,fs,rt          if (rt == 0) fd = fs;
                           /* rt is an integer register */
movn.d fd,fs,rt          if (rt != 0) fd = fs;
```

The FP condition code called `fpcondition(cc)` is a hard-to-avoid forward reference; you'll see more in Section 7.9.7. If you want to know why conditional move instructions are useful, see Section 8.4.3.

7.9.3 *Three-Operand Arithmetic Operations*

Note the following points:

- All arithmetic operations can cause any IEEE exception type and may result in an unimplemented trap if the hardware is not happy with the operands.

- All these instructions come in single-precision (32-bit, C `float`) and double-precision (64-bit, C double) versions; the instructions are distinguished by ".`s`" or ".`d`" on the op-code. We'll only show the double-precision version. Note that you can't mix formats; both source values and the result will all be either single or double. To mix singles and doubles you need to use explicit conversion operations.

    In all ISA versions:

```
add.d fd,fs1,fs2          fd = fs1 + fs2;
div.d fd,fs1,fs2          fd = fs1 / fs2;
mul.d fd,fs1,fs2          fd = fs1 × fs2;
sub.d fd,fs1,fs2          fd = fs1 - fs2;
```

Added in MIPS II:

```
sqrt.d fd,fs              fd = squarerootof(fs);
```

Added in MIPS IV for speed, and not IEEE accurate:

```
recip.d fd, fs           fd = 1/fs;
rsqrt.d fd, fs           fd = 1/(squarerootof(fs));
```

7.9.4 *Multiply-Add Operations*

These appeared in the MIPS IV version of the ISA, in response to Silicon Graphics's interest in achieving supercomputer-like performance in very high-end graphics systems (related to the 1995 SGI acquisition of Cray Research, Inc.). IBM's PowerPC chips seemed to get lots of FP performance out of their multiply-add, too. Although it's against RISC principles to have a single instruction doing two jobs, a combined multiply-add is widely used in common repetitive FP operations (typically the manipulation of matrices or vectors).

Moreover, it saves a significant amount of time by avoiding the intermediate rounding and renormalization step that IEEE mandates when a result gets written back into a register.

Multiply-add comes in various forms, all of which take three register operands and an independent result register:

```
madd.d  fd, fs1, fs2, fs3          fd = fs2 × fs3 + fs1;
msub.d  fd, fs1, fs2, fs3          fd = fs2 × fs3 - fs1;
nmadd.d fd, fs1, fs2, fs3          fd = -(fs2 × fs3 + fs1);
nmsub.d fd, fs1, fs2, fs3          fd = -(fs2 × fs3 - fs1);
```

IEEE754 does not rule specifically for multiply-add operations, but to conform to the standard the result produced should be identical to that coming out of a two-instruction multiply-then-add sequence. Since every FP operation may involve some rounding, this means that IEEE754 mandates somewhat poorer precision for multiply-add than could be achieved. The MIPS R8000 supercomputer chip set falls into this trap, and its multiply-add instructions do not meet (but exceed) the accuracy prescribed by IEEE. The R10000 and all subsequent implementations are IEEE compatible.

7.9.5   *Unary (Sign-Changing) Operations*

Although nominally arithmetic functions, these operations only change the sign bit and so can't produce most IEEE exceptions. They can produce an invalid trap if fed with a signalling NaN value. They are as follows:

```
abs.d  fd, fs            fd = abs(fs)
neg.d  fd, fs            fd = -fs
```

7.9.6   *Conversion Operations*

Note that "convert from single to double" is written "`cvt.d.s`"—and as usual the destination register is specified first. Conversion operators work between data in the FP registers: When converting data from CPU integer registers, the move from FP to CPU registers must be coded separately from the conversion operation. Conversion operations can result in any IEEE exception that makes sense in the context.

Originally, all this was done by the one family of instructions

```
cvt.x.y fd, fs
```

where *x* and *y* specify the destination and source format, respectively, as one of the following:

s C *float*, IEEE single, 32-bit floating point

d C *double*, IEEE double, 64-bit floating point

w C *int*, "word," 32-bit integer

l C *long long*, "long," 64-bit integer (available in MIPS III and higher CPUs only)

The instructions are as follows:

```
cvt.s.d fd, fs   /* double fs -> float, leave in fd */
cvt.w.s fd, fs   /* float fs -> int, leave in fd */
cvt.d.l fd, fs   /* long long fs -> double, leave in fd */
```

There's more than one reasonable way of converting from floating-point to integer formats, and the result depends on the current rounding mode (as set up in the **FCR31** register, described in Section 7.7). But FP calculations quite often want to round to the integer explicitly (for example, the ceiling operator rounds upward), and it's a nuisance trying to generate code to modify and restore **FCR31**. So at MIPS II, explicit rounding conversions were introduced.

Conversions to integer with explicit rounding:

```
round.x.y fd, fs        /* round to nearest */
trunc.x.y fd, fs        /* round toward zero */
ceil.x.y fd, fs         /* round up */
floor.x.y fd, fs        /* round down */
```

These instructions are only valid with **x** representing an integer format.

7.9.7 *Conditional Branch and Test Instructions*

The FP branch and test instructions are separate. We'll discuss the test instructions below—they have names like **c.le.s**, and they compare two FP values and set the FPA condition bit accordingly.

The branch instructions, therefore, just have to test whether the condition bit is true (set) or false (zero):

```
bc1t label         if (fpcondition(0)) branch-to-label;
bc1t cc, label     if (fpcondition(cc)) branch-to-label;
bc1f 0, label      if (!fpcondition(0)) branch-to-label;
bc1f cc, label     if (!fpcondition(cc)) branch-to-label;
```

Instructions added by MIPS II (see Section 8.4.4):

```
bc1tl label        /* branch-likely form of bc1t ... */
bc1fl label
```

Like the CPU's other instructions called branch, the target **label** is encoded as a 16-bit signed word displacement from the next instruction plus one (pipelining works in strange ways). If **label** was more than 128KB away, you'd be in trouble and you would have to resort to a **jr** instruction.

MIPS CPUs up to and including MIPS III had only one FP condition bit, called "C," in the FP control/status register **FCR31**. In MIPS IV there are 7 extra condition bits, called FCC7-1. If you leave the **cc** specification out of branch or compare instructions, you implicitly pick the old "C" bit, which has the honorary title of FCC0. That's compatible with older instruction set versions. (See Section 8.4.7 if you're interested in why this extension was introduced.) In all the instruction sets, **cc** is optional.

But before you can branch, you have to set the condition bit appropriately. The comparison operators are as follows:

```
c.cond.d fs1,fs2     /* compare fs1 and fs2 and set C */
c.cond.d cc, fs1,fs2 /* compare fs1 and fs2; set FCC(cc) */
```

In these instructions, **cond** can be a mnemonic for any of 16 conditions. The mnemonic is sometimes meaningful (**eq**) and sometimes more mysterious (**ult**). Why so many? It turns out that when you're comparing FP values there are four mutually incompatible outcomes:

```
fs1 < fs2
fs1 == fs2
fs1 > fs2
unordered (fs1, fs2)
```

The IEEE standard sometimes defines unordered as true when either of the operands is an IEEE NaN value.

It turns out we can always synthesize greater than by reversing the order of the operands or by setting up a less than or equal to and inverting the test, so we've got three outcomes to allow for. MIPS provides instructions to test for any "or" combination of the three conditions. On top of that, each test comes in two flavors, one that takes an invalid trap if the operands are unordered and one that never takes such a trap.

We don't have to provide tests for conditions like not equal; we test for equal but then use a **bc1f** rather than a **bc1t** branch. Table 7.4 may help.

The compare instruction produces its result too late for the branch instruction to be the immediately following instruction; thus a delay slot is required. In MIPS IV and later CPUs the delay is enforced with an interlock, but in earlier CPUs the branch instruction will misfire if run directly after the test.

TABLE 7.4 FP test instructions

"C" bit is set if...			Mnemonic	
			No trap	Trap
always false			**f**	**sf**
		unordered(fs1,fs2)	**un**	**ngle**
fs1 == fs2			**eq**	**seq**
	fs1 == fs2 ||	unordered(fs1,fs2)	**ueq**	**ngl**
fs1 < fs2			**olt**	**lt**
fs1 < fs2	||	unordered(fs1,fs2)	**ult**	**nge**
fs1 < fs2 ||	fs1 == fs2		**ole**	**le**
fs1 < fs2 ||	fs1 == fs2 ||	unordered(fs1,fs2)	**ule**	**ngt**

Note the following examples:

```
if (f0 <= f2) goto foo;      /* and don't branch if unordered */

    c.le.d  $f0, $f2
    nop             # the assembler will do this for you
    bc1t    foo

if (f0 > f2) goto foo;       /* and trap if unordered */

    c.ole.d $f0, $f2
    nop             # the assembler will do this for you
    bc1f    foo
```

Fortunately, you usually leave the compiler to cope with this!

7.10 Instruction Timing Requirements

Normal FP arithmetic instructions are interlocked, and there is no need to interpose **nop**s or to reorganize code for correctness. But to get the best performance the compiler should lay out FP instructions to make the best use of overlapped execution of integer instructions and of the FP pipeline.

However, the compiler, the assembler, or (in the end) the programmer must take care about the timing of the following:

- *Operations on the FP control and status register*: When altering **FCR31** take care with the pipeline. Its fields can affect any FP operation, which may be running in parallel. Make sure that at the point you write **FCR31** there are no FP operations live (started, but whose results have not yet been collected). The register is probably written late, too, so it's wise to allow one or two instructions to separate the **ctc1 rd, FCR31** from an affected computational instruction.

- *Moves between FP and general-purpose registers*: These complete late, and the resulting value cannot be used in the following instruction. On moves to FP registers (and on all kinds of moves in MIPS III and subsequent CPUs), this is interlocked.

- *FP register loads*: Like integer loads, these take effect late. The value can't be used in the following instruction.

- *Test condition and branch*: The test of the FP condition bit using the **bc1t**, **bc1f** instructions must be carefully coded, because the condition bit is tested a clock cycle earlier than you might expect. So the conditional branch cannot immediately follow a test instruction.

7.11   Instruction Timing for Speed

All MIPS FPAs take more than one clock cycle for most arithmetic instructions, hence the pipelining becomes visible. The pipeline can show up in three ways:

- *Hazards*: These occur where the software must ensure the separation of instructions to work correctly.

- *Interlocks*: These occur where the hardware will protect you by delaying use of an operand until it is ready. Knowledgeable rearrangement of the code will improve performance.

- *Visible pipelining*: This occurs where the hardware is prepared to start one operation before another has completed (provided there are no data dependencies). Compilers, and determined assembler programmers, can write code that works the hardware to the limit by keeping the pipeline full.

Hazards and interlocks arise when instructions fail to stick to the general MIPS rule of taking exactly one clock period between needing operands and making results ready. Some instructions either need operands earlier (branches, particularly), or produce results late (you've already met this in loads).

7.12   Initialization and Enabling on Demand

From reset you will normally have initialized the CPU's **SR** register to disable all optional coprocessors, which includes the FPA (coprocessor 1). The **SR** bit CU1 has to be set for the FPA to work. For MIPS III and subsequent FPAs, you can either use the registers in pairs (for MIPS I compatibility) or as 32 separate 64-bit registers.

You should read the FPA implementation register; if it reads zero, no FP is fitted and you should run the system with CU1 off.

Once CU1 is switched on you should set up the control/status register **FCR31** with your choice of rounding modes and trap enables. Anything except round to nearest and all traps disabled is uncommon. With MIPS III CPUs there's also the choice of setting the FS bit to cause very small results to be returned as zero, saving a trap to the emulator. This is not IEEE compatible, but the hardware can't produce the specified denormalized result.

Once the FPA is operating, you need to ensure that the FP registers are saved and restored during interrupts and context switches. Since this is (relatively) time consuming, you can optimize this, as some UNIX systems do, by doing the following:

- Leave the FPA disabled by default when running a new task. Since the task cannot now access the FPA, you don't have to save and restore registers when scheduling or parking it.

- On a CU1-unusable trap, mark the task as an FP user and enable the FP before returning to it.

- Disable FP operations while in the kernel or in any software called directly or indirectly from an interrupt routine. Then you can avoid saving FP registers on an interrupt; instead, FP registers need to be saved only when you are context-switching to or from an FP-using task.

7.13   Floating-Point Emulation

Some low-cost MIPS CPUs (including all ASIC cores to date) do not have a hardware FPA. Floating-point functions for these processors are provided by software and are perhaps 50–300 times slower than the hardware. Software FP is useful for systems where floating point is employed in some rarely used routines.

There are two approaches, as follows:

- *Soft float*: Some compilers can be requested to implement floating-point operations with software. FP arithmetic operations are likely to be implemented with a hidden library function, but housekeeping tasks such as moves, loads, and stores can be handled in line.

■ *Run-time emulation*: The compiler can produce the regular FP instruction set. The CPU will then take a trap on each FP instruction that is caught by the FP emulator. The emulator decodes the instruction and performs the requested operation in software. Part of the emulator's job will be emulating the FP register set in memory.

As described here, a run-time emulator is also required to back up FP hardware for very small operands or obscure operations; since the architecture is deliberately vague about the limits of the hardware's responsibility, the emulator is usually complete. However, it will be written to ensure exact IEEE compatibility and is only expected to be called occasionally, so it will probably be coded for correctness rather than speed.

Compiled-in floating point is much more efficient; the emulator has a high overhead on each instruction from the trap handler, instruction decoder, and emulated register file.

Some compilers don't offer soft float operation: The history of the MIPS architecture is in workstations where FP hardware was mandatory.

Chapter

8

Complete Guide to the MIPS Instruction Set

Chapter 8 and Chapter 9 are written for the programmer who wants to understand or generate assembly code (whether in person or indirectly because you're writing or fixing a compiler). While Chapter 9 discusses real assembler language programming, this chapter only concerns itself with assembler language instructions; broadly speaking, you can skip Chapter 9 if you only want to read disassembly listings. We begin with a simple piece of MIPS code and an overview.

8.1 A Simple Example

This is an implementation of the C library function strcmp(1), which compares two character strings and returns zero on equal, a positive value if the first string is greater (in string order) than the second, and a negative value otherwise. Here's a naive C algorithm:

```
int strcmp (char *str1, char *str2)
{
    char c1, c2;

    do {
        c1 = *str1++;
        c2 = *str2++;
    } while (c1 != 0 && c2 != 0 && c1 == c2);

    return c1 - c2; /* cunning: 0, +ve or -ve appropriately */
}
```

In assembler code the two arguments of the C function arrive in the registers called **a0** and **a1**. (See Table 2.1 if you've forgotten about the naming conventions for registers; the MIPS standard calling convention is described in detail in Section 10.1). A simple subroutine like this one is free to use the temporary registers **t0** and so on without saving and restoring their values, so they're the obvious choices for temporaries. The function returns a value, which by convention needs to be in the register **v0** at the time we return. So let's have a go at it:

```
strcmp:
1:
    lbu     t0, 0(a0)
    addu    a0, a0, 1
    lbu     t1, 0(a1)
    addu    a1, a1, 1

    beq     t0, zero,.t01   # end of first string?
    beq     t1, zero,.t01   # end of second string?
    beq     t2, t1, 1b

.t01:
    subu    v0, t0, t1
    j       ra
```

We will examine it from the top:

- *Labels*: "strcmp" is a familiar named label, which in assembler can define a function entry point, an intermediate branch, or even a data storage location.

    ".t01" is a legitimate label; the full-stop "." character is legal in labels and must not be confused with a C name elsewhere in your program.

    "1:" is a numeric label, which most assemblers will accept as a local label. You can have as many labels called "1" as you like in a program; "1f" refers to the next one in sequence and "1b" the previous one. This is useful.

- *Register names*: The unadorned names shown here are common usage, but they require that the assembly code be passed through some kind of macroprocessor before getting to the real MIPS assembler: Typically, the C preprocessor is used and most toolkits have ways to make this straightforward.

It would hardly be worth writing such a function in assembler as this; the compiler will probably do a better job. But we'll see later (Section 9.1) how much more clever we could have been.

8.2   Assembler Mnemonics and What They Mean

This section consists of a long list of all legal mnemonics in most MIPS assemblers up to and including MIPS IV instructions. After some agonizing and experimentation, I decided that this table should contain a mixture of real machine operations and the assembler's synthesized instructions. So for each instruction we'll list the following:

- *Assembler format*: How the instruction is written.

- *Machine instructions generated*: For assembler instructions that are aliases for machine code or expanded into a sequence of machine instructions, we'll put a "→" to show a macro expansion and list typical instructions in an expansion.

- *Function*: A description of what the instruction does, in pseudo-C code, which is meant to combine precision with brevity. C typecasts, where used, are necessary.

Not every possible combination of instruction and operands is listed, because it gets too long. So we won't list the following:

- *Two-operand forms of three-operand instructions*: For example, MIPS assemblers allow you to write

  ```
  addu $1, $2              # $1 = $1 + $2
  ```

  which would otherwise have to be written as:

  ```
  addu $1, $1, $2
  ```

  You can do that pretty much anywhere it makes sense.

- *All possible load/store address formats (addr)*: MIPS machine instructions always generate addresses for load/store operations using just the contents of a register plus a 16-bit signed displacement,[1] written, for example, `lw $1, 14($2)`. MIPS assemblers support quite a few other addressing mode formats; notably `lw $1, thing`, which loads data from the location whose assembler code label (or external C name) is "thing." See Section 9.4 for details; note that all of these modes are quietly available to any assembler instruction that specifies a memory address. We'll just write `lw t, addr` for the assembler instruction and the base+displacement format for the machine code.

---

1. Someone always has to break things; the MIPS IV ISA adds register+register address formats but only for load/stores with floating-point registers. This is done in deference to the importance of multidimensional-array organizations in floating-point codes.

The **la** (load address) instruction provided by the assembler uses the same addressing-mode syntax, even though it loads or stores nothing— it just generates the address value in the destination register.

When synthesizing some address formats (particularly on stores) the assembler needs a scratch register and quietly uses **at**. Programmers working at a very low level need to take care.

- *Immediate versions of instructions*: A constant value embedded within an instruction is, by ancient convention, called an immediate value. MIPS CPUs offer some real hardware instructions supporting immediates of up to 16 bits in size;[1] however, the assembler allows you to specify a constant source operand (always as the last operand) for any instruction. You'll see the immediate forms when we're discussing machine instructions (Table 8.6, for example) and in disassembly listings.

  Moreover, in assembly language you're not limited to 16 bits; if you write an arbitrary constant, the assembler will synthesize away, as described in Section 9.3.2.

  Once again, the assembler may need to use the temporary register **at** for some complicated cases.

8.2.1 *U and Non-U Mnemonics*

Before we get started, there's a particularly confusing thing about the way instruction mnemonics are written. A "**u**" suffix on the assembler mnemonic is usually read as "unsigned." But that's not always what it means (at least, not without a big stretch of your powers of imagination). There are a number of subtly different meanings for a "**u**" suffix, depending on context:

- *Overflow trap vs. no trap*: In most arithmetic operations U denotes "no overflow test." Unsuffixed arithmetic operations like **add** cause a CPU exception if the result overflows into bit 31 (the sign bit when we're thinking of integers as signed). The suffixed variant **addu** produces exactly the same result for all combinations of operands but never takes an exception. If you're dealing with unsigned numbers, the overflow test is certainly unwelcome; however, if you're writing C, C++, and assembler the overflow test is probably unwelcome anyway, and you are unlikely to ever generate anything but the suffixed versions.

- *Set if*: The universal test operations **slt** (set if less than) and **sltu** (set if less than, unsigned) have to produce genuinely different results when confronted by operands, one of which has the top bit set and the other doesn't.

---

1. These are recognized by the assembler as real instructions, so you can write them if you like; but probably only compilers generating assembler intermediate code should ever do so.

- *Multiply and divide*: Integer multiply operations produce a result with twice the precision of the operands, and that means that they need to produce genuinely different results for signed and unsigned inputs: hence there are two instructions **mult** and **multu**. Note that the low part of the result, left in the **lo** register, will be the same for both the signed and the unsigned version; it's the way that overflows into **hi** are handled that differs.

  Integer divide instructions are also sign dependent (think about dividing 0xFFFFFFFE by 2), so there's a **div** and a **divu**. The same variation exists for shift right instructions (shift right by one is really just divide by two), but this was obviously a U too far; the shift instructions are called **sra** (shift right arithmetic, suitable for signed numbers) and **srl** (shift right logical). The world is indeed a wonderful place.

- *Partial-register loads*: Loads of less-than-register-size chunks of data must decide what to do with the excess bits in the register. For the unsigned instructions such as **lbu**, the byte value is loaded into the register and the remaining bits are cleared to zero (we say that the value has been *zero-extended*). If the byte value represented a signed number, its top bit would tell us if it was negative. In this case we'll translate to the corresponding register-sized representation by filling the remaining bits of the register with copies of the sign bit, using the instruction **lb**. That's called *sign-extending*.

8.2.2   *Divide Mnemonics*

We've mentioned earlier that in machine code for integer multiply and divide there are separate initiation and result-collecting instructions. The assembler likes to cover this up, generating macro expansions for a three-operand format and doing a divide-by-zero check at the same time. This would be OK except that unfortunately the assembler macro name for divide is **div**, which is also the name for the basic machine code instruction. That means there's no way to write a machine code divide instruction in assembler; this is kludged by defining that a three-operand assembler divide with **zero** as the destination should just produce the machine start-divide operation and nothing else.

For reasons of consistency the assembler multiply instruction mnemonic **mul** behaves similarly—even though there's a distinct mnemonic **mult** for the machine code in this case.

Some toolchains have offered a better way out of this mess, by defining new mnemonics **divd** (divide direct) to mean just the hardware operation and **divo** (divide with overflow check) for the complicated macro. This didn't catch on, but you may see it in some codes.

8.2.3 *Inventory of Instructions*

In the assembler descriptions we use the conventions given in Table 8.1. Table 8.2 gives a full inventory of the instruction descriptions in mnemonic order.

TABLE 8.1 Conventions used in instruction tables

Word	Used for
s, *t*	CPU registers used as operands.
d	CPU register that receives the result.
j	"Immediate" constant.
label	The name of an entry point in the instruction stream.
offs	The 16-bit PC-relative word offset representing the distance in instructions to a label.
addr	One of a number of different legitimate data address expressions usable when writing load/store (or load address) instructions in assembler. (See Section 9.4 for a description of how the assembler implements the various options.)
at	The assembler temporary register, which is really $1.
zero	This register, $0, always contains a zero value.
ra	The return address register $31.
hilo	The double-precision integer multiply result formed by concatenating **hi** and **lo**. Each of **hi** and **lo** holds the same number of bits as a machine register, so **hilo** can hold a 64-bit integer on a 32-bit machine and a 128-bit result on a 64-bit machine.
MAXNEG32BIT MAXNEG64BIT	The most negative number representable in twos complement arithmetic, 32- and 64-bit, respectively. It's a feature of twos complement numbers that the positive number −MAXNEG32BIT is not representable in 32 bits.
cd	Coprocessor register that is written by instruction.
cs	Coprocessor register that is read by instruction.
exception(CAUSE, code) exception(CAUSE)	Take a CPU trap; CAUSE determines the setting of the **Cause(ExcCode)** register field. "code" is a value not interpreted by the hardware, but rather one encoded in a don't-care field of the instruction, where system software can find it by reading the instruction. Not every such instruction sets a "code" value, so sometimes we'll leave it out.
*const*31..16	Denotes the number obtained by just using bits 31 through 16 of the binary number "const." The MIPS books use a similar convention.

TABLE 8.2 Assembler instructions in alphabetical order

Assembler/machine code	Description

abs *d*,*s* →
   sra at,*s*,31
   xor *d*,*s*,at
   sub *d*,*d*,at
	`d = s < 0 ?  -s:  s;`

add *d*,*s*,*j* → **addi** *d*,*s*,*j*	`d = s + (signed)j; /* trap on overflow, rare */`
add *d*,*s*,*t*	`d = s + t; /* trap on overflow, rare */`

addciu *t*,*r*,*j*	`/* LSI MiniRISC only - "add with circular mask`
	`immediate," an instruction for computing circular`
	`buffer index values.` **CMASK** `is a special`
	`coprocessor 0 register, which holds a number`
	`between 0 and 15.   */`
	`t = ((unsigned)r + (unsigned)j) % (2**CMASK);`

addu *d*,*s*,*j* → **addiu** *d*,*s*,*j*	`d = s + (signed)j;` `/* more complex unless -32768 ≤ j < 32768 */`
addu *d*,*s*,*t*	`d = s + t;`
and *d*,*s*,*j* → **andi** *d*,*s*,*j*	`d = s & (unsigned) j; /* more complex unless 0 ≤` `j < 65535 */`
and *d*,*s*,*t*	`d = s & t;`
b *label* → **beq** zero,zero,*offs*	`goto label;`
bal *label* → **bgezal** zero,*offs*	Function call (limited range but PC-relative addressing). Note that the return address that is left in **ra** is that of the next instruction but one: The next instruction in memory order is in the branch delay slot and gets executed before the function is invoked.
bc0f *label* **bc0fl** *label* **bc0t** *label* **bc0tl** *label*	Branch on coprocessor 0 condition. On early 32-bit CPUs, this tested the state of a CPU input pin; on more modern CPUs there's no pin and the instruction is useless. The **l** suffix is for branch-likely variants; see Section 8.4.4.

continued

TABLE 8.2 *continued*

Assembler/machine code	Description
bc1f *label* bc1f *N,label* bc1fl *label* bc1fl *N,label* bc1t *label* bc1t *N,label* bc1tl *label* bc1tl *N,label*	Branch on floating-point (coprocessor 1) condition set/true (**t**) or clear/false (**f**); described in Section 7.9.7. From MIPS IV there are multiple FP condition bits, selected by N = 0..7. Suffix **l** as in **bc1fl** means branch-likely instructions; see Section 8.4.4.
bc2f *label* bc2fl *label* bc2t *label* bc2tl *label*	Branch on coprocessor 2 condition. Useful only if a CPU uses the CP2 instruction set or offers an external pin.
beq *s,t,label*	if (s == t) goto label;
beql *s,t,label*	Branch-likely variants of conditional branches above. The delay slot instruction is only executed if the branch is taken; see Section 8.4.4.
beqz *s,label* → beq *s,$zero,offs*	if (s == 0) goto label;
beqzl	Branch-likely variant of **beqz**; see Section 8.4.4.

bge *s,t,label* →
  slt at,*s,t*
  beq at,$zero,*offs*
	if ((signed) s ≥ (signed) t) goto label;

bgel *s,t,label* →
  slt at,*s,t*
  beql at,$zero,*offs*
	"Likely" form of **bge**, deprecated. Macro forms are of dubious use: Branch-likely is really for compilers and demon tuners to optimize out branch delay slots, and you can't realistically do that with macro-instructions. See Section 8.4.4.

bgeu *s,t,label* →
  sltu at,*s,t*
  beq at,$zero,*offs*
	if ((unsigned) s ≥ (unsigned) t)
	goto label;

bgeul *s,t,label*	Deprecated branch-likely macro; see Section 8.4.4.

TABLE 8.2 *continued*

Assembler/machine code	Description
bgez *s,label*	if (s ≥ 0) goto label;
bgezal *s,label*	if (s ≥ 0) label();
bgezall *s,label*	Branch-likely variant; see Section 8.4.4.
bgezl *s,label*	Branch-likely variant; see Section 8.4.4.

bgt *s,t,label* →
   slt at,*t,s*
   bne at,$zero,*offs*
	if ((signed) s > (signed) t)
	goto label;

bgtl *s,t,label*	Deprecated branch-likely macro; see Section 8.4.4.

bgtu *s,t,label* →
   slt at,*t,s*
   beq at,$zero,*offs*
	if ((unsigned) s > (unsigned) t)
	goto label;

bgtul *t,s,label*	Deprecated branch-likely macro; see Section 8.4.4.
bgtz *s,label*	if (s > 0) goto label;
bgtzl *s,label*	Branch-likely version of **bgtz**; see Section 8.4.4.

ble *s,t,label* →
   sltu at,*t,s*
   beq at,$zero,*offs*
	if ((signed) s ≤ (signed) t)
	goto label;

blel *s,t,label*	Deprecated branch-likely macro; see Section 8.4.4.

bleu *s,t,label* →
   sltu at,*t,s*
   beq at,$zero,*offs*
	if ((unsigned) s ≤ (unsigned) t)
	goto label;

bleul *s,t,label*	Deprecated branch-likely macro; see Section 8.4.4.
blez *s,label*	if (s ≤ 0) goto label;
blezl *s,label*	Branch-likely variant of **blez**; see Section 8.4.4.

blt *s,t,label* →
   slt at,*s,t*
   bne at,$zero,*offs*
	if ((signed) s < (signed) t)
	goto label;

bltl *s,t,label*	Deprecated branch-likely macro; see Section 8.4.4.

continued

TABLE 8.2 *continued*

Assembler/machine code	Description

bltu *s,t,label* →
  sltu at,*s,t*
  bne at,$zero,*offs*
	if ((unsigned) s < (unsigned) t)
	 goto label;

bltul *s,t,label*	Deprecated branch-likely macro; see Section 8.4.4.
bltz *s,label*	if (s < 0) goto label;
bltzal *s,label*	if (s < 0) label();
bltzall *s,label*	Branch-likely variant; see Section 8.4.4.
bltzl *s,label*	Branch-likely variant; see Section 8.4.4.
bne *s,t,label*	if (s != t) goto label;
bnel *s,t,label*	Branch-likely variant; see Section 8.4.4.
bnez *s,label*	if (s != 0) goto label;
bnezl *s,t,label*	Branch-likely variant; see Section 8.4.4.
break *code*	Breakpoint instruction. The value *code* has no hardware effect, but the breakpoint exception routine can retrieve it by reading the exception-causing instruction.
cache *k,addr*	Do something to a cache line, as described in Section 4.10 above. Available only from MIPS III on.
cfc0 *t,cs* cfc1 *t,cs* cfc2 *t,cs*	Move data from coprocessor control register **cs** to general-purpose register **t**. Only useful for a coprocessor that uses the auxiliary control register set: So far this means only the floating-point coprocessor CP1, which has just one control register—the floating-point control and status register.
ctc0 *t,cd* ctc1 *t,cs* ctc2 *t,cs*	Move data from general-purpose register **t** to coprocessor control register **cs**.

dabs *d,s* →
  dsra at,*s,*31
  xor *d,s,*at
  dsub *d,d,*at
	d = s < 0: -s: s; /* 64-bit */

dadd *d,s,t*	d = s + t; /* 64-bit, overflow trap, rare */
daddi *d,s,j*	d = s + j; /* 64-bit, overflow trap, rare */
daddiu *d,s,j*	d = s + j; /* 64-bit */

TABLE 8.2 *continued*

Assembler/machine code	Description
daddu *d,s,t*	`d = s + t; /* 64-bit */`

ddiv $zero,*s,t* →
 ddiv *s,t*
	`/* plain 64-bit hardware divide instruction */`
	`lo = (long long) s / (long long) t;`
	`hi = (long long) s % (long long) t;`

ddiv *d,s,t* →
   bnez *t,*1f
   ddiv $zero,*s,t*
   break 0x7
 1:
   li at,-1
   bne *t,***at,**2f
   lui at,32768
   dsll32 at,at,0
   bne *s,***at,**2f
   nop
   break 0x6
 2:
   mflo *d*
	`/* 64-bit signed divide with checks */ lo = (long`
	`long) s / (long long) t; hi = (long long) s % (long`
	`long) t; if (t == 0) exception (BREAK, 7); if (t ==`
	`-1 && s = MAXNEG64BIT) /* result overflows */`
	`exception (BREAK, 6); d = lo;`

ddivd *s,t*	Another way of writing plain hardware instruction, but use **ddiv** **$zero,**…instead.
ddivdu *s,t*	Another way of writing plain hardware instruction, but use **ddivu** **$zero,***s, t* instead.

ddivu $zero,*s,t* →
   ddivu *s,t*
	`/* plain unsigned 64-bit hardware divide instruction`
	`*/`
	`lo = (unsigned long long) s / (unsigned long long) t;`
	`hi = (unsigned long long) s % (unsigned long long) t;`

ddivu *d,s,t* →
   divu *s,t*
   bne *t,***$zero,**1f
   nop
   break 7
 1:
   mflo *d*
	`/* 64-bit unsigned divide with check */`
	`lo = (unsigned long long) s / (unsigned long long) t;`
	`hi = (unsigned long long) s % (unsigned long long) t;`
	`if (t == 0) exception(BREAK,7);`
	`d = lo;`

div $zero,*s,t* →
   div *s,t*
	`/* plain signed 32-bit hardware divide */`
	`lo = s / t;`
	`hi = s % t;`

continued

TABLE 8.2 *continued*

Assembler/machine code	Description

`div d,s,t` →
   `div s,t`
   `bne t,$zero,1f`
   `nop`
   `break 7`
 `1:`
   `li at,-1`
   `bne t,at,2f`
   `nop`
   `lui at,0x8000`
   `bne s,at,2f`
   `nop`
   `break 6`
 `2:`
   `mflo d`
	`/* signed 32-bit division with checks */`
	 `lo = s/t;`
	 `hi = s % t;`
	 `if (t == 0) exception(BREAK,7);`
	 `if (t == -1 && s == MAXNEG32BIT)`
	   `exception(BREAK, 6); /* result overflows */`
	 `d = lo;`

`divd s,t`	Sometimes gives hardware instruction, but use **div $zero,s,t** instead.
`divdu s,t`	Hardware division, not available in all toolchains; use **divu $zero,s,t** instead.
`divo d,s,t` `divou d,s,t`	Same as **div/divu**, but the name explicitly reminds you about overflow check.

`divu d,s,t` →
   `divu s,t`
   `bne t,$zero,1f`
   `nop`
   `break 7`
 `1:`
   `mflo d`
	`/* unsigned divide with check */`
	 `lo = (unsigned) s / (unsigned) t;`
	 `hi = (unsigned) s % (unsigned) t;`
	 `if (t == 0) exception(BREAK,7);`
	 `d = lo;`

`divu $zero, s,t` →
   `divu s,t`
	`/* $zero as destination means no checks */`
	 `lo = s/t;`
	 `hi = s % t;`

`dla t, addr` → `# various ...`	Load 64-bit address; see Section 9.4.

TABLE 8.2 *continued*

Assembler/machine code	Description

`dli t, const →`
`  # biggest case:`
`  lui t, const63..48`
`  ori t, const47..32`
`  dsll t, 16`
`  ori t, const31..16`
`  dsll t, 16`
`  ori t, const15..0`
	Load 64-bit constant. Separate mnemonic from `li` required only for values between 0x8000 0000 and 0xFFFF FFFF, where 32→64 bit transition rules require `li` to flood the high-order 32 bits with ones.

`dmadd16 s,t`	`/* found only on NEC Vr4100 CPU */`
	`(long long)lo = (long long)lo + ((short)s *`
	`(short)t);`

`dmfc0 t,cs`
`dmfc1 t,fs`
`dmfc2 t,fs`
	Move 64 bits from coprocessor register **cs** to general-purpose register **t**. **dmfc1** is for floating-point registers.

`dmtc0 t,cd`
`dmtc1 t,cs`
`dmtc2 t,cs`
	Move 64 bits from general-purpose register **t** to coprocessor register **cs**.

`dmul d,s,t →`
`  dmultu s,t`
`  mflo d`
	`/* no overflow check - and with a 64-bit result`
	`from 64-bit operands, a signed and unsigned`
	`version will do the same thing */`
	`d = (long long) s * (long long) t;`

`dmulo d,s,t →`
`  dmult s,t`
`  mflo d`
`  dsra32 d,d,31`
`  mfhi at`
`  beq d,at,1f`
`  nop`
`  break 0x6`
`1:`
`  mflo d`
	`/* signed multiply, trap if result overflows`
	`64-bit signed limit */`
	`hilo = (long long) s * (long long) t;`
	`if ((lo ≥ 0 && hi != 0) || (lo < 0 && hi != -1))`
	`  exception(BREAK, 6);`
	`d = lo;`

`dmulou d,s,t →`
`  dmultu s,t`
`  mfhi at`
`  mflo d`
`  beqz at,1f`
`  nop`
`  break 0x6`
	`/* unsigned multiply, trap if result overflows`
	`64-bit limit */`
	`hilo = (long long) s * (long long) t;`
	`if (hi != 0)`
	`  exception(BREAK, 6);`
	`d = lo;`

continued

TABLE 8.2 *continued*

Assembler/machine code	Description
dmult *s,t*	/* machine instruction: "hi" correct for signed 64-bit multiplication */ hilo = (long long) s * (long long) t;
dmultu *s,t*	/* machine instruction: "hi" correct for unsigned 64-bit multiplication */ hilo = (unsigned long long) s * (unsigned long long) t;
dneg *d,s* → dsub *d,$zero,s*	(long long) d = -(long long) s; /* trap on overflow */
dnegu *d,s* → dsubu *d,$zero,s*	(long long) d = -(long long) s;

drem *d,s,t* →
 bnez *t*,1f
 ddiv $zero,*s,t*
 break 0x7
1:
 li at,-1
 bne *t*,at,2f
 lui at,32768
 dsll32 at,at,0
 bne *s*,at,2f
 nop
 break 0x6
2:
 mfhi *d*
	/* 64-bit remainder with overflow check */
	if (t == 0) exception(BREAK,7); /* divide by zero? */
	/* result overflows 64-bit signed value? */
	if (s == MAXNEG64BIT && t == -1)
	  exception(BREAK,6);
	d = (long long) s % (long long) t;

dremu *d,s,t* →
 bnez *t*,1f
 ddivu $zero,*s,t*
 break 0x7
1:
 mfhi *d*
	/* 64-bit unsigned remainder */
	if (t == 0) exception(BREAK, 7); /* divide by zero? */
	d = (unsigned long long) s % (unsigned long long) t;

dret	Special exception return; only applies to the obsolete R6000 CPU.
drol *d,s,t* → dnegu at,*t* dsrlv at,*s*,at dsllv *d,s,t* or *d,d*,at	/* 64-bit rotate left */ d = (s << t)	(s >> (64-t));

TABLE 8.2 *continued*

Assembler/machine code	Description

dror *d,s,t* →
  dnegu at,*t*
  dsllv at,*s*,at
  dsrlv *d,s,t*
  or *d,d,*at
	/* 64-bit rotate right */
	d = (s >> t) | (s << (64-t));

dsll *d,s,shft*	d = (long long) s << shft /* 0 ≤ shft < 31 */
dsll *d,s,shft* → dsll32 *d,s,shft-32*	d = (long long) s << shft /* 32 ≤ shft < 63 */
dsll *d,s,t* → dsllv *d,s,t* dsllv *d,s,t*	d = (long long) s << (t % 64);
dsll32 *d,s,shft*	d = (long long) s << (shft+32) /* 0 ≤ shft < 31 */
dsra *d,s,shft*	/* 0 ≤ shft < 31 */ /* algebraic shifting, which replicates old bit 63 into top bits, producing a correct division by power of 2 for negative numbers */ d = (long long signed) s >> shft%32;
dsra *d,s,shft* → dsra32 *d,s,shft-32*	As above, for 32 ≤ shft < 63.
dsra32 *d,s,shft*	/* 64-bit shift right arithmetic by 32-63 bits */ d = (long long signed) s >> (shft%32 + 32)
drsa *d,s,t* → drsav *d,s,t* drsav *d,s,t*	d = (long long signed) s >> (t%64)
dsrl *d,s,shft*	/* 0 ≤ shft < 31 */ d = (long long unsigned) s >> shft%32;
dsrl *d,s,shft* → dsrl32 *d,s,shft-32*	As above, for 32 ≤ shft < 63.
dsrl *d,s,t* → dsrlv *d,s,t* dsrlv *d,s,t*	d = (long long unsigned) s >> (t%64)

continued

TABLE 8.2 *continued*

Assembler/machine code	Description
`dsrl32 d,s,shft`	`/* 64-bit shift right arithmetic by 32-63 bits */` `d = (long long unsigned) s >> (shft%32 + 32)`
`dsub d,s,t`	`d = s - t; /* 64-bit, trap on overflow, rarely used */`
`dsubu d,s,t`	`d = s - t; /* 64-bit */`
`eret`	Return from exception (MIPS III on). Clears the **SR(EXL)** bit and branches to the location saved in **EPC**. See Section 12.3.
`ffc d,s` `ffs d,s`	Find first clear/set. LSI MiniRISC 4010 CPUs only. Sets **d** to the lowest numbered bit that is 0/1, respectively in **s**.
`flushd`	Invalidate entire cache (LSI MiniRISC only).
`j label`	`/* limited to a label within 2**28-byte "page" */` `goto label;`
`j r` `jr r`	Jump to the instruction pointed to by register **r**.

`j s →`
  `jr s`
`jr s`
	Go to the address found in **s**. This is the only way of transferring control to an arbitrary address, since all the address-in-instruction formats span less than 32 bits.

`jal d,addr →`
  `la at,addr`
  `jalr d,at`
	Call with nonstandard return address. Synthesized with `jalr`. It's cheating to use the instruction `la` in the machine code expansion, as `la` is itself a macro. That's to avoid dealing with addressing modes here (see Section 9.4 instead).

`jal label`	Subroutine call, with return address in **ra** (**$31**). Note that the return address is the next instruction but one: The immediately following instruction position is the branch delay slot, and the instruction there is always executed before you reach the subroutine.
`jalr d,s`	Call the subroutine whose address is in **s**, but put the return address in **d**.

`jal s →`
  `jalr $31, s`
`jalr s →`
  `jalr $31, s`
	Uses **ra** if **d** is not specified.

TABLE 8.2 *continued*

Assembler/machine code	Description
`la d,addr →` `  # many options`	Load address. `la` will work with any of the addressing modes described in Section 9.4.
`lb t,addr`	`/* load byte and sign-extend */` `t = *((signed char *) addr);`
`lbu t,addr`	`/* load byte and zero-extend */` `t = *((unsigned char *)addr);`
`ld t,addr`	`/* will trap if address is not 8 byte aligned */` `t = *((long long *)addr);`
`ldl t,addr` `ldr t,addr`	Load double left/right—the two halves of a 64-bit unaligned load (see Section 2.5.2).

`ldxc1 fd,t(b)`	`/* indexed load to floating-point`
	`register--MIPS IV only.  Note that the role of the`
	`two registers is not quite symmetrical--b is`
	`expected to hold an address and t an offset, and`
	`it's an offense for (b + t) to end up in a`
	`different section of the overall MIPS address map`
	`than b (defined by the top 2 bits of the 64-bit`
	`address).  */`
	`fd = *((double *) (b+t)); /* b, t both registers`
	`*/`

`lh t,addr`	`/* load 16 bit (halfword) and sign-extend */` `t = *((short *)addr);`
`lhu t,addr`	`/* load 16 bit (halfword) and zero-extend */` `t = *((unsigned short *)addr);`
`li d,j →` `  ori d,$zero,j`	Load register with constant value. This expansion is for $0 \leq j < 65535$.
`li d,j →` `  addiu d,$zero,j`	This one is for $-32768 \leq j < 0$.

`li d,j →`
`  lui d, hi16(j)`
`  ori d, d, lo16(j)`
	This one is for any other value of j that is representable as a 32-bit integer.

continued

TABLE 8.2 *continued*

Assembler/machine code	Description
`ll t,addr` `lld t,addr`	Load-linked. Load 32 bits/64 bits respectively with link side effects; used together with **sc** or **scd** to implement a lockless semaphore (see Section 8.4.2).

`lui t,u`	`/* load upper immediate (constant u is`
	`sign-extended into 64-bit registers) */`
	`t = u << 16;`

`lw t,addr`	`/* 32-bit load, sign-extended for 64-bit CPUs */` `t = *((* int)(addr));`
`lwc1 fd,addr`	Load FP single to FP register file—more often called **l.s**. Instructions to load other coprocessors' registers are defined but have never been implemented.
`lwl t,addr` `lwr t,addr`	Load word left/right. See Section 2.5.2 for how these instructions work together to perform an unaligned 32-bit load operation.

`lwu t,addr`	`/* 32-bit zero-extending load, only found on`
	`64-bit CPUs */`
	`t = (unsigned long long)*((unsigned int *)addr);`

`lwxc1 fd,t(b)`	`/* load FP single with indexed (register+register)`
	`address */`
	`fd = *((float *)(t+b));`

`madd d,s,t`	`/* genuine three-operand integer`
	`multiply-accumulate, as implemented on Toshiba`
	`3900 series cores */`
	`hilo += (long long) s * (long long) t;`
	`d = lo;`

`maddu d,s,t`	`/* unsigned version */`

`mad s,t`
`madu s,t`
	`/* 32-bit integer multiply-accumulate, as`
	`implemented on IDT R4640/50.  Encoding and action`
	`are compatible with the R3900 form, so long as` **d**
	`is actually` **zero**. **mad** `is for signed operands,`
	madu `for unsigned.   */`
	`hilo = hilo + ((long long) s * (long long) t);`

TABLE 8.2 *continued*

Assembler/machine code	Description
madd *s,t* **maddu** *s,t*	LSI MiniRISC name for integer multiply-accumulate. Encoding is incompatible with other versions, clashing with the MIPS III code for **dmult**. Signed and unsigned version.
madd16 *s,t*	/* NEC Vr4100 integer multiply-accumulate; handles only 16-bit operands */ lo = lo + ((short)s * (short)t);
max *d,s,t*	/* LSI MiniRISC only */ d = (s > t) ? s: t;
mfc0 *t,cs* **mfc1** *t,fs* **mfc2** *t,cs*	Move 32-bit contents of coprocessor register **cs** into general-purpose register **t**. **mfc0** is vital for access to the CPU control registers, **mfc1** for putting floating-point unit data back into integer registers. **mfc2** is only useful if coprocessor 2 is implemented, which never happens on standard CPUs.
mfhi *d* **mflo** *d*	Move integer multiply unit results to general-purpose register **d**. **lo** contains the result of a division, the least-significant 32 bits of the result of a **mul**, or the least-significant 64 bits of the result of a **dmul**. **hi** contains the remainder of a division or the most-significant bits of a multiplication. These instructions stall the pipeline if the multiply/divide operation is still in progress.
min *d,s,t*	/* LSI MiniRISC only */ d = (s < t) ? s: t;
move *d,s* → or *d,s,$zero*	d = s;
movf *d,s,N*	if (!fpcondition(N)) d = s;
movn *d,s,t*	if (t) d = s;
movt *d,s,N*	if (fpcondition(N)) d = s;
movt.d *fd,fs,N* **movt.s** *fd,fs,N*	if (fpcondition(N)) fd = fs;
movz *d,s,t*	if (!t) d = s;
msub *s,t* **msubu** *s,t*	/* 32-bit integer multiply-subtract for LSI MiniRISC only; see **madd** instruction */ hilo = hilo - ((long long) s * (long long) t);

continued

TABLE 8.2 *continued*

Assembler/machine code	Description

`mtc0 t,cd`
`mtc1 t,cs`
`mtc2 t,cs`
	Move 32 bits from general-purpose register **t** to coprocessor register **cd**. Note that this instruction doesn't obey the usual convention of writing the destination register first.
	mtc0 is for the CPU control registers, **mtc1** is for putting integer data into floating-point registers (although they're more often loaded directly from memory), and **mtc2** is implemented only if the CPU uses coprocessor 2 instructions (very rare).

`mthi s` `mtlo s`	Move contents of general-purpose register **s** into the multiply-unit result registers **hi** and **lo**, respectively. This may not seem useful, but they are required to restore the CPU state when returning from an exception.
`mul d,s,t` `mulu d,s,t`	`/* genuine three-operand 32-bit integer multiply, available on IDT R4650 and some other CPUs; signed and unsigned versions */ hilo = (long long) s * (long long) t;` `d = lo;`

`mul d,s,t →`
`    multu s,t`
`    mflo d`
	`d = (signed)s*(signed)t; /* no checks */`

`mulo d,s,t →`
`    mult s,t`
`    mflo d`
`    sra d,d,31`
`    mfhi at`
`    beq d,at,1f`
`    nop`
`    break 6`
`1:`
`    mflo d`
	`/* 32-bit multiply with overflow check */`
	`lo = (signed)s * (signed)t;`
	`if ((s ≥ 0 && hi != 0) || (s < 0) && hi != -1)`
	`    exception(BREAK, 6);`

`mulou d,s,t →`
`    multu s,t`
`    mfhi at`
`    mflo d`
`    beq at,$zero,1f`
`    nop`
`    break 6`
	`/* 32-bit unsigned multiply with overflow check */`
	`hilo = (unsigned)s * (unsigned)t;`
	`if (hi != 0)`
	`    exception(BREAK, 6);`

`mult s,t`	`hilo = (signed)s * (signed)t;`
`multu s,t`	`hilo = (unsigned)s * (unsigned)t;`

TABLE 8.2 *continued*

Assembler/machine code	Description
neg *d,s* → **sub** *d,*$zero*,s*	`d = -s; /* trap on overflow, rare */`
negu *d,s* → **subu** *d,*$zero*,s*	`d = -s;`
nop → **sll** $zero*,*$zero*,*$zero	`/* no-op, instruction code == 0 */`
nor *d,s,t*	`d = ~(s | t);`
not *d,s* → **nor** *d,s,*$zero	`d = ~s;`
or *d,s,t*	`d = s	t;`
or *d,s,j* → **ori** *d,s,j* **ori** *t,r,j*	`d = s	(unsigned) j;`
pref *hint,addr* **prefx** *hint,t(b)*	Prefetch instruction, for memory reference optimization (MIPS IV and later). The cache line that contains the addressed item might be prefetched into the cache while the CPU keeps running. No side effects (other than the possible load into the cache) will occur. Implementations are entitled to treat this as a no-op—the R5000 does, for example. *hint* says something to the hardware about how the data will be used; see Section 8.4.8. The two versions use ordinary base+offset or register+register indexed addressing.
r2u *s*	LSI ATMizer-II only; converts to strange floating-point format. Result appears in **lo**.
radd *s,t*	LSI ATMizer-II only; strange floating-point add. Result appears in **lo**.

continued

TABLE 8.2 *continued*

Assembler/machine code	Description

rem *d,s,t* →
   bnez *t*,1f
   div $zero,*s,t*
   break 0x7
 1:
   li at,-1
   bne *t*,at,2f
   lui at,32768
   bne *s*,at,2f
   nop
   break 0x6
 2:
   mfhi *d*
	`/* 32-bit remainder with overflow check */`
	 `lo = s / t;`
	 `hi = s % t;`
	 `if (t == 0) exception(BREAK, 7);`
	 `if (t == -1 && s == MAXNEG32BIT)`
	 `   exception(BREAK, 6); /* result overflows */`
	 `d = hi;`

remu *d,s,t* →
   bnez *t*,1f
   divu $zero,*s,t*
   break 0x7
 1:
   mfhi *d*
	`/* as above, only divide-by-zero check */`

rfe	Restore CPU state when returning from exception—MIPS I only. Pops the interrupt-enable/kernel-state stack inside the status register **SR**. Can only be sensibly used in the delay slot of a **jr** instruction that is returning from the exception handler. See Section 3.1 and Section 3.3.2.
rmul *s,t*	LSI ATMizer-II only; strange floating-point multiply. Result appears in **lo**.

rol *d,s,t* →
   negu at,*t*
   srlv at,*s*,at
   sllv *d,s,t*
   or *d,d*,at
	`/* d = s rotated left by t */`

ror *d,s,t* → negu at,*t* sllv at,*s*,at srlv *d,s,t* or *d,d*,at	`/* d = s rotated right by t */`
rsub *s,t*	LSI ATMizer-II only; strange floating-point multiply. Result appears in **lo**.

TABLE 8.2 *continued*

Assembler/machine code	Description
sb *t,addr*	`*((char *)addr) = t;`
sc *t,addr* **scd** *t,addr*	Store word/double conditional; explained in Section 8.4.2.
sd *t,addr*	`*((long long *)addr) = t;`
sdbbp *c*	Extra breakpoint. LSI MiniRISC only.
sdc1 *ft,addr*	Store floating-point double register to memory; more often called **s.d**. **sdc0** and **sdc2** (store 64-bit coprocessor register) are defined but have never been implemented.
sdl *t,addr* **sdr** *t,addr*	Store double left/right; see Section 2.5.2 for an explanation.
sdxc1 *fs,t(b)*	`/* indexed FP store double (both t and b are registers), usually written s.d */` `*((double *)(t+b)) = fs;`
selsl *d,s,t*	`/* LSI MiniRISC instruction.  Combine and shift.` `Uses ROTATE register (CP0 register 23), of which` `only bits 4:0 are used.   */` `long long dbw;` `dbw = ((long long) s << 32	t);` `d = (((long long) 0xffffffff & (dbw << ROTATE))` `>> 32);`
selsr *d,s,t*	`/* as above, but shifting right */` `long long dbw;` `dbw = ((long long) s << 32	t);` `d = (unsigned) 0xffffffff & (dbw >> ROTATE);`

seq *d,s,t* →
  xor *d,s,t*
  sltiu *d,d,*1
	`d = (s == t) ? 1 :  0;`

sge *d,s,t* →
  slt *d,s,t*
  xori *d,d,*1
	`d = ((signed)s ≥ (signed)t) ? 1 :  0;`

sgeu *d,s,t* →
  sltu *d,s,t*
  xori *d,d,*1
	`d = ((unsigned)s ≥ (unsigned)t) ? 1 :  0;`

continued

TABLE 8.2 *continued*

Assembler/machine code	Description
sgt *d,s,t* → **slt** *d,t,s*	d = ((signed)s > (signed)t) ? 1 : 0;
sgtu *d,s,t* → **sltu** *d,t,s*	d = ((unsigned)s > (unsigned)t) ? 1 : 0;
sh *t,addr*	/* store halfword */ *((short *)addr) = t;

sle *d,s,t* →
  slt *d,t,s*
  xori *d,d,1*
	d = ((signed)s ≤ (signed)t) ? 1 : 0;

sleu *d,s,t* →
  sltu *d,t,s*
  xori *d,d,1*
	d = ((unsigned)s ≤ (unsigned)t) ? 1 : 0;

sll *d,s,shft*	d = s << shft; /* 0 ≤ shft < 32 */
sll *d,t,s* → **sllv** *d,t,s* **sllv** *d,t,s*	d = t << (s % 32);
slt *d,s,t*	d = ((signed) s < (signed) t) ? 1 : 0;
slt *d,s,j* → **slti** *d,s,j* **slti** *d,s,j*	/* j constant */ d = ((signed) s < (signed) j) ? 1 : 0;
sltiu *d,s,j*	/* j constant */ d = ((unsigned) s < (unsigned) j) ? 1 : 0;
sltu *d,s,t*	d = ((unsigned) s < (unsigned) t) ? 1 : 0;
sne *d,s,t* → **sltu** *d,$zero,d*	d = (s == t) ? 1 : 0;
sra *d,s,shft*	/* 0 ≤ shft < 31 */ /* algebraic shifting, which replicates old bit 31 into top bits, producing a correct division by power of 2 for negative numbers */ d = (signed) s >> shft;
sra *d,s,t* → **srav** *d,s,t* **srav** *d,s,t*	d = (signed) s >> (t%32)

TABLE 8.2 *continued*

Assembler/machine code	Description
srl *d,s,shft*	d = (unsigned) s >> shft; /* 0 ≤ shft < 32 */
srl *d,s,t* → **slrv** *d,s,t* **srlv** *d,s,t*	d = (unsigned) s >> (t % 32);
standby	Enter one of the power-down modes. NEC Vr4100 CPU only.
sub *d,s,t*	d = s - t; /* trap on overflow, little used */
subu *d,s,j* → **addiu** *d,s,-j*	d = s - j;
subu *d,s,t*	d = s - t;
suspend	Enter one of the power-down modes. NEC Vr4100 CPU only.
sw *t,addr*	/* store word */ *((int *)addr) = t;
swc1 *ft,addr*	Floating-point store single; more often written **s.s**. The instruction set defines **swc0** and **swc2** for coprocessor 0 and 2 registers, but neither have ever been implemented.
swl *t,addr* **swr** *t,addr*	Store word left/right; see Section 2.5.2.
swxc1 *fs,t(b)*	/* store floating-point single; indexed (two-register) addressing; usually written with **s.s** */ *((float *)(t + b)) = fs;
sync	Load/store barrier for multiprocessors; see Section 8.4.9.
syscall *B*	/* system call exception */ exception(SYSCALL, B);
teq *s,t*	/* conditional trap instructions, which generate a trap exception if the appropriate condition is satisfied; this one is...*/ if (s == t) exception(TRAP);
teqi *s,j*	if (s == j) exception(TRAP);
tge *s,t*	if ((signed) s ≥ (signed) t) exception(TRAP);
tgei *s,j*	if ((signed) s ≥ (signed) j) exception(TRAP);

continued

TABLE 8.2 *continued*

Assembler/machine code	Description
tgeiu *s,j*	if ((unsigned) s $\geq$ (unsigned) j) exception(TRAP);
tgeu *s,t*	if ((unsigned) s $\geq$ (unsigned) t) exception(TRAP);
tlbp	TLB maintenance; see Chapter 6. If the virtual page number currently in **EntryLo** matches a TLB entry, sets **Index** to that entry. Otherwise sets **Index** to the illegal value 0x8000.0000 (top bit set).
tlbr	TLB maintenance; see Chapter 6. Copies information from the TLB entry selected by **Index** into the registers **EntryLo**, **EntryHi1** and **EntryHi0**, and **PageMask**.
tlbwi **tlbwr**	TLB maintenance; see Chapter 6. Writes the TLB entry selected by **Index** (instruction **tlbwi**) or **Random** (instruction **tlbwr**), respectively, using data from **EntryLo**, **EntryHi1** and **EntryHi0**, and **PageMask**.
tlt *s,t*	/* more conditional traps */ if ((signed) s < (signed) t) exception(TRAP);
tlti *s,j*	if ((signed) s < (signed) j) exception(TRAP);
tltiu *s,j*	if ((unsigned) s < (unsigned) j) exception(TRAP);
tltu *s,t*	if ((unsigned) s < (unsigned) t) exception(TRAP);
tne *s,t*	if (t != s) exception(TRAP);
tnei *s,j*	if (t != j) exception(TRAP);
u2r *s*	LSI ATMizer-II only; converts unsigned to strange floating point. Result appears in **lo**.
uld *d,addr* → **ldl** *d,addr* **ldr** *d,addr*+7	Unaligned load double, synthesized from load-left and load-right as detailed in Section 2.5.2 (shown for big-endian only).
ulh *d,addr* → **lb** *d,addr* **lbu** at,*addr*+1 **sll** *d,d*,8 **or** *d,d*,at	Unaligned load halfword and sign-extend. Expansion may be more complex, depending on addressing mode.

TABLE 8.2 *continued*

Assembler/machine code	Description

`ulhu d,addr →`
  `lbu d,addr`
  `lbu at,addr+1`
  `sll d,d,8`
  `or d,d,at`
	Unaligned load halfword and zero-extend.

`ulw d,addr →`
  `lwl d,addr`
  `lwr d,addr+3`
	Load word unaligned; sign-extend if 64 bits (shown for big-endian only). See Section 2.5.2.

`usd d,addr →`
  `sdl d,addr`
  `sdr d,addr+7`
	Unaligned store double.

`ush addr →`
  `sb d,addr+1`
  `srl d,d,8`
  `sb d,addr`
	Unaligned store half.

`usw s,addr →`
  `swl s,addr`
  `swr s,addr+3`
	Store word unaligned; see Section 2.5.2.

`waiti`	Suspend execution until an interrupt is activated. LSI MiniRISC only.
`wb addr`	Write back the eight-word cache line containing this address if it's dirty. LSI MiniRISC only. On R4000 and similar CPUs this would be done with a `cache` instruction.
`xor d,s,t`	`d = s^t;`

`xor d,s,j →`
  `xori d,s,j`
`xori d,s,j`
	`d = s ^ j;`

8.3   Floating-Point Instructions

There's a relatively small and sensible set of MIPS floating-point instructions (see Tables 8.3 and 8.4 on pages 202 and 203), but they quickly develop their own complications. Note the following points:

- Pretty much every FP instruction comes in a single-precision version and a double-precision version, distinguished by `.s` or `.d` in the mne-

TABLE 8.3 Floating-point register and identifier conventions

Word	Used for
fs, **ft**	Floating-point register operands.
fd	Floating-point register which receives the result.
fdhi **fdlo**	Pair of adjacent FP registers in a 32-bit processor, used together to store an FP double. Use of the high-order (odd-numbered) register is implicit in normal arithmetic instructions.
M	The floating-point condition bit found in the FP control/status register and tested by the **bc1f** and **bc0t** instructions. There's been evolution here; the MIPS I through III ISAs have 1 condition bit but MIPS IV has 8. An instruction that omits to specify which condition bit to use will quietly use the original one.

monic. Table 8.4 only lists single-precision versions, so long as the double-precision version requires no special extra description.

■ The FP instruction set has evolved much more than the integer instruction set ever did (at user level, the integer instruction set has been remarkably stable), so it's more important to keep clear what version is what.

■ FP computational and type conversion instructions can cause exceptions. This is true both in the IEEE sense, where they detect conditions that a programmer may be interested in, and in a low-level architecture sense: MIPS FP hardware, if faced with a combination of operands and an operation it can't do correctly, will take an unimplemented exception with the aim of getting a software routine to carry out the FP operation for it.

Data movement instructions (loads, stores, and moves between registers) don't ever cause exceptions. Neither do the **neg.s**, **neg.d**, **abs.s**, or **abs.d** instructions (which just flip the sign bit without inspecting the contents).

8.4 Peculiar Instructions and Their Purposes

MIPS has never avoided innovation, and the instruction set contains features whose ingenuity might go unheeded (and unused) because they are hard to understand and have not been well explained. This section discusses those features.

TABLE 8.4 Floating-point instruction descriptions in mnemonic order

Assembler code	ISA number	Function
abs.s *fd*, *fs*	I	`fd = (fs < 0) ? -fs`
add.s *fd*, *fs*, *ft*	I	`fd = fs + ft;`
bc1f *label* **bc1t** *label*	I	Several branch on FP condition instructions, all found in Table 8.2.
c.eq.s *M*, *fs*, *ft* **c.f.s** *M*, *fs*, *ft* **c.le.s** *M*, *fs*, *ft* **c.lt.s** *M*, *fs*, *ft* **c.nge.s** *M*, *fs*, *ft* **c.ngl.s** *M*, *fs*, *ft* **c.ngt.s** *M*, *fs*, *ft* **c.ole.s** *M*, *fs*, *ft* **c.olt.s** *M*, *fs*, *ft* **c.seq.s** *M*, *fs*, *ft* **c.sf.s** *M*, *fs*, *ft* **c.ueq.s** *M*, *fs*, *ft* **c.ule.s** *M*, *fs*, *ft* **c.ult.s** *M*, *fs*, *ft* **c.un.s** *M*, *fs*, *ft*	I	FP compare instructions, which compare fs and ft and store a result in FP condition bit M. They are described at length in Section 7.9.7.
ceil.l.d *fd*, *fs* **ceil.l.s** *fd*, *fs*	III	Convert FP to equal or next-higher signed 64-bit integer value.
ceil.w.d *fd*, *fs* **ceil.w.s** *fd*, *fs*	II	Convert FP to equal or next-higher signed 32-bit integer value.
cvt.d.l *fd*, *fs*	III	Floating-point type conversions, where the types **d**, **l**, **s**, and **w** (double, long long, float, and int, respectively) are the destination and source type in that order.
cvt.d.s *fd*, *fs* **cvt.d.w** *fd*, *fs*	I	Where the conversion is losing precision, the rounding mode currently defined by the field **FCR31(RM)** in the floating-point status register is used to determine how the approximation is done. For integer conversions where the desired approximation is specific to the algorithm, you're better off writing instructions like **floor.w.s** and so on; however these will just be assembler macros for MIPS I machines, since the specific conversion instructions were only introduced with MIPS II.
cvt.l.d *fd*, *fs* **cvt.l.s** *fd*, *fs*	III	
cvt.s.d *fd*, *fs*	I	
cvt.s.l *fd*, *fs*	III	
cvt.s.w *fd*, *fs* **cvt.w.d** *fd*, *fs* **cvt.w.s** *fd*, *fs*	I	
div.s *fd*, *fs*, *ft*	I	`fd = fs/ft;`
dmfc1 *rs*, *fd*	III	Move 64-bit value from floating point (coprocessor 1) to integer register with no conversion.

continued

TABLE 8.4 *continued*

Assembler code	ISA number	Function
`dmtc1 rs,fd`	III	Move 64-bit value from integer to floating point (coprocessor 1) register with no conversion or validity check.
`floor.1.d fd,fs` `floor.1.s fd,fs`	III	Convert FP to equal or next-lower 64-bit integer value.
`floor.w.d fd,fs` `floor.w.s fd,fs`	II	Convert FP to equal or next-lower 32-bit integer value.
`l.d fd,addr →` `ldc1 fd,addr`	II	`/* load FP double, must be 8 byte aligned */` `fd = *((double *)(o+b));`

`l.d fd,addr →`
  `lwc1 fdhi,addr`
  `lwc1 fdlo,addr+4`
	I	`/* load FP double into register pair; note`
		`that the expansion (which half goes at what`
		`address) depends on CPU endianness */`
		`fd = *((double *) addr);`

`l.s fd,addr →` `lwc1 fd,addr`	I	`/* load FP single, must be 4 byte aligned */` `fd = *((float *)(o+b));`
`ldc1 fd, disp(rs)`	III	Deprecated equivalent of `l.d`.
`ldxc1 fd, ri(rs)`	IV	Explicit machine instruction for double-indexed load; preferred to use `l.d` with the appropriate address mode.
`li.s fd,const` `li.d fd,const`	I	Load floating-point constant, synthesized by placing the constant in a memory location and loading it.
`lwc1 fd, disp(rs)`	III	Deprecated equivalent of `l.s`.
`lwxc1 fd, ri(rs)`	IV	Explicit double-indexed load instruction; usually better to use `l.s` with the appropriate address mode.
`madd.s fd,fr,fs,ft`	IV	`fd = fr + fs*ft;`
`mfc1 rs,fd`	I	Move 32-bit value from floating point (coprocessor 1) to integer register with no conversion.
`mov.s fd,fs`	IV	`fd = fs;`
`movf.s fd,fs,N`	IV	`if (!fpcondition(N)) fd = fs;`
`movn.s fd,fs,t`	IV	`if (t != 0) fd = fs; /* t is a GPR */`
`movt.s fd,fs,N`	IV	`if (fpcondition(N)) fd = fs;`
`movz.s fd,fs,t`	IV	`if (t == 0) fd = fs; /* t is a GPR */`
`msub.s fd,fr,fs,ft`	IV	`nfd = fs*ft - fr;`

TABLE 8.4 *continued*

Assembler code	ISA number	Function
`mtc1 rs,fd`	I	Move 32-bit value from integer to floating point (coprocessor 1) register with no conversion or validity check.
`mul.s fd,fs,ft`	I	`fd = fs*ft;`
`neg.s fd,fs`	I	`fd = -fs;`
`nmadd.s fd,fr,fs,ft`	IV	`nfd = -(fs*ft + fr);`
`nmsub.s fd,fr,fs,ft`	IV	`nfd = fr - fs*ft;`
`recip.s fd,fs`	IV	`fd = 1/fs; /* fast but not IEEE accurate */`
`round.l.d fd,fs` `round.l.s fd,fs`	III	Convert FP to equal or closest 64-bit integer value.
`round.w.d fd,fs` `round.w.s fd,fs`	II	Convert FP to equal or closest 32-bit integer value.
`rsqrt.s fd,fs`	IV	`/* fast but not IEEE accurate */ fd = sqrt(1/fs);`
`s.d ft,addr →` 　`sdc1 ft,addr`	III	`/* FP store double; address must be 8 byte aligned ʌ/`

`s.d ft,addr →`
　`swc1 fthi,addr`
　`swc1 ftlo,addr+4`
	I	`*((double *)addr) = ft;`
		`/* synthesized for 32-bit CPUs */`

`s.s ft,addr →` 　`swc1 ft,addr`	I	`/* FP store single; address must be 4 byte aligned */` `*((float *)addr) = ft;`
`sdc1 fd, disp(rs)`	III	Deprecated equivalent to **s.d**.
`sdxc1 fd, ri(rs)`	IV	Explicit double-indexed store double; usually better to write **s.d** with an appropriate addressing mode.
`sqrt.s fd,fs`	III	`fd = sqrt(fs); /* IEEE compliant */`
`sub.s fd,fs,ft`	I	`fd = fs - ft;`
`swc1 fd, disp(rs)`	III	Deprecated equivalent to **s.s**.
`swxc1 fd, ri(rs)`	IV	Explicit double-indexed store of 32-bit FP value; usually better to write **s.s** with an appropriate addressing mode.
`trunc.l.d fd,fs` `trunc.l.s fd,fs`	III	Convert FP to equal or next-nearest-to-zero 64-bit integer value.
`trunc.w.d fd,fs` `trunc.w.s fd,fs`	II	Convert FP to equal or next-nearest-to-zero 32-bit integer value.

8.4.1 *Load Left/Load Right: Unaligned Load and Store*

Any CPU is going to be more efficient if frequently used data as arranged in memory is aligned on memory boundaries that fit the hardware. For a machine with a 32-bit bus, this favors 32-bit data items that are stored on an aligned 32-bit boundary; similarly, a 64-bit bus favors 64-bit data items stored on an aligned 64-bit boundary.

If a CPU must fetch or store unaligned data, it will need two bus cycles. RISC pipeline simplicity will not let the CPU perform two bus cycles for one instruction, so an unaligned transfer will take at least two instructions.

The ultimate RISC attitude is that we've got byte-sized operations and that any unaligned operation you like can be built out of those. If a piece of data (formatted as a 4- or 8-byte integer value) might be unaligned, the programmer/compiler can always read it as a sequence of byte values and then use shift/mask operations to build it up in a register. The sequence for a word-sized load looks something like this (assuming a big-endian CPU, and without optimizing for the load delay in the CPU pipeline):

```
lbu     rt,o(b)
sll     rt,rt,24
lbu     rtmp,o+1(b)
sll     rtmp,rtmp,16
or      rt,rt,rtmp
lbu     rtmp,o+2(b)
sll     rtmp,rtmp,8
or      rt,rt,rtmp
lbu     rtmp,o+3(b)
or      rt,rt,rtmp
```

That's 10 instructions, four loads, and needs a temporary register and is likely to be quite a performance hit if you do it a lot. The MIPS solution to this is a pair of instructions, each of which can obtain as much of the unaligned word as fits into an aligned word-sized chunk of memory.

The instructions that MIPS invented are used to perform a relatively efficient unaligned load/store (word or double size) operation and were mentioned in Section 2.5.2.

The hardware that accesses the memory (or cache) transfers 4 or 8 bytes of aligned data. Partial-word stores are implemented either by a hardware signal that instructs the memory controller to leave certain bytes unchanged or by a read-modify-write (RMW) sequence on the entire word/doubleword. MIPS CPUs mostly have RMW hardware available for writes to the data cache, but don't do that for memory—the memory controller must implement partial-word writes for itself.

We said that there need to be two instructions, because there are two bus cycles. The instructions are called load word left and load word right (mnemonics **lwl** and **lwr**) for 32-bit operations; they are called load double left and load double right (**ldl** and **ldr**) for 64-bit operations. The "left" instruction deals with the high-order bits of the unaligned integer, and the "right" instruction fetches the low-order bits, so "left" is used in the same sense as in "shift left." Because the instructions are defined in terms of more-significant and less-significant bits but must deal with a byte-addressed memory, their detailed use depends on the endianness of the CPU (see Section 11.6). A big-endian CPU keeps more-significant bits earlier, in lower byte addresses, and a little-endian CPU keeps more-significant bits later, in higher addresses.

Figure 8.1 is an attempt to show what's happening for a big-endian CPU when the unaligned pseudo-operation **uld** *rd*, **0(***rb***)** is coded as

```
ldl     rd, 0(rb)
ldr     rd, 7(rb)
```

What's going on in Figure 8.1?

- **ldl** *rd*, **0(***rb***)**: The 0 offset marks the lowest byte of the unaligned doubleword, and since we're big-endian that's the 8 most-significant bits. **ldl** is looking for bits to load into the left (most-significant bits) of the register, so it takes the addressed byte and then the ones after it in memory to the end of the word. They're going up in memory address, so they're going down in significance; they want to be butted up against the high-numbered end of the register as shown.

- **ldr** *rd*, **7(***rb***)**: The 7 is a bit odd, but it points at the highest byte of the doubleword—*rb*+8 would point at the first byte of the next doubleword, of course. **ldl** is concerned with the rightmost, least-significant bits; it takes the remaining bytes of our original data and butts them against the low-numbered bits of the register, and the job's done.

If you're skeptical about whether this works for words in any alignment, go ahead and try it. Note that in the case where the address is in fact correctly aligned (so the data could have been loaded with a conventional **ld** instruction), **uld** loads the same data twice; this is not particularly interesting but usually harmless.

The situation can get more confusing for people who are used to little-endian integer ordering because little-endians often write data structures with the least-significant bits to the left. Once you've done that, the "left" in the instruction name becomes "right" on the picture (though it's still movement toward more-significant bits). On a little-endian CPU the roles of **ldl/ldr**

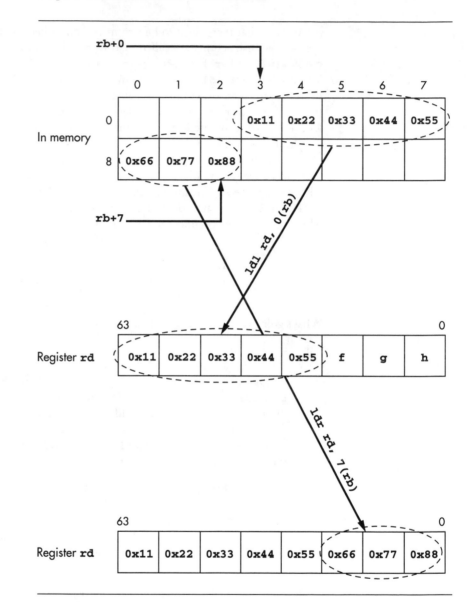

FIGURE 8.1 Unaligned load double on a big-endian CPU

are exchanged, and the code sequence is

```
ldr     rd, 0(rb)
ldl     rd, 7(rb)
```

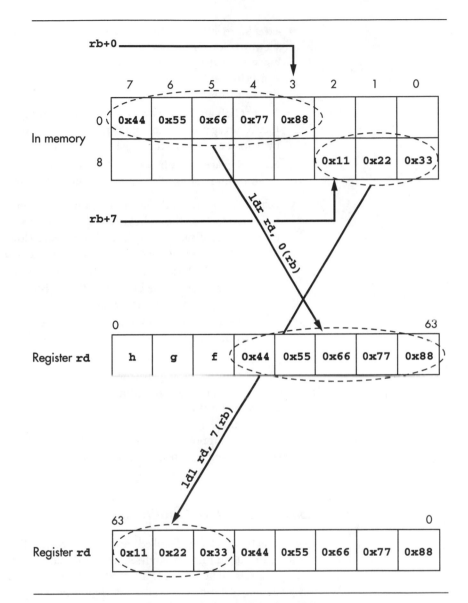

FIGURE 8.2 Unaligned load double on a little-endian CPU

Figure 8.2 shows you what happens: The most significant bits are reluc-
tantly kept on the left, so it's the mirror image of the diagram I'd "naturally"
have drawn.

With these figures in front of us, we can try to formulate an exact description of what the instructions do:

■ *Load/store left*: Find the addressed byte and enclosing word (or doubleword, for 64-bit operations). Operate on the addressed byte and
any more bytes between it and the least-significant end of that memory
word (higher byte addresses for big-endian and lower byte addresses for
little-endian).

Load: Grab all those bytes and shift them to higher bit numbers until
they're up against the top of the register. Leave any lower-bit-numbered
byte positions within the register unchanged.

Store: Replace those bytes with as many bytes of the register as there's
room from, starting at the most-significant byte in the register.

■ *Load/store right*: Find the addressed byte and enclosing word/double-
word. Operate on the addressed byte and any more bytes between it and
the most-significant end of that memory word (lower byte addresses for
big-endian and higher byte addresses for little-endian).

Load: Grab all those bytes and shift them to lower bit numbers until
they're down against the bottom of the register. Leave any higher-bit-
numbered byte positions within the register unchanged.

Store: Replace those bytes with as many bytes of the register as there's
room from, starting with the least-significant byte in the register.

The load/store left/right instructions do not require the memory controller
to offer selective operations on arbitrary groups of bytes within a word; the
active byte lanes are always together at one end of a word or doubleword.

Note that these instructions do not perform all possible realignments;
there's no special support for unaligned load half (which has to be implemented
with byte loads, shifts, masks, and combines).

8.4.2 *Load-Linked/Store-Conditional*

The instructions **ll** (load-linked) and **sc** (store-conditional) provide an alternative to the atomic test-and-set sequence that is part of most traditional
instruction sets. They provide a test-and-set sequence that operates without
any guarantee of atomicity but that succeeds (and tells you it's succeeded) only
if it turned out to be atomic. See Section 5.8.4 for what they're for and how
they're used.

Here's how they work. The instruction **ll rt, o(b)** performs a 32-bit
load from the usual base+offset address. But as a side effect it remembers that
a load-link has happened (setting an otherwise-invisible linked status bit inside
the CPU). It also keeps the address of the load in the register **LLAddr**.

A subsequent **sc rt, o(b)** first checks whether it can be sure that the
read-modify-write sequence that began with the last-executed **ll** will complete
atomically. If it can be sure, then the value of **rt** is stored into the location and

the "true" value 1 is returned in **rt**. If it can't be sure that the operation was atomic, no store happens and **rt** is set 0.

CAUTION!   The test for atomicity is unlikely to be exhaustive. The instruction is not defined to fail only if the memory location really has been changed by another CPU or task but to fail if it might have been.

There are two reasons why **sc** could fail. The first is that the CPU took an exception somewhere between executing the **ll** and the **sc**. Its exception handler, or a task switch triggered by the exception, might have done something non-atomic.

The second type of failure happens only in a multiprocessor, when another CPU has written the memory location or one near it (commonly in the same line, but some implementations may monitor the whole memory translation page). For efficiency reasons this detector is only enabled when both participating CPUs have agreed to map this data as a shared area—strictly, if the other CPU has completed a coherent store to the sensitive block.

Let's emphasize again: The failure of the **sc** is *not* evidence that some other task or CPU has in fact written the variable; implementations are encouraged to trade off a fair number of false warnings against simplicity or performance.

Multiprocessor CPUs must keep track of the address used by the last **ll**, and they keep it in the coprocessor 0 register **LLAddr** where software can read and write it. But the only reasons to read and write this register are diagnostic; on a CPU without multiprocessor features it is redundant. You're recommended not to rely on its existence.

Note that this is the only part of the MIPS III specification that has been regarded as optional by one chip vendor: NEC omitted **ll/sc** instructions from its core Vr4100 CPU, probably unaware that uniprocessors can benefit from these instructions too.

8.4.3   *Conditional Move Instructions*

A conditional move instruction copies data from one register to another, but only if some condition is satisfied—otherwise it does nothing. They were featured in other RISC architectures (ARM may have been first) before making a MIPS debut with the MIPS IV instruction set (first implemented in the R8000, R10000, and R5000 in 1995–96). Conditional moves allow compilers to generate code with fewer conditional branches because conditional branches are bad for pipeline efficiency.

CPUs built with the simple five-stage pipeline described in Chapter 1 don't have much trouble with branches; the branch delay slot instruction is usually executed, and the CPU then moves straight to the branch target. With these simple CPUs, most branches are free (provided the branch delay slot contains a useful instruction) and the others cost only one clock cycle.

But more extravagant implementations of the MIPS ISA may lose many instruction-execution opportunities while waiting for the branch condition to be resolved and the target instruction to be fetched. The long-pipeline R4400, for example, always pays a two-clock-cycle penalty on every taken branch. In the highly superscalar R10000 (which can issue four instructions per clock cycle) you might lose seven instruction issue opportunities waiting for the branch condition to be resolved. To reduce the effect of this the R10000 has special branch prediction circuits that guess the branch outcome and run ahead accordingly, while keeping the ability to back off from those speculative instructions. This is quite complicated: If the compiler can reduce the frequency with which it relies on the complicated features, it will run faster.

How do conditional move instructions get rid of branches? Consider a piece of code generating the minimum of two values:

```
n = (a < b) ? a: b;
```

Assuming that the compiler has managed to get all the variables into registers, this would normally compile to a sequence like the following (this is logical assembler language sequence, before making pipeline adjustments for delay slots):

```
    slt t0, a, b
    move n, a
    bne $0, t0, 1f
    move n, b
1:
```

On a MIPS IV CPU we can replace this with

```
    slt t0, a, b
    addu n, a, $0
    movz n, b, t0
```

Although the conditional move instruction **movz** looks strange, its role in the pipeline is exactly like any other register/register computational instruction. A branch has been removed and our highly pipelined CPU will go faster.

8.4.4 *Branch-Likely*

Another pipeline optimization, this one introduced with MIPS II, is branch-likely.

Compilers are generally reasonably successful in filling branch delay slots, but they have the hardest time at the end of small loops. Such loop-closing branches are the most frequently executed, so **nop**s in their delay slots are significant; however, the loop body is often full of dependent code that can't be reorganized.

The branch-likely instruction nullifies the branch delay slot instruction when the branch is not taken. An instruction is nullified by preventing its write-back stage from happening—and in MIPS that's as if the instruction had never been executed. By executing the delay slot instruction only when the branch is taken, the delay slot instruction becomes part of the next go around the loop.

So any loop

```
loop:
    first
    second
    ...
    blez t0, loop
    nop
```

can be transformed to

```
loop:
    first
loop2:
    second
    ...
    blezl t0, loop2
    first
```

This means we can fill the branch delay slot on loops almost all the time, greatly reducing the number of **nop**s actually executed.

You'll see it implied in some manufacturers' documentation that branch-likely instructions, by eliminating **nop**s, make programs smaller; this is a misunderstanding. You can see from the example that the **nop** is typically replaced by a duplicated instruction, so there's no gain in program size. The gain is in speed.

8.4.5 Integer Multiply-Accumulate and Multiply-Add Instructions

Many multimedia algorithms include calculations that are basically a sum of products. In the inner loops of something like a JPEG image decoder, the calculation is intensive enough to keep the CPU's arithmetic units fully utilized.

The calculations break down into a series of multiply-accumulate operations, each of which looks like this:

```
a = a + b*c;
```

Although the RISC principles described in Chapter 1 would appear to imply that it is better to build this calculation out of simple, separate functions, this is probably a genuine exception to that rule. It's probably because multiply is a multiple-clock-cycle operation, leaving a simple RISC with the problem of scheduling the subsequent (quick) add: If you attempt the add too early, the machine stalls; if you leave it until too late, you don't keep the critical arithmetic units busy. In a floating-point unit, there's an additional advantage in that some housekeeping associated with every instruction can be shared between the multiply and add stages.

Such operations have been added as vendor-specific extensions by a number of different manufacturers in a number of different implementations. But there's a subset of compatible operations to be found on IDT, Toshiba, and QED CPUs. They operate in the independently clocked integer multiply unit and so are all multiply-accumulate operations,[1] accumulating in the multiply unit output registers **lo** and **hi**. Confusingly, all vendors have called their instructions **mad** or **madd**, though they should have been called "mac."

8.4.6 *Floating-Point Multiply-Add Instructions*

All the arguments above apply to floating-point calculations too, though the critical applications here are 3D graphics transformations. In a floating-point unit, there's an additional advantage to a dual operation, in that some housekeeping associated with every instruction can be shared between the multiply and add stages.

There's no gainsaying actual benchmark performance, and the multiply-add at the heart of most PowerPC floating-point units has certainly produced some very impressive figures.

The floating-point operations **madd**, **msub**, **nmadd**, and **nmsub** got included in the MIPS IV instruction set. These are genuine four-operand multiply-add instructions, performing operations such as

```
a = b + c*d;
```

They're aimed at large graphic/numeric-intensive applications on SGI workstations and heavyweight numerical processing in SGI's range of supercomputers.

---

1. Toshiba's R3900 and some other CPUs have a three-operand multiply-add but even there the addend is constrained to come from **lo/hi**. The IDT and QED CPUs offer a two-operand instruction that is identical to Toshiba's in the special case where the destination register is **$0**.

8.4.7 *Multiple FP Condition Bits*

Prior to MIPS IV, all tests on floating-point numbers communicated with the main instruction set through a single condition bit, which was set explicitly by compare instructions and tested explicitly by special conditional branch instructions. The architecture grew like this because in the early days the floating-point unit was a separate chip, and the FP condition bit was implemented with a signal wire that passed into the main CPU.

The trouble with the single bit is that it creates dependencies that reduce the potential for launching multiple instructions in parallel. There is an unavoidable write-to-read dependency between the compare instruction that creates a condition and the branch instruction that tests it, while there's an avoidable read-to-write interaction where a subsequent compare instruction must be delayed until the branch has seen and acted on its previous value.

FP array calculations benefit from a compilation technique called *software pipelining*, where a loop is unrolled and the computations of successive loop iterations are deliberately interleaved to make maximum use of multiple FP units. But if something in the loop body requires a test and branch, the single condition unit will make this impossible, hence multiple conditions can make a big difference.

MIPS IV provides 8 bits, not just 1; previously reserved fields in compare and FP conditional branch instructions have been found that can specify which condition bit should be used. Older compilers set reserved fields to zero, so old code will run correctly using just condition code zero.

8.4.8 *Prefetch*

New in MIPS IV, **pref** provides a way for a program to signal the cache/memory system that data is going to be needed soon. Implementations that take advantage of this can prefetch the data into a cache. It's not really clear how many applications can foresee what references are likely to cause cache misses; prefetch is useful for large-array arithmetic functions, however, where chunks of data can be prefetched in one loop iteration so as to be ready for the next go-around.

The first argument to **pref** is a small-integer coded "hint" about how the program intends to use the data. Legal values are as shown in Table 8.5.

Some newer CPUs (R10000) implement a nonblocking load in which execution continues after a load cache miss, just so long as the load target register is not referenced. However, the **pref** instruction is better applied to longer-range prediction of memory accesses.

MIPS IV CPUs are free to ignore **pref** but of course must not take an illegal op-code trap; CPUs that aren't interested treat it as a **nop**.

TABLE 8.5 Prefetch "hint" codes

Value	MIPS name	What it means
0	load	We don't expect to write this location.
1	store	Probably will be written.
2–3	—	Reserved.
4	load_streamed	Part of a memory area that will be accessed sequentially. It would be reasonable to allow prefetched locations to overwrite each other in succession.
5	store_streamed	
6	load_retained	A location that is expected to be used heavily for quite a while, which may be worth avoiding replacing in the cache: In particular, it would not be sensible to replace it with data marked "streamed."
7	store_retained	
8–31	—	Reserved.

8.4.9 *Sync: A Load/Store Barrier*

Suppose we have a program that consists of a number of cooperating sequential tasks, each running on a different processor and sharing memory. We're probably talking about a multiprocessor using sophisticated cache coherency algorithms, but the cache management is not relevant right now.

Any task's robust shared memory algorithm will be dependent on when shared data is accessed by other tasks: Did they read that data before I changed it? Have they changed it yet?

Since each task is strictly sequential, why is this a problem? It turns out that the problem occurs because CPU tuning features often interfere with the logical sequence of memory operations; by definition this interference must be invisible to the program itself, but it will show up when viewed from outside. There can be good reasons for breaking natural sequence. For optimum memory performance, reads—where the CPU is stalled waiting for data—should overtake pending writes. As long as the CPU stores both the address and data on a write, it may defer the write for a while. If a CPU does that, it had better check that the overtaking read is not for a location for which a write is pending; that can be done.

Another example is when a CPU that implements nonblocking loads ends up with two reads active simultaneously: For best performance the memory system should be allowed to choose which one to complete first.

CPUs that allow neither of these changes of sequence, performing all reads and writes in program order, are called *strongly ordered*. Most MIPS CPUs, when configured as uniprocessors, are strongly ordered. But there are exceptions: Even some early R3000 systems would allow reads to overtake pending writes (after checking that the read was not for any pending-write location).

On a MIPS III or subsequent CPU that is not strongly ordered, a **sync** instruction defines a load/store barrier. You are guaranteed that all load/stores initiated before the **sync** will be seen before any load/store initiated afterward.

Note that in a multiprocessor we have to insist that the phrase "be seen" means "be seen by any task in the system that correctly implements the shared memory caching system." This is usually done by ensuring that **sync** produces a reordering barrier for transactions between the CPU and the cache/memory/bus subsystem.

There are limitations. There is no guarantee about the relative timing of load/stores and the execution of the **sync** itself; it merely separates load/stores before the instruction from those after. **sync** does not solve the problem of ensuring some timing relationship between the CPU's program execution and external writes, which we mentioned in Section 4.13.

And inside a multiprocessor **sync** works only on certain access types (uncached and *coherent* cached accesses). Much "normal" cached memory is noncoherent; any data space that is known not to be shared is safe, and so is anything that is read-only to the sharing tasks.

sync does not need to do anything on CPUs that are strongly ordered; in such cases it is a **nop**.

8.5   Instruction Encodings

All MIPS instructions (up to and including the MIPS IV ISA) are listed in order of encoding in Table 8.6. Subsections 8.5.1–8.5.3 provide further notes on the material in this table.

Most MIPS manuals say there are only three instruction formats used. I daresay this corresponds to some reality in the original internal design of the chip, but it never looked like that to the user, to whom it appears that different instructions use the fields for quite different purposes. Newer instructions use more complex encodings.

The table tells you the binary encoding, the mnemonic of the instruction in assembler code, and the MIPS instruction set level when the instruction was introduced. Occasionally this last column will have the name of a specific CPU that offers a special instruction or will be left blank when the instruction was implemented with the original instruction.

8.5.1   *Fields in the Instruction Encoding Table*

The following notes describe the fields in Table 8.6 (starting on page 219).

Field 31–26   The primary op-code "op," which is 6 bits long. Instructions that are having trouble fitting in 32 bits (like the "long" **j** and **jal** instructions or arithmetic with a 16-bit constant) have a unique "op" field. Other instructions come in groups that share an "op" value, distinguished by other fields.

Field 5–0   Subcode field used for the three-register arithmetical/logical group of instructions (major op-code zero).

Field 25–21   Yet another extended op-code field, this time used by coprocessor-type instructions.

rs, **rt**, **rw**   One or two fields identifying source registers.

o(b), **offset**, **rb**   "o" is a signed offset that fits in a 16-bit field; "b" is a general-purpose base register whose contents are added to "o" to yield an address for a load or store instruction.

rd   The destination register, to be changed by this instruction.

shft   How far to shift, used in shift-by-constant instructions.

broffset   A 16-bit signed offset defining the destination of a PC-relative branch. Offset zero is the delay slot instruction after the branch, so a branch-to-self has an offset of -1.

target   A 26-bit *word* address to be jumped to (it corresponds to a 28-bit byte address, which is always word-aligned). The long jump **j** instruction is rarely used, so this format is pretty much exclusively for function calls (**jal**).

The high-order 4 bits of the target address can't be specified by this instruction and are taken from the address of the jump instruction. This means that these instructions can reach anywhere in the 256MB region around the instructions' location. To jump further, use a **jr** (jump register) instruction.

constant   A 16-bit integer constant for immediate arithmetic or logic operations. It's interpreted as signed or unsigned according to the instruction context.

cs/cd   Coprocessor register as source or destination, respectively. Each coprocessor section of the instruction set may have up to 32 data registers and up to 32 control registers.

fr/fs/ft   Floating-point unit source registers.

fd   Floating-point destination register (written by the instruction).

N/M   Selector for FP condition code—"N" when it's being read, and "M" when it's being written by a compare instruction. The field is absent from assembler language and zero in the machine instructions before MIPS IV; hence all the floating-point compare instructions have the "M" field as zero in pre–MIPS IV guise.

hint   A hint for the prefetch instruction, described in Section 8.4.8.

cachop   This is used with the **cache** instruction and encodes an operation to be performed on the cache entry discovered by the instruction's address. See Table 4.2 in Section 4.10.

8.5.2 *Notes on the Instruction Encoding Table*

- *Double use of instruction encoding*: LSI's MiniRISC core CPU defines instructions whose encodings clash with standard instructions in MIPS III and higher. We've listed both interpretations.

- *Instruction aliases*: Mostly we have suppressed all but one possible mnemonic for the same instruction, but occasionally we leave them in. Instructions such as **nop** and **l.s** are so ubiquitous that it seems simpler to include them than to leave them out.

- *Coprocessor instructions*: Instructions that were once defined but are no longer have been expunged. Coprocessor 3 was never used by any MIPS I CPU and is not usable with MIPS III or higher—and some of the compulsory coprocessor op-codes, including memory loads, have been recycled for different uses.

TABLE 8.6 Machine instructions in order of encoding

31	26 25	21 20 18 17 16 15	11 10	8 7 6 5	0	Assembler name	ISA level
0	0	0	0	0	0	**nop**	
0	0	*rw*	*rd*	*shft*	0	**sll** *d,w,shft*	
0	*rs*	*N* 0	*rd*	0	1	**movf** *d,s,N*	MIPS IV
0	*rs*	*N* 1	*rd*	0	1	**movt** *d,s,N*	MIPS IV
0	*rs*	*rt*	*rd*	0	1	**selsr** *d,s,t*	MiniRISC-4010
0	0	*rw*	*rd*	*shft*	2	**srl** *d,w,shft*	
0	0	*rw*	*rd*	*shft*	3	**sra** *d,w,shft*	
0	*rs*	*rt*	*rd*	0	4	**sllv** *d,t,s*	
0	*rs*	*rt*	*rd*	0	5	**selsl** *d,s,t*	MiniRISC-4010
0	*rs*	*rt*	*rd*	0	6	**srlv** *d,t,s*	
0	*rs*	*rt*	*rd*	0	7	**srav** *d,t,s*	
0	*rs*	0	0	0	8	**jr** *s*	

continued

TABLE 8.6 *continued*

31 26	25 21	20 18 17 16	15 11	10 8 7 6	5 0	*Assembler name*	*ISA level*
0	rs	0	31	0	9	jalr s	
0	rs	0	rd	0	9	jalr d,s	
0	rs	×	rd	0	10	ffs d,s	MiniRISC-4010
0	rs	rt	rd	0	10	movz d,s,t	MIPS IV
0	rs	×	rd	0	11	ffc d,s	MiniRISC-4010
0	rs	rt	rd	0	11	movn d,s,t	MIPS IV
0	code				12	syscall code	
0	code		×		13	break code	
0	code		×		14	sdbbp code	R3900
0	0	0	0	0	15	sync	MIPS II
0	0	0	rd	0	16	mfhi d	
0	rs	0	0	0	17	mthi s	
0	0	0	rd	0	18	mflo d	
0	rs	0	0	0	19	mtlo s	
0	rs	rt	rd	0	20	dsllv d,t,s	MIPS III
0	rs	rt	rd	0	22	dsrlv d,t,s	MIPS III
0	rs	rt	rd	0	23	dsrav d,t,s	MIPS III
0	rs	rt	0	0	24	mult s,t	
0	rs	rt	0	0	25	multu s,t	
0	rs	rt	0	0	26	div s,t	
0	rs	rt	0	0	27	divu s,t	
0	rs	rt	0	0	28	dmult s,t	MIPS III
0	rs	rt	0	0	28	madd s,t	MiniRISC-4010
0	rs	rt	0	0	29	dmultu s,t	MIPS III

TABLE 8.6 *continued*

31	26 25	21 20 18 17 16 15	11 10	8 7 6 5	0	Assembler name	ISA level
0	rs	rt	0	0	29	maddu s,t	MiniRISC-4010
0	rs	rt	0	0	30	ddiv s,t	MIPS III
0	rs	rt	0	0	30	msub s,t	MiniRISC-4010
0	rs	rt	0	0	31	ddivu s,t	MIPS III
0	rs	rt	0	0	31	msubu s,t	MiniRISC-4010
0	rs	rt	rd	0	32	add d,s,t	
0	rs	rt	rd	0	33	addu d,s,t	
0	rs	rt	rd	0	34	sub d,s,t	
0	rs	rt	rd	0	35	subu d,s,t	
0	rs	rt	rd	0	36	and d,s,t	
0	rs	rt	rd	0	37	or d,s,t	
0	rs	rt	rd	0	38	xor d,s,t	
0	rs	rt	rd	0	39	nor d,s,t	
0	rs	rt	0	0	40	madd16 s,t	Vr4100
0	rs	rt	0	0	41	dmadd16 s,t	Vr4100
0	rs	rt	rd	0	42	slt d,s,t	
0	rs	rt	rd	0	43	sltu d,s,t	
0	rs	rt	rd	0	44	dadd d,s,t	MIPS III
0	rs	rt	rd	0	45	daddu d,s,t	MIPS III
0	rs	rt	rd	0	46	dsub d,s,t	MIPS III
0	rs	rt	rd	0	47	dsubu d,s,t	MIPS III
0	rs	rt	×		48	tge s,t	MIPS II
0	rs	rt	×		49	tgeu s,t	MIPS II
0	rs	rt	×		50	tlt s,t	MIPS II
0	rs	rt	×		51	tltu s,t	MIPS II
0	rs	rt	×		52	teq s,t	MIPS II
0	rs	rt	×		54	tne s,t	MIPS II

continued

TABLE 8.6 *continued*

31	26 25	21 2018171615	11 10 8765	0	*Assembler name*	*ISA level*
0	0	*rw*	*rd*	*shft* 56	`dsll d,w,shft`	MIPS III
0	0	*rw*	*rd*	*shft* 58	`dsrl d,w,shft`	MIPS III
0	0	*rw*	*rd*	*shft* 59	`dsra d,w,shft`	MIPS III
0	0	*rw*	*rd*	*shft* 60	`dsll32 d,w,shft`	MIPS III
0	0	*rw*	*rd*	*shft* 62	`dsrl32 d,w,shft`	MIPS III
0	0	*rw*	*rd*	*shft* 63	`dsra32 d,w,shft`	MIPS III

31	26 25	21		0	*Assembler name*	*ISA level*
1	*rs*	0	*broffset*		`bltz s,p`	
1	*rs*	1	*broffset*		`bgez s,p`	
1	*rs*	2	*broffset*		`bltzl s,p`	MIPS II
1	*rs*	3	*broffset*		`bgezl s,p`	MIPS II
1	*rs*	8	*constant*		`tgei s,j`	MIPS II
1	*rs*	9	*constant*		`tgeiu s,j`	MIPS II
1	*rs*	10	*constant*		`tlti s,j`	MIPS II
1	*rs*	11	*constant*		`tltiu s,j`	MIPS II
1	*rs*	12	*constant*		`teqi s,j`	MIPS II
1	*rs*	14	*constant*		`tnei s,j`	MIPS II
1	*rs*	16	*broffset*		`bltzal s,p`	
1	*rs*	17	*broffset*		`bgezal s,p`	
1	*rs*	18	*broffset*		`bltzall s,p`	MIPS II
1	*rs*	19	*broffset*		`bgezall s,p`	MIPS II

31	26 25		0	*Assembler name*	*ISA level*
2	*target*			`j target`	
3	*target*			`jal target`	

31	26 25	21 2018		0	*Assembler name*	*ISA level*
4	*rs*	*rt*	*broffset*		`beq s,t,p`	
5	*rs*	*rt*	*broffset*		`bne s,t,p`	

TABLE 8.6 *continued*

31 26 25	21 20 18 17 16 15	11 10 8 7 6 5	0	Assembler name	ISA level
6	rs	0	broffset	blez s,p	
7	rs	0	broffset	bgtz s,p	
8	rs	rd	(signed) const	addi d,s,const	
9	rs	rd	(signed) const	addiu d,s,const	
10	rs	rd	(signed) const	slti d,s,const	
11	rs	rd	(signed) const	sltiu d,s,const	
12	rs	rd	(unsigned) const	andi d,s,const	
13	rs	rd	(unsigned) const	ori d,s,const	
14	rs	rd	(unsigned) const	xori d,s,const	
15	0	rd	(unsigned) const	lui d,const	

31 26 25	21	20 18 17 16 15	11 10	8 7 6 5	0	Assembler name	ISA level
16	0	rt	cs	0	0	mfc0 t,cs	
16	1	rt	cs	0	0	dmfc0 t,cs	MIPS III
16	2	rt	cs	0	0	cfc0 t,cs	
16	4	rt	cd	0	0	mtc0 t,cd	
16	5	rt	cd	0	0	dmtc0 t,cd	MIPS III
16	6	rt	cd	0	0	ctc0 t,cd	
16	16	0	0	0	1	tlbr	
16	16	0	0	0	2	tlbwi	
16	16	0	0	0	6	tlbwr	
16	16	0	0	0	8	tlbp	
16	16	0	0	0	16	rfe	MIPS I only
16	16	0	0	0	24	eret	MIPS III
16	16	0	0	0	31	dret	MIPS II only
16	16	0	0	0	32	waiti	MiniRISC-4010
16	16	0	0	0	33	standby	Vr4100
16	16	0	0	0	34	suspend	Vr4100

continued

TABLE 8.6 *continued*

31	26 25	21 20181716 15		11 10	8 7 6 5	0	*Assembler name*	*ISA level*
16	8	0	*broffset*				bc0f p	
16	8	1	*broffset*				bc0t p	
16	8	2	*broffset*				bc0fl p	MIPS II
16	8	3	*broffset*				bc0tl p	MIPS II
17	0	*rt*	*fs*	0	0		mfc1 t,fs	
17	1	*rt*	*fs*	0	0		dmfc1 t,fs	MIPS III
17	2	*rt*	*cs*	0	0		cfc1 t,cs	
17	4	*rt*	*cs*	0	0		mtc1 t,cs	
17	5	*rt*	*cs*	0	0		dmtc1 t,cs	MIPS III
17	6	*rt*	*cs*	0	0		ctc1 t,cs	
17	16	*ft*	*fs*	*fd*	0		add.s fd,fs,ft	
17	17	*ft*	*fs*	*fd*	0		add.d fd,fs,ft	
17	16	*ft*	*fs*	*fd*	1		sub.s fd,fs,ft	
17	17	*ft*	*fs*	*fd*	1		sub.d fd,fs,ft	
17	16	*ft*	*fs*	*fd*	2		mul.s fd,fs,ft	
17	17	*ft*	*fs*	*fd*	2		mul.d fd,fs,ft	
17	16	*ft*	*fs*	*fd*	3		div.s fd,fs,ft	
17	17	*ft*	*fs*	*fd*	3		div.d fd,fs,ft	
17	16	0	*fs*	*fd*	4		sqrt.s fd,fs	MIPS II
17	17	0	*fs*	*fd*	4		sqrt.d fd,fs	MIPS II
17	16	0	*fs*	*fd*	5		abs.s fd,fs	
17	17	0	*fs*	*fd*	5		abs.d fd,fs	
17	16	0	*fs*	*fd*	6		mov.s fd,fs	
17	17	0	*fs*	*fd*	6		mov.d fd,fs	
17	16	0	*fs*	*fd*	7		neg.s fd,fs	
17	17	0	*fs*	*fd*	7		neg.d fd,fs	

TABLE 8.6 *continued*

31	26 25	21 2018 17 16 15	11 10	8 7 6 5	0	Assembler name	ISA level
17	16	0	*fs*	*fd*	8	round.l.s *fd,fs*	MIPS III
17	17	0	*fs*	*fd*	8	round.l.d *fd,fs*	MIPS III
17	16	0	*fs*	*fd*	9	trunc.l.s *fd,fs*	MIPS III
17	17	0	*fs*	*fd*	9	trunc.l.d *fd,fs*	MIPS III
17	16	0	*fs*	*fd*	10	ceil.l.s *fd,fs*	MIPS III
17	17	0	*fs*	*fd*	10	ceil.l.d *fd,fs*	MIPS III
17	16	0	*fs*	*fd*	11	floor.l.s *fd,fs*	MIPS III
17	17	0	*fs*	*fd*	11	floor.l.d *fd,fs*	MIPS III
17	16	0	*fs*	*fd*	12	round.w.s *fd,fs*	MIPS II
17	17	0	*fs*	*fd*	12	round.w.d *fd,fs*	MIPS II
17	16	0	*fs*	*fd*	13	trunc.w.s *fd,fs*	MIPS II
17	17	0	*fs*	*fd*	13	trunc.w.d *fd,fs*	MIPS II
17	16	0	*fs*	*fd*	14	ceil.w.s *fd,fs*	MIPS II
17	17	0	*fs*	*fd*	14	ceil.w.d *fd,fs*	MIPS II
17	16	0	*fs*	*fd*	15	floor.w.s *fd,fs*	MIPS II
17	17	0	*fs*	*fd*	15	floor.w.d *fd,fs*	MIPS II
17	16	*N* 0	*fs*	*fd*	17	movf.s *fd,fs,N*	MIPS IV
17	16	*N* 1	*fs*	*fd*	17	movt.s *fd,fs,N*	MIPS IV
17	17	*N* 0	*fs*	*fd*	17	movf.d *fd,fs,N*	MIPS IV
17	17	*N* 1	*fs*	*fd*	17	movt.d *fd,fs,N*	MIPS IV
17	16	*rt*	*fs*	*fd*	18	movz.s *fd,fs,t*	MIPS IV
17	17	*rt*	*fs*	*fd*	18	movz.d *fd,fs,t*	MIPS IV
17	16	*rt*	*fs*	*fd*	19	movn.s *fd,fs,t*	MIPS IV
17	17	*rt*	*fs*	*fd*	19	movn.d *fd,fs,t*	MIPS IV
17	16	0	*fs*	*fd*	21	recip.s *fd,fs*	MIPS IV

continued

TABLE 8.6 *continued*

31 26	25 21	20 18 17 16 15	11 10	8 7 6 5	0	*Assembler name*	*ISA level*
17	17	0	*fs*	*fd*	21	`recip.d fd,fs`	MIPS IV
17	16	0	*fs*	*fd*	22	`rsqrt.s fd,fs`	MIPS IV
17	17	0	*fs*	*fd*	22	`rsqrt.d fd,fs`	MIPS IV
17	17	0	*fs*	*fd*	32	`cvt.s.d fd,fs`	
17	20	0	*fs*	*fd*	32	`cvt.s.w fd,fs`	
17	21	0	*fs*	*fd*	32	`cvt.s.l fd,fs`	MIPS III
17	16	0	*fs*	*fd*	33	`cvt.d.s fd,fs`	
17	20	0	*fs*	*fd*	33	`cvt.d.w fd,fs`	
17	21	0	*fs*	*fd*	33	`cvt.d.l fd,fs`	MIPS III
17	16	0	*fs*	*fd*	36	`cvt.w.s fd,fs`	
17	17	0	*fs*	*fd*	36	`cvt.w.d fd,fs`	
17	16	0	*fs*	*fd*	37	`cvt.l.s fd,fs`	MIPS III
17	17	0	*fs*	*fd*	37	`cvt.l.d fd,fs`	MIPS III
17	16	*ft*	*fs*	*M* ×	48	`c.f.s M,fs,ft`	MIPS IV if M!=0
17	17	*ft*	*fs*	*M* ×	48	`c.f.d M,fs,ft`	MIPS IV if M!=0
17	16	*ft*	*fs*	*M* ×	49	`c.un.s M,fs,ft`	MIPS IV if M!=0
17	17	*ft*	*fs*	*M* ×	49	`c.un.d M,fs,ft`	MIPS IV if M!=0
17	16	*ft*	*fs*	*M* ×	50	`c.eq.s M,fs,ft`	MIPS IV if M!=0
17	17	*ft*	*fs*	*M* ×	50	`c.eq.d M,fs,ft`	MIPS IV if M!=0
17	16	*ft*	*fs*	*M* ×	51	`c.ueq.s M,fs,ft`	MIPS IV if M!=0
17	17	*ft*	*fs*	*M* ×	51	`c.ueq.d M,fs,ft`	MIPS IV if M!=0
17	16	*ft*	*fs*	*M* ×	52	`c.olt.s M,fs,ft`	MIPS IV if M!=0
17	17	*ft*	*fs*	*M* ×	52	`c.olt.d M,fs,ft`	MIPS IV if M!=0
17	16	*ft*	*fs*	*M* ×	53	`c.ult.s M,fs,ft`	MIPS IV if M!=0
17	17	*ft*	*fs*	*M* ×	53	`c.ult.d M,fs,ft`	MIPS IV if M!=0
17	16	*ft*	*fs*	*M* ×	54	`c.ole.s M,fs,ft`	MIPS IV if M!=0

TABLE 8.6 *continued*

31	26 25	21 20 18 17 16 15	11 10 8 7 6 5	0	*Assembler name*	*ISA level*
17	17	*ft*	*fs*	*M*	×	54	c.ole.d *M,fs,ft*	MIPS IV if M!=0
17	16	*ft*	*fs*	*M*	×	55	c.ule.s *M,fs,ft*	MIPS IV if M!=0
17	17	*ft*	*fs*	*M*	×	55	c.ule.d *M,fs,ft*	MIPS IV if M!=0
17	16	*ft*	*fs*	*M*	×	56	c.sf.s *M,fs,ft*	MIPS IV if M!=0
17	17	*ft*	*fs*	*M*	×	56	c.sf.d *M,fs,ft*	MIPS IV if M!=0
17	16	*ft*	*fs*	*M*	×	58	c.seq.s *M,fs,ft*	MIPS IV if M!=0
17	17	*ft*	*fs*	*M*	×	58	c.seq.d *M,fs,ft*	MIPS IV if M!=0
17	16	*ft*	*fs*	*M*	×	59	c.ngl.s *M,fs,ft*	MIPS IV if M!=0
17	17	*ft*	*fs*	*M*	×	59	c.ngl.d *M,fs,ft*	MIPS IV if M!=0
17	16	*ft*	*fs*	*M*	×	60	c.lt.s *M,fs,ft*	MIPS IV if M!=0
17	17	*ft*	*fs*	*M*	×	60	c.lt.d *M,fs,ft*	MIPS IV if M!=0
17	16	*ft*	*fs*	*M*	×	61	c.nge.s *M,fs,ft*	MIPS IV if M!=0
17	17	*ft*	*fs*	*M*	×	61	c.nge.d *M,fs,ft*	MIPS IV if M!=0
17	16	*ft*	*fs*	*M*	×	62	c.le.s *M,fs,ft*	MIPS IV if M!=0
17	17	*ft*	*fs*	*M*	×	62	c.le.d *M,fs,ft*	MIPS IV if M!=0
17	16	*ft*	*fs*	*M*	×	63	c.ngt.s *M,fs,ft*	MIPS IV if M!=0
17	17	*ft*	*fs*	*M*	×	63	c.ngt.d *M,fs,ft*	MIPS IV if M!=0

31	26 25	21 20 18 17 16 15		0	*Assembler name*	*ISA level*
17	8	0	*broffset*		bc1f *p*	
17	8	1	*broffset*		bc1t *p*	
17	8	2	*broffset*		bc1fl *p*	MIPS II
17	8	3	*broffset*		bc1tl *p*	MIPS II

31	26 25	21 20 18	17 16 15	0	*Assembler name*	*ISA level*
17	8	*N*	0	*broffset*	bc1f *N,p*	MIPS IV
17	8	*N*	1	*broffset*	bc1t *N,p*	MIPS IV
17	8	*N*	2	*broffset*	bc1fl *N,p*	MIPS IV
17	8	*N*	3	*broffset*	bc1tl *N,p*	MIPS IV

continued

TABLE 8.6 *continued*

31	26 25	21 2018	1716 15	11 10 8	7 6 5	0	Assembler name	ISA level
18	0	rt	cs	0		0	mfc2 t,cs	
18	2	rt	cs	0		0	cfc2 t,cs	
18	4	rt	cs	0		0	mtc2 t,cs	
18	6	rt	cs	0		0	ctc2 t,cs	
18	8	0	broffset				bc2f p	
18	8	1	broffset				bc2t p	
18	8	2	broffset				bc2fl p	MIPS II
18	8	3	broffset				bc2tl p	MIPS II
19	rb	rt	0	fd		0	lwxc1 fd,t(b)	MIPS IV
19	rb	rt	0	fd		1	ldxc1 fd,t(b)	MIPS IV
19	rb	rt	fs	0		8	swxc1 fs,t(b)	MIPS IV
19	rb	rt	fs	0		9	sdxc1 fs,t(b)	MIPS IV
19	rb	rt	hint	0		15	prefx hint,t(b)	MIPS IV
19	fr	ft	fs	fd		32	madd.s fd,fr,fs,ft	MIPS IV
19	fr	ft	fs	fd		33	madd.d fd,fr,fs,ft	MIPS IV
19	fr	ft	fs	fd		40	msub.s fd,fr,fs,ft	MIPS IV
19	fr	ft	fs	fd		41	msub.d fd,fr,fs,ft	MIPS IV
19	fr	ft	fs	fd		48	nmadd.s fd,fr,fs,ft	MIPS IV
19	fr	ft	fs	fd		49	nmadd.d fd,fr,fs,ft	MIPS IV
19	fr	ft	fs	fd		56	nmsub.s fd,fr,fs,ft	MIPS IV
19	fr	ft	fs	fd		57	nmsub.d fd,fr,fs,ft	MIPS IV
20	rs	rt	broffset				beql s,t,p	MIPS II
21	rs	0	broffset				bnezl s,p	MIPS II
21	rs	rt	broffset				bnel s,t,p	MIPS II
22	rs	0	broffset				blezl s,p	MIPS II

TABLE 8.6 *continued*

31 26	25 21	20 18 17 16 15 11 10 8 7 6 5 0	Assembler name	ISA level
23	*rs*	0 | *broffset*	bgtzl *s,p*	MIPS II
24	*rs*	*rd* | (signed) *const*	daddi *d,s,const*	MIPS III
25	*rs*	*rd* | (signed) *const*	daddiu *d,s,const*	MIPS III
26	*rb*	*rt* | *offset*	ldl *t,o(b)*	MIPS III
27	*rb*	*rt* | *offset*	ldr *t,o(b)*	MIPS III
28	*rs*	*rt* | 0 | 0 | 0	mad *s,t*	R4650
28	*rs*	*rt* | *rd* | 0 | 0	mad *d,s,t*	R3900
28	*rs*	*rt* | 0 | 0 | 1	madu *s,t*	R4650
28	*rs*	*rt* | *rd* | 0 | 2	mul *d,s,t*	R4650
28	*rs*	*rt* | *constant*	addciu *t,r,j*	MiniRISC-4010
32	*rb*	*rt* | *offset*	lb *t,o(b)*	
33	*rb*	*rt* | *offset*	lh *t,o(b)*	
34	*rb*	*rt* | *offset*	lwl *t,o(b)*	
35	*rb*	*rt* | *offset*	lw *t,o(b)*	
36	*rb*	*rt* | *offset*	lbu *t,o(b)*	
37	*rb*	*rt* | *offset*	lhu *t,o(b)*	
38	*rb*	*rt* | *offset*	lwr *t,o(b)*	
39	*rb*	*rt* | *offset*	lwu *t,o(b)*	MIPS III
40	*rb*	*rt* | *offset*	sb *t,o(b)*	
41	*rb*	*rt* | *offset*	sh *t,o(b)*	
42	*rb*	*rt* | *offset*	swl *t,o(b)*	
43	*rb*	*rt* | *offset*	sw *t,o(b)*	
44	*rb*	*rt* | *offset*	sdl *t,o(b)*	MIPS III
45	*rb*	*rt* | *offset*	sdr *t,o(b)*	MIPS III
46	*rb*	*rt* | *offset*	swr *t,o(b)*	

continued

TABLE 8.6 *continued*

31	26 25	21 2018 17 16 15	11 10 8 7 6 5	0	Assembler name	ISA level
47	0	1	0	0	0	`flushi`	MiniRISC-4010
47	0	2	0	0	0	`flushd`	MiniRISC-4010
47	0	3	0	0	0	`flushid`	MiniRISC-4010

31	26 25	21 2018 17 16 15	11 10 8 7 6 5	0	Assembler name	ISA level
47	*rb*	4	*offset*	`wb o(b)`	MiniRISC-4010
47	*rb*	*cachop*	*offset*	`cache cachop,o(b)`	MIPS III
48	*rb*	*rt*	*offset*	`ll t,o(b)`	MIPS II
49	*rb*	*ft*	*offset*	`l.s t,o(b)`	
50	*rb*	*cd*	*offset*	`lwc2 cd,o(b)`	
51	*rb*	*hint*	*offset*	`pref hint,o(b)`	MIPS IV
52	*rb*	*rt*	*offset*	`lld t,o(b)`	MIPS III
53	*rb*	*ft*	*offset*	`l.d ft,o(b)`	MIPS II
54	*rb*	*cd*	*offset*	`ldc2 cd,o(b)`	MIPS II
55	*rb*	*rt*	*offset*	`ld t,o(b)`	MIPS III
56	*rb*	*rt*	*offset*	`sc t,o(b)`	MIPS II
57	*rb*	*ft*	*offset*	`s.s ft,o(b)`	
57	*rb*	*ft*	*offset*	`swc1 ft,o(b)`	
58	*rb*	*cs*	*offset*	`swc2 cs,o(b)`	
60	*rb*	*rt*	*offset*	`scd t,o(b)`	MIPS III
61	*rb*	*ft*	*offset*	`s.d ft,o(b)`	MIPS II
61	*rb*	*ft*	*offset*	`sdc1 ft,o(b)`	MIPS II
62	*rb*	*cs*	*offset*	`sdc2 cs,o(b)`	MIPS II
63	*rb*	*rt*	*offset*	`sd t,o(b)`	MIPS III

8.5.3   *Encodings and Simple Implementation*

If you look at the encodings of the instructions you can sometimes see how the CPU is designed. Although there are variable encodings, those fields that are required very early in the pipeline are encoded in a totally regular way:

- Source registers are always in the same place, so that the CPU can fetch two operands from the integer register file without any conditional decoding. In some instructions, both registers will not be needed, but since the register file is designed to provide two source values on every clock cycle nothing has been lost.

- The 16-bit constant is always in the same place, permitting the appropriate instruction bits to be fed directly into the ALU's input multiplexer without conditional shifts.

8.6   Instructions by Functional Group

We've divided the instruction set into reasonable chunks, in this order:

- Nop
- Register/register moves: widely used, if not exciting; includes conditional moves added in MIPS IV
- Load constant: integer immediate values and addresses
- Arithmetical/logical instructions
- Integer multiply, divide, and remainder
- Integer multiply-accumulate
- Loads and stores
- Jumps, subroutine calls, and branches
- Breakpoint and trap
- CP0 functions: instructions for CPU control
- Floating point
- ATMizer-II floating point: obscure special instructions

8.6.1   *Nop*

nop: The MIPS instruction set is rich in nops, since any instruction with **zero** as a destination is guaranteed to do nothing. The favored one is **sll zero,zero,zero** whose binary encoding is a zero-valued word.

8.6.2 *Register/Register Moves*

move: Usually implemented with an **or** with the **$zero** register. A few CPUs—where for some reason adding is better supported than logical operations—use **addu.**[1]

Conditional Move

Useful branch-minimizing addition to instruction set in MIPS IV (see Section 8.4.3).

movf, movt: conditional move of integer register, testing floating-point condition code.

movn, movz: Conditional move of integer register subject to state of another register.

8.6.3 *Load Constant*

dla, la: Macro-instructions to load the address of some labelled location or variable in the program. You only need **dla** when using 64-bit pointers (which you'll only do in big unix-type systems). These instructions accept the same addressing modes as do all loads and stores (even though they do quite different things with them).

dli, li: Load constant immediate. **dli** is the 64-bit version, not supported by all toolchains, and is only needed to load unsigned numbers too big to fit in 32 bits. This is a macro whose length varies according to the size of the constant.

lui: Load upper immediate. The 16-bit constant is loaded into bits 16–31 of a register, with bits 32–63 (if applicable) set equal to bit 31 and bits 0–15 cleared. This instruction is one half of the pair of machine instructions that load an arbitrary 32-bit constant. Assembler programmers will probably never write this explicitly; it is used implicitly for macros like **li** (load immediate), **la** (load address), and above all for implementing useful addressing modes.

8.6.4 *Arithmetical/Logical*

The arithmetical/logical instructions are further broken down into the following types:

---

1. For example, some LSI MiniRISC CPUs have the ability to run two instructions at once under some circumstances and adds a pair with more instructions than logical operations do.

Add

add, addi, dadd, daddi: Obscure and rarely used alternate forms of **addu**, which trap when the result would overflow. Probably of use to Cobol compilers.

addciu: Add-with-carry instruction, specific to the LSI MiniRISC core.

addu, addiu, daddu, daddiu: Addition, with separate 32-bit and 64-bit versions. Here and throughout the instruction set, 64-bit versions of instructions are marked with a leading "d" (for doubleword); also, you don't need to specify the "immediate" mnemonic—you just feed the assembler a constant. If the constant you need can't be represented in the 16-bit field provided in the instruction, then the assembler will produce a sequence of instructions.

dsub, sub: Subtract variants that trap on overflow.

dsubu, subu: Regular 64- and 32-bit subtraction (there isn't a subtract-immediate, of course, because the constant in add-immediate can be negative).

Miscellaneous Arithmetic

abs, dabs: Absolute value; expands to set and branch (or conditional move if there is one).

dneg, neg, dnegu, negu: Unary negate; mnemonics without U will trap on overflow.

max, min: Only available on LSI MiniRISC CPUs.

Bitwise Logical Instructions

and, andi, or, ori, xor, xori, nor: Three-operand bitwise logical operations. Don't write the "immediate" types—the assembler will generate them automatically when fed a constant operand. Note that there's no **nori** instruction.

not: Two-operand instruction implemented with **nor**.

Shifts and Rotates

drol, dror, rol, ror: Rotate right and left; expand to two-instruction sequence.

dsll, dsll32, dsllv: 64-bit (double) shift left, bringing zeroes into low bits. The three different instructions provide for different ways of specifying the shift amount: by a constant 0–31 bits, by a constant 32–63 bits, or by using the low 6 bits of the contents of another register. Assembler programmers should just write the **dsll** mnemonic.

dsra, dsra32, dsrav: 64-bit (double) shift right arithmetic. This is "arithmetic" in that it propagates copies of bit 63—the sign bit—into high bits. That means it implements a correct division by a power of two when applied to signed 64-bit integer data. Always write the **dsra** mnemonic; the assembler will choose the instruction format according to how the shift amount is specified.

dsrl, dsrl32, dsrlv: 64-bit (double) shift right logical. This is "logical" in that it brings zeros into high bits. Although there are three different instructions, assembler programmers should always use the **dsrl** mnemonic; the assembler will choose the instruction format according to how the shift amount is specified.

sll, sllv: 32-bit shift left. You only need to write the **sll** mnemonic.

sra, srav: Shift right arithmetic (propagating the sign bit). Always write **sra**.

srl, srlv: Shift right logical (bringing zeros into high bits). Always write **srl**.

Set if...

slt, slti, sltiu, sltu: Hardware instructions, which write a 1 if the condition is satisfied and a 0 otherwise. Write **slt** or **sltu**.

seq, sge, sgeu, sgt, sgtu, sle, sleu, sne: Macro-instructions to set the destination according to more complex conditions.

Obscure Bit-Related Instructions

ffc, ffs: Find first clear bit, find first set bit (LSI MiniRISC only instructions).

selsl, selsr: Provided only on LSI MiniRISC CPUs. Using two registers to hold a 64-bit bitfield, rotate left/rotate right and select a 32-bit result. The rotate amount comes from the special CP0 register **ROTATE**, which is CP0 register **23** and holds a number between 0 and 31, for which only bits 0–4 are implemented. This kind of shift is useful for dealing with bits moving between words in bitmap graphic applications. It also provides a true rotate operation if the same register is used for both source operands.

8.6.5 *Integer Multiply, Divide, and Remainder*

The integer multiply and divide machine instructions are unusual, because the MIPS multiplier is a separate unit not built in to the normal pipeline and takes much longer to produce results than regular integer instructions. Machine instructions are available to fire off a multiply or divide, which then proceeds in parallel with the instructions.

Integer multiply-accumulate and multiply-add instructions are built with the same mechanism (see Section 8.6.6).

As a result of being handled by a separate unit, multiply/divide instructions don't include overflow or divide-by-zero tests (they can't cause exceptions because they are running asynchronously) and don't usually deliver their results into general-purpose registers (it would complicate the pipeline by fighting a later instruction for the ability to write the register file). Instead, multiply/divide results appear in the two separate registers **hi** and **lo**. You can only access these values with the two special instructions **mfhi** and **mflo**. Even in the earliest MIPS CPUs, the result registers are interlocked: If you try to read the result before it is ready, the CPU is stalled until the data arrives.

However, when you write the usual assembler mnemonics for multiply/divide, the CPU will generate a sequence of instructions that simulate a three-operand instruction and perform overflow checking. A **div** (signed divide) may expand into as many as 13 instructions. The extra instructions run in parallel with the hardware divider so that, usually, no time is wasted (the divide itself takes 35–75 cycles on most MIPS CPUs).

MIPS Corporation's assembler will convert constant multiplication, and division/remainder by constant powers of two, into the appropriate shifts, masks, etc. But the assembler found in most toolchains is likely to leave this to the compiler.

By a less-than-obvious convention, a multiply or divide written with the destination register **zero** (as in **div zero, s, t**) will give you the raw machine instruction.[1] It is then up to you to fetch the result from **hi** and/or **lo** and to do any checking you need.

Following is the comprehensive list of multiply/divide instructions.

ddiv, ddivu, div, divu: Three-operand macro-instruction for integer division, with 64-/32-bit and signed/unsigned options. All trap on divide-by-zero; signed types trap on overflow. Use destination **zero** to obtain just the divide-start instruction.

ddivd, ddivdu, divd, divdu: Mnemonics for raw machine instruction provided by some toolchains. It is better to use **ddiv zero,...** instead.

divo, divou: Explicit name for divide with overflow check, but really just the same as writing **div, divu**.

dmul, mul, mulu: Three-operand 64-/32-bit multiply macro-instruction. There is no overflow check; as a result, there doesn't need to be an unsigned version of the macro—the truncated result is the same for signed and unsigned interpretation.

---

1. Some toolkits interpret special mnemonics, **mult** for multiplication and **divd** for division, for the machine instructions. However, specifying **zero** as the destination, though bizarre, is more portable.

Toshiba's R3900, IDT's R4640/R4650, and QED CPUs implement three-operand multiply directly; the instruction is called **mul**. It is completely equivalent to the macro, in that **hi** and **lo** still get set, but the least-significant 32 bits of the result are also put directly into the general-purpose register **d**. The CPUs implementing **mul** also have a **mulu**; it always returns the same result in the destination register, but it leaves an appropriate extension in **hi**.

mulo, mulou, dmulo, dmulou: Multiply macros that trap if the result overflows beyond what will fit in one general-purpose register.

dmult, dmultu, mult, multu: The machine instruction that starts off a multiply, with signed/unsigned and 32-/64-bit variants. The result never overflows, because there's 64 and 128 bits' worth of result respectively. The least significant part of a result gets stored in **lo** and the most significant part in **hi**.

drem, dremu, rem, remu: Remainder operations, implemented as a divide followed by **mfhi**. The remainder is kept in the **hi** register.

mfhi, mflo, mthi, mtlo: Move from **hi**, etc. These are instructions for accessing the integer multiply/divide unit result registers **hi** and **lo**. You won't write the **mflo**/ **mfhi** instructions in regular code if you stick to the synthetic **mul** and **div** instructions, which retrieve result data for themselves.

MIPS integer multiply, **mult** or **multu**, always produces a result with twice the bit length of the general-purpose registers, eliminating the possibility of overflow. The high-order and low-order register-sized pieces of the result are returned in **hi** and **lo**, respectively.

Divide operations put the result in **lo** and the integer remainder in **hi**. **mthi** and **mtlo** are used only when restoring the CPU state after an exception.

8.6.6 *Integer Multiply-Accumulate*

Some MIPS CPUs have various forms of integer multiply-accumulate instructions—none of them in a MIPS standard instruction set. All these instructions take two general-purpose registers and accumulate into **lo** and **hi**. As usual, "u" denotes an unsigned variant, but otherwise the mnemonic (and instruction code) is specific to a particular CPU implementation.

dmadd16, madd16: Specific to NEC Vr4100, these variants gain speed by only accepting 16-bit operands, making them of very limited use to a C compiler. **dmadd16** accumulates a 64-bit result in the 64-bit **lo** register.

mad, madu: Found in Toshiba R3900, IDT R4640/4650, and QED CPUs, these take two 32-bit operands and accumulate a 64-bit result split between the **lo** and **hi** registers. The Toshiba R3900 allows a three-operand version, **mad** **d, s, t**, in which the accumulated value is also transferred to the general-purpose register **d**.

madd, maddu, msub, msubu: These do the same thing as the corresponding **mad** etc. instructions, but have different encodings. Found only in LSI's MiniRISC-4010 and derivative core CPUs.

8.6.7   *Loads and Stores*

This subsection lists all the assembler's integer load/store instructions and anything else that addresses memory. Note the following points:

- There are separate instructions for the different data widths supported: 8 bit (byte), 16 bit (halfword), 32 bit (word), and 64 bit (doubleword).

- For data types smaller than the machine register, there's a choice of zero-extending ("u" suffix for unsigned) or sign-extending the operation.

- All the instructions listed here may be written with any addressing mode the assembler supports (see Section 9.4).

- A store instruction is written with the source register first and the address register second to match the syntax for loads; this breaks the general rule that in MIPS instructions the destination is first.

- Machine load instructions require that the data be naturally aligned (halfwords on a 2-byte boundary, words on a 4-byte boundary, doublewords on an 8-byte boundary). But the assembler supports a complete set of macro-instructions for loading data that may be unaligned, and these instructions have a "u" prefix (for unaligned).

  All data structures that are declared as part of a standard C program will be aligned correctly. But you may meet unaligned data from addresses computed at run time, data structures declared using a nonstandard language extension, data read in from a foreign file, and so on.

- All load instructions deliver their result at least one clock cycle later in the pipeline than computational instructions. In MIPS I CPUs, use of loaded data in the immediately following instruction is illegal; however, for any MIPS CPU efficiency is maximized by filling the load delay slot with a useful but nondependent instruction. For MIPS I all decent assemblers should guarantee this by inserting a **nop** if necessary.

Following is a list of the instructions.

lb, lbu: Load byte then sign-extend or zero-extend, respectively, to fill the whole register.

ld: Load doubleword (64 bits). This machine instruction is available only on 64-bit CPUs, but assemblers for 32-bit targets will often implement it as a macro-instruction that loads 64 bits from memory into two consecutive integer registers. This is probably a really bad idea, but someone wanted some compatibility.

ldl, ldr, lwl, lwr, sdl, sdr, swl, swr: Load/store left/right, in word/ doubleword versions. Used in pairs to implement unaligned load/store operations like **ulw**, though you can always do it for yourself (see Section 8.4.1).

lh, lhu: Load halfword (16 bits), then sign-extend or zero-extend to fill the register.

ll, lld, sc, scd: Load-linked and store-conditional (32- and 64-bit versions); strange instructions for semaphores (see Section 8.4.2).

lw, lwu: Load word (32 bits), then sign-extend or zero-extend to fill the register. **lwu** is found only in 64-bit CPUs.

pref, prefx: Prefetch data into the cache (see Section 8.4.8). This is only available in MIPS IV and higher ISAs and is a nop on many of those CPUs. While **pref** takes the usual addressing modes, **prefx** adds a register+register mode implemented in a single instruction.

sb: Store byte (8 bits).

sd: Store doubleword (64 bits). This may be a macro (storing two consecutive integer registers into a 64-bit memory location) for 32-bit CPUs.

sh: Store halfword (16 bits).

sw: Store word (32 bits).

uld, ulh, ulhu, ulw, usd, ush, usw: Unaligned load/store macros. The doubleword and word versions are implemented as macro-instructions using the special load left/load right instructions; halfword operations are built as byte memory accesses, shifts, and **or**s. Note that normal delay slot rules do not apply between the constituent load left/load right of an unaligned operation; the pipeline is designed to let them run head to tail.

Floating-Point Load and Store

l.d, l.s, s.d, s.s: Load/store double (64-bit format) and single (32-bit format). Alignment is required, and no unaligned versions are given here. On 32-bit CPUs, **l.d** and **s.d** are two-instruction macros that load/store two 32-bit chunks of memory into/from consecutive FP registers (see Section 7.5). These instructions are also called **ldc1, lwc1, sdc1,** and **swc1** (load/store word/double to coprocessor 1), but don't write them like that.

ldxc1, lwxc1, sdxc1, swxc1: Base register + offset register addressing mode loads and stores, introduced with MIPS IV. In the instruction **ldxc1 *fd, ri(rb)*,** the full address must lie in the same program memory region as is pointed to by the base register **rb** or bad things might happen.

If your toolkit will accept syntax like **l.d** *fd, ri(rb)*, then use it.

8.6.8 *Jumps, Subroutine Calls, and Branches*

The MIPS architecture follows Motorola nomenclature for these instructions, as follows:

- PC-relative instructions are called "branch" and absolute-addressed instructions "jump"; the operation mnemonics begin with **b** or **j**.

- A subroutine call is "jump and link" or "branch and link," and the mnemonics end ... **al**.

- All the branch instructions, even branch and link, are conditional, testing one or two registers. Unconditional versions can be and are readily synthesized, for example **beq $0, $0, label**.

j: This instruction transfers control unconditionally to an absolute address. Actually, **j** doesn't quite manage a 32-bit address: The top 4 address bits of the target are not defined by the instruction and the top 4 bits of the current PC value are used instead. Most of the time this doesn't matter; 28 bits still gives a maximum code size of 256MB.

To reach a long way away, you must use the **jr** (jump to register) instruction; which is also used for computed jumps. You can write the **j** mnemonic with a register, but it's quite popular not to do so.

jal, jalr: These implement a direct and indirect subroutine call. As well as jumping to the specified address, they store the return address (the instruction's own address + 8) in register **ra**, which is the alias for **$31**.[1] Why add 8 to the program counter? Remember that jump instructions, like branches, always execute the immediately following branch delay slot instruction, so the return address needs to be the instruction *after* the branch delay slot. Subroutine return is done with a jump to register, most often **jr ra**.

Position-independent subroutine calls can use the **bal**, **bgezal**, and **bltzal** instructions.

b: Unconditional PC-relative (though relatively short-range) branch.

bal: PC-relative function call.

bc0f, bc0fl, bc0t, bc0tl, bc2f, bc2fl, bc2t, bc2tl: Branches that test the coprocessor 0 or coprocessor 2 condition bit, neither of which exist on most modern CPUs. On older CPUs these test an input pin.

---

1. In fact the **jalr** machine instruction allows you to specify a register other than **$31** to receive the return address, but this is seldom useful, and the assembler will automatically put in **$31** if you do not specify one.

bc1f, bc1fl, bc1t, bc1tl: Branch on floating-point condition bit (multiple in MIPS IV and later CPUs).

beq, beql, beqz, beqzl, bge, bgel, bgeu, bgeul, bgez, bgezl, bgt, bgtl, bgtu, bgtul, bgtz, bgtzl, ble, blel, bleu, bleul, blez, blezl, blt, bltl, bltu, bltul, bltz, bltzl, bne, bnel, bnez, bnezl: A comprehensive set of two- and one-operand compare-and-branch instructions, most of them macros.

bgezal, bgezall, bltzal, bltzall: Raw machine instructions for conditional function calls, if you ever need to do such a thing.

8.6.9 *Breakpoint and Trap*

break: Causes an exception of type "break." It is used in traps from assembler-synthesized code and by debuggers.

sdbbp: Additional breakpoint instruction (only in LSI MiniRISC CPUs).

syscall: Causes an exception type conventionally used for system calls.

teq, teqi, tge, tgei, tgeiu, tgeu, tlt, tlti, tltiu, tltu, tne, tnei: Conditional exception, testing various one- and two-operand conditions. These are for compilers and interpreters that want to implement run-time checks to array bounds and so on.

8.6.10 *CP0 Functions*

CP0 functions can be classified under the following types:

Move To/From

cfc0, ctc0: Move data in and out of CP0 control registers, of which there are none in any MIPS CPUs defined to date. But there may be such registers one day soon.

mfc0, mtc0, dmfc0, dmtc0: Move data between CP0 registers and general-purpose registers.

cfc2, ctc2, dmfc2, dmtc2, mfc2, mtc2: Instructions for coprocessor 2, if implemented. It has not often been done.

Special Instructions for CPU Control

eret: Return from exception, as used by all MIPS III and higher CPUs to date (see Chapter 5).

dret: Return from exception (R6000 version). This instruction is obsolete and not described in this book.

rfe: Restore status register at end of exception; to be placed in the branch delay slot of the **jr** instruction, which returns control to the exception victim after an exception in any MIPS I CPU built to date (see Chapter 5).

cache: The polymorphic cache control instruction, introduced with MIPS III (see Section 4.10).

sync: Memory access synchronizer for CPUs that might perform load/stores out of order (see Section 8.4.9).

tlbp, tlbr, tlbwi, tlbwr: Instructions to control the TLB, or memory translation hardware (see Section 6.4).

flushd, wb: Cache control instructions specific to LSI MiniRISC CPUs. Consult your CPU manual for details.

waiti: Enter power-down mode (LSI MiniRISC CPUs).

standby, suspend: Enter power-down mode (NEC Vr4100 CPUs).

8.6.11   *Floating Point*

Floating-point instructions are listed under the following types:

Move Between FP and Integer

cfc1, ctc1: Access to FP control registers (ID and control/status).

dmfc1, dmtc1, mfc1, mtc1: Move data between FP and general registers.

Move Between FP Registers

mov.s, mov.d: Regular moves.

movt.d, movt.s, movf.s, movf.d: Move only if some FP condition bit is set or clear.

movn.s, movz.s, movn.d, movz.d: Move only if some general register is zero/nonzero.

Load Constant

li.d, li.s: Macro to load a floating-point constant, which is usually implemented by planting a constant in an initialized data area and then loading from it.

FP Sign Fiddling

These instructions can't ever cause an FP exception, because they don't examine the data at all—they just flip the sign bit.

abs.s, abs.d: Absolute value.

neg.s, neg.d: Negate.

FP Arithmetic

add.s, add.d, div.s, div.d, mul.s, mul.d, sub.s, sub.d: Three-operand arithmetic.

madd.s, madd.d, msub.s, msub.d, nmadd.s, nmadd.d, nmsub.s, nmsub.d: Four-operand multiply-add, plus subtract and negate-result options.

sqrt.s, sqrt.d: IEEE754-accurate square root.

FP Arithmetic (Approximate)

These instructions produce results fast but not to the accuracy required by IEEE754.

recip.s, recip.d: Reciprocal.

rsqrt.s, rsqrt.d: Reciprocal square root.

FP Test

c.eq.s etc...: A vast set of compare-and-set-flag instructions (see Section 7.9.7).

FP Conversions

ceil.T.F, floor.T.F, round.T.F, trunc.T.F: Familiar floating point to integer conversions in a variety of formats. The machine instructions appeared in MIPS III; in MIPS I they're implemented as macros that set the rounding mode and then use **cvt.T.F**. Note also that floating point to integer interconversion is performed exclusively between values in FP registers—data is never converted by the move instruction.

cvt.T.F: Generic floating-point format conversion, with many different T (to) and F (from) formats allowed.

8.6.12 ATMizer-II Floating Point

A 15-bit floating-point format specific to ATM communications applications gives rise to these instructions, which will only be implemented by a few assemblers.

r2u, u2r: Convert between integer and fixed point.

radd, rmul, rsub: Arithmetic functions.

Chapter

9 Assembler Language Programming

This chapter tells you how to read and write MIPS assembler code. This is different from just looking at the list of machine instructions for several reasons:

- MIPS assemblers provide a large number of extra macro-instructions, so the assembler instruction set is much more extensive than the list of machine instructions.

- There are a lot of strange incantations (called "directives" or "pseudo-ops" in assembler circles) used to start and end functions, define data, control instruction ordering and optimization, and so on.

- It's common (though not compulsory) to pass assembler code through the C preprocessor before handing it to the assembler itself. The C preprocessor includes files of definitions and replaces macro names with their definitions, allowing the language to be less restricted.

Before you read too much further, it may be a good idea to go back and refresh your memory of Chapter 2, which describes the low-level machine instruction set, data types, addressing modes, and conventional register usage.

9.1   A Simple Example

We'll use the same example as in Chapter 8: an implementation of the C library function strcmp(1). But this time we'll include essential elements of assembler syntax and also show some hand-optimized and -scheduled code. The algorithm shown is somewhat cleverer than a naive strcmp() function. Its starting point is a simple algorithm, but with all operations separated out to make them easier to play with, as follows:

```
int
strcmp (char *a0, char *a1)
{
    char t0, t1;
    while (1) {
        t0 = a0[0];
        a0 += 1;
        t1 = a1[0];
        a1 += 1;
        if (t0 == 0)
            break;
        if (t0 != t1)
            break;
    }
}
```

Its speed of running will be reduced by the two conditional branches and two loads per loop iteration, because there isn't enough work to fill the branch and load delay slots. It will also be reduced because as it zooms along a string it's taking a loop-closing branch on every byte. By unrolling the loop to perform two comparisons per iteration and juggling a load down to the tail of the loop, we can rewrite it so that every load and branch gets something useful to put in its delay slot:

```
int
strcmp (char *a0, char *a1)
{
    char t0, t1, t2;

    /* first load moved to loop end,
       so load for first iteration here */
    t0 = a0[0];

    while (1) {
        /* first byte */
        t1 = a1[0];
        if (t0 == 0)
            break;
        a0 += 2;
        if (t0 != t1)
            break;

        /* second byte */
        t2 = a0[-1]; /* we already incremented a0 */
        t1 = a1[1];  /* didn't increment a1 yet */
```

```
        if (t2 == 0)
            /* label t02 in assembler */
            return t2-t1;
        a1 += 2;
        if (t1 != t2) {
            /* label t02 in assembler */
            return t2-t1;
        t0 = a0[0];
        }

    /* label t01 in assembler */
    return t0-t1;
    }
}
```

So now let's translate this code into assembler:

```
#include <mips/asm.h>
#include <mips/regdef.h>

LEAF(strcmp)
    .set    nowarn
    .set    noreorder
    lbu     t0, 0(a0)
1:  lbu     t1, 0(a1)
    beq     t0, zero,.t01       # load delay slot
    addu    a0, a0, 2           # branch delay slot
    bne     t0, t1, .t01
    lbu     t2, -1(a0)          # branch delay slot
    lbu     t1, 1(a1)           # load delay slot
    beq     t2, zero,.t21
    addu    a1, a1, 2           # branch delay slot
    beq     t2, t1, 1b
    lbu     t0, 0(a0)           # branch delay slot

.t21: j    ra
    subu    v0, t2, t1          # branch delay slot

.t01: j    ra
    subu    v0, t0, t1          # branch delay slot
    .set    reorder
END(strcmp)
```

Even without all the scheduling, there's quite a lot of material here. Let's examine it in order:

- *#include*: This file relies on the C preprocessor *cpp* as a good way of giving mnemonic names to constants and of defining simple text-substitution macros. Here *cpp* is being used to put two header files in line before submitting the text to the assembler; `mips/asm.h` defines the macros LEAF and END (discussed further below), and `mips/regdef.h` defines the conventional register names like **t0** and **a0** (Section 2.2.1).

- *Macros*: We're using two macros defined in `mips/asm.h`, **LEAF** and **END**. Here is the basic definition for **LEAF**:

```
#define LEAF(name) \
    .text; \
    .globl  name; \
    .ent    name; \
name:
```

LEAF is used to define a simple subroutine (one that calls no other subroutine and hence is a "leaf" on the calling tree (see Section 10.9.1). Nonleaf functions have to do much more work saving variables, return addresses, and so on, but you might go through your whole MIPS career without needing to write a nonleaf function in assembler. Note the following:

- **.text** says that what the assembler produces is to be kept in the object code section called ".text," which is the section name that C functions use for their instructions.

- **.globl** declares "name" as global, to be included in the module's symbol table as a name that should be unique throughout the whole program. This mimics what the C compiler does to function names (unless they are marked "static").

- **.ent** has no effect on the code produced but tells the assembler to mark this point as the beginning of a function called "name" and to use that information in debug records.

- **name** makes "name" a label for this point in the assembler's output and marks the place where a subroutine call to function "name" will start.

END defines two more assembler items, neither strictly necessary:

```
#define END(name) \
    .size name,.-name; \
    .end    name
```

- **.size** means that in the symbol table, "name" will now be listed with a size that corresponds to the number of bytes of instructions used.

- **.end** delimits the function for debug purposes.

- **.set** *directives*: These are used to tell the assembler how to do its work. In this case, **noreorder** asks it to refrain from attempting to fill branch and load delay slots and to leave the instruction sequence exactly as written—something you're likely to want to do in a carefully tuned library function.

  nowarn asks the assembler not to try to figure out what's going on with all these interleaved loads and branches and to trust that the programmer has got it right. This is not a good idea until you're sure it is right, but after that it quiets unnecessary diagnostics.

- *Labels*: "1:" is a numeric label, which most assemblers will accept as a local label. You can have as many labels called "1" as you like in a program; a reference to "1f" (forward) will get the next one in sequence and "1b" (back) the previous one. This can be useful.

- *Instructions*: You'll notice some unexpected sequences, since the **.set noreorder** has exposed the underlying branch delay slots and requires us to ensure that load data is never used by the following instruction.

  For example, note the use of register **t2** in the second half of the unrolled loop. It's only necessary to use the second register because the **lbu t2, -1(a0)** is in the delay slot of the preceding branch instruction and can't overwrite **t0**, which will be used at the branch target.

Now that we've examined an example, let's get a bit more systematic.

9.2 Syntax Overview

In Appendix B you will find a formal syntax for the original MIPS Corporation assembler; most assemblers from other vendors follow this pattern, although they may differ in their support of certain directives. If you've used an assembler from a unix-like system before, then it should all look fairly familiar.

9.2.1 *Layout, Delimiters, and Identifiers*

For this, you need to be familiar with C. If you are, note that writing in assembler is different from C for the following reasons:

- Assembler code is basically line oriented, and an end-of-line delimits an instruction or directive. You can have more than one instruction/directive on each line, however, as long as they are separated by semicolons.

- All text from a "#" to the end of the line is a comment and is ignored. But don't put a "#" in the leftmost column: It activates the C preprocessor *cpp*, and you will probably want to use that. If you know your code is going to be run through *cpp*, you can use C-style comments: /* ... */. These can be multiline if you like.

- Identifiers for labels and variables can be anything that's legal in C and can also contain "$" and ".".

- In code you can use a number (decimal between 1 and 99) as a label. This is treated as temporary, and you can use the same number as many times as you like. In a branch instruction "1f" (forward) refers to the next "1:" label in the code and "1b" (back) refers to the previous "1:" label. This saves you thinking about names for little branches and loops. Reserve named labels for subroutine entry points or for exceptionally big jumps.

- The MIPS/SGI assembler provided the conventional register names (**a0**, **t5**, etc.) as C preprocessor macros, so you must pass your source through the C preprocessor and include the file mips/regdef.h. Algorithmics assembler knows the names already, but don't depend on that.

- You can put in pointer values; in a word context, a label (or any other relocatable symbol) is replaced with its address. The identifier "**.**" (dot) represents the current location counter. You can even do some limited arithmetic with these things.

- Character constants and strings can be defined as in C.

9.3 General Rules for Instructions

The MIPS assembler allows some convenient shortcuts by behaving nicely when you provide fewer operands than the machine instruction needs, or put in a constant where the machine instruction really needs a register. You'll see this very frequently in real assembler code, so this section summarizes the common cases.

9.3.1 *Computational Instructions: Three-, Two-, and One-Register*

MIPS computational machine instructions are three-register operations, i.e., they are arithmetic or logical functions with two inputs and one output. For example,

```
rd = rs + rt
```

is written as **addu rd,rs,rt**.

We mentioned as well that any or all of the register operands may be identical. To produce a CISC-style, two-operand instruction you just have to use the destination register as a source operand: The assembler will do this for you automatically if you omit **rs**: **addu** *rd, rs* is the same as **addu** *rd, rd, rs*.

Unary operations like **neg, not** are always synthesized from one or more of the three-register instructions. The assembler expects a maximum of two operands for these instructions, so **negu** *rd, rs* is the same as **subu** *rd, zero, rs* and **not** *rd* will be assembled as **nor** *rd, zero, rd*.

Probably the most common register-to-register operation is **move** *rd, rs*. This ubiquitous instruction is implemented by an **or** *rd, zero, rs*.

9.3.2 *Immediates: Computational Instructions with Constants*

In assembler or machine language, a constant value encoded within an instruction is called an *immediate* value. Many of the MIPS arithmetical and logical operations have an alternative form that uses a 16-bit immediate in place of **rt**. The immediate value is first sign-extended or zero-extended to 32 bits; the choice of how it's extended depends on the operation, but in general arithmetical operations sign-extend and logical operations zero-extend.

Although an immediate operand produces a different machine instruction from its three-register version (e.g., **addi** instead of **add**), there is no need for the programmer to write this explicitly. The assembler will spot when the final operand is an immediate and use the correct machine instruction:

```
addu     $2, $4, 64      →    addiu    $2, $4, 64
```

If an immediate value is too large to fit into the 16-bit field in the machine instruction, then the assembler helps out again. It automatically loads the constant into the *assembler temporary register* **at/$1** and then performs the operation using that:

```
add      $4, 0x12345     →    li       at, 0x12345
                              add       $4, $4, at
```

Note the **li** (load immediate) instruction, which you won't find in the machine's instruction set; **li** is a heavily used macro-instruction that loads an arbitrary 32-bit integer value into a register without the programmer having to worry about how it gets there.

When the 32-bit value lies between ±32K it can use a single **addiu** with **$0**; when bits 16–31 are all zero it can use **ori**; when bits 0–15 are all zero it will be **lui**; and when none of these are possible it will be a **lui/ori** pair:

```
li    $3, -5          →    addiu    $3, $0, -5
li    $4, 0x8000      →    ori      $4, $0, 0x8000
li    $5, 0x120000    →    lui      $5, 0x12
li    $6, 0x12345     →    lui      $6, 0x1
                          ori      $6, $6, 0x2345
```

9.3.3 *Regarding 64-Bit and 32-Bit Instructions*

We described how the MIPS architecture extends to 64 bits (Section 2.7.3) by ensuring that programs running only 32-bit (MIPS II) instructions behave exactly as they would on old CPUs by maintaining the top half of all registers as all ones or all zeros (according to the value of bit 31). Many 32-bit instructions carry over directly to 64-bit systems—all bitwise logical operations, for example—but arithmetic functions don't. Adds, subtracts, shifts, multiplies, and divides all need new versions. The new instructions are named by prefixing the old mnemonic with **d** (double): For example, the 32-bit addition instruction **addu** is augmented by the new instruction **daddu**, which does full 64-bit-precision arithmetic. A leading "d" in an instruction mnemonic generally means "double."

9.4 Addressing Modes

As noted previously, the hardware supports only the one addressing mode *base_reg+offset*, where *offset* is in the range −32768 to 32767. However, the assembler will synthesize code to access data at addresses specified in various other ways:

- *Direct*: a data label or external variable name supplied by you
- *Direct+index*: an offset from a labeled location specified with a register
- *Constant*: just a large number, interpreted as an absolute 32-bit address
- *Register indirect*: just register+offset with an offset of zero

When these methods are combined with the assembler's willingness to do simple constant arithmetic at compile time, and the use of a macro processor, you are able to do most of what you might want. Here are some examples:

Instruction			Expands to	
lw	$2, ($3)	→	lw	$2, 0($3)
lw	$2, 8+4($3)	→	lw	$2, 12($3)
lw	$2, *addr*	→	lui	at, %hi(*addr*)
			lw	$2, %lo(*addr*)(at)
sw	$2, *addr*($3)	→	lui	at, %hi(*addr*)
			addu	at, at, $3
			sw	$2, %lo(*addr*)(at)

The symbol **addr** in the above examples can be any of the following:

- A relocatable symbol—the name of a label or variable (whether in this module or elsewhere)

- A relocatable symbol ± a constant expression (the assembler/linker can handle this at system build time)

- A 32-bit constant expression (e.g. the absolute addres of a device register)

The constructs %hi() and %lo() are provided in the MIPS assembler but not in some others. They represent the high and low 16 bits of the address. This is not quite the straightforward division into low and high halfwords that it looks, because the 16-bit offset field of an lw is interpreted as signed. So if the *addr* value is such that bit 15 is a 1, then the %lo(*addr*) value will act as negative and we need to increment %hi(*addr*) to compensate:

addr	%hi(addr)	%lo(addr)
0x12345678	0x1234	0x5678
0x10008000	0x1001	0x8000

The la (load address) macro-instruction provides a similar service for addresses as the li instruction provides for integer constants:

```
la      $2, 4($3)       →       addiu   $2, $3, 4

la      $2, addr        →       lui     at, %hi(addr)
                                addiu   $2, at, %lo(addr)

la      $2, addr($3)    →       lui     at, %hi(addr)
                                addiu   $2, at, %lo(addr)
                                addu    $2, $2, $3
```

In principle, la could avoid messing around with apparently negative %lo( ) values by using an ori instruction. But the linker is already equipped with the ability to fix up addresses in the signed %lo(*addr*) format found for load/store instructions, so la uses the add instruction to avoid the linker having to understand two different fix-up types.

The instruction mnemonic dla is documented by SGI for loading a 64-bit pointer; it will only be necessary in environments that support both 32- and 64-bit pointer representations—which is probably a lot more useful than it sounds. So far, no off-workstation toolkit has needed to implement this.

9.4.1   *Gp-Relative Addressing*

A consequence of the way the MIPS instruction set is crammed into 32-bit operations is that accesses to compiled-in locations usually require at least two instructions, for example:

```
lw      $2, addr        →       lui     at, %hi(addr)
                                lw      $2, %lo(addr)(at)
```

In programs that make a lot of use of global or static data, this can make the compiled code significantly fatter and slower.

Early MIPS compilers introduced a fix for this, which has been carried into most MIPS toolchains. It's usually called *gp-relative addressing*. This technique requires the cooperation of the compiler, assembler, linker, and run-time startup code to pool all of the "small" variables and constants into a single memory region; then it sets register **$28** (known as the *global pointer* or **gp** register) to point to the middle of this region. (The linker creates a special symbol **_gp** whose address is the middle of this region. The address of **_gp** must then be loaded into the **gp** register by the startup code, before any load or store instructions are used.) So long as all the variables together take up no more than 64KB of space, all the data items are now within 32KB of the midpoint, so a load turns into

```
lw      $2, addr        →       lw      $2, addr - _gp(at)
```

The problem is that the compiler and assembler must decide what variables can be accessed via **gp** at the time the individual modules are compiled. The usual test is to include all objects of less than a certain size (8 bytes is the usual default). This limit can usually be controlled by the "**-G n**" compiler/assembler option; specifying "**-G 0**" will switch this optimization off altogether.

While it is a useful trick, there are some pitfalls to watch out for. You must take special care when writing assembler code to declare global data items consistently and correctly:

- Writable, initialized small data items must be put explicitly into the **.sdata** section.

- Global common data must be consistently declared with the correct size:
```
.comm   smallobj, 4
.comm   bigobj, 100
```

- Small external variables should also be explicitly declared
```
.extern smallext, 4
```

- Most assemblers will not act on a declaration unless it precedes the use of the variable.

In C you must declare global variables correctly in all modules that use them. For external arrays, either omit the size, like this,

```
extern int extarray[];
```

or give the correct size:

```
int cmnarray[NARRAY];
```

Sometimes the way programs are run means this method can't be used. Some real-time operating systems, and many PROM monitors, are built with a separately linked chunk of code implementing the kernel, and applications invoke kernel functions with regular subroutine calls. There's no cost-effective method by which you could switch back and forth between the two different values of **gp** that will be used by the application and OS, respectively. In this case either the applications or the OS (but not necessarily both) must be built with **-G 0**.

When the **-G 0** option has been used for compilation of any set of modules, it is usually essential that all libraries linked in with them should be compiled that way. If the linker is confronted with modules that disagree whether a named variable should be put in the small or regular data sections, it's likely to give you peculiar and unhelpful error messages.

9.5   Assembler Directives

We've summarized the directives under functional headings. You can also find a list (without explanations) in Appendix B.

9.5.1   *Selecting Sections*

The names of and support for conventional code and data sections may differ from one toolchain to another. Hopefully most will at least support the original MIPS conventions, which are illustrated (for ROMmable programs) in Figure 9.1.

Within an assembler program the sections are selected as described in the groupings that follow:

.text, .rdata, and .data

Simply put the appropriate section name before the data or instructions, as shown in this example:

```
    .rdata
msg:.asciiz "Hello world!\n"

    .data
table:
    .word    1
```

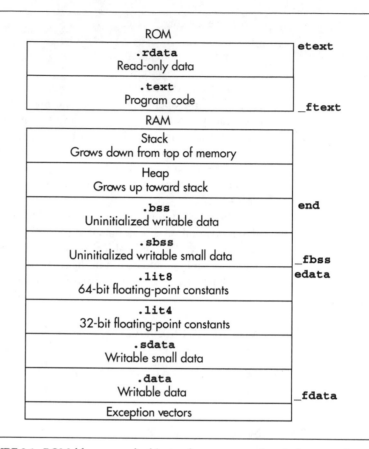

FIGURE 9.1 ROMable program's object code segments and typical memory layout

```
        .word   2
        .word   3

        .text
func:sub    sp, 64
    ...
```

.lit4 and .lit8 Sections: Floating-Point Implicit Constants

You can't write these section names as directives. They are read-only data sections created implicitly by the assembler to hold floating-point constants that are given as arguments to the **li.s** or **li.d** macro instructions. Some assemblers and linkers will save space by combining identical constants.

.bss, .comm, and .lcomm Data

This section name is also not used as a directive. It is used to collect all uninitialized data declared in C modules. It's a feature of C that multiple same-named definitions in different modules are acceptable so long as not more than one of them is initialized. The **.bss** section is used for data that is not initialized anywhere. Fortran programmers would recognize this as what is called *common* data, motivating the name of the directives.

You always have to specify a size for the data (in bytes): When the program is linked, the item will get enough space for the *largest* size. If any module declares it in an initialized data section, all the sizes are used and that definition is used:

```
.comm    dbgflag, 4       # global common variable, 4 bytes
.lcomm   sum, 4           # local common variable, 8 bytes
.lcomm   array, 100       # local common variable, 100 bytes
```

"Uninitialized" is actually a misnomer: Although these sections occupy no space in the object file, the C language assumes that the run-time startup code or operating system will clear the **.bss** area to zero before entering your program; many C programs rely on this behavior.

.sdata, Small Data, and .sbss

These sections are used as alternatives to the **.data** and **.bss** sections above by toolchains that want to separate out smaller data objects. MIPS toolchains do this because the resulting small-object section is compact enough to allow an efficient access mechanism that relies on maintaining a data pointer in a reserved register **gp**, as described in Section 9.4.1.

Note that the **.sbss** is not a legal directive; data is allocated to the **.sbss** section when declared with **.comm** or **.lcomm**, and it is smaller than the **-G** parameter size fed to the assembler program.

.section

Start an arbitrarily named section and supply control flags (which are object code specific and probably toolkit specific). See your toolkit manuals, and always use the specific section name directives above for the common sections.

9.5.2   Practical Program Layout Including Stack and Heap

The program layout illustrated in Figure 9.1 might be suitable for a ROM program running on a bare CPU. The read-only sections are likely to be located in an area of memory remote from the lower read/write sections.

The stack and heap are not real sections that are recognized by the assembler or linker. Typically they are initialized and maintained by the run-time system. The stack is defined by setting the **sp** register to the top of available memory (aligned to an 8-byte boundary). The heap is defined by a global pointer variable used by functions like malloc functions; it's often initialized to the **end** symbol, which the linker has calculated as the highest location used by declared variables.

Special Symbols

Figure 9.1 also shows a number of special symbols that are automatically defined by the linker to allow programs to discover the start and end of their various sections. They are descended from conventions that grew up in unix-style OSs, and some are peculiar to the MIPS environment. Your toolkit might or might not define all of them; those marked with a $\sqrt{}$ in the following list are pretty certain to be there:

Symbol	Standard?	Value
_ftext		Start of text (code) segment
etext	$\sqrt{}$	End of text (code) segment
_fdata		Start of initialized data segment
edata	$\sqrt{}$	End of initialized data segment
_fbss		Start of uninitialized data segment
end	$\sqrt{}$	End of uninitialized data segment

9.5.3 Data Definition and Alignment

Having selected the correct section, you will then specify the data objects themselves using the directives described in this section.

.byte, .half, .word, and .dword

These directives output integers that are 1, 2, 4, or 8 bytes long, respectively.[1] A list of values may be given, separated by commas. Each value may be repeated a number of times by following it with a colon and a repeat count, for example:

```
.byte 3            # 1 byte:      3
.half 1, 2, 3      # 3 halfwords: 1 2 3
.word 5 : 3, 6, 7  # 5 words:     5 5 5 6 7
```

Note that the position of this data (relative to the start of the section) is automatically aligned to the appropriate boundary before the data is output. If

---

1. Some toolchains, even those supporting 64-bit processors, may fail to provide the **.dword** directive.

you really want to output unaligned data, then explicit action must be taken using the `.align` directive described below.

.float and .double

These output single- or double-precision floating-point values, respectively:

```
.float     1.4142175      # 1 single-precision value
.double    1e+10, 3.1415  # 2 double-precision values
```

Multiple values and repeat counts may be used in the same way as the integer directives.

.ascii and .asciiz

These directives output ASCII strings, without and with a terminating null character, respectively. The following example outputs two identical strings:

```
.ascii     "Hello\0"
.asciiz    "Hello"
```

.align

This directive allows you to specify an alignment greater than that normally required for the next data directive. The alignment is specified as a power of two:

```
    .align  4       # align to 16-byte boundary (2^4)
var:
    .word   0
```

If a label (**var** in this case) comes immediately before the `.align`, then the label will still be aligned correctly. For example, the following is exactly equivalent to the above case:

```
var:
    .align  4       # align to 16-byte boundary (2^4)
    .word   0
```

For packed data structures this directive allows you to override the automatic alignment feature of `.half`, `.word`, etc. by specifying a zero alignment. This will stay in effect until the next section change, for example:

```
    .half   3       # correctly aligned halfword
    .align  0       # switch off auto-alignment
    .word   100     # word aligned on halfword boundary
```

.comm and .lcomm

These directives declare a *common*, or *uninitialized*, data object by specifying the object's name and size.

An object declared with **.comm** is available to all modules that declare it: It is allocated space by the linker, which uses the largest declared size. But if any module declares it in one of the initialized **.data**, **.sdata**, or **.rdata** sections, then all the sizes are ignored and the initialized definition is used instead.

.comm is useful in that it avoids the asymmetry of having to declare something in one place and then refer to it everywhere else, when it's got no special attachment to any one file. But it's really there because Fortran defines common variables with these semantics, and we want to be able to compile Fortran programs via assembly language.

An object declared with **.lcomm** is local and is allocated space in the uninitialized **.bss** (or **.sbss**) section by the assembler, but it is otherwise invisible from outside the module:

```
.comm    dbgflag, 4  # global common variable, 4 bytes
.lcomm   array, 100  # local uninitialized object, 100 bytes
```

.space

The **.space** directive increments the current section's location counter by a number of bytes, for example:

```
struc: .word 3
    .space   120      # 120-byte gap
    .word    -1
```

For normal data and text sections the space will be zero-filled; however, if your assembler allows you to declare sections whose content is not defined in the object file (like **.bss**), the space just affects the offset of subsequent labels and variables.

9.5.4 Symbol-Binding Attributes

Symbols (labels in one of the code or data segments) can be made visible and used by the linker that joins separate modules into a single program. The linker binds a symbol to an address and substitutes the address for assembler language references to the symbol.

Symbols can have three levels of visibility:

- *Local*: These are invisible outside the module they are declared in and unused by the linker. You don't have to worry about whether the same local symbol is used in another module.

- *Global*: These are made public for use by the linker. Using the **.extern** directive, you can refer to a global symbol in another module without defining any local space for it.

- *Weak global*: This obscure feature is provided by some toolchains using the directive **.weakext**. It allows you to define a symbol that will link to a global symbol of the same name if one is found but that will quietly default to being a local object otherwise. You shouldn't use this feature where **.comm** would do the job.

.globl

Unlike C, where module-level data and functions are automatically *global* unless declared with the `static` keyword, ordinary assembler labels have *local* binding unless explicitly modified by the **.globl** directive. You don't need **.globl** for objects declared with the **.comm** directive; these automatically have global binding. Use the directive as follows:

```
    .data
    .globl  status      # global variable
status: .word   0

    .text
    .globl  set_status  # global function
set_status:
    subu    sp,24
    ...
```

.extern

All references to labels that are not defined within the current module are automatically assumed to be references to globally bound symbols in another module (*external* symbols). In some cases the assembler can generate better code if it knows how big the referenced object is (see Section 9.4.1). An external object's size is specified using the **.extern** directive, as follows:

```
.extern index, 4
.extern array, 100
lw      $3, index       # load a 4-byte (1-word) external
lw      $2, array($3)   # load part of a 100-byte external
sw      $2, value       # store in an unknown-size external
```

.weakext

Some assemblers and toolchains support the concept of *weak* global binding. This allows you to specify a provisional binding for a symbol, which may be overridden if a normal (*strong*) global definition is encountered, for example:

```
    .data
    .weakext errno
errno: .word   0

    .text
    lw      $2, errno   # may use local or external definition
```

This module, and others that access **errno**, will use this local definition of **errno** unless some other module also defines it with a **.globl**.

It is also possible to declare a local variable with one name but to make it weakly global with a different name:

```
    .data
myerrno: .word   0
    .weakext errno, myerrno

    .text
    lw      $2,myerrno  # always use local definition
    lw      $2,errno    # may use local definition or other
```

9.5.5 Function Directives

You can generate correct assembler code for a MIPS function by using a global label for its entry point and returning from it with a **jr** instruction. However, MIPS assemblers generally expect you to use special directives to mark the start and end of each function and to describe the stack frame that it uses.

.ent and .end

These directives mark the start and end of a function. A trivial leaf function might look like this:

```
    .text
    .ent    localfunc
localfunc:
    addu    v0,a1,a2    # return (arg1 + arg2)
    j       ra
    .end    localfunc
```

The label name may be omitted from the **.end** directive, which then defaults to the name used in the last **.ent**. Specifying the name explicitly allows the assembler to check that you haven't missed any earlier **.ent** or **.end** directives.

.aent

Some functions may provide multiple, alternative entry points. The **.aent** directive identifies labels as such, for example:

```
        .text
        .globl  memcpy
        .ent    memcpy
memcpy: move    t0,a0           # swap first two arguments
        move    a0,a1
        move    a1,t0

        .globl  bcopy
        .aent   bcopy
bcopy:  lb      t0,0(a0)        # very slow byte copy
        sb      t0,0(a1)
        addu    a0,1
        addu    a1,1
        subu    a2,1
        bne     a2,zero,bcopy
        j       ra
        .end    memcpy
```

.frame, .mask, and .fmask

Most functions need to allocate a stack frame in which to

- Save the return address register **ra**
- Save any of the registers **s0–s9** and **$f20–$f31** that they modify (known as the *callee-saves* registers)
- Store local variables and temporaries
- Pass arguments to other functions

In some CISC architectures, the stack frame allocation and possibly register saving are done by special-purpose *enter* and *leave* instructions, but in the MIPS architecture the allocation has to be coded by the compiler or assembly language programmer. However, debuggers need to know the layout of each stack frame to do stack back-traces and so on, and in the original MIPS Corporation toolchain these directives provided this information. In other toolchains they may be quietly ignored and the stack layout determined at run time by disassembling the function prologue. Putting these directives in your code is therefore not always essential but can do no harm. Many toolchains supply a header file, probably called asm.h, which provides C-style macros to generate a number of standard directives as required (see Section 10.1).

The .frame directive takes three operands:

```
.frame      framereg, framesize, returnreg
```

- *framereg*: This is the register used to access the local stack frame—usually $sp.

- *returnreg*: This register holds the return address. Some compilers indicate $0, when the return address is stored in the stack frame (some compilers convey this with the .mask directive instead); all use $31 if this is a *leaf* function (i.e., it doesn't call any other functions) and the return address is not saved.

- *framesize*: This is the total size of stack frame allocated by this function: It should always be the case that $sp + *framesize* = previous $sp.

The .mask directive indicates where the function saves general registers in the stack frame; .fmask does the same for floating-point registers:

```
.mask   regmask, regoffs
.fmask  fregmask, fregoffs
```

Their first argument is *regmask*, a bitmap of which registers are being saved (i.e., bit 1 set = $1, bit 2 set = $2, etc.); the second argument is *regoffs*, the distance from *framereg* + *framesize* to the start of the register save area.

How these directives relate to the stack frame layout, and examples of their use, can be found in Section 10.9. Remember that the directives do not create the stack frame, they just describe its layout; that code still has to be written explicitly by the compiler or assembly language programmer.

9.5.6 *Assembler Control (.set)*

The original MIPS Corporation assembler is an ambitious program that performs intelligent macro expansion, delay slot filling, peephole optimization, and sophisticated instruction reordering (scheduling) to minimize pipeline stalls. Most other assemblers will be less complex: modern optimizing compilers usually prefer to do these sort of optimizations themselves. In the interest of source code compatibility and to make the programmer's life easier, however, all MIPS assemblers should at least perform macro expansion, insert extra **nop**s as required to hide branch and load delay slots, and prevent pipeline hazards in normal code.

With a reordering assembler it is sometimes necessary to restrict the reordering to guarantee correct timing or to account for side effects of instructions that the assembler cannot know about (e.g., enabling and disabling interrupts). The **.set** directives provide this control.

.set noreorder/reorder

By default the assembler is in *reorder* mode, which allows it to reorder your instructions to avoid pipeline hazards and (perhaps) to achieve better performance; in this mode it will not allow you to insert your own **nop**s. Conversely, code that is in a *noreorder* region will not be optimized or changed in any way. This means that you can completely control the instruction order, but the disadvantage is that you must now schedule the code yourself and fill load and branch delay slots with useful instructions or **nop**s. For example:

```
.set    noreorder
lw      t0, 0(a0)
nop                     # in the load delay slot
subu    t0, 1
bne     t0, zero, loop
nop                     # in the branch delay slot
.set    reorder
```

.set volatile/novolatile

Any load or store instruction within a **volatile** region will not be moved (in particular, with respect to other loads and stores). This can be important for accesses to memory-mapped device registers, where the order of reads and writes is important. For example, if the following fragment did not use **.set volatile**, then the assembler might decide to move the second **lw** before the **sw** to fill the first load delay slot:

```
.set    volatile
lw      t0,0(a0)
sw      t0,0(a1)
lw      t1,4(a0)
.set    novolatile
```

Hazard avoidance and other optimizations are not affected by this option.

.set noat/at

The assembler reserves register **$1** (known as the *assembler temporary*, or **at**, register) to hold intermediate values when performing macro expansions; if you attempt to use the register yourself, you will receive a warning or error message. It is not always obvious when the assembler will use **at**, and there are certain circumstances when you may need to ensure that it does not (for example, in exception handlers before **$1** has been saved). Switching on **noat** will make the assembler generate an error message if it needs to use **$1** in a macro expansion, and will allow you to use it explicitly without receiving warnings, for example:

```
xcptgen:
    .set    noat
    subu    k0,sp,XCP_SIZE
    sw      at,XCP_AT(k0)
    .set    at
```

.set nomacro/macro

Most of the time you will not care whether an assembler statement generates more than one real machine instruction, but of course there are exceptions. For instance, when you are manually filling a branch delay slot in a *noreorder* region, it would almost certainly be wrong to use a complex macro-instruction; if the branch were taken, then only the first instruction of the macro would be executed. Switching on **nomacro** will cause a warning if any statement expands to more than one machine instruction. For example, compare the following two fragments:

```
    .set    noreorder
    blt     a1,a2,loop
    li      a0,0x12345  # should be the branch delay slot
    .set    reorder


    .set    noreorder
    blt     a1,a2,loop
    .set    nomacro
    li      a0,0x12345
    .set    macro
    .set    reorder
```

The first will generate what is probably incorrect code, because the **li** is expanded into two machine instructions (**lui** and **ori**) and only the **lui** will be executed in the branch delay slot. With the second instruction you'll get an error message. Some assemblers will flag the scheduling mistake automatically, but you cannot rely on that.

.set nobopt/bopt

Setting the **nobopt** control prevents the assembler from carrying out certain types of branch optimization. It is usually used only by compilers.

9.5.7 *Compiler/Debugger Support*

Found in autogenerated files, such as the output from a compiler or preprocessor, the directive **.file** is used by the assembler to attribute any errors back to the generating source file.

9.5.8 *Additional Directives in SGI Assembly Language*

In this chapter I've tried to stick to a subset of assembly language that I believe most toolkits will support. However, SGI's assembler (supporting the SGI n32/n64 standards for register use) defines a whole lot more. Try not to rely on these, but here's what they mean.

.2byte, .4byte, and .8byte

These define data, but whereas the similar directives **.half**, **.word**, and **.dword** pack out the section to align the data appropriately, these don't. You can achieve the same effect with **.align 0** followed by a regular declaration followed by a redefinition of the section name to get natural alignment switched back on.

.cpadd, .cpload, .cplocal, .cprestore, .cpreturn, .cpsetup, .gpvalue, and .gpword

These directives facilitate generation of the kind of position-independent code used to build shared libraries on SGI systems and are not expected to be useful for embedded systems.

.dynsym

This is some kind of ELF-specific name aliasing for a symbol.

.lab

This defines a label that might contain characters that would be illegal in front of a colon.

.loc

This directive cross-references another file, like the **.file** directive above—but this one allows you to select a column number within the source line of the generating program.

.origin

This changes the current position in the section by a supplied offset.

.set [no]transform

This marks code that must not be modified by SGI's pixie program. pixie takes any MIPS application and generates a version of it with profiling counters built in. It is irrelevant to non-UNIX code.

.size and .type

These directives allow you to specify the size and/or type of a symbol. In most object code formats, each symbol is associated with a size and the linker may check that the importer and exporter of a symbol agree about its size or type.

Chapter

10

C Programming on MIPS

This chapter discusses things you are likely to need to know when building a complete MIPS system using C code. Perversely, that means a lot of this chapter is not about what you see when you write in the C language (which I'm assuming you know or can find out about elsewhere), but what shows up in the assembler language that is produced by the C compiler. To avoid turning this chapter into a whole new book, I've tried to limit the discussion to issues that are particularly likely to confront you when you first write or port code for MIPS.

An efficient C run-time environment relies on conventions (enforced by compilers, and therefore mandatory for assembly language programmers) about register usage within C-compatible functions. Refer to Section 2.2.1 for the overall conventions as to register use. In this chapter we'll cover

- *The stack, subroutine linkage, and argument passing*: how these processes are implemented for MIPS and how they support everything while avoiding unnecessary work

- *Shared and nonshared libraries*: a note on the complex mechanisms used by shared-library OSs

- *An introduction to compiler optimization*: as it might affect you

- *Hints about device access from C*: since that's how most device-driving code is written

Regarding other high-level languages, I realize that some of you may not be writing in C. However, if you are producing compiled code for MIPS that is to link with standard libraries, much of this chapter is still relevant to you. I haven't dealt specifically with any other language, because I don't understand them well and I can't figure out where I should stop.

10.1 The Stack, Subroutine Linkage, and Parameter Passing

Many MIPS programs are written in mixed languages—for embedded systems programmers, this is most likely to be a mix of C (maybe C++) and assembler.

From the very start MIPS Corporation established a set of conventions about how to pass arguments to functions (this is C-speak for "pass parameters to subroutines") and about how to return values from functions. These conventions can look very complex, but partly that's just appalling documentation. The conventions follow logically from an unappreciated underlying principle.

The basic principle is that all arguments are allocated space in a data structure on the stack, but the contents of the first few stack locations are placed in CPU registers—the corresponding memory locations are left undefined. In practice, this means that for most calls the arguments are all passed in registers; however, the stack data structure is the best starting point for understanding the process.

Since about 1995 Silicon Graphics has introduced changes into the calling conventions, in a search for higher performance. They have named these calling conventions as follows:

- *o32:* The traditional MIPS convention ("o" for old); described in detail below. This convention (not including features SGI added to support shared libraries) is still pretty much universally used by embedded toolchains; however, it seems likely that the two new models may be supported as options by other toolchains sometime soon.

- *n64:* New convention for 64-bit programs. SGI's 64-bit model implies that both pointers and C long integer types are compiled as 64-bit data items. The longer pointers represent nothing but extra overhead for embedded applications, so it's questionable whether this convention will be taken up outside the workstation environment. However, n64 also changes the conventions for using registers and the rules for passing parameters; and because it puts more arguments in registers, it improves performance.

- *n32:* This convention has identical rules to n64 for passing parameters, but leaves pointers and the C long data types implemented as 32 bits. However, SGI and other compilers support an extended integer data type long long, which is a hardware-supported 64-bit integer. This compilation model is becoming quite popular in embedded systems.

We'll describe the o32 standard first and then point out the changes with n32 and n64. The changes are summarized in Section 10.8.

There are other standards in discussion as this book goes to press, most of which seem to be called MIPS EABI. The overall MIPS EABI project is aimed at producing a range of standards to make embedded toolkits interwork better, which is a really good idea; however, the new calling conventions seem to have arisen from a proprietary project to build something like SGI's n32 (but simpler and regrettably incompatible). We hope something good comes out of this—but for the time being you can reasonably use o32 compilers for embedded applications and you won't lose a lot.

10.2   Stack Argument Structure

This and subsequent sections describe the original MIPS conventions which SGI now calls o32. We'll summarize the changes implicit in the new standards in Section 10.8.

The MIPS hardware does not directly support a stack, but the calling convention requires one. The stack is grown downward and the current stack bottom is kept in register **sp** (alias **$29**). Any OS that is providing protection and security will make no assumptions about the user's stack, and the value of **sp** doesn't really matter except at the point where a function is called. But it is conventional to keep **sp** at or below the lowest stack location your function has used.

At the point where a function is called, **sp** must be 8 byte aligned (not required by 32-bit MIPS hardware, but essential for compatibility with 64-bit CPUs and part of the rules). Subroutines can fit in with this by always adjusting the stack pointer by a multiple of eight.[1]

To call a subroutine according to the MIPS standard, the caller creates a data structure on the stack to hold the arguments and sets **sp** to point to it. The first argument (leftmost in the C source) is lowest in memory. Each argument occupies at least one word (32 bits); 64-bit values like floating-point `double` and (for some CPUs) 64-bit integer values must be aligned on an 8-byte boundary (as are data structures that contain a 64-bit scalar field).

The argument structure really does look like a C `struct`, but there are some more rules. Firstly, you should allocate a minimum of 16 bytes of argument space for any call, even if the arguments would fit in less. Secondly, any partial-word argument (`char` or `short`) is "promoted" to an `int` and passed as a 32-bit object. This does not apply to partial-word fields inside a `struct` argument.

10.3   Using Registers to Pass Arguments

Any arguments allocated to the first 16 bytes (four words) of the argument structure are passed in registers, and the caller can and does leave the first 16

---

1. SGI's n32 and n64 standards call for the stack to be maintained with 16-byte alignment.

bytes of the structure undefined. The stack-held structure must still be reserved; the called function is entitled to save the register-held argument values back into memory if it needs to (perhaps because someone generates a pointer to the arguments—in C, arguments are variables and you can form a pointer to any variable).

The four words of register argument values go in **a0** through **a3** (**$4** through **$7**), respectively, except where the caller can be sure that the data would be better loaded into floating-point (FP) registers.

The criteria for deciding when and how to use FP registers look peculiar. Old-fashioned C had no built-in mechanism for checking that the caller and callee agreed on the type of each argument to a function. To help programmers survive this, the caller converted arguments to fixed types, int for integer values and double for floating point. There was no way of saving a programmer who confused floating-point and integer arguments, but at least some possibilities for chaos were averted.

Modern C compilers use function prototypes available to all callers, which define all the argument types. But even with function prototypes, there are routines—notably the familiar printf()—where the type of arguments is unknown at compile time; printf() discovers the number and type of its arguments at run time.

MIPS made the following rules.

Unless the first argument is a floating-point type, no arguments can be passed in FP registers. This is a kludge that ensures that traditional functions like printf() still work: Its first argument is a pointer, so all arguments are allocated to integer registers and printf() will be able to find all its argument data (regardless of the argument type). The rule is also not going to make common math functions inefficient, because they mostly take only FP arguments.

Where the first argument is a floating-point type, it will be passed in an FP register, and in this case so will any other FP types that fit in the first 16 bytes of the argument structure. Two doubles occupy 16 bytes, so only two FP registers are defined for arguments—**fa0** and **fa1**, or **$f12** and **$f14**. Evidently nobody thought that functions explicitly defined to have lots of single-precision arguments were frequent enough to make another rule.

Another peculiarity is that if you define a function that returns a structure type that is too big to be returned in the two registers normally used, then the return-value convention involves the invention of a pointer as the implicit first argument before the first (visible) argument (see Section 10.7).

If you're faced with writing an assembler routine with anything but a simple and obvious calling convention, it's probably worth building a dummy function in C and compiling it with the "-S" option to produce an assembler file you can use as a template.

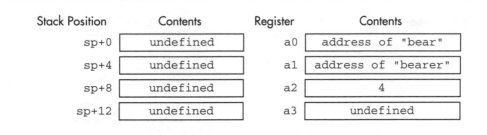

FIGURE 10.1   Argument structure, three non-FP operands

10.4   Examples from the C Library

Here is a code example:

```
thesame =  strncmp("bear", "bearer", 4);
```

We'll draw out the argument structure and the registers separately (see Figure 10.1), though in this case no argument data goes into memory; but later we'll see examples where it does.[1]

There are fewer than 16 bytes of arguments, so they all fit in registers.

That seems a ridiculously complex way of deciding to put three arguments into the usual registers! But let's try something a bit more tricky from the math library:

```
double ldexp (double, int);

y = ldexp(x, 23); /* y = x * (2**23) */
```

Figure 10.2 on page 272 shows the corresponding structure and register values.

10.5   An Exotic Example: Passing Structures

C allows you to use structure types as arguments (it is much more common practice to pass pointers to structures instead, but the language supports both). To fit in with the MIPS rules, the structure being passed just becomes part of the argument structure. Inside a C structure, byte and halfword fields are packed

---

1. After much mental struggle, I decided it was best to have the arguments ordered top to bottom in these pictures. Because the stack grows down that means memory addresses increase down the page, which is opposite from how I've drawn memory elsewhere in the book.

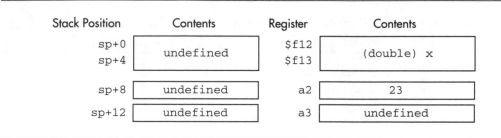

FIGURE 10.2 Argument passing: A floating-point argument

together into single words of memory, so when we use a register to pass the data that conceptually belongs to the stack-resident structure, we have to pack the register with data to mimic the arrangement of data in memory.

So if we have

```
struct thing {
    char letter;
    short count;
    int value;
} = {"z", 46, 100000};

(void) processthing (thing);
```

then the arguments show in in Figure 10.3 will be generated.

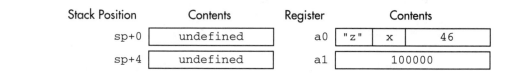

FIGURE 10.3 Arguments when passing a structure type

Note that because MIPS C structures are always laid out with fields so their memory order matches the order of definition (though padded where necessary to conform to the alignment rules), the placement of fields inside the register follows the byte order exposed by load/store instructions, which differs according to the CPU's endianness. The layout in Figure 10.3 is inspired by a big-endian CPU, when the `char` value in the structure should end up in the most-significant 8 bits of the argument register but is packed together with the `short`.

If you really want to pass structure types as arguments, and they must contain partial-word data types, you should try this out and see whether your compiler gets it right.

10.6   Passing a Variable Number of Arguments

Functions for which the number and type of arguments are determined only at run time stress conventions to their limits. Consider this example:

```
printf ("length = %f, width = %f, num = %d\n", 1.414, 1.0, 12);
```

The rules above allow us to see that the argument structure and register contents will be as shown in Figure 10.4.

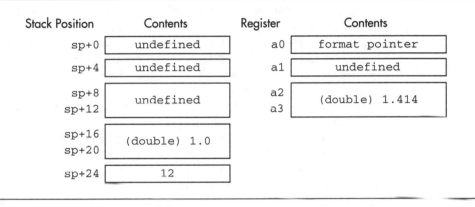

FIGURE 10.4 Argument passing for *printf()*

There are two things to note. Firstly, the padding at **sp+4** is required to get correct alignment of the double values (the C rule is that floating-point arguments are always passed as double unless you explicitly decide otherwise with a typecast or function prototype). Note that padding to an 8-byte boundary can cause one of the standard argument registers to be skipped.

Secondly, because the first argument is not a floating-point value, the rules tell us not to use any FP registers for arguments. So the data for the second argument (coded as it would be in memory) is loaded into the two registers **a2** and **a3**.

This is much more useful than it looks!

The printf() subroutine is defined with the stdarg.h macro package, which provides a portable cover for the register and stack manipulation involved in accessing an unpredictable number of operands of unpredictable types. The printf() routine picks off the arguments by taking the address of the first or second argument and advancing through memory up the argument structure to find further arguments.

To make this work we need to persuade the C compiler working on the printf() routine to store the registers **a0** through **a3** into their "shadow" locations in the argument structure. Some compilers will see you taking the address of an argument and take the hint; ANSI C compilers should react to "..."

in the function definition; others may need some horrible "pragma" which will be decently concealed by the macro package.

Now you can see why it was necessary to put the double value into the integer registers; that way stdarg and the compiler can just store the registers **a0–a3** into the first 16 bytes of the argument structure, regardless of the type or number of the arguments.

10.7 Returning a Value from a Function

An integer or pointer return value will be in register **v0** (**$2**). By MIPS/SGI-defined convention, register **v1** (**$3**) is reserved, even though many compilers don't use it. However, expect it to be used in 32-bit code for returning 64-bit, non-floating-point, values. Some compilers may define a 64-bit data type (often called long long) and some may use **v1** when returning a structure value that fits in 64 bits but not in 32.

Any floating-point result comes back in register **$f0** (implicitly using **$f1** in a 32-bit CPU, if the value is double precision).

If a function is declared in C as returning a structure value that is too big to fit into the return registers **v0** and **v1**, something else has to be done. In this case the caller makes room on its stack for an anonymous structure variable, and a pointer to that structure is prepended to the explicit arguments; the called function copies its return value to the template. Following the normal rules for arguments, the implicit first argument will be in register **a0** when the function is called. On return, **v0** points to the returned structure too.

10.8 Evolving Register-Use Standards: SGI's n32 and n64

For the purposes of this section (calling conventions and integer register usage) the n32 and n64 ABIs are identical.[1] The n32/n64 ABIs are applicable only to MIPS III CPUs which have 64-bit registers.

Despite the significant attempts to keep the register conventions similar, o32 and n32/n64 are deeply incompatible and functions compiled in different ways will not link together successfully. The following points summarize the n32/n64 rules:

- They provide for up to eight arguments to be passed in registers.
- Argument slots and therefore argument registers are 64 bits in size. Shorter integer arguments are promoted to a 64-bit register.

---

1. Under the n64 convention long and pointer types are compiled as 64-bit objects; with n32 only long long types are 64 bits.

- They do not require the caller to allocate stack space for arguments passed in registers.

- They pass structures and arrays in registers where possible (like the old standard does).

- They pass any floating-point variable that fits into the first eight argument slots in an FP register. In fact, these rules will also use an FP register for aligned `double` fields in arrays and structures, so long as the field isn't in a `union` and isn't a variable argument to `printf()` or a similar variable-argument function.

When life gets complicated (as when passing structures or arrays), the use of the registers is still figured out from a ghostly argument structure, even though it doesn't now have any stack space reserved.

The n32/n64 conventions abandon o32's first-argument-not-FP kludge which o32 uses to identify floating-point arguments as special cases for `printf()` and so on. The new conventions require that both caller and callee code be compiled with full knowledge of the number and type of arguments and therefore that they need function prototypes.

For a function like `printf()`, where the type of arguments is unknown at compile time, all the variable arguments are actually passed in integer registers.

The n32/n64 organization has a different set of register-use conventions; Table 10.1 compares the use of integer registers with the o32 system. There is only one material difference: four registers that used to be regarded purely as temporaries should now be used to pass the fifth through the eighth arguments. I'm puzzled by the arbitrary and apparently unnecessary reallocation of names among the temporary registers, but this is how they did it.

You might think that compiled code would suffer from losing four registers that were previously available for temporary storage, but this is only appearance. All argument registers and the **v0** and **v1** registers are available for the compiler to use as temporaries most of the time. Also, the change to n32/n64 has not affected which of the registers are designated as "saved" (i.e., the registers whose value may be assumed to survive a subroutine call).[1]

The floating-point register conventions (shown in Table 10.2) change more dramatically; this is not surprising, since the n32/n64 conventions are for MIPS III CPUs which have 16 extra FP registers to play with—recall that use of an even-numbered register in the old architecture usually implied use of the next-

---

1. This is not quite true. In SGI computers functions manipulate the **gp** register to help implement position-independent code (see Section 10.11.2 for details). In o32 each function could do what it liked with **gp**, which meant that you might have to restore the register after each function call. In n32/n64 the **gp** register is now defined as "saved." Most embedded systems leave **gp** constant, so the differences are academic.

TABLE 10.1 Integer register usage evolution in newer SGI tools

Register number	Name	Use			
$0	zero	Always zero			
$1	at	Assembler temporary			
$2, $3	v0, v1	Return value from function			
$4–$7	a0–a3	Arguments			
		o32		*n32/n64*	
	Name	*Use*		*Name*	*Use*
$8–$11	t0–t3	Temporaries		a4–a7	Arguments
$12–$15	t4–t7			t0–t3	Temporaries
$24, $25	t8, t9			t8, t9	
$16–$23	s0–s7	Saved registers			
$26, $27	k0, k1	Reserved for interrupt/trap handler			
$28	gp	Global pointer			
$29	sp	Stack pointer			
$30	s8/fp	Frame pointer if needed (additional saved register if not)			
$31	ra	Return address for subroutine			

up odd-numbered one.[1] While SGI could have interleaved the new registers and maintained some vestiges of compatibility, the company decided instead to tear up most of the existing rules and start again.

In addition to the larger number of arguments that can be passed in registers, the n32/n64 standard doesn't make any rules dependent on whether the first argument is a floating-point type. Instead, arguments are allocated to registers according to their position in the argument list. Here again is one of the examples used above:

```
double ldexp (double, int);

y = ldexp(x, 23); /* y = x * (2**23) */
```

Figure 10.5 shows the corresponding n32/n64 structure and register values.

---

1. MIPS III CPUs have a mode switch that makes their FP behavior totally compatible with earlier 32-bit CPUs; n32/n64 assume that the CPU is running with that switch off.

TABLE 10.2   FP register usage with o32 and n32/n64 conventions

Register number	o32 use
$f0, $f2	Return values; **fv1** is used only for complex data type and is not available in C
$f4, $f6, $f8, $f10	Temporaries—functions can use without any need to save
$f12, $f14	Arguments
$f16, $f18	Temporaries
$f20, $f22, $f24, $f26, $f28, $f30	Saved registers—functions must save and restore any of these registers they want to write, making them suitable for long-lived values that persist across function calls

Register number	n32 use	n64 use
$f0, $f2	Return values—**$f2** is used only when returning a structure of exactly two floating-point values; this is a special case that deals with Fortran complex numbers	
$f1, $f3		
$f4–$f10	Temporaries	
$f12–$f19	Arguments	
$f20–$f23	Evens (from $f20-$f30) are temporary; odds (from $f21-$f31) are saved	Temporaries
$f24–$f31		Saved registers

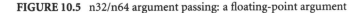

	Stack Position	Contents		Register	Contents
	sp+0	undefined		$f12	(double) x
	sp+4				
	sp+8	undefined		a1	23

FIGURE 10.5   n32/n64 argument passing: a floating-point argument

Although n32/n64 can handle an arbitrary mix of floating-point and other values and still put any double types that are in the first eight arguments in FP registers, there are some careful rules. Any argument that is touched by a union (and that therefore might not really be a double) is excluded and so are any of the variable arguments of a variable-number-of-arguments function. Note that this decision is made on the basis of having a function prototype;

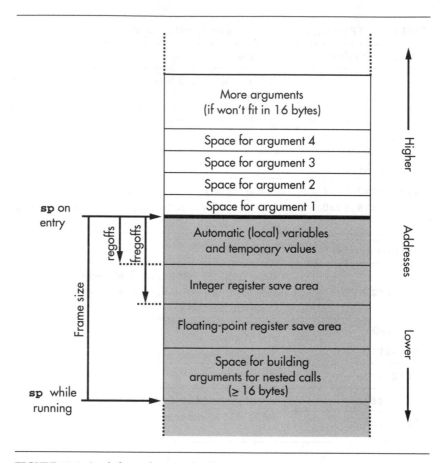

FIGURE 10.6 Stack frame for a nonleaf function

with no prototype, you can break things. SGI's linker will usually detect this and warn you.

10.9   Stack Layouts, Stack Frames, and Helping Debuggers

Figure 10.6 gives a diagrammatic view of the stack frame of a MIPS function. (We're back to having the stack growing down, with higher memory at the top.) You should recognize the slots reserved for the first four words of the function's arguments as required by the traditional MIPS function calling convention— newer calling conventions will only provide any space they actually need.

The gray areas of the diagram show stack space used by the function itself; the white area, above the bold line, belongs to the caller. *All* the gray components of the stack frame are optional, and some functions need none of them;

such a simple function does not need to do anything to the stack. We'll see some of those in the examples through the rest of the chapter.

Apart from the arguments (whose layout must be agreed with the caller), the stack structure is private to the function. The only reason we need a standard arrangement is for debugging and diagnostic tools, which want to be able to navigate the stack. If we interrupt a running program for debugging, we'd very much like to be able to run backward up the stack, displaying a list of the functions that have been called en route to our breakpoint and the arguments passed to those functions. Moreover, we'd like to be able to step the debugger context back up the stack a few positions and in that context to discover the value of variables—even if that piece of code was maintaining the variable's data in a register, as optimizing compilers should.

To perform this analysis, the debugger must know a standard stack layout and must be fed information that allows it to see the size of each stack frame component and the internal layout of each of those components. If a function somewhere up the stack saved the value of **s0** in order to use it, the debugger needs to know where to find the saved value.

In CISC architectures, there is often a complex function call instruction that maintains a stack frame similar to that in Figure 10.6 but with an additional frame pointer register that corresponds to the position marked "sp on entry" on our diagram. In such a CPU, the caller's frame pointer will be stored at some known stack position, allowing a debugger to skip up the stack by analyzing a simple linked list. But in a MIPS CPU, all this extra run-time work is eliminated; most of the time a compiler knows how much to decrement the stack pointer at the head of a function and how much to increment it before return.

So in the minimal MIPS stack frame, where is a debugger to find out where data is stored? Some debuggers are quite heroic and will even interpret the first few instructions of a function to find how large the stack frame is and to locate the stored return address. But most toolchains pass at least some stack frame information in the object code, written there by suitable assembler directives.

Since the mixture of directives is quite dependent on the toolkit, it's worth defining prologue and epilogue macros that both save you from having to remember the details and make it easier to change to another toolkit if you need to. Most toolkits will come with some macros ready to use; you'll see simple ones called **LEAF** and **NESTED** used in the examples below.

We haven't fully documented the SGI conventions, but the examples that follow (using the recommended function prologue and epilogue macros) are compatible with old versions of the SGI tools and therefore are probably compatible with most embedded toolkits.

The key directives are **.frame** and **.mask**, and you can read more about them in Section 9.5.

We can divide up functions into three classes and prescribe three different approaches, which will probably cover everything you need.

10.9.1 *Leaf Functions*

Functions that contain no calls to other functions are called *leaf functions*. They don't have to worry about setting up argument structures and can safely maintain data in the nonpreserved registers **t0–t7**, **a0–a3**, and **v0** and **v1**. They can use the stack for storage if they feel like it but can and should leave the return address in register **ra** and return directly to it.[1]

Most functions that you may write in assembler for tuning reasons or as convenience functions for accessing features not visible in C will be leaf functions; many of them will use no stack space at all. The declaration of such a function is very simple, for example:

```
#include <mips/asm.h>
#include <mips/regdef.h>

LEAF(myleaf)
    . . .
    <your code goes here>
    . . .
    j        ra
END(myleaf)
```

Most toolchains can pass your assembler source code through the C macro preprocessor before assembling it—unix-style tools decide based on the filename extension. The files mips/asm.h and mips/regdef.h include useful macros (like **LEAF** and **END**, shown above) for declaring global functions and data; they also allow you to use the software register names, e.g., **a0** instead of **$4**. If you are using the old MIPS or SGI toolchain, the above fragment would be expanded to

```
    .globl   myleaf
    .ent     myleaf,0
    . . .
    <your code goes here>
    . . .
    j        $31
    .end     myleaf
```

Other toolchains may have different definitions for these macros, as appropriate to their needs.

---

1. Storing the return address somewhere else may work perfectly well, but the debugger won't be able to find it.

10.9.2 *Nonleaf Functions*

Nonleaf functions are those that contain calls to other functions. Normally the function starts with code (the function prologue) to reset **sp** to the low-water mark of argument structures for any functions that may be called and to save the incoming values of any of the registers **s0–s8** that the function uses. Stack locations must also be reserved for **ra**, automatic (i.e., stack-based local) variables, and any further registers whose value this function needs to preserve over its own calls. (If the values of the argument registers **a0–a3** need to be preserved, they can be saved into their standard positions on the argument structure.)

Note that since **sp** is set only once (in the function prologue) all stack-held locations can be referenced by fixed offsets from **sp**.

To illustrate this, we will walk through the following nonleaf function (in conjunction with the picture of the stack frame in Figure 10.6):

```
#include <mips/asm.h>
#include <mips/regdef.h>


#
# myfunc (arg1, arg2, arg3, arg4, arg5)
#

# framesize = locals + regsave (ra,s0) + pad + fregsave (f20/21) + args + pad
myfunc_frmsz    = 4 + 8 + 4 + 8 + (5 * 4) + 4

NESTED(myfunc, myfunc_frmsz, ra)
    subu     sp,myfunc_frmsz
    .mask    0x80010000, -4
    sw       ra,myfunc_frmsz-8(sp)
    sw       s0,myfunc_frmsz-12(sp)
    .fmask   0x00300000, -16
    s.d      $f20,myfunc_frmsz-24(sp)
    ...
    <your code goes here, e.g.>
    # local = otherfunc (arg5, arg2, arg3, arg4, arg1)
    sw       a0,16(sp)                # arg5 (out) = arg1 (in)
    lw       a0,myfunc_frmsz+16(sp)   # arg1 (out) = arg5 (in)
    jal      otherfunc
    sw       v0,myfunc_frmsz-4(sp)    # local = result
    ...
    l.d      $f20,myfunc_frmsz-24(sp)
    lw       s0,myfunc_frmsz-12(sp)
    lw       ra,myfunc_frmsz-8(sp)
    addu     sp,myfunc_frmsz
```

```
    jr        ra
END(myfunc)
```

To begin with, the function myfunc expects five arguments: On entry the first four of these will be in registers **a0–a3** and the fifth will be at **sp+16**. The next code is

```
# framesize = locals + regsave (ra,s0) + pad + fregsave (f20/21) + args + pad
myfunc_frmsz   = 4 + 8 + 4 + 8 + 20 + 4
```

The total frame size is calculated as follows:

- **locals** *(4 bytes)*: We are going to keep one local variable on the stack, rather than in a register; perhaps we need to pass the address of the variable to another function.

- **regsave** *(8 bytes)*: We need to save the return address register **ra**, because we are calling another function; we also plan to use the callee-saved register **s0**.

- **pad** *(4 bytes)*: The rules say that double-precision floating point must be 8 byte aligned, so we add one word of padding to align the stack.

- **fregsave** *(8 bytes)*: We plan to use **$f20**, which is one of the callee-saved floating-point registers.

- **args** *(20 bytes)*: We are going to call another function that needs five argument words; this size must never be less than 16 bytes if a nested function is called, even if it takes no arguments.

- **pad** *(4 bytes)*: The rules say that the stack pointer must always be 8 byte aligned, so we add another word of padding to align it.

The next piece of code is

```
NESTED(myfunc, myfunc_frmsz, ra)
    subu      sp,myfunc_frmsz
```

In the MIPS Corporation toolchain this would be expanded to

```
.globl   myfunc
.ent     myfunc,0
.frame   $29,myfunc_frmsz,$0
subu     $29,myfunc_frmsz
```

This declares the start of the function and makes it globally accessible. The **.frame** function tells the debugger the size of stack frame we are about to create and the **subu** instruction creates the stack frame itself.

This is followed by

```
.mask    0x80010000, -4
sw       ra,myfunc_frmsz-8(sp)
sw       s0,myfunc_frmsz-12(sp)
```

We must save the return address and any callee-saved integer registers that we use in the stack frame. The **.mask** directive tells the debugger which registers we are going to save (**$31** and **$20**) and the offset from the top of the stack frame to the top of the save area: This corresponds to **regoffs** in Figure 10.6. The **sw** instructions then save the registers; the higher the register number, the higher up the stack it is placed (i.e., the registers are saved in order). The next code is

```
.fmask   0x00300000, -16
s.d      $f20,myfunc_frmsz-24(sp)
```

We do the same thing for the callee-saved floating-point registers **$f20** and (implicitly) **$f21**. The **.fmask** offset corresponds to **fregoffs** in Figure 10.6 (i.e., local variable area + integer register save area + padding word).

Next comes

```
# local = otherfunc (arg5, arg2, arg3, arg4, arg1)
sw       a0,16(sp)                # arg5 (out) = arg1 (in)
lw       a0,myfunc_frmsz+16(sp)   # arg1 (out) = arg5 (in)
jal      otherfunc
```

We call function otherfunc. Its arguments 2 to 4 are the same as our arguments 2 to 4, so these can pass straight through without being moved. We have to swap our argument 5 and its argument 1, however, so we copy our arg1 (in register **a0**) to the arg5 position in the outgoing argument build area (new **sp+16**) and our arg5 (at old **sp+16**) to outgoing argument 1 (register **a0**).

Then in the code

```
sw       v0,myfunc_frmsz-4(sp)    # local = result
```

the return value from otherfunc is stored in the local (automatic) variable, allocated in the top 4 bytes of the stack frame.

Finally, we have

```
l.d      $f20,myfunc_frmsz-24(sp)
lw       s0,myfunc_frmsz-12(sp)
lw       ra,myfunc_frmsz-8(sp)
addu     sp,myfunc_frmsz
jr       ra
END(myfunc)
```

Here the function epilogue reverses the prologue operations: It restores the floating-point, integer, and return address registers; pops the stack frame; and returns.

10.9.3 *Frame Pointers for More Complex Stack Requirements*

In the stack frames described above, the compiler has been able to manage the stack with just one reserved register, **sp**. Those of you who are familiar with other architectures will know that they often use two stack maintenance registers, an **sp** to mark the stack low-water point and a frame pointer to point to the data structures created by the function prologue. However, so long as the compiler can allocate all the stack space needed by the function in the function prologue code, it should be able to decrement **sp** in the prologue and leave it pointing to a constant stack offset for the life of the function. If so, everything on the local stack frame is at a compile-time-known offset from **sp** and no frame pointer is needed. But sometimes you want to mess with the stack pointer at run time: Figure 10.7 shows how MIPS allocates a frame pointer to cope with this need.

What leads to an unpredictable stack pointer? In some languages, and even in some extensions to C, dynamic variables can be created whose size varies at run time. And many C compilers can allocate stack space on demand through the useful built-in function alloca().[1] In this case the function prologue grabs another register, **s8** (which has a regular alias of **fp**), and sets it to the incoming value of **sp**.

Since **fp** (in its other guise as **s8**) is one of the saved registers, the prologue must also save its old value, which is done just as if we were using **s8** as a subroutine variable. In a function compiled with a frame pointer, all local stack frame references are made via **fp**, so if the compiler needs to lower **sp** to make space for variables of run-time-computed size, it can go right ahead.

Note that if the function has a nested call that uses so many arguments that it needs to pass data on the stack, that will be done with relation to **sp**.

One ingenious feature of this trick is that neither the caller of a frame pointer function, nor anything called by it, see it as anything special. Functions it calls are obliged to preserve the value of **fp** because it's a callee-saved register; and the callee-visible part of the stack frame looks like it should.

Assembler buffs may enjoy the observation that, when you create space with alloca() the address returned is actually a bit higher than **sp**, since the compiler has still reserved space for the largest argument structure required by any function call.

---

1. Actually, some implementations of alloca() don't just make space on the local stack, and some are pure library functions (which means that you never need go without alloca() for portability reasons). But compilers that implement alloca() using stack space go faster.

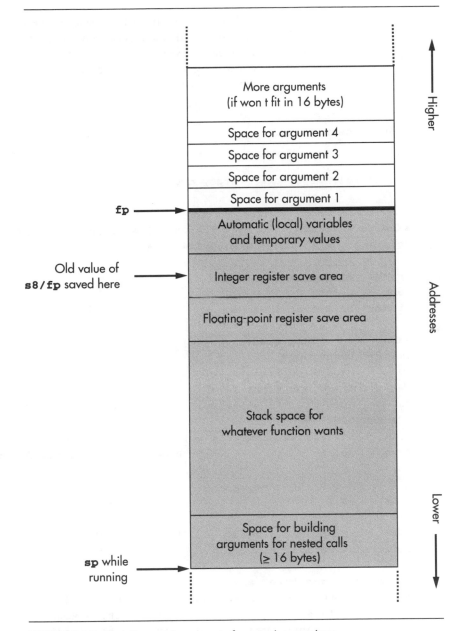

FIGURE 10.7   Stack frame using separate frame pointer register

Some tools also employ an **fp**-based stack frame when the size of the local variables grows so large that some stack frame objects are too far from **sp** to be accessed in a single MIPS load/store instruction (with its ±32KB offset limit).

So let's look at a slightly modified version of the example function used in the last section, with the addition of a call to alloca():

```
#include <mips/asm.h>
#include <mips/regdef.h>


#
# myfunc (arg1, arg2, arg3, arg4, arg5)
#

# framesize = locals + regsave (ra,s8,s0) + fregsave (f20/21) + args + pad
myfunc_frmsz   = 4 + 12 + 8 + (5 * 4) + 4

      .globl  myfunc
      .ent    myfunc,0
      .frame  fp,myfunc_frmsz,$0

      subu    sp,myfunc_frmsz
      .mask   0xc0010000, -4
      sw      ra,myfunc_frmsz-8(sp)
      sw      fp,myfunc_frmsz-12(sp)
      sw      s0,myfunc_frmsz-16(sp)
      .fmask  0x00300000, -16
      s.d     $f20,myfunc_frmsz-24(sp)
      move    fp,sp                    # save bottom of fixed frame
      ...
      # t6 = alloca (t5)
      addu    t5,7                     # make sure that size
      and     t5,~7                    #   is a multiple of 8
      subu    sp,t5                    # allocate stack
      addu    t6,sp,20                 # leave room for args
      ...
      <your code goes here, e.g.>
      # local = otherfunc (arg5, arg2, arg3, arg4, arg1)
      sw      a0,16(sp)                # arg5 (out) = arg1 (in)
      lw      a0,myfunc_frmsz+16(fp)   # arg1 (out) = arg5 (in)
      jal     otherfunc
      sw      v0,myfunc_frmsz-4(fp)    # local = result
      ...
      move    sp,fp                    # restore stack pointer
      l.d     $f20,myfunc_frmsz-24(sp)
      lw      s0,myfunc_frmsz-16(sp)
```

```
      lw      fp,myfunc_frmsz-12(sp)
      lw      ra,myfunc_frmsz-8(sp)
      addu    sp,myfunc_frmsz
      jr      ra
END(myfunc)
```

Let's look at what is different from the previous example:

```
      .globl  myfunc
      .ent    myfunc,0
      .frame  fp,myfunc_frmsz,$0
```

We can't use the **NESTED** macro any more, since we are using a separate frame pointer which must be explicitly declared using the **.frame** directive. We are going to modify **fp** (which is, of course, the same as **s8** or **$30**), so we must save it in the stack frame too:

```
      .mask   0xc0010000, -4
      sw      ra,myfunc_frmsz-8(sp)
      sw      fp,myfunc_frmsz-12(sp)
      sw      s0,myfunc_frmsz-16(sp)
```

The sequence

```
      # t6 = alloca (t5)
      addu    t5,7            # make sure that size
      and     t5,~7           #   is a multiple of 8
      subu    sp,t5           # allocate stack
      addu    t6,sp,20        # leave room for args
```

allocates a variable number of bytes on the stack and sets a register (**t6**) to point to it. Notice how we must make sure that the size is rounded up to a multiple of 8, so that the stack stays correctly aligned. Notice also how we add 20 to the stack pointer to leave room for the five argument words that will be used in future calls.

When building another function's arguments we use the **sp** register, but when accessing our own arguments or local variables we must use the **fp** register:

```
      sw      a0,16(sp)                  # arg5 (out) = arg1 (in)
      lw      a0,myfunc_frmsz+16(fp)     # arg1 (out) = arg5 (in)
      jal     otherfunc
      sw      v0,myfunc_frmsz-4(fp)      # local = result
```

Finally, at the start of the function epilogue, we restore the stack pointer to its post-prologue position and then restore the registers (not forgetting to restore the old value of **fp**, of course):

```
move    sp,fp                        # restore stack pointer
l.d     $f20,myfunc_frmsz-24(sp)
lw      s0,myfunc_frmsz-16(sp)
lw      fp,myfunc_frmsz-12(sp)
```

10.10 Variable Number of Arguments and stdargs

If you need to build a new function that takes a variable number of arguments, use your toolkit's stdarg.h macro package (compulsory for ANSI compatibility). The macro package delivers the macros—or possibly functions—va_start(), va_end(), and va_arg(). To see how they're used, look at how the Algorithmics SDE-MIPS package implements printf():

```
int printf(const char *format,... )
{
    va_list arg;
    int n;

    va_start(arg, format);
    n = vfprintf(stdout, format, arg);
    va_end(arg);

    return n;
}
```

Once we've called va_start(), we can extract any argument we like. So somewhere in the middle of the code that implements the format conversions for printf(), you'll see the following code used to pick up the next argument, supposing it to be a double-precision floating-point type:

```
    . . .
    d = va_arg(ap, double);
    . . .
```

Never try to build an assembler function that takes a variable number of arguments—it isn't worth the portability hassle.

10.11   Sharing Functions between Different Threads and Shared Library Problems

A C object library is a collection of precompiled modules, which are automatically linked into your program's binary when you refer to a function or variable whose name is defined in the module. Standard C functions like printf are just functions provided in libraries.

Although libraries provide a simple and powerful way of extending the language, they can cause trouble when used within a multitasking OS. Most often, you want library functions to behave like the code you write—just as if each task had its own copy. But we'd like to be able to share at least the library function's code, to avoid consuming memory space with multiple copies of the same thing. Library functions may be huge: The graphics interface libraries to the widely used X window system add about 300KB to the size of a MIPS object.

Most MIPS operating systems provide some way in which library code may be shared between different tasks. To understand the problems of sharing functions, we'll distinguish a number of different classes of data used by functions:

- *Read-only code and data*: This can be freely shared so long as each thread can find it.

- *Dynamic data*: Arguments, function variables, saved registers, and other information that a function keeps on the stack will remain safely thread specific. Every task has its own stack space: Even a thread sharing address space with other threads must have its own stack. Such data vanishes when the function returns.

- *Static transient data*: These are static data items whose value is not expected to persist between invocations of the functions. In principle these could be eliminated in favor of dynamic data—though not trivially, if the data is shared by several subfunctions—but that would mean rewriting the code and we'd rather be able to simply recompile it.

- *Per-thread persistent data*: These are static data items that persist between invocations of library functions, but where a separate copy must be kept for each client thread. The global errno variable (which holds an error code after a unix-style file I/O function is called) is one of these.

- *Global persistent data*: These are static persistent data items that track state changes in the system being organized by the library function. Once a library routine starts deliberately keeping multitask state information, it's well on its way to being part of the operating system; that's beyond the scope of this book.

The strategies for these classes of data are quite different according to whether the client threads are running in a common address space or each has its own independent address space.

10.11.1 *Sharing Code in Single-Address-Space Systems*

In a single-address-space OS like most real-time OSs, a shared library function's code and static data are shared at fixed addresses; there's no new problem for the client to find the function nor for the function itself to find its own data. However, the libraries must be written to be *re-entrant*: They may be used by different tasks, and one task may be suspended in the middle of a library function and that function reused by another. Dynamic data is safe enough, so simpler routines that don't keep state will often work correctly unmodified.

Static transient data accesses should be protected by semaphores to serialize the code from before the first access to the data until after the last access (see Section 5.8.4). The semaphore operations can be dummied out when we know there's only one thread active. Most often library functions for shared address multitasking systems will be built with some reprogramming to eliminate static transient data; when that's too difficult, the code section relying on the static data should be protected from being re-entered with a semaphore. Quite often, the library will also have been reprogrammed in some OS-dependent way to maintain some global persistent data.

10.11.2 *Sharing Library Code in the MIPS ABI*

In a protected OS where separate applications run in separate virtual address spaces, the problems are quite different. We'll outline the way in which unix-style systems conforming to the MIPS ABI standard provide libraries that can be shared between different applications, with no restriction on how the libraries and applications can be programmed.

Every MIPS ABI application runs in its own virtual address space, and the shared library facility makes no provision for multiple threads in one address space. The application's own compiled code is fixed to particular locations in this address space when it is linked. Library code is not built in: The application carries a table of the names of library functions and variables it wants to use, but those names are not yet resolved to addresses. In addition, the application binary file includes a table that defines public symbols in the application for use by library functions; under the MIPS ABI, library routines may freely refer to public data, or call public functions, in application code.[1]

---

1. Though this probably isn't ideal programming practice, it allows for the recompilation of unmodified library functions that attached themselves to such globals; consider the way a library function like `malloc()` uses the _end symbol.

In the MIPS ABI model the section of memory that holds binary instructions may not be modified; there's another level of code sharing, implemented by the virtual memory system, that allows multiple copies of the same application to use the same physical memory for their code.

The MIPS ABI doesn't try to predefine the virtual addresses at which a library's code or data will be located—libraries are built into the application's virtual address space starting at a fixed-by-convention location well away from where the function's data might grow up to or the stack grow down to.[1] That means that the library must be compiled to *position-independent code* (PIC)— it must run correctly regardless of its location in program memory. To make the program independent of its code location, all branches, jumps, and other instructions that reference code labels must operate correctly anywhere. All MIPS branch instructions are PC relative, but the regular jump and subroutine call instructions **j** and **jal** are useless. Within a library module, branch-like instructions such as **bal** provide a PC-relative function call—so long as the module isn't too big. But it's also possible to load a label's address in a PC-relative way, by using a branch-and-link instruction as a dummy call for the side effect that loads its return address into the **ra** register:

```
la      rd, label   →       bgezal  zero, 1f
                            nop
                    1:      addu    rd, $31, label - 1b
```

PIC is suitable for references to code within a single module of a library, because the module's code is loaded as a single entity into consecutive virtual addresses. Data, or external functions, will be at locations that cannot be determined until the application and library are loaded, and so their addresses cannot be embedded in the program text.

Such addresses are held in a table built in the application's address space as the application and libraries are loaded—the *global offset table* (GOT). There's one GOT for each chunk of modules that were linked at compile time— typically, one for the application and one for each module of related library functions. At the start of any function, the address of its own GOT is loaded into the **gp** register.

A MIPS ABI function refers to a dynamically linked variable or external function through the GOT at a table index fixed when the group of modules sharing the GOT was compiled and linked. A load of the external integer variable **errno** will come out as

---

1. Since most applications have quite a lot of virtual address to spare, it's tempting to try to fix a library's code and data to well known addresses—and this was quite common in early shared library systems. But with different applications building in different combinations of library functions, this requires a commitment to find a unique memory space for each shared library module we ever use. For a 32-bit system, virtual memory isn't big enough to use like this.

```
lw      rd, errno      →      lw      rd, errno_offset(gp)
                              nop
                              lw      rd, 0(rd)
```

Note the two loads: The double indirection is necessary because the GOT holds pointers, not the data items themselves.

Similarly, invocation of the shared library function `exit()` would look like this (assuming we've already set up the arguments):

```
jal     exit           →      lw      t9, exit_offset(gp)
                              nop
                              jalr    t9
```

The register **gp** is a good choice for the table base. Because of its role in providing fast access to short variables, it is not modified by standard functions. As an optimization, it is calculated only once per function (in the function prologue). That in turn depends upon making a fixed convention that at the point a function is entered the function's own address will be in **t9**. We don't care that **t9** itself may be reused by any subroutine, because once we've used it to compute the GOT address we won't use it again.

The function group's GOT is located in the first page of memory after the code of the function group; wherever a library gets loaded, the distance between the function entry point and the GOT is constant, and we can get the linker to figure that out at compile/link time. So a position-independent function prologue might start like this:

```
func:
    la      gp, _gp_disp
    addu    gp, gp, t9
    addu    sp, sp, framesize
    sw      gp, 32(sp)
```

In the above example, **_gp_disp** is a magic symbol that is recognized by the linker when building a shared library: Its value will be the offset between the instruction and the GOT. The **gp** value is saved on the stack and must be restored from there after a call to an external function, since that function may itself have modified **gp**.

There is much more that could be said about the way in which the MIPS ABI implementation is optimized. For example, no attempt is made to link in libraries when an application is first loaded into memory; dummy GOT entries that point to illegal memory addresses are used instead. When and if the application uses a library module, the illegal reference is caught by the OS, recognized as a GOT dummy entry, and fixed up. If necessary, the appropriate library function is paged in first.

10.12   An Introduction to Compiler Optimization

In saying anything at all about compiler optimization we're straying from the main path of this book, so we'll keep it brief. This section focuses on optimization as a process that does things that a programmer may need to know about. Interested readers will find a large literature on compiler techniques.

Compilers are not nearly as clever as you might think. The compiler writer's first responsibility is to ensure that the generated code does precisely what the language semantics say it should; and that is hard enough. It has for a long time been accepted good practice that cunning improvements to code should be made as a sequence of transformations to an internal representation of the program, with each individual optimization leaving a transformed but equivalent program. This approach has the merit of allowing programs to be built either including or leaving out a particular optimization step, thus containing the complexity of the compiler debugging job.

Once you can do that, of course, it makes sense for the basic compiler to ignore performance, generating dumb-but-correct code. The first optimization stage will factor out the stupid code; however, by doing it in two stages we expose even that first optimization stage to our debugging strategy.

It's nice to imagine a compiler making a smooth transition from the front end (concerned with syntax and program semantics) through to the back end (concerned with representing the program using the machine code of the target). Unfortunately, it's not like that; even during early compilation some overall features of the machine are likely to change the direction of compilation: Is it stack oriented? Does it have special-purpose registers? Conversely, the use of a machine-specific transformation down at the back end can often open up a good opportunity for rerunning a machine-independent optimization stage. The optimizers run with one eye on the logic of the program and another on the limitations and opportunities of the target architecture.

The data structure representing the unit of compilation (a function, if you're compiling C) is typically a tree whose branch structure shows the control flow in the function and whose nodes are individual operations. GNU C's RTL nodes specify the operation concerned in a machine-independent language, but usually also have a fragment of assembler attached to them that will do the job. The assembler language is explicitly associated with the target machine; more subtly, the operation itself has been chosen by the compiler as one available, in a general sense, on this target.

10.12.1   *Common Optimizations*

Most compilers will do all of the following. Occasionally, the assembler may perform some of these, too.

■ *Common subexpression elimination (CSE)*: This detects when the code is doing the same work twice. At first sight this looks like it is just making up for dumb programming,[1] but in fact CSE is critically important and tends to be run many times to tidy up after other stages:

- It is CSE that gives the compiler the ability to optimize globally across the function. The basic code generator works through your code expression by expression; even if you write very neat code the expansion of simple C statements into multiple MIPS instructions will lead to a lot of duplicated effort. The very first CSE pass factors out the stupid duplication and clears the way for register allocation. Older compilers often allocated registers before CSE, and when some temporary results were no longer required they ended up with spare registers they were unable to benefit from.

- Most memory-reference optimization is actually done by CSE. The code that fetches a variable from memory is itself a subexpression.

The enemy of CSE is unpredictable flow of control: the conditional branch. Once code turns into spaghetti, the compiler finds it difficult to know which computation has run before which other one; with some straightforward exceptions, CSE can really only operate inside *basic blocks* (a piece of code delimited by, but not containing, either an entry point or a branch). CSE markedly improves both code density and run-time performance.

Similar to CSE are the optimizations of constant folding, constant propagation, and arithmetic simplification. These precompute arithmetic performed on constants and modify other expressions using standard algebraic rules so as to permit further constant folding and better CSE.

■ *Jump optimization*: This removes redundant tests and jumps. Code produced by the earlier compiler stages often contains jumps to jumps, jumps around unreachable code, redundant conditional jumps, and so on. These optimizations will remove this redundancy.

■ *Strength reduction*: This means the replacement of computationally expensive operations by cheaper ones. For example, multiplication by a constant value can be replaced by a series of shifts and adds. This actually tends to increase the code size while reducing run time.

■ *Loop optimization*: This studies loops in your code, starting with the inner ones (which, the compiler guesses, will be where most time is spent). There are a number of useful things that can be done:

- Subexpressions that depend on variables that don't change inside the loop can be precomputed before the loop starts.

---

1. Here and elsewhere no disrespect is attached to dumb programming. Dumb programming is often the best programming, and it's really stupid to be unnecessarily clever.

– Expressions that depend in some simple way on a loop variable can be simplified. For example, in

```
int i, x[NX];

for (i = 0; i < NX; i++)
    x[i]++;
```

the array access (which as written would involve a multiplication and addition) can be implemented by an incrementing pointer. This kind of optimization will usually recognize only a particular set of stylized opportunities (a skeptic would point out that it is much better at improving performance on benchmarks than it is on your real code).

– Loops can be unrolled, allowing the work of two to a few iterations of the loop to be performed in line. On some processors where branches are inherently slow, this is valuable in itself, but branches are cheap on most MIPS CPUs. However, the unrolled loop offers much better pickings for other optimizations (CSE and register allocation being the main beneficiaries).

Loop unrolling may significantly increase the size of your compiled program, and you will usually have to request it with a specific compiler option.

■ *Function inlining*: The compiler may guess that some small functions can be usefully expanded in line, like a macro, rather than calling them. This is another optimization that increases the size of your program to give better performance and that usually requires an explicit compiler option. Some compilers may recognize the `inline` keyword (formalized in C++; an implementation-defined extension in C) to allow the programmer to specify which functions' invocations can be replaced by inlined code.

■ *Register allocation*: It's absolutely critical to good performance to make the best possible use of the 32 general-purpose registers, to make your code faster and smaller. The compiler identifies global variables (static and external data stored in memory); automatic variables (defined within a function, and notionally stored on the stack); and intermediate products of expression evaluation.

Any variable must be assigned to a machine register, and input data must be copied to that register, before you can do anything useful with it. The register allocator's job is to minimize the amount of work done in shuffling data in and out of registers; it does this by maintaining some variables in registers for all or part of a function's run time.

There are several points about register allocation that you should note:

- This process usually entirely ignores the old-fashioned C register attribute. It might be used as a hint, but most compilers figure out for themselves which variables are best kept in registers and when.
- The MIPS compiler has nine registers, **s0–s8**, which can be freely used as automatic variables. Any function using one of these must save its value on entry and restore it on exit. These registers tend to be suitable for long-term storage of user variables.

  It also has a set of 10 temporary registers, **t0–t9**, which are typically used for intermediate values in expression evaluation. The argument registers **a0–a3** and result registers **v0** and **v1** can be freely used too. However, these values don't survive a function call; if data is to be kept past a function call it is more efficient to use one of the callee-saved registers **s0–s8**, because then the work of saving and restoring the value will be done only if a called function really wants to use that register.

- C's loose semantics mean that any assignment through a pointer could potentially dump on essentially any memory location and hence change pretty much any declared variable. Since the programmer might have meant this to happen, the compiler's ability to maintain a variable in a register is strictly limited. It is safe to do so for any function variable (automatic variable) that is nowhere subject to the "address of" operator "&". And a variable value can be left in a register during any piece of code where there is neither a store-through-pointer operation nor a function call.

■ *Pipeline reorganization*: The compiler or assembler can sometimes move the logical instruction flow around so as to make good use of the branch and load delay slots referred to so often in this book. In practice, the delay slots are fine grained and tied to specific machine instructions; this can only be done late in the compilation process.

The most obvious techniques are as follows:

- If the instruction succeeding a load doesn't depend on the loaded value, just leave out the **nop**.
- Move the logically preceding instruction around. You may be able to find an instruction a few positions preceding the branch or load, provided that there are no intervening entry points. The register-register architecture makes it fairly simple to pick out instructions that depend on each other and cannot be resequenced.
- For a load, you may be able to find an instruction in the code after the load that is independent of the load value and is able to be moved.
- Move the instruction just before a branch into the branch delay slot.
- Duplicate the instruction at a branch target into the branch delay slot, and fix up the branch to go one more instruction forward. This is particularly effective with loop-closing instructions. If the branch

is conditional, though, you can only do it if the inserted instruction can be seen to be harmless when the branch is not taken.

10.12.2 *Optimizer-Unfriendly Code and How to Avoid It*

Certain kinds of C programs will cause problems to a MIPS CPU and its optimizing compiler and will cause unnecessary loss of performance. Some things to avoid include the following:

- *Subword arithmetic*: Use of short or char variables in arithmetic operations is not helpful. The MIPS CPU lacks subword arithmetic functions and will have to do extra work to make sure that your expressions overflow and wrap around when they should. The int data type represents the optimum arithmetic type for your machine; most of the time short and char values can be correctly manipulated by int automatic variables.

- *Taking the address of a local variable*: The compiler will now have to consider the possibility that any function call or write through a pointer might have changed the variable's value, so it won't live long in a machine register. Perhaps the best way of seeing this is observing that a variable defined locally to a function (and whose address is not taken) is essentially free. It will be assigned to a register, which would have been needed in any case for the intermediate result.

- *Function calls*: In the MIPS architecture the direct overhead of a function call is very small (2–3 clock cycles). But the function call makes it difficult for the compiler to make good use of registers, so it may be much more costly in the long run. So a nested call inside a function with a fairly complex set of local variables is probably as slow as a typical CISC function call, and it adds a lot of code.

10.12.3 *The Limits of Optimization*

Compilers have been much studied for a long time. Modern compilers tend to use only a fraction of the ideas and techniques that academics have come up with; partly this is appropriate conservatism, in that a compiler that generates incorrect code at just one point in your 100,000-line program isn't much good to you, even if the code it got right is 10% smaller and 10% faster. But another reason for avoiding fancy techniques is that most of them deliver very little improvement. There are some really bad compilers in use, so if you are using one of those you may see a big improvement by changing; reasonable compilers, however, perform about equally.

Big-time improvements are traditionally possible in certain specific types of programming. Notably, many big floating-point programs are somewhat "vectorizable" and can be sped up a lot by the use of supercomputer CPUs that perform the same operation to a whole array of variables at one time. It turns out that the vector optimizer can also make improvements in code for CPUs that can't actually perform the operations in parallel but whose pipelines permit one operation to start before the last one finishes. MIPS floating-point operations are like that.

For example, SGI has been tuning its own compilers to the MIPS architecture for years, whereas the GNU C compiler is a peculiar public-domain collaboration and MIPS is just one of many architectures. On plain integer code there is some evidence that the GNU compiler slightly outpaces SGI's; where this is true it's probably evidence of better register allocation. But on floating-point code the SGI compilers, with their supercomputer heritage, are often 20% or more faster.

10.13 Hints about Device Access from C

Most of you will be writing code that accesses I/O registry in C—you certainly shouldn't be using assembler code. As C evolves, it becomes more high level and increases the risk that the compiler won't do what you think you're telling it to do. Here are some well-trodden hints.

10.13.1 *Using "volatile" to Inhibit Destructive Optimization*

I might write a piece of code that is intended to poll the status register of a serial port and to send a character when it's ready:

```
unsigned char *usart_sr = (unsigned char *) 0xBFF00000;
unsigned char *usart_data = (unsigned char *) 0xBFF20000;
#define TX_RDY 0x40

void putc (ch)
char ch;
{
    while ((*usart_sr & TX_RDY) == 0)
        ;
    *usart_data = ch;
}
```

I'd be upset if this sent two characters and then looped forever, but that would be quite likely to happen. The compiler sees the memory-mapped I/O reference implied by *usart_sr as a loop-invariant fetch; there are no stores in the while loop so this seems a safe optimization. Your compiler has recognized that your C program is equivalent to

```
void putc (ch)
char ch;
{
    tmp = (*usart_sr & TX_RDY);

    while (tmp)
        ;
    *usart_data = ch;
}
```

With ANSI-compliant compilers,[1] you could prevent this particular problem by defining your registers as follows:

```
volatile unsigned char *usart_sr = (unsigned char *) 0xBFF00000;
volatile unsigned char *usart_data = (unsigned char *) 0xBFF20000;
```

A similar situation can exist if you examine a variable that is modified by an interrupt or other exception handler. Again, declaring the variable as volatile should fix the problem.

I don't know whether to tell you that this will *always* work: The C bible describes the operation of volatile as implementation dependent. I suspect, though, that compilers that ignore the volatile keyword are implicitly not allowed to optimize away loads.

Programmers have some trouble using volatile. The thing to remember is that it behaves just like any other C type modifier—just like unsigned in the example above. You need to avoid syndromes like this:

```
typedef char * devptr;
volatile mypointer devptr;
```

You've now told the compiler that it must keep loading the pointer value from the variable devptr, but you have said nothing about the behavior of the register you're using it to point at. More useful would be the following:

```
typedef volatile char * devptr;
mypointer devptr;
```

Once you've dealt with this, the most common reason why optimized code breaks will be that you have tried to drive the hardware too fast. There are often timing constraints associated with reads and writes of hardware registers, and you'll often have to deliberately slow your code to fit in.

---

1. And most others, too; this particular ANSI feature is a must.

What is the moral of this section? While it's easier to write and maintain hardware driver code in C than in assembler, it's your responsibility to understand enough about the translation of that code to be sure it hasn't introduced something you didn't want.

10.13.2 *Unaligned Data from C*

Some C compilers give you the chance to mark structure data as being "packed"—that is, with no padding to enforce alignment—and will generate code to cope.[1]

What's more unusual is a compiler that understands that the main source of potentially unaligned data is not the data you've declared, but data that has arrived from somewhere else. But you can probably code a routine that will read an unaligned datum, something like this:

```
int unalignedload (ptr)
    void *ptr;
{
#pragma pack (1)
    /* define what you like here, with no assumptions about alignment */

    struct unaligned {
        int conts;
    } *ip;

#pragma pack ()
/* back to default behavior */

    ip = (struct unaligned *) ptr;

    /* can now generate an unaligned load of int size */
    return ip->conts;
}
```

The `pragma` syntax shown is an ANSI-approved escape mechanism, which means that while the syntax is standard, the meaning probably isn't. The parameter to pack determines the level of alignment to enforce: `#pragma pack(1)` proposes alignment on 1-byte boundaries (i.e., no padding at all); you could also use `#pragma pack(2)` to have 2-byte and larger entities aligned on 2-byte boundaries, though I can't see where this would be useful. The closing `#pragma pack()` is used to restore the default alignment rules.

---

1. All reasonable versions of GNU C will do this, but only compilers based on code currently on prerelease for gcc version 2.8 or some earlier versions from Algorithmics will generate reasonably efficient code for unaligned accesses.

Portability Considerations and C Code

There are not many completely new programs in the world, and most applications for MIPS will have formerly run on some other microprocessor. *Portability* refers to the ease with which a piece of software can be transferred successfully and correctly to a new environment, particularly a new instruction set. We all know that so-called portable computers can make your arms ache; portability is relative, and porting a substantial application is rarely easy.

All applications that have grown up in one particular environment are likely to present some portability problems, both deliberate and inadvertent. The object of this chapter is to draw your attention to areas that are particularly likely to give problems.

Much of this chapter is necessarily somewhat vague and polemical; experienced programmers may feel that they are just being fed motherhood and apple pie. Feel free to skip most of it; but take a look at the sections on data alignment (different for every architecture) and endianness (which somehow is so slippery that everyone, myself included, always makes mistakes).

Those parts of a system that drive relatively low-level hardware are necessarily unportable; it isn't cost effective or sensible to insist that the hardware/software interface be preserved as you make faster and faster laser printers, for example.

But outside those areas, C code is frequently inadvertently unportable. C is often lax about semantics in search of performance, implementability, and functionality.[1] If a language abstraction stands between the programmer and a potentially useful machine feature, the abstraction had better be efficient and universal. C's strength is that when such abstractions commanded a wide con-

---

1. This is not a reason for using other languages. Pascal, for example, is a much more prescriptive language, but the consequent inability to do some vital things has encouraged a welter of incompatible dialects. C's semantic looseness (and some other cultural factors) has allowed enough room to breathe that a single language standard has survived.

sensus (like block structure, loop controls, and subroutine calls) it used them; and when they did not (the semantics of pointers and pointer-dereference operations, for example) it just provided the machine feature, perhaps slightly cleaned up.

However, while C encourages portability by allowing a huge range of software to be implemented with the same syntax, portability issues can creep back in through the many machine-dependent gaps in C's coverage.

11.1 Porting to MIPS: A Checklist of Frequently Encountered Problems

The following are problems that have come up fairly frequently in our practice at Algorithmics:

- *Need for explicit cache management*: In many cases, the customer's previous system either didn't have caches or used a CPU and peripherals that snoop direct memory accesses (DMA) to hide them from software. We'll describe what to do about this in Section 11.7.

- *Timing consequences of a faster CPU*: Some problems happen just because the software is now going so much faster. There's no general solution for this, so you'll need to be vigilant.

- *Data alignment and memory layout*: Your program may make unportable assumptions about the memory layout of data declared in C. It's almost always unportable to use C struct declarations to map input files or data received through a communication link, for example. Danger can lurk in a program that employs multiple views of private data with differently typed pointers or unions.

  You should review and check your declarations. MIPS CPUs have more rigid alignment requirements than some other CPUs, so you may find that data structures change significantly.

  We'll describe how to understand what MIPS compilers usually do in Section 11.5.

- *Endianness*: The computer world is divided into little- and big-endian camps, and a gulf of incomprehension falls between them. The MIPS CPU can be set up to do either, but you probably ought to understand this problem; read much more about it in Section 11.6.

- *Negative pointers*: When running unmapped code on a MIPS CPU, all pointers are in the kseg0 or kseg1 areas, and both use pointers whose 32-bit value has the top bit set. Unmapped programs on most other architectures are dealing with physical addresses, which are invariably a lot smaller than 2GB!

Such pointer values could cause trouble when pointer values are being compared, if the pointer were implicitly converted to a signed integer type. Any implicit conversions between integer and pointer types (quite common in C) should be made explicit and should specify an unsigned integer type (you should use `unsigned long` for this).

Most compilers will warn about pointer-to-integer conversions, though you may have to specify an option.

■ *Signed vs. unsigned characters*: In early C compilers, the `char` type used for strings was usually equivalent to `signed char`; this is consistent with the convention for larger integer values. However, as soon as you have to deal with character encodings using more than 7-bit values, this is dangerous when converting or comparing. Modern compilers usually make `char` equivalent to `unsigned char` instead.

If you discover that your old program depends on the default sign-extension of `char` types, good compilers offer an option that will restore the traditional convention.

■ *Moving from 16-bit int*: A significant number of programs are being moved up from 16-bit x86 or other CPUs where the standard `int` is a 16-bit value. Such programs may rely, much more subtly than you think, on the limited size and overflow characteristics of 16-bit values. Although you can get correct operation by translating such types into `short`, that will be inefficient. In most cases you can let variables quietly pick up the MIPS `int` size of 32 bits, but you should be particularly aware of places where signed comparisons are used to catch 16-bit overflow.

■ *Programming that depends on the stack*: Some kind of function invocation stack and data stack are implicit in C's block structure. Despite the MIPS hardware's complete lack of stack support, MIPS C compilers implement a fairly conventional stack structure. Even so, if your program thinks it knows what the stack looks like, it won't be portable. Don't try to fix it by replacing the old assumptions with new ones.

Two respectable and standards-conforming macro/library operations are available that may tackle what your software was trying to do before:

– `stdargs`: Use this include-file-based macro package to implement routines with a variable number of parameters. Your C code should make no other assumptions about the calling stack.

– `alloca()`: To allocate memory at run time, use this library function, which is "on the stack" in the sense that it will be automatically freed when the function allocating the memory returns. Some compilers implement `alloca()` as a built-in function that actually extends the stack; otherwise there are pure-library implementations available. But don't assume that such memory is actually at an address with some connection with the stack.

- *Argument passing, autoconversions*: Arguments passed to a function, and not explicitly defined by a function prototype, are often "promoted"; typically, for subword integers, to an int type. This can cause surprises, particularly when you are promoting data unexpectedly interpreted as signed.

  It's time your software used function prototypes everywhere!

- *Ambiguous behavior of library functions*: Library functions may behave unexpectedly at the margins. A classic example is using the memcpy() routine (defined in many C environments) to copy bytes and accidentally feeding it a source and destination area that overlap—this is forbidden by definition. A simple sequential loop that copies bytes from source to destination one at a time behaves fairly gracefully with overlapping pointers, but a tuned routine is likely to pick up multiple bytes at once.

  Your problem is that if you are using a lightly tuned library, as you port your code bizarre things may start happening as incorrect library usage is exposed. Some test suites may have debug versions of library routines that check for possible problems.

- *Include file usage*: This is closer to a system dependency, but you can spend hours trying to untangle an incompatible forest of ".h" files. This is probably an unavoidable chore when porting a program of any size. We'll give some general words of wisdom.

Before we get onto the more thorny problems in detail, let's describe how Mr. Perfect might go about porting a program. You will rarely have the chance to do it this way, of course, but at least you can point at this book to explain where it went wrong!

11.2 An Idealized Porting Process

It is unlikely that the source code you have to port is literally the complete system. Most programs depend on an environment implemented by underlying third-party software; this may be bound in at run time (an operating system or system monitor) or at link time (library functions, include files). Quite often you won't have sources; sometimes you will have source code, but this part of the system will just be more trouble to port than to reproduce.

This is the point at which you can appreciate the purpose of attempts to standardize a C run-time library. If only your old and new environments provided something like the same application program interface, the job would be trivial. It isn't, usually.

Two Golden Rules

While you're porting a program, don't make any functional change. None at all. Not even a little bit.

You'll have quite enough trouble getting the new program to behave just like the old one without trying to make it behave better; one of the few advantages porters have over green-field software engineers is that the old system provides a rigid and unarguable specification.

Here's another golden rule: Use every tool you have to make better maps of the system. If you've got tools that will figure out call trees or variable cross-references, use them. If you haven't got them, now would be a good time to get them; many are available free.

11.2.1   *Three Porting Choices*

You're going to consider every source module in the old system and decide its fate: port, reimplement, or discard:

- *Port.* This is a part of your application or its essential superstructure, and its basic job is machine independent. You will make no CPU- or hardware-dependent changes to such a module; any changes you make will be to correct portability errors and will not prevent your new module from being used to rebuild your old system. You won't change the logic of such a module in any way, so with care you shouldn't introduce many bugs.

- *Reimplement.* This is a "glue" function that provides a service (as a set of functions or data items) to portable code but whose implementation depends on the way the old system works. You'll produce a new version of this module that exports the same service (possibly taking advantage of cut-and-pasted code from the old one).

- *Discard.* This is a module whose service interface is no longer relevant to the new system. Perhaps it was supplied as part of an OS you won't be using, as a library function that is not available (with *exactly* the same semantics) in the new compilation system, or perhaps it is even not licensed for use on your target system.

This is art as well as science; there is no single right way to do it. Your objective will be to minimize the scope for introducing new errors, while minimizing the amount of work you have to do. To do this job right requires skill, insight, and experience; programming is a hard craft and not quickly learned.

Usually, you should make your decision on whole existing modules. Where it seems that a single module really contains a mixture of "port" and "reimplement" functions, try splitting it in two as cleanly as possible and then reclassify each half.

The modules identified for reimplementation are likely to represent a small fraction of the code but will absorb a lot of your effort. It will be easier if your new target and its toolkit provide a high-quality run-time system and libraries that can provide an easy base for those reimplementations.

The other large source of effort in reimplementation is most characteristic of device drivers: It's often very difficult to figure out how the hardware works. It probably isn't specified properly, and in any case it doesn't adhere to its specifications. If your software system is large and your hardware is new and minimal, it's often a good idea to write a test program to allow you to weigh empirical evidence against the lies and blandishments of documentation. The test program will also let you become familiar with the new toolkit and CPU.

11.2.2 *Fixing Up Dependencies*

Once you've made your divisions among the three porting choices, you begin by recompiling the "port" modules on the new system, fixing minor portability problems as you go. When you link them together you'll get a list of unresolved definitions that need to be patched up. Some of these, when investigated, will turn out to be used only in code that really fell into the "reimplement" category; move the boundary and iterate until the list of unresolved names makes sense.

Then tackle the reimplement modules. You have two choices for each function. The first is to recompile the function, adding some "underglue" definitions or functions to mimic the behavior of the old environment using the new one. (In a sense, you're pragmatically deciding that what was seen as glue is better pushed back into the port category.) Alternatively, you can discard the old function and write a new one (using the old one for inspiration and as a source for cut and paste), aiming to mimic the function as a black box.

For each function or module, choose one of these strategies. It is nearly always a bad idea to mix strategies in the same module.

11.2.3 *Isolating Nonportable Code*

No complete and useful program can be written portably. Two systems may both implement the same OS and may allow you to carry programs between them; but this is only because the OS writer has taken on the burden of the nonportable bits.

The best you can do is to herd the nonportable parts of your code together into modules, whose interfaces consist of stable data declarations and functions whose operation can be expressed succinctly and clearly. You've got it right when no potential user of a nonportable function ever feels the need to look inside to see what it does!

11.2.4 *When to Use Assembler*

There are three reasons for using assembler:

- *Efficient implementation of critical functions*: Removing the last unnecessary clock cycle from any much-used piece of code, even if it's as simple as a `strcpy()`, may well be worthwhile. But you should always keep a portable C version alongside. In fact, since you're going to keep the portable version, don't write the assembler yet: Wait until you've built a complete system and measured it to see whether this function is really heavily used enough to justify the effort. Never change the assembler version without changing the portable version too.

- *Access to features not available to compiled code*: Routines may need to access CPU control registers, for example. Sometimes these may be appropriately implemented as C functions built on tiny subroutines and sometimes by C `asm` statements. Tiny subroutines are particularly apt when—although the implementation will be completely machine dependent—the desired effect is machine independent, such as a preference for a disable interrupts function to a set status register bits function.

- *Some critical environmental deficiency*: Most commonly, this is the inability to provide the free use of CPU registers and the stack that the compiler relies on. Classic examples are startup code (where you may not want to rely on memory for the stack) or the early part of an interrupt handler (before you've saved the interrupted program's registers). Make it a priority, in these situations, to build an environment from which you can call C functions.

11.3   Portable C and Language Standards

C does not meet the academic ideal of a high-level programming language. It is one of a class of languages that were evolved by working programmers who were trying to obtain (on simple minicomputers that were unsuited to the large run-time system or the inefficiency of early high-level languages) the kind of programming ease available from block-structured, purists' high-level languages.

Algol or its successors (Pascal, Modula-2, and even Ada) set out to make portability compulsory; these languages attempted to ensure that program behavior was exactly specified by the source code, so they certainly couldn't be dependent on what kind of CPU was being used. C lets the underlying implementation show through and in doing so makes itself usable for a larger range of programming tasks. But that very power means that while it is possible to write portable C by programming discipline, it doesn't happen by accident.

An example of this is how basic data types change in their size (and therefore the number of bits of precision) between different implementations. Another is that C's pointers (inevitably implemented as real machine pointers) expose the memory layout of data, which is implementation dependent.

Some things have gotten easier with time: Early C implementations had to target machines with 7-, 8-, and 9-bit char types and with 36-bit machine words. Most of you can safely assume that all the targets you ever want to compile for have an 8-bit char as the smallest addressable unit of memory; other basic types will be 16, 32, or 64 bits in size.

C has evolved continuously since its early days. It has definitely evolved to a higher level: Most changes have tended to increase the amount of abstraction and checking. Like species, languages probably evolve more by "punctuated equilibrium" than at a constant rate, so you can get quite a good fix on any C dialect by fixing its position relative to three relatively stable and famous variants.

First is traditional C, often called "K&R" from the authors (Kernighan and Ritchie) of the *C Programming Manual*, first version.[1] This reflects the standard used for the first few years' of Unix's life and the influence of a single implementation: the AT&T Bell Labs Portable C compiler. It has little type checking, many defaults, and the compilers do little to check your code. However, it provides a useful lingua franca: Most compilers will (sometimes unwillingly and with warnings) correctly translate programs written to K&R.

Second is the ANSI standard, which collects together improvements made over the years and regulates them. ANSI adopted syntax that allows you to make far more well-defined declarations of functions and then checks your usage against them. ANSI compilers are much noisier, with a tendency to produce warning messages.

ANSI C is very much a commercial standard, and in many cases it standardized ahead of current practice. Moreover, it contains features that many users dislike: Users respond by using a not-quite-ANSI dialect, and compiler suppliers respond by permitting the use of such a dialect with command line options. Surprisingly, the outcome of this process seems to have left the C language in better shape than it used to be.

Third is the Free Software Foundation's GNU compiler, which is available for a huge range of hosts and is encouraging the emergence of a new dialect.[2] (Of course, Microsoft's PC-oriented C and C++ compilers are more widely used, but are much more rarely used off-desktop.) The GNU compiler, though fully ANSI compliant, is often deployed to implement a language, liked by its protagonists, that keeps some important ANSI features but ignores others.

1. One of the best pieces of writing in computer science, this book gives a comprehensive and comprehensible description of the world's most useful language in a remarkably small space. It's been updated for new language standards, which has made it fatter but hasn't spoiled it. If you haven't got one, go out and buy it now!

2. GNU C is also an extraordinary experiment; it is a major piece of ingenuity and intellectual work that is being maintained and continually developed by a large, loose knit, worldwide community of workers, many of them volunteers. No other piece of free software has filtered quite so far into the body of the computer industry.

The virtue of this is that the protagonists of GNU C are themselves serious programmers.

GNU also adds a number of very valuable extensions that extend the scope of the language—examples include function inlining, a robust `asm` statement, and the `alloca()` routine which allocates memory dynamically from the program stack. If you can standardize on GNU, you minimize language portability problems, with (probably) minimal loss of ability to move to novel and exotic hardware. It's tempting. However, most programmers needing portability are writing ANSI-compliant C that has function prototypes but would otherwise be acceptable to a K&R compiler.

11.4   C Library Functions and POSIX

C supports separate compilation of modules, and you can link together the resulting object code without recourse to the source. C libraries are bunches of precompiled object code defining common functions. The "standard" C library of everyday functions is to all intents and purposes part of the language.

The ANSI standard addresses a subset of common library functions and defines their functions. But this deliberately steers clear of OS-dependent functions and that means avoiding even the simplest input/output routines.

The POSIX standard (IEEE1003.4) is probably the best candidate for defining a standard C language interface to a workable I/O system. POSIX has its problems: It only includes a subset of OS features (probably a good thing), and because its definers occasionally felt obliged to standardize an improvement of current practice, full POSIX compliance is still hard to find even in big OSs.[1] Moreover, Microsoft has steadfastly discouraged the use of POSIX standards; its Win32 application programming interface was invented after the POSIX system call interface had stabilized but is pointlessly incompatible. But you can get software that implements a POSIX interface on top of Win32, and POSIX is a useful reference point for desktop tools.

POSIX is as yet much further from reality in embedded systems. The POSIX "threads" proposal is a reasonable and sensible attempt to standardize multitasking in one address space, but few embedded systems follow it.

11.5   Data Representations and Alignment

The MIPS architecture can only load multibyte data that is "naturally" aligned—a 4-byte quantity only from a 4-byte boundary, etc. Many CISC

---

1. A standards committee often finds it impossible to select one out of a number of competing solutions, each one of which is already provided by one vendor, because any selection will benefit one party at the expense of all the others.

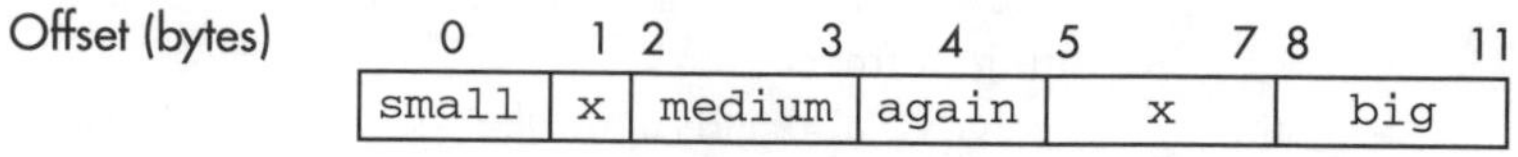

Offset (bytes)

FIGURE 11.1 Structure layout and padding in memory

architectures don't have this restriction. The MIPS compiler attempts to ensure that data lands in the right place; this requires far-reaching (and not always obvious) behaviors, such as leaving padding between fields of data structures and ensuring that complex data structures are aligned to the largest unit to which the architecture is sensitive (4 or 8 bytes in the MIPS architecture).

Your previous compiler may do this differently. Consider the following example:

```
struct foo {
    char small;
    short medium;
    char again;
    int big;
}
```

This will be laid out in memory as shown in Figure 11.1. A word of warning is in order here, however: Figure 11.1 is not necessarily correct for all MIPS compilers, and all these notes should be taken as typical of what a good compiler will do. A standard for interlinkable modules or binary-compatible programs would have to nail these down—as does, for example, the MIPS ABI standard. But beware—a compiler *could* still be fully compliant with C standards and use bizarre and wholly counterintuitive data representations, so long as these were internally consistent. Following are some typical behaviors:

■ *Alignment of structure base address*: The data structure shown in Figure 11.1 will always be placed on a 4-byte boundary; a structure's alignment is that of its most demanding record. `struct foo` contains an `int` requiring 4-byte alignment, so the structure itself will be 4 byte aligned.

Where memory is allocated dynamically, either implicitly on the stack or explicitly by software routines such as `malloc()`, the resulting pointers could give rise to alignment problems; hence they are specified to return pointers aligned to the largest size the architecture cares about. In the case of 32-bit MIPS CPUs, this need only be 4 bytes, but the common convention is to align to 8 bytes for compatibility with 64-bit implementations. Stack alignment is maintained by only altering the **sp** value by a multiple of 8 bytes if needed.

- *Memory order*: Fields within structures are stored in memory in the order declared.

- *Padding*: This is generated whenever the next field would otherwise have the wrong alignment with respect to the structure's base address.

- *Endianness*: This has no effect on the picture shown in Figure 11.1. Endianness determines how an integer value is related to the values of its constituent bytes (when they are considered separately); it does not affect the relative byte locations used for storing those values.[1] Endianness does have some effect on the layout of C bitfields; this is discussed in Section 11.6.2.

There's an irrefutable, pure, and correct position on data structures and portability: The memory representation of data is compiler dependent, and you have no right to expect it to be in any way portable, even between two different compilers for the same architecture. But in the real world it would be hopelessly inefficient to make sure that all data ever exchanged or published by programs was universally represented, and nonportable C is often a better way of defining data than anything else at your disposal.

However, there are some tools that may help. ANSI compilers may support an option using the pack pragma:[2]

```
#pragma pack(1)
struct foo {
    char small;
    short medium;
    char again;
    int big;
}
#pragma pack()
```

This has the effect of causing the compiler to omit all padding, producing the layout shown in Figure 11.2. A structure packed like this has no inherent alignment, so in addition to the lack of any padding, the structure base address may also be unaligned. The compiler is therefore obliged to generate load and store sequences to its fields that are alignment independent (and therefore to some extent inefficient)—even though, in this particular case, the `big` field happens to have the correct 4-byte alignment from the structure base.

The `#pragma pack()` at the end restores the default alignment rules.

---

1. If you find this difficult to believe, it's probably because big-endians and little-endians draw pictures differently.

2. GNU C users have a nicer, more specific syntax for this inside individual field declarations; for example `int n attribute((packed))` would declare a field as an integer but avoid any padding before it.

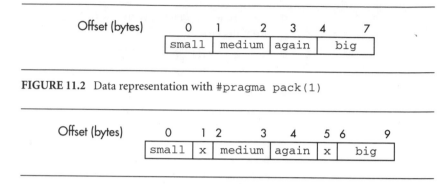

Offset (bytes)

0	1	2	3	4		7
small	medium	again	big			

FIGURE 11.2 Data representation with #pragma pack(1)

Offset (bytes)

0	1	2	3	4	5	6	9
small	x	medium	again	x	big		

FIGURE 11.3 Data representation with #pragma pack(2)

The 1 in pack(1) refers to the maximum alignment that must be respected, so pack(2) means align only to 2-byte boundaries. Hence the code string

```
#pragma pack(2)
struct foo {
    char small;
    short medium;
    char again;
    int big;
}
#pragma pack()
```

has the effect of causing the compiler to pad items of 2 bytes or larger to 2-byte boundaries, producing the layout shown in Figure 11.3.

The #pragma pack() feature would be more appealing if most compilers supported it, and if when they did, they generated tolerably efficient code using the MIPS instructions that are designed for unaligned accesses (see Section 8.4.1). It would also help if there weren't another quite different source of incompatibility of data representation: endianness (Section 11.6). Nonetheless, used with care the "pragma pack" feature can make it easier to configure a source module between two or more different architectures. It's less likely to be a good choice for a one-off conversion.

11.6 Endianness: Words, Bytes, and Bit Order

The word *endianness* was introduced to computer science by Danny Cohen (Cohen 1980). In a paper of rare humor and readability, Cohen observed that computer architectures had divided up into two camps, based on an arbitrary choice of the way in which byte addressing and integer definitions are related. The name comes from *Gulliver's Travels*, where the little-endians and big-endians fought a war over the correct end at which to start eating a boiled egg. The satire highlights the inability of the protagonists to comprehend the arbitrary nature of their difference. The joke was appreciated, and the name has stuck.

Computer programs are always dealing with sequence and order of different types of data: iterating in order over the characters in a string, the words in an array, or the bits in a binary representation. C programmers tend to make the pervasive assumption that all these variables are stored in a memory that is itself visible as a sequence of bytes—memcpy() will copy any data type. And C's I/O system models all I/O operations as bytes; you can also read() and write() any chunk of memory containing any data type.

So one computer can write out some data, and another computer can read it: Suddenly we're interested in whether the second computer can understand what the first one wrote.

We understand (from Section 11.5) that we need to be careful with padding and alignment. And it's probably too much to expect that complex data types like floating-point numbers will always transfer intact. But we'd hope at least to see simple twos complement integers coming across OK; the curse of endianness is that they don't. The 32-bit integer whose hexadecimal value was written as 0x12345678 quite often reads in as 0x78563412.

A 32-bit binary integer is represented by a sequence of bits, with each bit having a different significance. The least significant bit is "ones," then "twos," then "fours"—just as a decimal representation is "ones," "tens," and "hundreds." To represent a number you have to agree on which bits are significant— and some computers put the least-significant bit "first" (that is, in lower memory locations) and some put the most-significant bit first, i.e., they're either little-endian or big-endian. When I first came into computers in 1976 DEC's minicomputers were little-endian and IBM mainframes were big-endian; neither camp was about to give way.

But wait a moment. Surely, since 0x12345678 is also 00010010 00110100 01010110 01111000 in binary, when seen with the opposite ordering convention it should be the number you get by reversing all the bits, which is 00011110 01101010 00101100 01001000 (and, in hex, 0x1e6a2c48)? That would be logical and could arise in some circumstances; IBM always called the most-significant bit "bit 0"—i.e., a totally consistent big-endian approach. But sometime in the 70s, when 8-bit bytes were winning out as a universal base unit for both computers and computerized communications systems, the war ended at the byte level. Since then bytes have bits numbered 0 through 7, and the most-significant bit is 7. IBM's documentation stood out against this, but it so happens that IBM didn't really sell anything with a byte-wide interface—neither hardware, software, or cross-platform communication protocols. IBM could not have been converted but was just bypassed.

When Motorola introduced the 68000 microprocessor around 1978, it made the fateful decision to reflect IBM's mainframe architecture. Motorola couldn't go against the prevailing bits-within-bytes convention (every 8-bit peripheral would have had to be connected with its data bus backward) but when storing 16- and 32-bit integers Motorola put the byte containing the most-significant bits at the lowest memory address. The bits and bytes were numbered in opposite directions.

Danny Cohen's paper is careful to be neutral, but I don't have to be; if any single decision can be held responsible for the trouble detailed in this section it was Motorola's.

There is software trouble when porting software or moving data between incompatible machines; there is hardware trouble when connecting incompatible components or buses. We'll take the software and hardware problems separately.

Here's a software-oriented definition: A CPU/compiler system where the lowest addressed byte of a multibyte integer holds the least-significant bits is called little-endian; a system where the lowest addressed byte of a multibyte integer holds the most significant bits is called big-endian. The CPU/compiler is strictly correct—a compiler can always produce the effect of reversed endianness and on some architectures the decision is fairly arbitrary.[1] But on a 32-bit byte-addressable CPU like MIPS, the compiler can't reasonably cover over the hardware; thus we talk of the endianness of the CPU.

11.6.1 *Endianness and the Programmer*

You can very easily find out if you have a big-endian, or little-endian, CPU, by running a piece of deliberately nonportable code:

```
union either {
    int as_int;
    short as_short[2];
    char as_char[4];
};

either.as_int = 0x12345678;

if (sizeof(int) == 4 && either.as_char[0] == 0x78) {
    printf ("Little endian\n");
}
else if (sizeof(int) == 4 && either.as_char[0] == 0x12) {
    printf ("Big endian\n");
}
else {
```

1. A pure 8-bit micro has no built-in endianness; in fact, any computer whose memory addressing, registers, and operations all operate with the same width words has no built-in endianness.

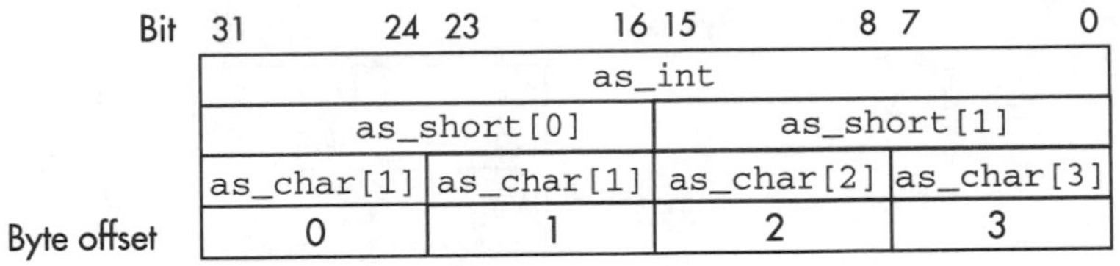

Bit	31	24	23	16	15	8	7	0
	as_int							
	as_short[0]				as_short[1]			
	as_char[1]	as_char[1]		as_char[2]		as_char[3]		
Byte offset	0		1		2		3	

FIGURE 11.4 Typical big-endian's picture

```
    printf ("Confused\n");
}
```

So long as binary data items are never imported into an application from elsewhere, and so long as you avoid the syndrome above where you access the same piece of data under two different integer types, your CPU's endianness is invisible (and your code is portable). You should be able to check an application in this respect with the type-checking facilities available with modern C compilers.

But that still leaves foreign data reads into your system and the memory view of memory-mapped hardware registers: For these, you need to know exactly how your compiler accesses memory.

11.6.2   *Endianness: The Pictures and the Intellectual Problem*

This all seems fairly harmless, but experience shows that of all data-mapping problems, endianness is uniquely confusing. I think this is because it is difficult even to describe the problem without taking a side. The origin of the two alternatives lies in two different ways of drawing the pictures and describing the data; both are natural in different contexts.

Big-endians typically draw their pictures organized around words (32 bits in a MIPS system), as shown in Figure 11.4 for the code following:

```
union either {
    int as_int;
    short as_short[2];
    char as_char[4];
};
```

What's more, big-endians see words as a sort of number, so they put the highest bit number (most significant) on the left, like our familiar Arabic numbers. And a big-endian sees memory as an array of words; to emphasize the separation of bit and word order, the words are likely to be drawn extending up and down the page (Figure 11.4).

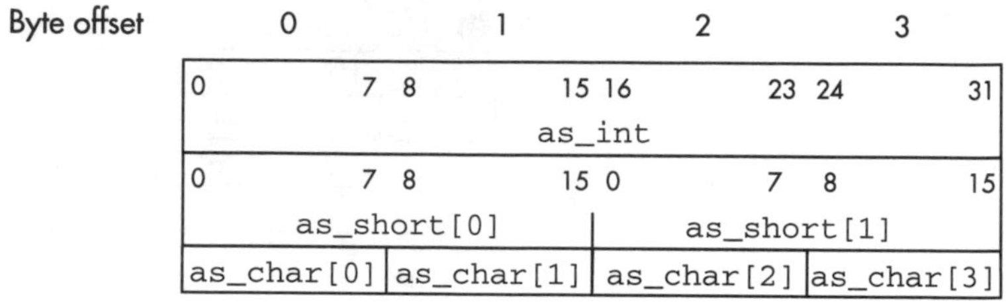

Byte offset	0	1	2	3

```
0            7 8           15 16          23 24          31
                          as_int
0            7 8           15 0           7 8            15
        as_short[0]        |         as_short[1]
as_char[0] | as_char[1] | as_char[2] | as_char[3]
```

FIGURE 11.5 Little-endian's picture

But little-endians generally want to abstract a computer memory as an array of bytes. So the same data structure looks like Figure 11.5. Little-endians don't think of computer data as primarily numeric, so they tend to put all the low numbers (bits, bytes, or whatever) on the left. A little-endian sees memory as extending off to the left and right of the picture.

You can't describe endianness without drawing pictures; however, the picture you draw immediately commits you to one camp or the other. This is the essence of the subject's capacity to confuse: You can't talk about it without getting caught in it first.

Bitfields, Floating Point, and Endianness

Before discussing solutions, let's look at one particularly messy issue. C permits you to define bitfields in structures; you may recall that in Section 7.9.3 we used a bitfield structure to map the fields of a single-precision IEEE floating-point value (a C float) stored in memory. An FP single value is multibyte, so you should probably expect this definition to be endianness dependent. The big-endian version looked like this:

```
struct ieee754sp_konst {
    unsigned    sign:1;
    unsigned    bexp:8;
    unsigned    mant:23;
};
```

C bitfields are always packed—that is, the fields are not padded out to yield any particular alignment. But compilers reject bitfields that span the boundaries of the C type used to hold them (in the example, that's an unsigned, which is short for unsigned int). Such fields are usually 32 bits for MIPS microprocessors, even 64-bit ones. Some compilers will let you get a field of up to 64 bits by using a long long as the basic type.

The structure and mapping for a big-endian CPU is shown in Figure 11.6 (using a typical big-endian's picture); a little-endian version is shown in Figure 11.7.

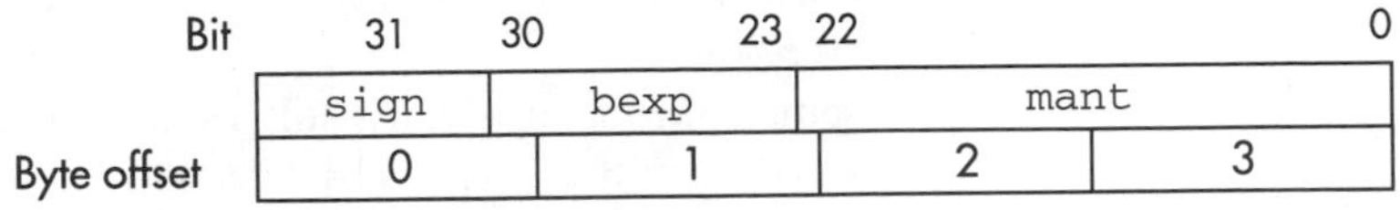

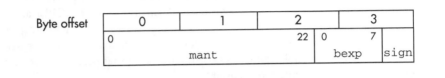

Bit	31	30		23	22			0
	sign		bexp			mant		
Byte offset	0		1		2		3	

FIGURE 11.6 Bitfields from the big-endian viewpoint

Byte offset	0	1	2	3

0		22	0	7	
	mant		bexp		sign

FIGURE 11.7 Bitfields from the little-endian viewpoint

The little-endian version of the structure has to define the fields in the other direction to be compatible with the way the hardware registers work; the C compiler insists that, even for bitfields, items declared first in the structure occupy lower addresses:

```
struct ieee754sp_konst {
    unsigned    mant:23;
    unsigned    bexp:8;
    unsigned    sign:1;
};
```

To see why that works, you can see from Figure 11.7 that in little-endian mode the compiler packs bits into structures starting from low-numbered bits.

It's probably not surprising that the CPU's endianness shows up when looking inside a floating-point number; we said earlier that accessing the same data with different C types often showed up the CPU's nature. But it does demonstrate that there is still a real and pervasive issue before we deal with foreign data or hardware.

11.6.3   *Endianness: The Hardware Problem*

We saw above that a CPU's native endianness only shows up when it offers direct support both for word-length numbers and a finer-resolution, byte-sized memory system. Similarly, your hardware system acquires a recognizable endianness when a byte-addressed system is wired up with buses that are multiple bytes wide. When you transfer multibyte data across the bus, each byte of that data has its own individual address.

If the lowest-address byte in the data travels on the eight bus lines ("byte lane") with the lowest bit numbers, the bus is *little-endian*. But if the lowest-address byte in the data travels on the byte lane with the highest bit numbers, the bus is *big-endian*.

In some IBM manuals you'll still see bit 0 used for the most-significant bit of a byte. But that's really obsolete, and for practical purposes everyone has decided to agree that high bit numbers are interpreted as the most significant. In hardware as in software, that means there's general agreement on the interpretation of 8-bit bytes.

Byte-addressable CPUs announce themselves as either big- or little-endian every time they transfer data. Intel and DEC CPUs are little-endian; Motorola 680x0 and IBM CPUs are big-endian. MIPS CPUs can be either, as configured from power-up; most other RISCs have followed the MIPS lead and chosen to make endianness configurable, so that designers can choose what matches the CPU they're used to.

With all the CPUs I know, this matches up with the software-visible endianness.[1] Since this hardware endianness shows up when data is transferred on a bus, you can identify the endianness of any device that connects to more than 1 byte of a data bus.

So long as all the buses and devices in a system have the same endianness, there's no real problem for hardware engineers; you just connect up the data buses by matching up the numbers. Trouble strikes when your system includes buses, CPUs, or peripherals whose endianness doesn't match. In this case the choice is not a happy one; the system designer must choose the lesser of two evils:

- *Bit number consistent/byte address scrambled*: Most obviously, the designer can wire the two buses up according to their bit numbers, which will have the effect of preserving bit numbering within aligned "words." But since the relationship between bit numbers and bytes-within-words is different on the two buses, the two sides will see the sequence of bytes in memory differently.

  Byte-oriented data being transferred across the join will not make sense until the software byte-swaps each word unit of the data as required. This looks and feels different from the software endianness problem: In the software problem you have no problem finding data type boundaries; it's just that the data doesn't make sense. With this hardware problem the boundaries are scrambled too (unless the data happened to be aligned on bus-width "word" boundaries).

---

1. It doesn't have to match up, though. You *could* build a CPU interface where instead of having data bits numbered 0–31, you instead collected the data bits into byte lanes and perhaps called the signals *0D0–7, 1D0–7, 2D0–7, 3D0–7*, according to whether they were the bits of bytes at low→high addresses. There would be no endianness visible in such an interface.

If the data being passed across the interface is always aligned word-length integers, then this may even be useful; the word data can be converted from its opposite-endian fomrat to a this-endian format.

- *Byte address consistent/word scrambled*: The designer can decide to preserve byte addressing: That will mean connecting byte lanes that correspond to the same byte-within-word address, even though the numbering of the data lines in the byte lane doesn't match at all. Of course, that means that a bus-width-aligned integer (the "natural" unit of transfer) will get scrambled when travelling between the two buses; any multibyte data will require reinterpretation by software from the other side.

For most purposes, byte address scrambling is much more pernicious: When dealing with data representation and transfer problems, programmers will usually fall back on C's basic model of memory as an array of bytes, with other data types built up from that. When your assumptions about memory order don't work out, it's very hard to see what's going on.

Unfortunately, a bit number consistent/byte address scrambled connection looks much more natural on a schematic; it can be very hard to persuade hardware engineers to do anything else.

Not every connection in a system matters. Suppose we have a 32-bit-wide memory system bolted directly to a CPU. The CPU's system interface may not include a byte-within-word address—the address bus does not specify address bits 1 and 0. Instead, many CPUs have four "byte enables" that show that data is being transferred on particular byte lanes. The memory array is wired to the whole bus, and on a write the byte enables tell the memory array which of four possible byte locations within the word will actually get written. Internally, the CPU associates each of the byte lanes with a byte-within-word address, but that has no effect on the operation of the memory system. Effectively, the memory/CPU combination acts together and inherits the endianness of the CPU; where byte-within-word 0 actually goes in memory doesn't matter, so long as the CPU can read it back again.[1]

It's very important not to be seduced by this helpful characteristic of a RAM memory into believing that there's no intrinsic endianness in a simple CPU/RAM system. You can spot the endianness of any transfer on a wide bus. Here's a sample list of conditions in which you can't just ignore the CPU's endianness when building a memory system:

---

1. Hardware-familiarized engineers will recognize that this is a consequence of a more general rule: It's a property of a writable memory array that it continues to work despite arbitrary permutations of the address and data lines to it. It doesn't matter where any particular data goes, so long as when you feed the matching read address into the array you get back the same data you originally wrote.

- When a ROM memory is preprogrammed, the hardware address and byte lane connections need to match those used for programming the ROM, and the ROM data needs to match the CPU's software endianness.

- When a DMA device gets to transfer data directly into memory, then its notions of ordering will matter.

- When a CPU interface does not in fact use byte enables, but instead issues byte-within-word addresses with a byte-width code, then the endianness will matter. Many MIPS CPUs are like this.

Section 11.6.5 is a discussion for hardware engineers about how to set up a byte address consistent system and survive.

11.6.4 *Wiring a Connection between Opposite-Endian Camps*

Suppose we've got a big-endian 64-bit CPU, perhaps a MIPS R4x00 configured big-endian. And we've got a little-endian 32-bit bus, probably PCI.

Figure 11.8 shows how we'd wire up the data buses to achieve the recommended outcome of consistent byte addresses as seen by the big-endian CPU and the little-endian bus.

The numbers called "byte lane" show the byte-within-bus-width part of the address of the byte data travelling there. Writing in the byte lane numbers is the key to getting one of these connections right.

Since the CPU bus is 64 bits wide and the PCI bus 32 bits, you need to be able to connect each half of the wide bus to the narrow bus according to the "word" address—that's address bit 2, since address bits 1 and 0 are the byte-within-32-bit-word address. The 64-bit bus is big-endian, so its high-numbered bits carry the lower addresses, as you can see from the byte lane numbers.

If you look just at the bit numbering around the bus switch, you'd think it just couldn't be right. Such are the joys of endianness.

11.6.5 *Wiring an Endianness-Configurable Connection*

Suppose you want to build a board or bus switch device that is designed to handle MIPS CPUs of either endianness. How can we generalize the advice of Section 11.6.4?

We'd suggest that, if you can persuade your hardware designer, you should put a programmable byte lane swapper between the CPU and the I/O system. The way this works is shown diagrammatically in Figure 11.9; note that this is only a 32-bit configurable interface and it's an exercise for you to generalize it to a 64-bit CPU connection.

We call this a byte lane swapper, not a byte swapper, to emphasize that it does not discriminate on a per-transfer basis, and in particular to indicate

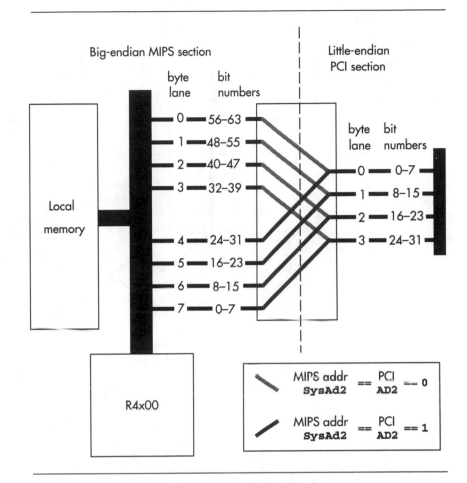

FIGURE 11.8 Wiring a big-endian CPU to a little-endian bus

that it is not switched on and off for transfers of different sizes. There are circumstances where it can be switched on and off for transfers to different address regions—mapping some part of the system as bit number consistent/byte address scrambled—but that's for you to make work.

What a byte lane swapper *does* achieve is to ensure that, when your CPU configuration is changed, the relationship between the CPU and the now-non-matching external bus or device can still be one where byte sequence is preserved.

You normally won't put the byte-lane swapper between the CPU and its local memory—this is just as well, because the CPU/local memory connection is fast and wide, which would make the byte swapper expensive. As mentioned above, so long as you can decode the CPU's system interface successfully you can treat the CPU/local memory as a unit and install the byte swapper between

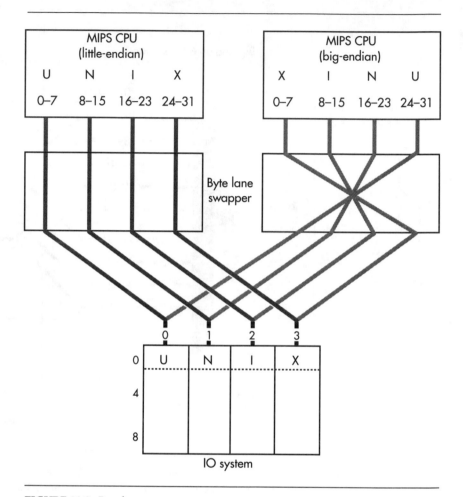

FIGURE 11.9 Byte lane swapper

the CPU/memory unit and the rest of the system. In this case the relationship between bit number and byte order inside the local memory changes with the CPU, but this fact is not visible from the rest of the world.

11.6.6 *Software to Cope with Both-Endianness of a MIPS CPU*

You may want to write software that will run correctly on MIPS CPUs with either endianness—either for a particular board that may be run either way or to create a portable device driver that may run on boards of either configuration. It's a bit tricky, but you can do a much better job by thinking it out in advance.

The MIPS CPU doesn't have to do too much to change endianness. The only parts of the instruction set that recognize objects smaller than 32 bits are partial-word loads and stores. On a MIPS CPU with a 32-bit bus, the instruction

```
lbu t0, 1(zero)
```

takes the byte at byte program address 1, loads it into the least-significant bits (0 through 7) of register **t0**, and fills the rest of the register with zero bits.

This description is endianness independent; indeed, the signals produced by the CPU are identical in the two cases: The address will be the appropriate translation of the program address "1" and the transfer-width code will indicate 1 byte. *In big-endian mode, however, the data loaded into the register will be taken from bits 16–23 of the CPU data bus; in little-endian mode, the byte is loaded from bits 8–15 of the CPU data bus.*

Inside the MIPS CPU, there are alternate data paths leading from each individual byte lane to bits 0–7 of the register so that the CPU can implement the normal four different load-byte cases; the MIPS CPU can change endianness by altering the choice of data path for each byte-within-word address.

It is the change in the relationship between the active byte lane and the address on partial-word loads and stores that characterizes the MIPS CPU's endianness. And complementing the chip's ability to reconfigure itself, most MIPS cross-compilers can produce code either way around based on a command line option.

If you just reconfigure a MIPS CPU to the wrong endianness for a particular system, then a couple of things will happen. Firstly, if you change nothing else the system will most likely stop working, since on any partial-word write the memory system will pick up the CPU's data from the wrong part of the bus and will store garbage; thus, at the same time as reconfiguring the CPU, we'd better reconfigure the logic that decodes CPU cycles.[1]

Once we've got around that, we'll find that the CPU's view of byte addressing becomes scrambled with respect to the rest of the system; in terms of the description above, we've implicitly opted for a bit number consistent/byte-address scrambled connection.

Of course, data written by the CPU after its sex change will seem fine to the CPU; if we only select endianness at power-up then volatile memory that is private to the CPU won't give us any trouble.

Note also that the CPU's view of bit numbering within aligned bus-width words continues to match the rest of the system. This is the choice we described as bit number consistent/byte address scrambled and discouraged above deprecated for general use. But in this particular case it has a useful side effect, because MIPS instructions are encoded as bitfields in 32-bit words. An instruction ROM that makes sense to a big-endian CPU will make sense to a little-

---

1. This first problem won't happen on some CPUs, like IDT's R3051 family, which signal partial-word transfers with independent byte lane enable signals.

	31	24 23	16 15	8 7	0
	r	e	m	E
Byte address from BE CPU	0	1	2	3
Byte address from LE CPU	3	2	1	0
	c	n	e	g
Byte address from BE CPU	4	5	6	7
Byte address from LE CPU	7	6	5	4
	x	x	\000	y
Byte address from BE CPU	8	9	10	11
Byte address from LE CPU	11	10	9	8

FIGURE 11.10 Garbled string storage when mixing modes; see text

endian CPU too, allowing us to share a bootstrap. Nothing works perfectly—in this case, any data in the ROM that doesn't consist of aligned 32-bit words will be scrambled. Algorithmics has never made a bi-endian bootstrap, but we do have just enough bi-endian code to detect that the main ROM program does not match the CPU's endianness and to print the helpful message:

```
Emergency - wrong endianness configured.
```

The word Emergency is held as a C string, null-terminated. You should now know enough to understand why the ROM startup code contains the enigmatic lines

```
.align  4
.ascii "remEcneg\000\000\000y"
```

That's what the string Emergency (with its standard C terminating null and two bytes of essential padding) looks like when viewed with the wrong endianness. It would be even worse if it didn't start on a 4-byte-aligned location. Figure 11.10 (drawn from the point of view of a confirmed big-endian) shows what is going on.

Note that just because you can write some bi-endian code doesn't mean it's going to be easy to load it into ROM. Typically, big-endian tools pack instruction words into the bytes of a load file with the most-significant bits first, and little-endian tools work the other way around. You need to figure out what you need and make sure you get it.

11.6.7   *Portability and Endianness-Independent Code*

By a fairly well-respected convention most MIPS toolchains define the symbol
BYTE_ORDER as follows:

```
#if BYTE_ORDER == BIG_ENDIAN
/* big-endian version... */
#else
/* little-endian version... */
#endif
```

However, wherever you can you should use endianness-independent code.
Particularly in a well-controlled situation (such as when writing code for a
MIPS system that may be initialized with the CPU in either mode) you can
get rid of a lot of dependencies by good thinking.

All data references that pick up data from an external source or device are
potentially endianness dependent. But according to how your system is wired
you may be able to produce code that works both ways. There are only two
ways of wiring the wrong endianness together: one preserves byte addresses
and the other bit numbers. For some particular peripheral register access in a
particular range of systems, there's a good chance that the endianness change
consistently sticks to one of these.

If your device is typically mapped to be byte address compatible, then you
should program it strictly with byte operations. If ever, for reasons of efficiency
or necessity, you want to transfer more than 1 byte at a time, you need to write
endianness-conditional code that packs or unpacks that data.

If your device is compatible at the word (32-bit) level—for example, it consists of registers wired (by however devious and indirect a route) to a fixed set
of MIPS data bus bits—then program it with bus-width read/write operations.
That will be 32-bit or 64-bit loads and stores. If the device registers are not
wired to MIPS data bus bits starting at 0, you'll probably want to shift the data
after a read and before a write. For example, 8-bit registers on a 32-bit bus in a
system originally conceived as big-endian are commonly wired via bits 31–24.

11.6.8   *Endianness and Foreign Data*

This is only a chapter on program porting, not a treatise on I/O and communications, so we'll keep this section brief. Any data that is not initialized in your
code, chosen libraries, and OS is foreign. It may be data you read from some
memory-mapped piece of hardware, data put into memory by DMA, data in a
preprogrammed ROM that isn't part of your program, or you may be trying to
interpret a byte stream obtained from an "abstract" I/O device under your OS.

The first stage is to figure out what this data looks like in memory; with
C that can usually be accomplished by mapping out what its contents are as
an array of unsigned char. Even if you know your data and compiler well

enough to guess what C structure will successfully map to the data, fall back to the array of bytes when something is not as you expect; it's far too easy to miss what is really going on if your data structure is incorrect.

Apart from endianness, the data may consist of data types that are not supported by your compiler/CPU; it may have similar types but with completely different encodings; it may have familiar data but be incorrectly aligned; or, falling under this section's domain, it may have the wrong endianness.

If the chain along which the data has reached you has preserved byte order at each stage, the worst that will happen is that integer data will be represented with an opposite order, and it's easy enough to build a "swap" macro to restore the 2, 4, or 8 bytes of an integer value.

But if the data has passed over a bit number consistent/byte address scrambled interface, it can be more difficult. In these circumstances you need to locate the boundaries corresponding to the width of the bus where the data got swapped, then taking groups of bytes within those boundaries swap them without regard to the underlying data type. If you do it right, the result should now make sense, with the correct byte sequence, although you may still need to cope with the usual problems in the data—including, possibly, the need to reswap multibyte integer data.

11.6.9 *False Cures and False Prophets for Endianness Problems*

Every design team facing up to endianness goes through the stage of thinking it's a hardware deficiency to be solved. It's not. Here are a few examples.

Configurable I/O Controllers

Some newer I/O controllers can themselves be configured into big-endian and little-endian modes. You're going to have to read the manual very carefully before using such a feature, particularly when you are using it not as a static (design time) option but rather as a jumper (reset time) option.

It is quite common for such a feature to affect only bulk data transfers, leaving the programmer to handle other endianness issues, such as access to bit-coded device registers or shared memory control fields. Also, the controller designer probably didn't have the benefit of this book—and confusion about endianness is widespread.

Hardware That Byte-Swaps According to Transfer Type

If you're designing in some byte-swap hardware, it seems appealing to try to solve the whole problem. If we just swapped byte data to preserve its addresses, but left words alone, couldn't we prevent the whole software problem? The answer is no, there aren't any hardware fixes for the software problem. For example, many of the transfers in a real system are of cache lines. They may contain a mixture of data types; how do we locate and fix them? Also, CPUs

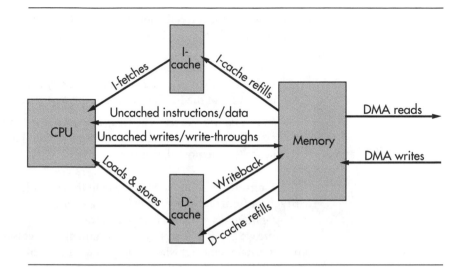

FIGURE 11.11   Data flow between CPU, memory, and caches

may sometimes deal with numeric data that spans memory-word boundaries; how would we swap that?

Conditional byte-swapping just adds confusion. Nothing except unconditional byte lane swapping is any good.

11.7   What Can Go Wrong with Caches and How to Stop It

We've looked at how to manage caches in Section 4.6. This section will focus on how you make sure that you always do the right thing to the cache when necessary.

Most of the time the caches are completely invisible to software, doing nothing except accelerating the system as they should. But when it comes to DMA devices and some other issues, it can be helpful to see the caches as independent extra buffer memories, as shown in Figure 11.11. When you're taking this view, it's important to remember that transfers between cache and memory fetch blocks of memory that fit the cache line structure—typically 16- or 32-byte-aligned blocks—so the cache may read and write data the CPU has not explicitly referenced.

Note that MIPS CPUs with simple write-through data caches don't need the line called "write back" in Figure 11.11.

For a simple life, we'd want to be sure that the state of the memory exactly reflects the operations the CPU has commanded and that all valid cache lines contain an exact copy of memory data. Unfortunately, such a simple life is not compatible with the positive effects of caches on performance. We'll assume that the caches are correctly initialized and that you avoid the dreaded cache aliases described in Section 4.14.2. So what can go wrong with the ideal picture?

- *Stale data in the cache*: Either cache can be holding data that has been updated in memory, by a DMA write, or by a CPU uncached write—or in the case of the I-cache, by a D-cache write back.
- *Stale data in memory*: The CPU may have written some locations with new data, but the data hasn't yet been written back from the D-cache, hence the memory data is stale.

The software weapons you have to fight these problems are a couple of standard subroutines that allow you to invalidate, or write back, any cache locations corresponding to a specified area of memory.

Before we go on to that, I want to comment on accesses to I/O registers and other external memories where you need total control over what gets read and written. Reads that hit in the cache or writes that hit in a write-back cache are nonevents outside the CPU/cache subsystem. Obviously, you will have planned that hardware register accesses are uncached, which can conveniently be done by accessing those registers through pointers in kseg1 or some other uncached space; if you use cached space for I/O, bad things will happen!

If (unusually) you need to use the TLB to map hardware register accesses, you can mark the page translation as uncached. That's useful if someone has built hardware whose I/O registers are not in the low 512MB of the physical memory space.

I suppose it's possible that one day you might want to map a device through cached space so as to benefit from the speed of the block reads and writes that the CPU only uses to implement cache refills and write backs. You'd have to explicitly manage the cache by invalidation and write back on every such access.

11.7.1 *Cache Management and DMA Data*

This is a common source of errors, and we've heard tales of lurking cache problems besetting MIPS OS ports done by experienced, hardened low-level programmers. But it's really not so bad.

When a DMA device puts data into memory (you're reading from a disk or receiving network data), the CPU/cache subsystem doesn't know about it. Your last system may not have been like this: Your last CPU may not have had a cache, or it may have snooped DMA transfers from its local bus and adjusted its caches accordingly. But the MIPS CPUs don't do that for you.

If any locations that have just been written by the DMA device are currently in either cache, then when the CPU goes to read the data it will get the old, stale data from the cache instead. This will be a disaster.

You need to invalidate any location in the cache where any of your DMA data may land. The invalidation must be inclusive, incorporating any odd remains of cache lines that are partially in the buffer. And that needs to be done between the last reference your program made to any of those locations and the point (after the DMA has finished) where you first try to read any of the DMA data.

Note that if the DMA locations don't completely fill the first or last cache line, you can inadvertently reload the cache line before the DMA is complete by referencing some other data in the line. It's best to segregate DMA data buffers on cache line boundaries. And remember that on many MIPS CPUs a write will bring something into the cache as surely as a read will.

In the other direction, before allowing a DMA device to take data out of memory (writing to a disk or sending to a network) you must make quite sure that none of the data that the CPU has prepared for this purpose is still lurking in your cache. After your program has finished writing the DMA buffer contents, but before setting off the DMA, you must write back all the DMA data in the buffer. This can't happen for an older CPU with a write-through cache.

It would save trouble to map the buffer memory uncached. But it will also cost performance. Even if your program access to the buffers is purely sequential, caching the buffers will mean that data gets read and written in efficient cache-line-sized bursts rather than single transfers. My general advice, also given in this book, is to cache everything. I'd make an exception for a small shared memory control structure like a status word maintained by a DMA master controller.

11.7.2   *Cache Management and Writing Instructions*

The writing of instructions is the other place where explicit cache management can bite you; this problem can't happen on a system with a unified (instruction and data) cache or one where the I-cache snoops all reads and writes.

On a MIPS CPU, after your program has written instructions to memory and before you try to execute them, you need to do a write back of the chunk of memory with instructions in it, followed by an I-cache invalidation to discard any stale copies of whatever used to be in memory at those locations.

11.7.3   *Cache Management and Uncached/Write-Through Data*

If you mix cached and uncached references to memory the hardware gives you no help. Uncached writes will leave stale data in the I-cache and D-cache, and uncached loads will bypass data that may have been updated in the D-cache, returning possibly stale data from memory.

If you feel that your system (beyond the bootstrap) needs to make uncached references to cacheable memory, then I strongly recommend that you divide memory into regions that are always accessed uncached and regions that are always accessed through the cache—and don't let them overlap. The region boundaries should not split a cache line block.

11.8   Different Implementations of MIPS

Although MIPS has grown up a long way, the path has been one of guaranteed compatibility for regular user-level programs and careful evolution of lower-level features. MIPS IV CPUs quite happily run MIPS I binaries; the biggest change (the change to 64 bits) is not normally important except for small chunks of embedded software, and occasional use of 64-bit data requires recompilation rather than program changes.

So we don't expect you to have large porting problems as you go up the MIPS CPU family. The software-visible differences you will find in these CPUs are listed following:

- *Type of cache*: Essentially all 32-bit MIPS CPUs used a write-through data cache, but 64-bit CPUs have used write-back caches. (The different types of cache are described in Chapter 4.) Write-back caches introduce a new caching hazard, where data that the CPU has written is held only in the cache but not in main memory and so is not available to a device that reads memory for itself.

  On the bright side, there have really only been two programming models for MIPS cache families, and once again the split coincides with the change from 32 to 64 bit; a 32-bit MIPS CPU probably has caches like an R3000 and a 64-bit CPU has caches like an R4000. See Section 12.2 for examples of a set of reasonable cache management functions implemented for both R3000- and R4000-type CPUs.

- *Raw speed*: This is most easily characterized as clock rate. MIPS pipeline clock rates have increased from 8MHz to 200MHz over the 10 years since the first commercial R2000 appeared. As CPUs speed up, you meet more occasions where you have to deliberately slow down accesses to devices.

- *64-bit support*: This is rarely a portability problem. Just because the CPU is 64 bit capable, there's no call to go changing all the data types used by your program. The 64-bit support does create new hardware alignment requirements for long data types, but your old compiler for MIPS probably anticipated that.

- *Cache size*: All CPUs have separate I- and D-caches, but they vary in size and some have separate primary and secondary caches. R4x00 CPUs have an authoritative cache size field in the **Config** register; for other types you should sense the cache size at system initialization. Do not infer cache size from the CPU type and revision fields in the ID register; nobody changes those fields when they spin a CPU variant with bigger caches.

- *Cache line size*: This is the number of bytes loaded into or written back from the cache in a unit; it varies from one word (4 bytes) for early data caches up to 32 bytes for many R4x00 I-caches. Management routines need to know the line size, of course; less obviously, the cache line size defines important boundaries for DMA data. Bear in mind that even the one-word "line" of the data cache in early R3000-style CPUs is a cache line; it can cause implicit loading of the other bytes in the same word.

- *Write buffer differences and* `wbflush()`: To make the write-through cache efficient, all CPUs have some kind of write buffer, which holds the address/data of a write while the CPU runs on. The operation of the write buffer should be invisible when writing and reading regular memory that is free of side-effects; but it can have effects when accessing I/O buffers.

  The programmer only needs an implementation of `wbflush()`, which is a routine defined not to return until all pending writes have been completed. There is no universal implementation of this; see Section 4.13.1 for a discussion.

- *FP hardware*: Some CPUs have this hardware; most 32-bit integrated CPUs don't. For occasional FP instruction use, trap-based software emulators exist: Because you really need an FP trap handler to make *any* use of the FPA, the use of the emulator can be completely software transparent. However, for any serious use, the emulator will be far too slow.

  Most compilation systems give you the option of compiling programs to use built-in subroutines to perform FP calculations.

- *MMU hardware*: If present, such hardware is always the same software-refilled TLB and control set (see Chapter 6). Some TLB-free CPUs recycle what would otherwise be the mapped program address spaces for other purposes, but portable software will use only the kseg0, kseg1 regions which are supported by all processors.

- *Integrated I/O devices*: Some CPUs integrate timers, watchpoint registers, DRAM controllers, DMA, and lots more. You're on your own with these; however, do isolate such code into "driver" modules, just as if you were dealing with external device controllers.

Chapter

12 Software Examples

This chapter is based on real workable chunks of software, which often means we sacrifice clarity and are less than concise; but then, real software is like that. We're going to cover the following:

- *Starting up MIPS*: getting the CPU and system going, to the point where you can run a C program

- *MIPS cache management*: an example of the system you might need to be able to invalidate and/or write back cache locations to make your I/O system work

- *MIPS exception handling*: grisly details from low-level interrupt to comfortable C handler

- *MIPS interrupts*: not particularly efficient, but showing the essential features; builds on the structures of the previous section

- *Tuning for MIPS*: a simple function rewritten in assembler with many tricks to improve bandwidth

12.1 Starting Up MIPS

Starting up a CPU from reset with code in ROM always involves a number of complicating factors:

- *Configuration*: We probably want to use the same ROM for many different board configurations, so we have to proceed warily until we've figured out what it is we're running on.

- *CPU initialization*: The CPU itself may not be prepared to do much until its own registers have been attended to. The ROM may have to cope with more than one type of CPU, too.

- *Memory initialization*: Most modern memory systems require some programming before they work, which means that we'll have to run from on-chip resources (registers, basically) until we've done that.

- *Traceability*: When something goes wrong, mere silence from a ROM bootstrap is undesirable. So the code should attempt to communicate with the user before relying on some part of the hardware that might not work.

- *Compatibility*: Running somewhere over the ROM there may be all sorts of old crusty software, which has its own idea of what the ROM should be doing.

It might be nice to show you an example without these complications, but then it wouldn't ever have been tested....

We'll look at software from Algorithmics SDE-MIPS, which comes in two modules. There's a generic from-reset ROM module (entered at **__reset**) and a hardware-specific module for the Algorithmics P-4032 prototyping board (which is only ever fitted with R4x00 and R5x00 CPUs) starting with **_sbd_reset**.

The MIPS reset-time entry point is at physical address `0x1fc0.0000`, which puts it at the start of a 16MB chunk of memory; no Algorithmics board has anything like 16MB of ROM, so the reset-time entry point is the very location in the ROM, which happens automatically because it's the first line of code in the first module linked into the ROM:

```
.text

.set   noreorder
b __reset; move k0, zero        /* RESET */
/* ... */
```

Starting with a branch is regarded as good form. If absolutely nothing works, we can watch the CPU address bus with a logic analyzer: If it goes to the reset location and then branches to the right place, a fair amount of the ROM and data bus system must be working.

This system uses **k0** (if it's nonzero) to hold the address of an alternate exception handler. From reset, if we get an unexpected exception, we want to handle it ourselves. So now let's go on:

```
/*
 * We jump here on a Reset Exception
 */
```

```
SLEAF(__reset)
    /*
     * Determine relocation factor and set $gp
     */
    bal       _rom_reloc
    la        gp,_gp

    /*
     * Call board-specific initialization code
     */
    bal       _sbd_reset
```

We'll ignore the **_rom_reloc** routine for now—it's used when the ROM code is running at an address different from where it was linked, which this ROM might want to do for reasons we won't go into. If necessary, this ROM uses the **s8** register to remember the difference between where we were linked and where we really are.

So it's off to **_sbd_reset**, in the board-specific module. We'll go through that in detail.

```
/*
 * P4032/sbdreset.S: low-level code for Algorithmics P4032 board
 * Copyright (c) 1996 Algorithmics Ltd.
 */

#include <mips/asm.h>
#include <mips/regdef.h>
#include <mips/cpu.h>
#include <mips/endian.h>

#include "sbd.h"
#include "rtc.h"
#include "v96xpbc.h"
#include "w83777f.h"
#include "z80pio.h"

#if !#cpu(r4000) && !#cpu(r5000)
# error Wrong CPU type selected
#endif
```

The #include files contain the following material:

■ mips/asm.h: some things for assembly language, like the **LEAF** macro used to introduce externally callable functions.

- `mips/regdef.h`: conventional register names for MIPS registers
- `mips/cpu.h`: coprocessor 0 register and bitfield constants for your CPU (with conditional compilation used to specialize this for a particular CPU type or family)

This usual collection of include files for low-level code is accompanied by

- `mips/endian.h`: some standard ways of deducing current endianness configuration
- `sbd.h`: characteristics of the board, its address map, and definitions of board-specific registers
- `v96xpbc.h`, etc.: registers and bitfields specific to the device

Here is a macro to write four characters to the onboard LED display:

```
#define DISPLAY(d0,d1,d2,d3)                 \
    li      t8,PA_TO_KVA1(LED_BASE);         \
    li      t9,d0;                           \
    sw      t9,LED(0)(t8);                   \
    li      t9,d1;                           \
    sw      t9,LED(1)(t8);                   \
    li      t9,d2;                           \
    sw      t9,LED(2)(t8);                   \
    li      t9,d3;                           \
    sw      t9,LED(3)(t8)
```

If the software dies, the last value so written will be left there, which will give us a clue about what happened.

These macros are used to access the battery-backed-up memory locations (about 100 bytes) that are implemented by this board's real-time clock chip, which is used as a scratch nonvolatile store:

```
#define WBFLUSH

#define MEG     0x100000

/*
 * Include standard memory test/clear code
 */
#define BUSWIDTH        4               /* 32-bit, noninterleaved */
#define MEMSTART        (32*MEG)        /* simm1 start */
#define MEMINCR         (8*MEG)         /* simm1 quanta */
#include "../share/memprobe.s"
```

```
/*
 * Basic board initialization, called straight from RESET.
 * It is only called if this program is built for ROM.
 * It can use any registers except s8, k0, and k1.
 *
 * Note that s8 holds a "relocation factor" (see ../share/romlow.sx)
 * that must be added to any address before it is used.  This
 * is to support relocatable roms.
 */

#define rtcptr   s2
#define crptr    s3
#define crval    s4
#define msize    s5
#define rasave   s6
#define RELOC    s8

#define RTC_STORE(rtcoffs,reg)        \
    li      t8,rtcoffs;               \
    sw      t8,RTC_ADDR(rtcptr);      \
    sw      reg,RTC_DATA(rtcptr)

#define RTC_LOAD(rtcoffs,reg)         \
    li      t8,rtcoffs;               \
    sw      t8,RTC_ADDR(rtcptr);      \
    lw      reg,RTC_DATA(rtcptr);     \
    and     reg,0xff
```

But here's the actual entry point; we're going to start with CPU registers that may cause trouble if left:

```
LEAF(_sbd_reset)
    move    rasave,ra

#if #cpu(r4300)
    /* set config register for kseg0 cacheable */
    mfc0    t1,C0_CONFIG
    or      t1,CFG_C_NONCOHERENT
    /* we can also control the endianness */
#if #endian(big)
    or      t1,CFG_BE
#else
    and     t1,~CFG_BE
#endif
```

```
     mtc0      t1,C0_CONFIG
#endif /* r4300 */


#ifdef C0_WATCHLO
     mtc0      zero,C0_WATCHLO
     mtc0      zero,C0_WATCHHI
#endif


#if #cpu(r4640)
     /* reset default cache algorithm and watchpoints */
     li        t1,0x22233333
     mtc0      t1,C0_CALG
     mtc0      zero,C0_IWATCH
     mtc0      zero,C0_DWATCH
#endif
```

This is all very CPU specific, but most MIPS CPUs from R4000 onward have a **Config** register that wants to be set early. The watchpoint registers are initialized because the manual suggests that hardly anything prevents a watchpoint exception, and we don't want unsolicited exceptions.

We need to set most fields in the status register **SR** to make sure the CPU runs OK; the **SR(SR)** (soft reset) bit distinguishes a nonmaskable interrupt from a hardware reset and may be important:

```
     mfc0      t1,C0_STATUS

     and       t1,SR_SR              # leave the SoftReset bit
     or        t1,SR_BEV             # force boot exceptions
1:   mtc0      t1,C0_STATUS
     mtc0      zero,C0_CAUSE
```

Cause is zeroed to make sure the software interrupt bits **Cause(IP0-1)** are inactive.

That's done enough to the CPU to prevent disasters (so long as we don't touch the caches, interrupts, or the TLB just yet), so we get on with the board:

```
     la        crptr,PA_TO_KVA1(BCR_BASE)
     la        rtcptr,PA_TO_KVA1(RTC_BASE)

     /* initialise board control register, toggling the V3 reset
        and making sure everything else is disabled */
     li        crval, BCR_V96X_ENABLE
     bal       crwrite
     move      crval, zero
     bal       crwrite
```

```
#if #endian(big)
    li      crval,BCR_LED_ON|BCR_V96X_ENABLE
#else
    li      crval,BCR_LED_ON|BCR_V96X_ENABLE|BCR_IO_LE
#endif
    bal     crwrite
    RTC_STORE(RTC_BCR, crval)
```

The assembler function **crwrite** sets the board control register (BCR), a collection of output-only bits, many of which are used to keep chunks of the logic in reset until needed. We keep a soft copy of the BCR in the real-time clock chip's (RTC's) little memory, because the value doesn't read back.[1]

reginittab (defined at the end of the section) is a list of address/data pairs; just take each data item and write it to the corresponding address:

```
    /* initialise I/O devices */
1:  la      a0,reginittab
    addu    a0,RELOC
1:  lw      v0,0(a0)            # reg addr
    lw      v1,4(a0)            # reg data
    beqz    v0,2f
    sw      v1,0(v0)
    addu    a0,8
    b       1b
2:
```

You can initialize a lot of hardware like that (at least to a first-pass, just-shut-up level).

We may even have to initialize some programmable logic devices here:

```
    /* load ICU firmware via JTAG interface */
    bal     icuload
```

---

1. There's a cautionary tale about hardware and software evolution here. It takes extra hardware resources to add a read-back port to a simple output register. That leads to the following:

   The software problem: To change only one bit of the port and leave the rest alone requires a global soft copy of the register—which is always hard to organize when several only loosely related pieces of software are used to initialize the board.

   The software solution: Keep a soft copy in a magic location—in this case, the NVRAM of the real-time clock chip. But the hardware engineers didn't know this so they came up with...

   The hardware solution: The board's BCR register is implemented as 8 separately writable bits, so there's no need to know the value of other bits when changing one. But, of course, the software was already written, so the bit-writable hardware produces...

   The software response: A subroutine **crwrite()** that loops around and writes all 8 bits.

Now that so much logic is designed into in-system programmable devices, logic that is not required for simple dumb ROM and I/O cycles can be loaded by the CPU.

MIPS CPUs (post-R4000) can have several different flavors of reset, from ground-up to nonmaskable interrupt:

```
/* skip memory size/clear if a soft reset */
mfc0    t1,C0_STATUS
and     t1,SR_SR
beqz    t1,1f

/* get previous memory size from rtc sram */
RTC_LOAD(RTC_MEMSZ, msize)
sll     msize,20
b       .noinit
1:
```

I don't think you can actually make a soft reset happen on the P-4032 board; however, if you could, it would skip the DRAM system reset, leaving the memory contents intact for postmortem debugging.

For the DRAM configuration we'll reassign the registers yet again:

```
/*
 * Determine DRAM bank arrangement and size
 */
#define aces    t0
#define fives   t1
#define base    t2
#define tval    t3
#define simmmap         t4
#define SIMM0_0         0x01
#define SIMM0_1         0x02
#define SIMM1_0         0x04
#define SIMM1_1         0x08
#define msize0 v0
#define msize1 v1

/* initialise DCR memory speed and type from option links */
lw      crval,PA_TO_KVA1(OPTION_BASE)
and     crval,DCR_SIMM1_DRAM|DCR_TYPE|DCR_DRAMFAST
```

What's this **PA_TO_KVA1()** macro? It takes a physical address (the header files define register locations as physical addresses) and adds some high-order bits to deliver the corresponding program address in kseg2, which will give us an uncached access.

Here, the program is reading a software image of a jumper block and will shortly write that value (stored in `crval`) to the DRAM configuration register, telling the hardware what sort of memories are fitted:

```
/* initialise registers */
move    msize0,zero
move    msize1,zero
li      aces,0xaaaaaaaa
not     fives,aces
li      base,PA_TO_KVA1(0)


/* make sure memory has started up properly */
/* configure for 4MB double sided and read at 4MB intervals */
or      crval,DCR_4MB
DISPLAY ('D','C','R','I')
li      crptr,PA_TO_KVA1(DCR_BASE)
bal     crwrite                     # write the BCR
```

At this stage any modules plugged in will store a minimum of 4MB per side (the SIMM modules have one or two banks of memory chips, and the second bank is usually soldered to the back of the board). Detect what's there first and figure out what it actually is:

```
DISPLAY ('M','E','M','I')
li      tval,8
.initmem:
    sw      zero,+0*MEG(base)
    sw      zero,+4*MEG(base)
    sw      zero,+8*MEG(base)
    sw      zero,12*MEG(base)
    subu    tval,1
    bnez    tval,.initmem
```

This eight-times-around loop seems to be paranoia about DRAM working right from the first cycle; this paranoia may or may not be justified in this particular system.

Then we'll write to each possible module and see which ones retain the data (and can therefore be assumed to be present):

```
/* now detect the presence of SIMMS and their sides */
DISPLAY ('S','L','O','T')

    sw      aces,+0*MEG(base)
    sw      aces,+4*MEG(base)
    sw      aces,+8*MEG(base)
```

```
sw      aces,12*MEG(base)

sw      fives,+0*MEG+4(base)
sw      fives,+4*MEG+4(base)
sw      fives,+8*MEG+4(base)
sw      fives,12*MEG+4(base)

sw      zero,+0*MEG+8(base)
sw      zero,+4*MEG+8(base)
sw      zero,+8*MEG+8(base)
sw      zero,12*MEG+8(base)
```

We've written three different values to the first three words of each of four possible banks. The last write (zero to the third word) is really intended to prevent a false-positive that you sometimes get in sizing memory, in which you appear to read data back successfully from memory that isn't there at all. The effect is caused by the stray capacitance of the memory bus, and is common with modern CMOS circuits: You're actually reading back from the bus wires the "ghost" of the last data you wrote.

So now we find where there are modules plugged in:

```
/* generate map of SIMM slots/sides */
move    simmmap,zero

        lw      tval,+0*MEG(base)
        bne     tval,aces,1f
        or      simmmap,SIMM0_0
1:
        lw      tval,+4*MEG(base)
        bne     tval,aces,1f
        or      simmmap,SIMM0_1
1:
        lw      tval,+8*MEG(base)
        bne     tval,aces,1f
        or      simmmap,SIMM1_0
1:
        lw      tval,+12*MEG(base)
        bne     tval,aces,1f
        or      simmmap,SIMM1_1
1:
        ...
```

You're probably getting the idea by now, so we're now going to skip the rest of the code that figures out how big each module is and that configures the addresses to make a nice sequential map.

The code string ends thus:

```
.noinit:
    DISPLAY ('R','U','N',' ')

    /* return to generic code, with available memory size */
    move    ra,rasave
    move    v0,msize
    j       ra
END(_sbd_reset)
```

That's it, apart from a couple of things jumped to from above that you might like to look at, starting with the fatal-error routine **_sbd_memfail()**, which never exits:

```
LEAF(_sbd_memfail)
    DISPLAY ('!','M','E','M')
1:  b       1b
    j       ra
END(_sbd_memfail)
```

Also, here is **crwrite()**, the subroutine designed to hide the hardware features we thought software engineers were calling for:

```
/* crwrite (base, val)
 *      Write 8-bit <val> to 8 consecutive 1-bit registers,
 *      starting at <base>
 * Uses:    t8, t9
 */
SLEAF(crwrite)
        move    t9,crval
        li      t8,8
1:  .set    noat
        and     AT,t9,1
        sw      AT,0(crptr)
        .set  at
        srl     t9,1
        subu    t8,1
        addu    crptr,4
        bnez    t8,1b

        subu    crptr,8*4       # reset pointer
        j       ra
SEND(crwrite)
```

Finally, here is **reginittab**:

```
#define INIT(addr,val) \
    .word PA_TO_KVA1(addr), val

    .rdata
reginittab:
    /* initial magic cycle for PCI bridge */
    INIT(V96XPBC_BASE+V96X_LB_IO_BASE, V96XPBC_BASE+V96X_LB_IO_BASE)
    /* led message */
    INIT(LED_BASE+LED(0), 'P')
    INIT(LED_BASE+LED(1), '4')
    INIT(LED_BASE+LED(2), '3')
    INIT(LED_BASE+LED(3), '2')
    /* program a 32KHz square wave from the RTC */
    INIT(RTC_BASE+RTC_ADDR, RTC_STATUSA)
    INIT(RTC_BASE+RTC_DATA, RTC_OSC_32KHz|RTC_RATE_NONE)
    INIT(RTC_BASE+RTC_ADDR, RTC_STATUSB)
    INIT(RTC_BASE+RTC_DATA, RTCSB_BINARY|RTCSB_24HR|RTCSB_SQWE)
    INIT(RTC_BASE+RTC_ADDR, RTC_INTR)
    INIT(RTC_BASE+RTC_DATA, RTCIR_32KE)
    /* disable the combi chip configuration registers */
    INIT(EFER, EFER_DISABLE)
    /* initialize the z80pio chip, B channel */
    INIT(ZPIO_BASE+ZPIO_B_CTL, ZPIO_MODE_CTRL)   # control mode
    INIT(ZPIO_BASE+ZPIO_B_CTL, ZPIOB_E2_DO)      # input mask
    INIT(ZPIO_BASE+ZPIO_B_DAT, 0)                # initial value
    .word 0,0                                     # terminate table
```

reginittab is the table we mentioned earlier on page 339; it contains pairs of entries consisting of a register address and a data value to be written to that register. Lots of obscure hardware can be adequately initialized by appropriate table entries.

12.2   MIPS Cache Management

We're going to look at two large, indigestible chunks of assembler code that are provided as part of the Algorithmics SDE-MIPS.[1] They implement the following functions:

---

1. Like the rest of this book, this software is copyrighted. You can obtain the right to use this software for commercial purposes from Algorithmics, Ltd.

- void mips_size_cache(): When first called, initialize cache and leave cache sizes in global variables. If called again, do nothing.

- void mips_init_cache(): Work out and record the size of I- and D-caches and initialize them.

- void mips_flush_cache (): Write back (if required) and invalidate all caches. I dislike the term "flush" because of its ambiguity, but in this case it's historical and derives from a time when caches were always write through and so never needed a write back.

- void mips_clean_cache (unsigned kva, size_t n):   Write back and invalidate the address range in all caches.

- void mips_flush_dcache (void): Write back and invalidate the entire contents of data cache.

- void mips_clean_dcache (unsigned kva, size_t n):   Write back and invalidate the address range in data caches.

- void r4k_hit_writeback_inv_dcache (unsigned kva, size_t n): Write back and invalidate the address range in the primary data cache.

- void mips_clean_icache (unsigned kva, size_t n):   Invalidate the address range in instruction caches.

The files retain their original (light) comments and are going to be interspersed with further commentary. But they're still assembler code and likely to be fairly hard going.

12.2.1   *Cache Operations: 32-Bit MIPS before Cache Instructions*

Before the **cache** instruction was invented, cache management was done by doing stores with the CPU in strange modes ("isolated" to access caches, "swapped" to write the I-cache rather than the D-cache). Here's how Algorithmics does it:

```
/*
 * r3kcache.S: generic R3000 cache support functions for SDE-MIPS
 */

#if !#cpu(r3000)
#error use -mcpu=r3000 option with this file
#endif

#include <mips/asm.h>
#include <mips/regdef.h>
#include <mips/r3kc0.h>
#include <mips/prid.h>
```

The #include files contain the following:

- asm.h: some things for assembly language, like the **LEAF** macro used to introduce externally callable functions
- regdef.h: conventional register names for MIPS registers
- r3kc0.h: register and bitfield constants for R3x00 coprocessor 0 registers
- prid.h: processor ID and revision values for MIPS CPUs

Declare some variables, make them global, and give them initial values:

```
#define DECL(x, val)       \
    EXPORTS(x, 4)          \
    .word val


    .sdata
DECL(mips_icache_size,-1)
DECL(mips_dcache_size,-1)
DECL(mips_scache_size,-1)
DECL(mips_tcache_size,-1)
DECL(mips_icache_linesize,-1)
DECL(mips_dcache_linesize,-1)
DECL(mips_tcache_linesize,-1)
DECL(mips_pcache_ways,1)
DECL(mips_scache_ways,1)
DECL(mips_tcache_ways,1)


/*
 * void mips_size_cache()
 * Initialise I- and D- caches and flush them, but only if size is unknown
 */
LEAF(mips_size_cache)
    lw      t0,mips_icache_size
    blez    t0,mips_init_cache
    j       ra
END(mips_size_cache)

/*
 * void mips_init_cache()
 *
 * work out size of I- and D-caches and flush them
 *
 * uses:    v0,v1,t0,t1,t2,t3,t4,t7,t8,ra
 * save regs:   t3,t7,t8,v1
```

```
 * calls:    _init_cache
 */
LEAF(mips_init_cache)
    move    t8,ra

    mfc0    t7,$sr
    and     t3,t7,SR_BEV               # disable interrupts
    mtc0    t3,$sr

    /* run uncached (but do it in pic form) */
    .set    noreorder
    bal     1f
    nop
1:  or      t1,ra,KSEG1_BASE
    addu    t1,16
    jr      t1
    nop
    .set    reorder
```

Note the following points:

- *Save* **ra**: By keeping the return address somewhere else, we can at least use one level of subroutine call instructions inside this module.

- *Disable interrupts*: We've zeroed everything in **SR** except for **SR(BEV)**, which is left in its previous state. Disabling interrupts is one of the side effects of this draconian action.

- **nop**s: Most of this code is *not* surrounded by **.set noreorder** directives, so we're going to let the assembler figure out when accesses to coprocessor 0 registers need **nop**s added. Not all MIPS assemblers do this.
  Sometimes we'll need to put in explicit **nop**s, for example where what we're doing affects the operation of the caches. No assembler is clever enough to figure that out.

- *Run uncached…*: We obviously don't want to be running code from cache while initializing it; however, the CPU doesn't have a mode, so we just force the address we're executing in to be in the kseg1 region.

- *…but do it in pic form*: This code needs to be position independent, so assembly language constructs can't give us our own location directly. The only way to get the real code address is to do a subroutine call instruction and retrieve the value from **ra**.

Almost all MIPS write buffers (see Section 4.13) flush all writes before attempting an uncached read: Here we're reading the instruction memory (we don't have any other known-valid pointer around at the moment).

```
/* Generic R3000 caches */

/* make sure write buffer is empty */
lw      zero, 0(t1)
```

Next comes the following:

```
/*
 * Size and initialise instruction cache
 */
or      t4,t3,SR_ISC|SR_SWC # isolate and swap cache (see Section 4.9)
mtc0    t4,$sr
bal     _init_cache         # ... which you'll find on page 349
move    v1,v0

/*
 * size and initialise data cache
 */
or      t4,t3,SR_ISC        # isolate cache
mtc0    t4,$sr
bal     _init_cache

.set  noreorder
mtc0    t7,$sr              # restore IE and ISC to normal
nop; nop; nop; nop; nop     # ...  can take a long time to settle
.set  reorder
```

The **nop** instructions delay the CPU for long enough that the cache behavior changes implicit in those **SR** changes will be fixed before the next instruction does anything at all to the caches.

Relying on the contents of the **PRID** register is not usually a good idea, but the I-cache line size for R3000s is otherwise opaque:

```
/* save results */
sw      v0,mips_dcache_size
sw      v1,mips_icache_size

/* most r3000 family CPUs have 1 word (4 bytes) per cache line */
mfc0    t2,$prid
li      t0,4
li      t1,4
```

```
        and     t2,0xff00
        srl     t2,8
        bne     t2,PRID_R3IDT,1f      # IDT core has 4 word/line I-cache
        li      t0,16
        /* can't identify other r30x1 variants, since PrID == R3000A */
1:      sw      t0,mips_icache_linesize
        sw      t1,mips_dcache_linesize
        move    ra,t8
        j       ra
END(mips_init_cache)
```

Next is an internal function to size and initialize an R3000 cache; the size is returned in **v0**. It works by writing address to address at all possible cache boundaries (256K down to 512). Due to address wraparound, whatever is found at cache location zero is the cache size.

Here is the code:

```
#define MIN_CACHE_SIZE                  (512)
#define MAX_CACHE_SIZE                  (256*1024)


/*
 * int _init_cache()
 *
 * returns size of one cache and flushes it
 *
 * uses:    v0,t1,t2,a0,a1,ra
 * save regs:   none
 * calls:   nothing
 */
SLEAF(_init_cache)
    .set  noreorder
    li      t1,MIN_CACHE_SIZE
    li      t2,MAX_CACHE_SIZE
    nop


1:  sw      t2,KSEG0_BASE(t2)
    bne     t2,t1,1b
    srl     t2,1                        # BDSLOT (branch delay slot)

    lw      v0,KSEG0_BASE(zero)         # get cache size

    /*
     * now flush the cache
     */
    li      a0,KSEG0_BASE
```

```
        addu    a1,a0,v0
1:      sw      zero,0(a0)                  # clear parity
        sw      zero,4(a0)
        sw      zero,8(a0)
        sw      zero,12(a0)
        sb      zero,0(a0)                  # invalidate
        sb      zero,4(a0)
        sb      zero,8(a0)
        addu    a0,16
        bne     a0,a1,1b
        sb      zero,-4(a0)                 # BDSLOT

        nop; nop; nop                       # pipe clear of stores
        .set    reorder
        j       ra
SEND(_init_cache)

#define SIZE_CACHE(which)       \
        lw      v0,which;       \
        move    t5,ra;          \
        bgez    v0,9f;          \
        bal     mips_init_cache; \
        lw      v0,which;       \
        move    ra,t5;          \
9:      blez    v0,9f
```

The **SIZE_CACHE()** macro is going to get used quite heavily. It tests to see whether the particular cache (referred to by its size variable) has been initialized, and if not it attempts initialization (saving **ra** around the call). It also jumps out to the label "**9f**," which by local convention is used to mark the end of each subroutine, so it will exit quietly (but leaving the size marker set to −1) if something goes wrong.

Next comes the following:

```
/*
 * void mips_clean_dcache (unsigned kva, size_t n)
 *
 * invalidate address range in data cache
 */
LEAF(mips_clean_dcache)
    SIZE_CACHE(mips_dcache_size)

    /* n = MIN(dcachesize,n) */
    bltu    a1,v0,1f
    move    a1,v0
```

```
1:
    /* disable interrupts */
    mfc0    v0,$sr
    and     v1,v0,SR_BEV
    mtc0    v1,$sr

    /* make sure write buffer is empty */
    la      v1,1b
    or      v1,KSEG1_BASE
    lw      zero, 0(v1)

    .set    noreorder

    /* r3000: isolate caches, no swap */
    or      v1,SR_ISC
    mtc0    v1,$sr

    /* make sure the address is inside kseg0 */
    and     a0,~KSEG1_BASE
    or      a0,KSEG0_BASE
```

That was just paranoia; with the caches isolated, all R3000 loads and stores hit the cache and only the cache.

More significant is what we *haven't* done, which is to make sure we're executing code from the uncached region—so we may well be running cached. The isolation of the cache affects only the data cache for loads and stores. This **mips_clean_dcache()** routine is regularly called by I/O functions that are cleaning up before or after DMA, and it needs to be efficient. Now we have the following:

```
    addu    a1,a0               /* length -> ending address */

    /* unrolled loop: flush 32 bytes at a time */
    /* r3000: 4-byte cache lines */
    /* store byte when isolated invalidates the cache entry */
1:  sb      zero,0(a0)
    sb      zero,4(a0)
    sb      zero,8(a0)
    sb      zero,12(a0)
    sb      zero,16(a0)
    sb      zero,20(a0)
    sb      zero,24(a0)
    addu    a0,32
    bltu    a0,a1,1b
    sb      zero,-4(a0)
```

```
        /* isolated stores out of pipe */
        nop; nop; nop
```

The three **nop** instructions make quite sure that all stores have finished and that the last cache line is invalidated before we reset **SR** and restore normal cache operation:

```
        /* restore status register (pipe clean) */
        mtc0    v0,$sr
        nop
        .set reorder

9:  j       ra
END(mips_clean_dcache)

/*
 * void mips_clean_icache (unsigned kva, size_t n)
 *
 * Invalidate address range in instruction cache
 */
LEAF(mips_clean_icache)
XLEAF(mips_clean_icache_indexed)
        SIZE_CACHE(mips_icache_size)

        /* n = MIN(icachesize, n) */
        bltu    a1,v0,1f
        move    a1,v0
1:
        /* disable intrs */
        mfc0    v0,$sr
        and     v1,v0,SR_BEV
        mtc0    v1,$sr

        /* run uncached */
        la      v1,1f
        or      v1,KSEG1_BASE
        jr      v1
1:
```

Note that we're not worrying here about position-independent code: Only the initialization functions may be called at the wrong address. We can therefore leave the assembler and linker to figure out the address for us.

We probably could run cached (but swapped) here in most cases. But this code is supposed to be safe and universal, so we take the coward's way out.

The rest of this code is just like the **mips_clean_dcache()** function described above.

```
        /* make sure write buffer is empty */
        lw      zero, 0(v1)

        .set    noreorder
        /* r3000: isolate caches and swap */
        or      v1,SR_ISC|SR_SWC
        mtc0    v1,$sr

        /* ensure address is inside kseg0 */
        and     a0,~KSEG1_BASE
        or      a0,KSEG0_BASE
        addu    a1,a0           /* length -> ending address */

        /* unrolled loop: flush 32 bytes at a time */
        /* r3000: 4-byte cache lines */
        /* store byte when isolated invalidates the cache entry */
1:      sb      zero,0(a0)
        sb      zero,4(a0)
        sb      zero,8(a0)
        sb      zero,12(a0)
        sb      zero,16(a0)
        sb      zero,20(a0)
        sb      zero,24(a0)
        addu    a0,32
        bltu    a0,a1,1b
        sb      zero,-4(a0)

        nop; nop; nop                   # pipe clear of stores

        /* restore status register (pipe clear) */
        mtc0    v0,$sr
        nop
        .set reorder

        /* restore cached mode */
9:      j       ra
END(mips_clean_icache)

/*
 * void mips_clean_cache (unsigned kva, size_t n)
 *
 * Invalidate address range in all caches
```

```
 */
LEAF(mips_clean_cache)
    move      t9,ra
    move      a2,a0
    move      a3,a1

    bal       mips_clean_dcache

    move      a0,a2
    move      a1,a3
    bal       mips_clean_icache

    move      ra,t9
    j         ra
END(mips_clean_cache)

/*
 * void mips_flush_cache ()
 *
 * Invalidate all caches
 */
LEAF(mips_flush_cache)
    move      t9,ra

    SIZE_CACHE(mips_dcache_size)
    li        a0,KSEG0_BASE
    move      a1,v0
    bal       mips_clean_dcache

9:  lw        a1,mips_icache_size
    li        a0,KSEG0_BASE
    blez      a1,9f
    bal       mips_clean_icache

9:  move      ra,t9
    j         ra
END(mips_flush_cache)
```

12.2.2 *Cache Operations: After MIPS III and Cache Instructions*

Things are much tidier from the R4x00 onward, and we don't expect them to ever revert to the R3000 cache access mechanisms. Here are the same functions implemented for the new version:

```
/*
 * r4kcache.s: R4000 cache support functions for SDE-MIPS
 */

#if !#cpu(r4000)
#error use -mcpu=r4k option with this file
#endif

#include <mips/asm.h>
#include <mips/regdef.h>
#include <mips/r4kc0.h>
#include <mips/prid.h>

#define NO      0
#define YES     1
#define MAYBE   2

#ifndef R4KSCACHE
#if #cpu(r4000sc) || #cpu(r4400sc) || #cpu(r4000mc) || #cpu(r4400mc)
#define R4KSCACHE YES
#else
#define R4KSCACHE NO
#endif
#endif


#ifndef R4KPC2WAY
#if #cpu(r4600) || #cpu(r4640) || #cpu(r4650) || #cpu(r4700)
#define R4KPC2WAY YES
#elif R4KSCACHE || #cpu(r4100) || #cpu(r4200) || #cpu(r4400) \
        || #cpu(cw4010) || #cpu(cw4001)
#define R4KPC2WAY NO
#else
#define R4KPC2WAY MAYBE
#endif
#endif
```

Those horrible macros are being used to try to figure out whether there's a secondary cache and whether the primary/secondary caches are direct mapped or two-way set associative.

Whether a secondary cache exists is of vital importance.

For most purposes, the set associativity of the cache does not matter. Neither the initialization nor the **clean_cache** functions need rely on it.

```
/*
 * R4000 cache operations
 *
 * The _flush and _clean functions are complex composites that do whatever
 * is necessary to flush/clean ALL caches, in the quickest possible way.
 * The other functions are targeted explicitly at a particular cache,
 * I-, D-, or SD; it is up to the user to call the correct set of functions
 * for a given system.
 */

#define DECL(x, val)    \
    EXPORTS(x, 4)    \
    .word val

.sdata
DECL(mips_icache_size,-1)
DECL(mips_dcache_size,-1)
DECL(mips_scache_size,-1)
DECL(mips_tcache_size,-1)
DECL(mips_icache_linesize,-1)
DECL(mips_dcache_linesize,-1)
DECL(mips_scache_linesize,-1)
DECL(mips_tcache_linesize,-1)
DECL(mips_pcache_ways,1)
DECL(mips_scache_ways,1)
DECL(mips_tcache_ways,0)
DECL(mips_scache_split,0)

/*
 * macros to automate cache operations
 */

#define addr    t0
#define maxaddr t1
#define mask    t2

#define cacheop(kva, n, linesize, op)    \
    .set   noreorder ;                   \
    /* check for bad size */             \
    blez    n,11f ;                      \
    addu    maxaddr,kva,n ;              \
    /* align to line boundaries */       \
    subu    mask,linesize,1 ;            \
    not     mask ;                       \
    and     addr,kva,mask ;              \
```

```
    addu      maxaddr,-1 ;                        \
    and       maxaddr,mask ;                      \
    /* the cacheop loop */                        \
10: cache         op,0(addr) ;                    \
    bne       addr,maxaddr,10b ;                  \
    addu      addr,linesize ;                     \
11: .set      reorder
```

The **cacheop()** macro applies the appropriate flavor of **cache** instruction on a bunch of cache lines. This makes most sense when **kva** is being used as the address of a memory region of which any cached copies should be treated.

```
/*
 * static void _size_cache()
 *
 * Internal routine to determine cache sizes by looking at R4000 config
 * register.  Sizes are returned in registers, as follows:
 */

#define icachesize      t2
#define dcachesize      t3
#define scachesize      t4
#define ilinesize       t5
#define dlinesize       t6
#define slinesize       t7
#define cacheflags      t8
#define CF_SCSPLIT      0x2
#define CF_PC2WAY       0x1


#define SCACHE_MIN_SIZE         0x010000        /* minimum S-cache:  64KB */
#define SCACHE_MAX_SIZE         0x400000        /* maximum S-cache:   4MB */

SLEAF(_size_cache)
    mfc0      t0,$config              # config register fields in Figure 3.4 above

    /* work out primary I-cache size */
    and       t1,t0,CFG_ICMASK
    srl       t1,CFG_ICSHIFT
    li        icachesize,0x1000
    sll       icachesize,t1

    /* work out primary I-cache line size */
    li        ilinesize,32
```

```
        and     t1,t0,CFG_IB
        bnez    t1,1f
        li      ilinesize,16
1:

        /* work out primary D-cache size */
        and     t1,t0,CFG_DCMASK
        srl     t1,CFG_DCSHIFT
        li      dcachesize,0x1000
        sll     dcachesize,t1

        /* work out primary D-cache line size */
        li      dlinesize,32
        and     t1,t0,CFG_DB
        bnez    t1,1f
        li      dlinesize,16
1:

        move    scachesize,zero
        move    slinesize,zero
        move    cacheflags,zero

#if R4KSCACHE
        /* no secondary cache if Config.SC = 1 */
        and     t1,t0,CFG_SC
        bnez    t1,9f

        /* note split cache */
        and     t1,t0,CFG_SS
        beqz    t1,1f
        or      cacheflags,CF_SCSPLIT


        /* work out secondary cache line size */
1:      and     t1,t0,CFG_SBMASK
        srl     t1,CFG_SBSHIFT
        li      slinesize,16
        sll     slinesize,t1

        /* disable all interrupts and cache exceptions */
        mfc0    t9,$sr
        li      t8,SR_BEV
        and     t8,t9
        or      t8,SR_DE
        .set    noreorder
```

```
        mtc0    t8,$sr
        nop; nop; nop
        mtc0    zero,$taglo                 # initial cache tag

        /* set initial zero marker */
        li      t8,KSEG0_BASE
        cache   Index_Store_Tag_SD,0(t8)    # sdcache[0].tag = 0

        /* check all secondary cache boundaries, until we wrap around */
        li      scachesize,SCACHE_MIN_SIZE
        li      t0,SCACHE_MAX_SIZE

2:      mtc0    scachesize,$taglo
        addu    t1,t8,scachesize            # calc &sdcache[size]
        cache   Index_Store_Tag_SD,0(t1)    # sdcache[size].tag = size
        nop; nop
        cache   Index_Load_Tag_SD,0(t8)     # check sdcache[0].tag == 0
        nop
        .set    reorder

        mfc0    t1,$taglo
        and     t1,TAG_STAG_MASK
        bnez    t1,8f                       # wrap around, got it
        sll     scachesize,1                # try next boundary
        bne     scachesize,t0,2b            # up to maximum size

8:      mtc0    t9,$sr
#endif /* R4KSCACHE */

9:
#if R4KPC2WAY == MAYBE
        /* have we got two-way set-associative primary caches? */
        mfc0    t0,$prid                    # get processor ID
        and     t0,0xff00                   # get implementation
        srl     t0,8
        seq     t1,t0,PRID_R4600            # r4600
        or      cacheflags,t1
        seq     t1,t0,PRID_R4700            # r4700
        or      cacheflags,t1
        seq     t1,t0,PRID_R4650            # r4650/r4640
        or      cacheflags,t1
        seq     t1,t0,PRID_R5000            # r5000
        or      cacheflags,t1
        seq     t1,t0,PRID_RM52XX           # rm52xx
        or      cacheflags,t1
```

```
#elif R4KPC2WAY == YES
    or      cacheflags,CF_PC2WAY
#endif

    j       ra
SEND(_size_cache)
```

It would probably have made better sense to assume that any **PrID(Impl)** field from R5000 up would be (at least) two-way set associative, so if you must read the CPU ID, do that.

```
/*
 * void size_cache()
 *
 * Work out size of I-, D-, and S-caches
 */
LEAF(mips_size_cache)
    lw      t0,mips_icache_size
    move    v0,ra
    bgtz    t0,8f                           # already known?
    bal     _size_cache
    move    ra,v0
    sw      icachesize,mips_icache_size
    sw      dcachesize,mips_dcache_size
    sw      scachesize,mips_scache_size
    sw      ilinesize,mips_icache_linesize
    sw      dlinesize,mips_dcache_linesize
    sw      slinesize,mips_scache_linesize
    and     t0,cacheflags,CF_SCSPLIT
    sw      t0,mips_scache_split
    and     t0,cacheflags,CF_PC2WAY
    move    t1,zero
    beqz    t0,1f
    li      t1,2
1:  sw      t1,mips_pcache_ways
8:  j       ra
END(mips_size_cache)

/*
 * void mips_init_cache()
 *
 * Work out size of and initialise I-, D-, and S-caches
 *
```

```
*     assumes that at least a cache's worth of memory has been initialised
*     with correct parity
*/
LEAF(mips_init_cache)
    /*
     * determine the cache sizes
     */
    move    v0,ra
    bal     _size_cache
    move    ra,v0

    /*
     * The caches may be in an indeterminate state,
     * so we force good parity into them by doing an
     * invalidate, load/fill, invalidate for each line.
     */

    /* disable all interrupts and cache exceptions */
    mfc0    v0,$sr
    li      a0,SR_BEV
    and     a0,v0
    or      a0,SR_DE
    .set noreorder
    mtc0    a0,$sr
    nop; nop; nop
    /* set up initial cache tag - certainly invalid! */
    mtc0    zero,$taglo
    nop
    .set reorder
```

The caches need to be invalidated, but all data fields must be filled with good parity data, or we'll get random cache parity errors while running the system. We work in this sequence:

1. Write cache tags to invalidate the secondary cache—we're going to fill the primary caches from memory and we don't want to pick up garbage from the secondary.

2. Invalidate the primary cache lines and load known-to-be-good data from memory into them.

3. Fill the secondary cache data lines by creating "dirty" primary cache lines and pushing them out. We can't fill the secondary cache from memory, because we may not have that much memory set up yet.

4. Leave all invalidated again.

```
#if R4KSCACHE
    /*
     * Initialise secondary cache tags (if present)
     */
    blez    scachesize,3f                   # S-cache present?

    /* first data/unified tags */
    li      a0,KSEG0_BASE
    addu    a1,a0,scachesize               # limit = base + S-cache size
    .set    noreorder
1:  addu    a0,slinesize
    bne     a0,a1,1b
    cache   Index_Store_Tag_SD,-4(a0)      # BDSLOT: clear tag
    .set    reorder

    and     a0,cacheflags,CF_SCSPLIT       # S-cache split?
    beqz    a0,3f
```

The R4000 cache can be programmed as split, so I- and D-cache accesses are directed to distinct blocks. If so, we need to do the I-cache section separately:

```
    /* then split I-cache, if present */
    li      a0,KSEG0_BASE
    addu    a1,a0,scachesize               # limit = base + S-cache size
    .set    noreorder
1:  addu    a0,slinesize
    bne     a0,a1,1b
    cache   Index_Store_Tag_SI,-4(a0)      # BDSLOT: clear tag
    .set    reorder
#endif
3:

    /*
     * assume bottom of RAM will generate good parity for the
     * primary caches (max 32K)
     */

    /*
     * initialise primary instruction cache
     */
    .set    noreorder
    li      a0,KSEG0_BASE
    addu    a1,a0,icachesize               # limit = base + I-cache size
```

```
1:  addu     a0,ilinesize
    cache    Index_Store_Tag_I,-4(a0)      # clear tag
    nop
    cache    Fill_I,-4(a0)                 # fill line
    nop
    bne      a0,a1,1b
    cache    Index_Store_Tag_I,-4(a0)      # BDSLOT: clear tag
    .set  reorder

    /*
     * Initialise primary data cache
     * (for R4600 2-way set-associative caches, we do it in 3 passes)
     */
```

You've seen this primary cache initialization algorithm before in Section 4.10.4. The comment above specifies two-way caches, but in fact this method copes with a cache of any level of set associativity, so long as it has a least recently accessed or least recently written replacement policy.

```
    /* 1: initialise D-cache tags */
    /* three separate loops, unlike I-cache: see Section 4.10 for why */
    .set  noreorder
    li       a0,KSEG0_BASE
    addu     a1,a0,dcachesize              # limit = base + D-cache size
1:  addu     a0,dlinesize
    bne      a0,a1,1b
    cache    Index_Store_Tag_D,-4(a0)      # BDSLOT: clear tag
    .set  reorder

    /* 2: fill D-cache */
    .set  noreorder
    li       a0,KSEG0_BASE
    addu     a1,a0,dcachesize              # limit = base + D-cache size
1:  addu     a0,dlinesize
    bne      a0,a1,1b
    lw       zero,-4(a0)                   # BDSLOT: fill line
    .set  reorder

    /* 3: clear D-cache tags */
    .set  noreorder
    li       a0,KSEG0_BASE
    addu     a1,a0,dcachesize              # limit = base + D-cache size
1:  addu     a0,dlinesize
    bne      a0,a1,1b
    cache    Index_Store_Tag_D,-4(a0)      # BDSLOT: clear tag
```

```
        .set   reorder

#if R4KSCACHE
    /*
     * Initialise the secondary data cache data array
     */
    blez    scachesize,3f                   # S-cache present?
```

This is rather ugly, because we're not prepared to assume the existence of enough correctly initialized memory to fill the whole secondary cache. Instead, we generate lines in the primary cache and push them out. This is seriously unportable and probably works only on R4x00 CPUs.

```
    li      a0,KSEG0_BASE
    addu    a1,a0,scachesize                # a1 = base + S-cache size

    .set   noreorder
    /* create matching dirty lines in primary and secondary */
1:  cache   Create_Dirty_Exc_SD,0(a0)
    nop; nop

    cache   Create_Dirty_Exc_D,0(a0)
    nop; nop

    /* write primary cache line, so it's modified */
    sw      zero,0(a0)
    nop; nop

    /* push primary cache line out to secondary */
    cache   Hit_Writeback_Inv_D,0(a0)
    nop; nop

    /* reset secondary tag */
    addu    a0,dlinesize
    bne     a0,a1,1b
    cache   Index_Store_Tag_SD,-4(a0)    # BDSLOT: clear tag
    .set   reorder

    /*
     * Initialise the secondary instruction cache data array
     */
    and     a0,cacheflags,CF_SCSPLIT        # S-cache split?
    beqz    a0,3f
```

```
        li      a0,KSEG0_BASE
        addu    a1,a0,scachesize                # a1 = base + S-cache size

        .set    noreorder

        /* fill primary I-cache from secondary (ignoring ecc) */
1:      cache   Fill_I,0(a0)
        nop; nop

        /* write primary I-cache to secondary */
        cache   Hit_Writeback_I,0(a0)
        nop; nop

        /* reset secondary tag */
        addu    a0,ilinesize
        bne     a0,a1,1b
        cache   Index_Store_Tag_SI,-4(a0)    # BDSLOT: clear tag
        .set    reorder
#endif

        /* we store the sizes only after the caches are initialised */
3:      sw      icachesize,mips_icache_size
        sw      dcachesize,mips_dcache_size
        sw      scachesize,mips_scache_size
        sw      ilinesize,mips_icache_linesize
        sw      dlinesize,mips_dcache_linesize
        sw      slinesize,mips_scache_linesize
        and     t0,cacheflags,CF_SCSPLIT
        sw      t0,mips_scache_split
        and     t0,cacheflags,CF_PC2WAY
        move    t1,zero
        beqz    t0,1f
        li      t1,2
1:      sw      t1,mips_pcache_ways

        mtc0    v0,$sr
        j       ra
END(mips_init_cache)

#define SIZE_CACHE(reg,which)           \
        lw      reg,which;              \
        move    v1,ra;                  \
        bgez    reg,9f;                 \
        bal     mips_size_cache;        \
```

```
        lw       reg,which;                          \
        move     ra,v1;                              \
9:      blez     reg,9f


/*
 * void mips_flush_cache (void)
 *
 * write back and invalidate all caches
 */
LEAF(mips_flush_cache)
#if R4KSCACHE
        /* secondary cacheops do all the work if present */
        SIZE_CACHE(a1,mips_scache_size)
        lw       a2,mips_scache_linesize
        lw       v1,mips_scache_split


        li       a0,KSEG0_BASE
        /* here we go with the macro (see above) */
        cacheop(a0,a1,a2,Index_Writeback_Inv_SD)


        beqz     v1,2f                            # split S-cache?
        cacheop(a0,a1,a2,Index_Invalidate_SI)


        b        2f


9:      lw       a1,mips_dcache_size
#else
        SIZE_CACHE(a1,mips_dcache_size)
#endif
        /* else flush primary caches individually */
        lw       a2,mips_dcache_linesize
        li       a0,KSEG0_BASE
        cacheop(a0,a1,a2,Index_Writeback_Inv_D)


        lw       a1,mips_icache_size
        lw       a2,mips_icache_linesize
        cacheop(a0,a1,a2,Index_Invalidate_I)


2:;9:   j        ra
END(mips_flush_cache)
```

The syntax **2:;9:** is a bit odd, but the assembler treats the semicolon as a line break for all purposes, including another label. We want two labels here because we need a **9:** at the end of every routine that uses the **cacheop()** macro.

```
/*
 * void mips_clean_cache (unsigned kva, size_t n)
 *
 * Write back and invalidate address range in all caches
 */
LEAF(mips_clean_cache)
#if R4KSCACHE
    /* secondary cacheops do all the work (if fitted) */
    SIZE_CACHE(a2,mips_scache_linesize)
    lw      v1,mips_scache_split

    cacheop(a0,a1,a2,Hit_Writeback_Inv_SD)

    beqz    v1,2f                           # split S-cache?
    cacheop(a0,a1,a2,Hit Invalidate_SI)

    b       2f

9:  lw      a2,mips_dcache_linesize
#else
    SIZE_CACHE(a2,mips_dcache_linesize)
#endif
    cacheop(a0,a1,a2,Hit_Writeback_Inv_D)

    lw      a2,mips_icache_linesize
    cacheop(a0,a1,a2,Hit_Invalidate_I)

2:;9:j      ra
END(mips_clean_cache)

/*
 * void mips_flush_dcache (void)
 *
 * Flush and invalidate data cache only
 */
LEAF(mips_flush_dcache)
#if R4KSCACHE
    /* use secondary cacheops if present */
    SIZE_CACHE(a1,mips_scache_size)
    lw      a2,mips_scache_linesize
    li      a0,KSEG0_BASE
```

```
        cacheop(a0,a1,a2,Index_Writeback_Inv_SD)
        b       2f

9:  lw      a1,mips_dcache_size
#else
        SIZE_CACHE(a1,mips_dcache_size)
#endif
        /* else flush primary data cache */
        lw      a2,mips_dcache_linesize
        li      a0,KSEG0_BASE
        cacheop(a0,a1,a2,Index_Writeback_Inv_D)

2:;9:j      ra
END(mips_flush_dcache)


/*
 * void mips_clean_dcache (unsigned kva, size_t n)
 *
 * Write back and invalidate address range in data caches
 */
LEAF(mips_clean_dcache)
#if R4KSCACHE
        /* secondary cacheops do all the work (if fitted) */
        SIZE_CACHE(a2,mips_scache_linesize)
        cacheop(a0,a1,a2,Hit_Writeback_Inv_SD)
        b       2f

9:  lw      a2,mips_dcache_linesize
#else
        SIZE_CACHE(a2,mips_dcache_linesize)
#endif
        cacheop(a0,a1,a2,Hit_Writeback_Inv_D)

2:;9:   j       ra
END(mips_clean_dcache)


/*
 * void r4k_hit_writeback_inv_dcache (unsigned kva, size_t n)
 *
 * Write back and invalidate address range in primary data cache
 */
LEAF(r4k_hit_writeback_inv_dcache)
        SIZE_CACHE(a2,mips_dcache_linesize)
        cacheop(a0,a1,a2,Hit_Writeback_Inv_D)
```

```
9:  j         ra
END(r4k_hit_writeback_inv_dcache)


/*
 * void mips_clean_icache (unsigned kva, size_t n)
 *
 * Write back and invalidate address range in instruction caches
 */
LEAF(mips_clean_icache)
#if R4KSCACHE
    /* secondary cacheops do all the work (if fitted) */
    SIZE_CACHE(a2,mips_scache_linesize)
    cacheop(a0,a1,a2,Hit_Invalidate_SI)
    b        2f

9:  lw        a2,mips_icache_linesize
#else
    SIZE_CACHE(a2,mips_icache_linesize)
#endif
    cacheop(a0,a1,a2,Hit_Invalidate_I)

2:;9:  j        ra
END(mips_clean_icache)
```

12.3   MIPS Exception Handling

The exception-handling routines are once again taken (sometimes simplified) with permission from the Algorithmics SDE-MIPS—note again that the code is copyrighted and not freely reusable for commercial purposes. In this case, the mechanism is called *xcption*; it connects MIPS machine-level exceptions through to C interrupt handlers and POSIX-like signal handlers.

12.3.1   *Xcption: What It Does for Programmers*

Firstly, we need to swallow a rather heroic C data type definition:

```
typedef int (*xcpt_t)(int, struct xcptcontext *);
```

The golden rule of C declarations is "read it backward from the name of the thing being declared"; thus the data type xcpt_t is a pointer to a function that returns an integer. Moreover, the parentheses after the function declaration give us the function's argument types; there's an `int` and a pointer to an exception context, saved on the stack after an exception.

An `xcpt_t` is just the thing to use in a table of function pointers. As used, they're often found bundled with some other data (not important here) in a structure called `xcptaction`.

A programmer can provide an `xcpt_t` as a pointer to a handler function, which will then be invoked whenever a low-level exception occurs with the field **Cause(ExcCode)** of the **Cause** register set to a particular value (there's a list of possible values in Table 3.3). In Section 12.4 we'll show you how this can be used to catch MIPS interrupts.

The xcption handler routine should return 0 if all goes as expected, but if it doesn't the value will be interpreted as a POSIX signal number and a signal will be delivered to the current application. That in turn provides a somewhat-portable way for applications to respond to asynchronous events.

The same mechanism also supports a GNU-standard debug stub, which allows unexpected exceptions to drop into the debugger rather than off the edge of the universe.

Note that all interrupts are disabled during exception processing, until and unless they are explicitly unmasked inside a user-supplied handler.

12.3.2 *Xcption: C Interface Code*

The C routine called from assembler to dispatch xcptions is short and simple:[1]

```
int
_xcpt_deliver (struct xcptcontext *xcp)
{
    int xcode, sig;

    xcode = (xcp->cr & CR_XMASK) >> 2;

    if (sig = (xcpthandlertab[xcode]) (xcode, xcp)) {
        _sig_raise (sig, xcp);
        }
    return 0;
}
```

What's going on here?

---

1. The real code is more opaque than this, because it abstracts register types and field positions and such to a larger extent. It can also invoke lower-level user handlers if they're linked in.

- xcode picks up the value that was in the **Cause(ExcCode)** field in the **Cause** register; CR_XMASK is defined in one of the CPU-family-specific include files.

- We look up that code in an array xcpthandlertab[] of pointers to handler functions. The function whose address has been loaded in the appropriate position will be called with two arguments: the **Cause(ExcCode)** value and the pointer to the exception context.

- If the handler function return value is nonzero, we invoke a signal.

12.3.3 *Xcption: Low-Level Module*

The foundation is an assembler routine that is entered from the MIPS general-exception entry point and that builds the environment to allow the user to supply an exception handler written to the xcption framework.

The module is fairly long; here are some signposts to find your way around:

- **LEAF(_xcpt_vecbev)** is the entry point of the exception-handling code (page 374).

- (Actually, the MIPS CPU jumps to one of its standard entry points; tiny fragments of code that jump to **_xcpt_vecbev** are defined at places like **_xcpt_vecutlb** on page 383, and then copied into the right place by the initialization routine.)

- **LEAF(_xcptlow_init)** sets up the vectors and initializes the CPU appropriately (page 384).

- Somewhere down on page 379 we finally have saved enough registers and built an environment suitable for C programs, and we branch to **_xcptcall** to go off and do something useful. But even then, **LEAF(_xcptcall)**, on page 386: fakes an indirect call to the C routine _xcpt_deliver() to help the debugger keep track of the stack when being used on exception-triggered code.

- Lastly, the single argument to the C code is a pointer to an exception-context structure. We use #ifdefs to vary the definition, but we'll show the structure for a CPU from the R4000 family.

A struct xcptcontext contains the saved value of all general-purpose registers and those coprocessor 0 registers that need saving:

```
struct xcptcontext {
    reg_t        sr;
    reg_t        cr;
    reg_t        epc;
    reg_t        vaddr;

    reg_t        regs[32];
```

```
    reg_t       mdlo;
    reg_t       mdhi;

#if #cpu(r4640) || #cpu(r4650)
    reg_t       iwatch;
    reg_t       dwatch;
#elif #cpu(cw4010)
    reg_t       dcs;
    reg_t       bda;
#elif !#cpu(r4600) && !#cpu(r4700)
    reg_t       watchlo;
    reg_t       watchhi;
#else
    reg_t       _spare0;
    reg_t       _spare1;
#endif

    struct xcptcontext  *prev;
    unsigned    xclass;
};
```

It also provides copies of the key exception-related CP0 registers **SR**, **Cause** (**cr**), **EPC**, and **BadVaddr** (**vaddr**). C exception code will pick up fields from those registers to decide what to do next.

Note that because it's convenient—particularly for emulators and debuggers that may need to reference the pre-exception values of registers—to define all 32 registers together, we'll store in the table the value of the register **$0**, which is hardly going to be a surprise, and the values of the reserved-for-exception registers **k0** and **k1**. These are completely useless and in any case can't reflect their real pre-exception values—they're going to be used early in the exception routine.

So here goes with the assembler code.

```
/*
 * xcptlowb.S: SDE-MIPS basic low-level exception handling
 *
 * This exception handler is not very sophisticated, but it is
 * simple and does what is required for most embedded code.
 *
 * It assumes that sp is at all times a valid, current stack pointer
 * into unmapped memory.  If your application has sp pointing into
 * possibly mapped memory (i.e., kuseg/kseg2), then you will need
 * something more like xcptlow.S. It does not save/restore
 * floating-point registers: This must be done explicitly if
 * exception-level code needs to use the FPA.
```

```
*/

#include <mips/asm.h>
#include <mips/regdef.h>
#include <mips/cpu.h>
#include <mips/xcpt.h>
#if #cpu(lr33k)
#include <lsi/lr33000.h>
#endif

#if __mips >= 3
#ifndef __mips64
    .set gp64      /* force 64-bit register support */
#endif
#define lr      ld
#define sr      sd
#if !#cpu(r4640) && !#cpu(r4650)
#define rmfc0   dmfc0
#define rmtc0   dmtc0
#endif
#define     RS      8
#else
#define lr      lw
#define sr      sw
#define     RS      4
#endif

#ifndef rmfc0
#define rmfc0   mfc0
#define rmtc0   mtc0
#endif
```

What we've done with these macros is to define a set of operators (load, store, and move between general-purpose and CP0 registers) that do *register-length* operations—64 bit if the system configuration requires us to load and save 64-bit registers, 32 bit otherwise.

Any system where users may have run 64-bit instructions has important data in the top half of registers, and the exception/interrupt system must always preserve the whole 64-bit register value. Conversely, if a system uses only 32-bit instructions, then the top half of registers is known to consist of just a sign extension (Section 2.7.3), and we need only save/restore 32 bits.

```
    .data
class:    .word    0

/*
 * Low-level flags controlling exception handling
 */
EXPORTS(_xcpt_flags,NXCPT*4)
    .word 0 : NXCPT

/*
 * We get here from ROM boot exception handler (k0 points here),
 * or from one of the RAM exception stubs below
 *
 * On entry, k1 = exception class
 *
 * Note: exceptions do not save and restore registers k0 or k1
 */
```

In this system, the cached exception entry points are just patched to branch to **_xcpt_vecbev**. Algorithmics' ROM exception entry points (not listed here) use a convention to allow ROM exceptions to be redirected too; if **k0** is nonzero on entry to the ROM exception routine, its contents are assumed to be the address of an alternative handler. While running the xcption system, it will point here.

Until this exception handler has saved enough state to permit nested exceptions, it will keep **k0** zero; that way if anything bad happens, the ROM handler will trap it and we won't get into an exception loop.

Also, before jumping here the exception vectors set **k1** to a value (which we call "exception class") that tells us which vector was used; think of that as an extension of the CPU **Cause** register. It gets stored in a global variable and eventually is copied into the exception frame.

```
LEAF(_xcpt_vecbev)
    .set noreorder
    .set noat

    /* save exception class in memory */
    la      k0,class
    sw      k1,0(k0)                # had better not trap!
    move    k0,zero                 # now boot exceptions will abort

    /* allocate exception stack frame (on 8-byte boundary) */
    subu    k1,sp,XCP_SIZE
```

```
    srl     k1,3
    sll     k1,3

    /* save enough registers to get by */
    sr      AT,XCP_AT(k1)
    sr      v0,XCP_V0(k1)
    sr      v1,XCP_V1(k1)
    sr      a0,XCP_A0(k1)
    sr      a1,XCP_A1(k1)
    sr      a2,XCP_A2(k1)
    sr      a3,XCP_A3(k1)
    sr      sp,XCP_SP(k1)
    sr      ra,XCP_RA(k1)

    /* fool modern exception code by pretending we are NOT nested */
    sw      zero,XCP_PREV(k1)
```

Every now and again, something is beyond explanation. That last line is one of those.

```
    /* get coprocessor 0 exception state */
    mfc0    a0,$cr
    mfc0    a1,$sr
    rmfc0   a2,$vaddr
    rmfc0   a3,$epc
#if #cpu(lr33k)
    mfc0    v1,$dcic
#endif
    /* we can safely use AT now */
    .set    at
```

We've now saved a good set of everyday registers, which we're now free to use, and we have got the exception state into some general registers where it's easy to look at.

We're now going to have lots of #ifdefs, dealing with things that only occur in some CPUs. You'll note that while some of these test for specific CPUs, where possible we'll use the existence/nonexistence of some register or feature. R3000-type CPUs depend on swapping data and instruction caches for I-cache manipulation, under the control of a status register bit **SR(SwC)** which is defined in the include file as SR_SWC; therefore, when we're testing for exceptions in cache managers (they're fatal) we prefer testing for SR_SWC to trying to list affected CPUs.

```
    /* switch to using sp to point at exception frame */
    move    sp,k1

#ifdef SR_SWC
    /* If SR_PZ || SR_SwC || SR_IsC are set then
     * the exception has occurred in some VERY hairy code such
     * as during cache handling and is unrecoverable.
     */
    and     v0,a1,SR_PZ|SR_SWC|SR_ISC
    bnez    v0,xcpt_hairy
    nop
#endif

#if #cpu(lr33k)
    /* save LR330x0 dcic register */
    sr      v1,XCP_DCIC(sp)
#endif

    /* save watchpoint registers and disable watchpoint */
#if defined(C0_DCIC)
    mfc0    v0,C0_DCIC
    mfc0    v1,C0_BDA
    mtc0    zero,C0_DCIC
    sr      v0,XCP_DCIC(sp)
    sr      v1,XCP_BDA(sp)
#elif defined(C0_DCS)
    mfc0    v0,C0_DCS
    mfc0    v1,C0_BDA
    mtc0    zero,C0_DCS
    sr      v0,XCP_DCS(sp)
    sr      v1,XCP_BDA(sp)
#elif defined(C0_WATCHLO)
    mfc0    v0,C0_WATCHLO
    mfc0    v1,C0_WATCHHI
    mtc0    zero,C0_WATCHLO
    sr      v0,XCP_WATCHLO(sp)
    sr      v1,XCP_WATCHHI(sp)
#elif defined(C0_IWATCH)
    mfc0    v0,C0_IWATCH
    mfc0    v1,C0_DWATCH
    mtc0    zero,C0_IWATCH
    mtc0    zero,C0_DWATCH
    sr      v0,XCP_IWATCH(sp)
    sr      v1,XCP_DWATCH(sp)
#endif
```

```
    /* stash exception class */
    lw      v0,class
    /* nothing sensible to store for k0/k1, store zero */
    sr      zero,XCP_K0(sp)
    sr      zero,XCP_K1(sp)
    or      v0,XCPC_USRSTACK         # we are still on the user stack
    sw      v0,XCP_XCLASS(sp)


    /*
     * We have now finished with the uninterruptible code
     * (using k0/k1, and saving exception state), so
     * we can permit nested exceptions; however, we cannot
     * permit device interrupts until the interrupt handler
     * does its prioritisation and sets SR_IMASK.
     */
    la      k0,_xcpt_vecbev         # restore rom boot exception hook
#if defined(SR_EXL)
    /* R4x00-style exceptions */
    and     v0,a1,~(SR_IMASK|SR_EXL|SR_KSU_MASK)
#elif defined(SR_IEC)
    /* R3x00-style exceptions */
    and     v0,a1,~(SR_IMASK)        # sr.SR_IMASK := 0
    srl     v1,a1,2                  # sr.SR_IEC   := sr.SR_IEP
    and     v1,SR_IEC
    or      v0,v1
#endif
    mtc0    v0,$sr


    .set  reorder


    /*
     * We are now interruptible: dump all remaining state
     * into the exception stack frame.
     */
```

Actually, interrupts are guaranteed to be disabled at this stage and will remain that way until and unless we invoke some kind of interrupt routine that can figure out which interrupt is active and service it. But a nested exception now would not overwrite any vital state, and we could return from it and to our user program intact.

```
    /* coprocessor exception state */
    sr      a0,XCP_CR(sp)
```

```
sr       a1,XCP_SR(sp)
sr       a2,XCP_VADDR(sp)
sr       a3,XCP_EPC(sp)

/* mdhi and mdlo */
mfhi     v0
mflo     v1
sr       v0,XCP_MDHI(sp)
sr       v1,XCP_MDLO(sp)
```

It's easy to forget the not-quite-registers **hi** and **lo** which are the results from the multiply unit. But you can't go trampling randomly on them every time there's an interrupt.

```
/*
 * Save all the other general registers.
 *
 * You might think that you don't need to save zero,
 * s0-s7, and s8, but software instruction emulators (required
 * for FP operation) and debuggers both rely on having all the
 * user's register values stored together in a well-defined
 * structure.
 */
sr       zero,XCP_ZERO(sp)
sr       t0,XCP_T0(sp)
sr       t1,XCP_T1(sp)
sr       t2,XCP_T2(sp)
sr       t3,XCP_T3(sp)
sr       t4,XCP_T4(sp)
sr       t5,XCP_T5(sp)
sr       t6,XCP_T6(sp)
sr       t7,XCP_T7(sp)
sr       s0,XCP_S0(sp)
sr       s1,XCP_S1(sp)
sr       s2,XCP_S2(sp)
sr       s3,XCP_S3(sp)
sr       s4,XCP_S4(sp)
sr       s5,XCP_S5(sp)
sr       s6,XCP_S6(sp)
sr       s7,XCP_S7(sp)
sr       t8,XCP_T8(sp)
sr       t9,XCP_T9(sp)
sr       gp,XCP_GP(sp)
sr       s8,XCP_S8(sp)
```

```
/* load our _gp pointer */
la      gp,_gp

/* and call the C exception handler */
move    a0,sp              # arg1 = &xcp
subu    sp,16              # (arg save area)
move    ra,zero            # fake return address
b       _xcptcall
```

Remember **gp**? It's the register that is maintained to point into the middle of the data area, so that a lot of static and extern data items can be loaded/stored with a single instruction (see Section 9.4.1).

The **subu sp,16** is an artifact of the MIPS convention for passing subroutine arguments (see Section 10.1).

The bizarre call to **_xcptcall** (a bit of code on page 386) with a zero return address is a bit of debugger-support trickery. It interposes a bogus stackframe (with a zero return address) between the C exception handler and the actual machine exception; innocent debuggers will stop a stack backtrace there, and xcption-aware debuggers can use it to invoke special knowledge to trace back over the exception event.

```
xcptrest:
    .set   noat
    addu    at,sp,16            # at points to exception frame
```

And here we are back again. We just have to restore all registers from where we saved them on entry, rewind the stack, and return. (The choice of **at** for the frame pointer here is rather arbitrary; we wanted to choose something we can restore last.)

```
xcptrest_other:
    /*
     * Restore all state
     */

    /* restore most general registers */
    lr      t0,XCP_T0(at)
    lr      t1,XCP_T1(at)
    lr      t2,XCP_T2(at)
    lr      t3,XCP_T3(at)
    lr      t4,XCP_T4(at)
    lr      t5,XCP_T5(at)
    lr      t6,XCP_T6(at)
    lr      t7,XCP_T7(at)
```

```
lr      s0,XCP_S0(at)
lr      s1,XCP_S1(at)
lr      s2,XCP_S2(at)
lr      s3,XCP_S3(at)
lr      s4,XCP_S4(at)
lr      s5,XCP_S5(at)
lr      s6,XCP_S6(at)
lr      s7,XCP_S7(at)
lr      t8,XCP_T8(at)
lr      t9,XCP_T9(at)
lr      gp,XCP_GP(at)
lr      s8,XCP_S8(at)

/* mdhi and mdlo */
lr      v0,XCP_MDHI(at)
lr      v1,XCP_MDLO(at)
mthi    v0
mtlo    v1

/* remaining general registers */
lr      a0,XCP_A0(at)
lr      a1,XCP_A1(at)
lr      a2,XCP_A2(at)
lr      a3,XCP_A3(at)
lr      ra,XCP_RA(at)

/*
 * Restore the exception-time status register, which has the
 * side effect of disabling interrupts.
 */
.set    noreorder
lr      v0,XCP_SR(at)
```

Now we have serious magic coming up. In MIPS CPUs, not much care is taken to hide the pipeline when you're doing control register updates; control bits in **SR** take effect when they take effect, and users are supposed to read a table of when that is in each case and to program accordingly. But it may still be unexpected that on R4000 CPUs the process of disabling interrupts implicitly by setting the exception level bit **SR(EXL)** takes one clock cycle longer than the process of enabling interrupts explicitly by clearing the interrupt enable bit **SR(IE)**. If you update **SR** to do both those things simultaneously, you can get an unwanted interrupt. An additional and worse implication is that by the time that interrupt event works its way up the pipeline, the CPU thinks it's at exception level and then it processes the interrupt exception as if it were a nested exception.

Although this behavior is bad, it can be documented not to be a bug by patching the table of control bit delays. It's easy enough to fix: Set **SR(EXL)** first and then wait a couple of clock cycles before restoring the start-of-exception value of **SR** (which most likely has interrupts enabled).

The #if uses the presence of the **SR(EXL)** bit as characteristic of R4x00-style exception handling.

```
#if defined(SR_EXL)
    # clear SR_IMASK before setting SR_EXL (nasty window)
    li      v1,~(SR_IMASK|SR_EXL)
    and     v1,v0
    mtc0    v1,$sr
    or      v0,SR_EXL                 # make sure that EXL really is set
    nop
#elif defined(SR_IEC)
    li      v1,~(SR_IEC|SR_KUC)       # make sure than interrupts are disabled
    and     v0,v1
#endif
    lr      v1,XCP_V1(at)
    mtc0    v0,$sr
```

An R3000-like CPU (with the **SR(IEc)** bit defined) is just cheerfully overwriting the status register to clear out the privilege and interrupt bits—can this be right? Yes, because when we return from the exception below, the **rfe** instruction is going to pop the **SR(KUx,IUx)** stack and lose the value we just overwrote in any case.

```
#if defined(C0_DCIC)
    lr      v0,XCP_BDA(at)
    lr      sp,XCP_DCIC(at)
    mtc0    v0,C0_BDA
    mtc0    sp,C0_DCIC
#elif defined(C0_DCS)
    lr      v0,XCP_BDA(at)
    lr      sp,XCP_DCS(at)
    mtc0    v0,C0_BDA
    mtc0    sp,C0_DCS
#elif defined(C0_WATCHLO)
    lr      v0,XCP_WATCHLO(at)
    lr      sp,XCP_WATCHHI(at)
    mtc0    v0,C0_WATCHLO
    mtc0    sp,C0_WATCHHI
#elif defined(C0_IWATCH)
```

```
        lr       v0,XCP_IWATCH(at)
        lr       sp,XCP_DWATCH(at)
        mtc0     v0,C0_IWATCH
        mtc0     sp,C0_DWATCH
#endif

        lr       v0,XCP_V0(at)
        lr       sp,XCP_SP(at)


        /*
         * We are now uninterruptible and can use k1 safely
         */
        lr       k1,XCP_EPC(at)
        lr       AT,XCP_AT(at)
#ifdef SR_EXL
        rmtc0    k1,$epc
        nop; nop
        eret
        nop
#else
        j        k1
        rfe
#endif
        .set  reorder
        .set  at
END(_xcpt_vecbev)


/*
 * See comment above about this catastrophe
 */


SLEAF(xcpt_hairy)
    b           xcpt_hairy              # no hope - loop forever
SEND(xcpt_hairy)
```

Let's return to exceptions. This generates pieces of code suitable to be copied to the MIPS standard exception entry points, which will jump into the handler above. Note that we use the same exception handler for every kind of event, including the TLB miss exceptions that the MIPS architecture so kindly separated out. Now we know why RISC architectures don't have multiple interrupt vectors.

Anyway, here are the branches. They don't look very exciting.

```
    .set noat
    .set noreorder
```

```
#ifndef XCPC_XTLBMISS

/* utlb exception code (copied to 0xa0000000) */
_xcpt_vecutlb:
    la      k1,_xcpt_vecbev
    j       k1
    li      k1,XCPC_TLBMISS
_xcpt_endutlb:

#else

/* tlbmiss exception code (copied to 0xa0000000) */
_xcpt_vectlb:
    la      k1,_xcpt_vecbev
    j       k1
    li      k1,XCPC_TLBMISS
_xcpt_endtlb:

/* xtlbmiss exception code (copied to 0xa0000080) */
_xcpt_vecxtlb:
    la      k1,_xcpt_vecbev
    j       k1
    li      k1,XCPC_XTLBMISS
_xcpt_endxtlb:

#endif

/* general exception code */
_xcpt_vecgen:
    la      k1,_xcpt_vecbev
    j       k1
    li      k1,XCPC_GENERAL
_xcpt_endgen:

#if #cpu(r4640) || #cpu(r4650) || #cpu(rm52xx) || #cpu(rm7000)
/* interrupt exception code (copied to 0xa0000200) */
/* XXX you could fast vector here */
_xcpt_vecint:
    la      k1,_xcpt_vecbev
    j       k1
    li      k1,XCPC_GENERAL
_xcpt_endint:
#endif
```

```
#if #cpu(lr33k)
/* debug exception code (copied to 0xa0000040) */
_xcpt_vecdbg:
    la      k1,_xcpt_vecbev
    j       k1
    li      k1,XCPC_DEBUG
_xcpt_enddbg:
#endif
    .set reorder
    .set at


#ifdef XCPC_CACHEERR
#include "xcptcache.s"
#endif


/* Macro to copy exception handler to UNCACHED low memory */
#define XCPTCOPY(offs,start,end)      \
    li      t0,KSEG1_BASE+offs;       \
    la      t1,start;                 \
    la      t2,end;                   \
1:  lw      t3,0(t1);                 \
    addu    t1,4;                     \
    sw      t3,0(t0);                 \
    addu    t0,4;                     \
    bne     t1,t2,1b
```

Why uncached? Because you can't execute instructions out of the data cache. In fact, you're also going to need to be sure that the I-cache does not already contain some previous contents of these locations. This code assumes that this cannot be the case.

```
/*
 * Low-level exception handler initialization function.
 * Call only when a stack is set up and memory valid.
 * RAM handler stubs are installed via UNCACHED memory;
 * also sets k0 = &_xcpt_vecbev for ROM BEV handler.
 *
 * It will normally not be called when running under a
 * PROM monitor, which we want to allow to continue
 * catching exceptions itself.
 */

LEAF(_xcptlow_init)
#if !#cpu(164360)
```

```
    /* disable all interrupts */
    mfc0    t4,$sr
    and     t4,~SR_IE
    mtc0    t4,$sr


    /* copy exception handlers down to low memory */
#ifndef XCPC_XTLBMISS
    XCPTCOPY(0x000, _xcpt_vecutlb, _xcpt_endutlb)
    XCPTCOPY(0x080, _xcpt_vecgen, _xcpt_endgen)
#else
    XCPTCOPY(0x000, _xcpt_vectlb, _xcpt_endtlb)
    XCPTCOPY(0x080, _xcpt_vecxtlb, _xcpt_endxtlb)
    XCPTCOPY(0x180, _xcpt_vecgen, _xcpt_endgen)
#endif
#ifdef XCPC_CACHEERR
    XCPTCOPY(0x100, _xcpt_veccache, _xcpt_endcache)
#endif
#if #cpu(lr33k)
    XCPTCOPY(0x040, _xcpt_vecdbg, _xcpt_enddbg)
#endif
#if #cpu(r4640) || #cpu(r4650) || #cpu(rm52xx) || #cpu(rm7000)
    XCPTCOPY(0x200, _xcpt_vecint, _xcpt_endint)
#endif


    lw      t0,_ram_based
    beqz    t0,1f


    /* using RAM-based handlers, so switch off boot exceptions */
    and     t4,~SR_BEV
    mtc0    t4,$sr
#endif /* !#cpu(l64360) */


    /* set up ROM BEV handler hook (always, cannot hurt) */
1:  la      k0,_xcpt_vecbev
    j       ra
END(_xcptlow_init)



/*
 * This function exists simply for the debugger.
 * The debugger can see that ra is the return address
 * and in the normal case it is zero so it looks no further.
 * It also recognises this special name "_xcptcall" and can
 * trace back across the exception frame.
 *
```

```
 * On entry: a0 == &xcp
 */


LEAF(_xcptcall)
    subu    sp,24
    sr      ra,16(sp)                   /* == 0 normally */

    /* punt out to xcpt_deliver */
    jal     _xcpt_deliver

    lr      ra,16(sp)
    addu    sp,24
    beqz    ra,xcptrest
    j       ra
END(_xcptcall)
```

12.4   MIPS Interrupts

The interrupt handler we're going to look at here is built on the exception handler described in Section 12.3. The interrupt handler is just one of the possible exception action routines, so we know that

```
xcpthandlertab[XCPTINTR] == &intrhandler
```

where XCPTINTR is actually zero, because that's the **Cause(ExcCode)** value for an interrupt.

Once an interrupt occurs and control transfers into intrhandler(), the handler looks for interrupts that are active and wanted and the handler can call a different routine for each of the MIPS CPU's eight possible interrupt flags. There are utility routines to keep a table of individual interrupt routines, to allow you to register drivers' interrupt routines, and to handle unregistered or spurious interrupts.

But here's the guts of the handler:

```
/*
 * low-level interrupt exception handler
 */
static int intrhandler (int xcptno, struct xcptcontext *xcp)
{
    unsigned int cr = XCP_CAUSE (xcp) & XCP_STATUS (xcp) & CR_IMASK;
```

The **Cause(IP)** interrupt active bits simply track the corresponding CPU inputs. The matching bits of the status register, **SR(IM)**, are individual active-high enables for those interrupts. So we've now computed a bit vector of interrupts that are trying to be active.

```
struct intraction *ia;
int sig = 0;
int intr;

while (cr != 0) {
    if ((cr & _intrmask) == 0) {
        _mon_printf ("\nUnregistered interrupt: epc=%p, sr=%x, cr=%x\n",
                    REG_TO_VA (xcp->epc), XCP_STATUS (xcp),
                    XCP_CAUSE (xcp));
        return SIGKILL;
    }
```

_intrmask is a soft interrupt mask, which enables only interrupts for which a registered interrupt handler exists. The xcption allows us to just return a nonzero value and will send a signal to the controlling application—in this case, it is usually fatal.

```
/* find highest-priority interrupt bit number */
intr = priotab[(cr & _intrmask) >> 8];
ia = &intrtab[intr];

/* call its handler at its ipl */
splx (ipltab[ia->ia_ipl].mask);
sig = (ia->ia_handler) (ia->ia_arg, xcp);
```

priotab is just a table to speed a find-first-set-bit operation. Then we can find a structure pointer ia relating to this interrupt input.

The splx() function adjusts the mask in the status register, **SR(IM)**, to disable this interrupt and all those lower in priority. Then we call the handler:

```
intrblock();
```

intrblock() disables all interrupts in the status register, to make sure no hardware interrupt can get in while we figure out what's happening.

```
/* check for a signal request */
if (sig)
    return sig;

/* fetch new cause register */
cr = mips_getcr () & XCP_STATUS (xcp) & CR_IMASK;
```

As we said before, the interrupt flags in the cause register just track input signals and may change at any time, so we recompute and go around again until there are really no active interrupts.

```
    }
    return 0;
}
```

12.5 Tuning for MIPS

The following example is the heavily used C library function memcpy(), tuned heroically. This is freely redistributable code from a BSD release, used with thanks to the University of California.

```
/*-
 * Copyright (c) 1991, 1993
 *        The Regents of the University of California.  All rights reserved.
 *
 * This code is derived from software contributed to Berkeley by
 * Ralph Campbell.
 *
 * Redistribution and use in source and binary forms, with or without
 * modification, are permitted provided that the following conditions
 * are met:
 * 1. Redistributions of source code must retain the above copyright
 *    notice, this list of conditions and the following disclaimer.
 * 2. Redistributions in binary form must reproduce the above copyright
 *    notice, this list of conditions and the following disclaimer in the
 *    documentation and/or other materials provided with the distribution.
 * 3. All advertising materials mentioning features or use of this software
 *    must display the following acknowledgement:
 *       This product includes software developed by the University of
 *       California, Berkeley and its contributors.
 * 4. Neither the name of the University nor the names of its contributors
 *    may be used to endorse or promote products derived from this software
 *    without specific prior written permission.
 *
 * THIS SOFTWARE IS PROVIDED BY THE REGENTS AND CONTRIBUTORS ``AS IS'' AND
 * ANY EXPRESS OR IMPLIED WARRANTIES, INCLUDING, BUT NOT LIMITED TO, THE
 * IMPLIED WARRANTIES OF MERCHANTABILITY AND FITNESS FOR A PARTICULAR PURPOSE
 * ARE DISCLAIMED.  IN NO EVENT SHALL THE REGENTS OR CONTRIBUTORS BE LIABLE
 * FOR ANY DIRECT, INDIRECT, INCIDENTAL, SPECIAL, EXEMPLARY, OR CONSEQUENTIAL
 * DAMAGES (INCLUDING, BUT NOT LIMITED TO, PROCUREMENT OF SUBSTITUTE GOODS
```

```
 * OR SERVICES; LOSS OF USE, DATA, OR PROFITS; OR BUSINESS INTERRUPTION)
 * HOWEVER CAUSED AND ON ANY THEORY OF LIABILITY, WHETHER IN CONTRAOT, STRICT
 * LIABILITY, OR TORT (INCLUDING NEGLIGENCE OR OTHERWISE) ARISING IN ANY WAY
 * OUT OF THE USE OF THIS SOFTWARE, EVEN IF ADVISED OF THE POSSIBILITY OF
 * SUCH DAMAGE.
 */

#include <mips/asm.h>
#include <mips/regdef.h>

/* use 64-bit operations if available */
#if __mips >= 3
#define L       ld
#define LL      ldl
#define LR      ldr
#define S       sd
#define SL      sdl
#define SR      sdr
#define RS      8
#else
#define L       lw
#define LL      lwl
#define LR      lwr
#define S       sw
#define SL      swl
#define SR      swr
#define RS      4
#endif


/* moving bytes in chunks, so endianness matters */
#ifdef MIPSEL
#       define LHI      LR
#       define LLO      LL
#       define SHI      SR
#       define SLO      SL
#endif
#ifdef MIPSEB
#       define LHI      LL
#       define LLO      LR
#       define SHI      SL
#       define SLO      SR
#endif
```

Let's review these definitions. The strange instructions like **ldr** and **ldl** are for unaligned accesses; these two act in a pair to load a doubleword from an arbitrarily aligned location.

What we have defined are the following:

Symbol	Means
L	Load a word-size chunk
S	Store a word-size chunk
RS	Size of a word, in bytes
LHI	Word-size unaligned load (higher addresses)
LLO	Word-size unaligned load (lower addresses)
SHI	Word-size unaligned store (higher addresses)
SLO	Word-size unaligned store (lower addresses)

We'll also use free registers. The **t0–t9** registers are by definition free for our use in a subroutine; so are the argument registers **a0–a3** and the return-value registers **v0** and **v1**.

```
/* memcpy(to, from, n) */
LEAF(memcpy)
    .set   noreorder
    move   v0,a0                     # save to for return
    beq    a2, zero, .ret
    sltu   t2, a2, 12                # check for small copy
    bne    t2, zero, .smallcpy       # do a small bcopy
```

We're going to consign small copies (12 bytes or less by measurement) to something simple.

memcpy()—by the rules of the C standards—doesn't have to handle overlapped regions, which would make life a lot more complicated.

The basic strategy is to try to do the bulk of the copy with aligned big chunks of data. Where the source and destination are aligned the same, that's good (we make it a special case); where they're not, we use unaligned loads and aligned stores.

```
    xor    v1, a1, a0                # compare low bits of addresses
    and    v1, RS-1
    subu   a3, zero, a0              # compute # bytes to word align address
    beq    v1, zero, .aligned        # addresses can both be word aligned
    and    a3, RS-1                  # BDSLOT - harmless if we branch

    beq    a3, zero, 1f
    subu   a2, a3                    # subtract from remaining count
```

```
        LHI     v1, 0(a1)                   # get next RS bytes (unaligned)
        LLO     v1, RS-1(a1)
        addu    a1, a3
        SHI     v1, 0(a0)                   # store 0..RS-1 bytes to align a0
        addu    a0, a3


        /* Try a 4X unrolled unaligned block copy */
1:      and     v1, a2, (RS*4)-1            # remaining size % blocksize
        subu    a3, a2, v1                  # size of remaining blocks
        beq     a3, zero, 1f                # none?
        move    a2, v1                      # bytes remaining after block copy
        addu    a3, a1                      # compute ending address

2:      LHI     v1, RS*0(a1)                # copy block a1 unaligned, a0 aligned
        LLO     v1, RS*0+RS-1(a1)
        LHI     t0, RS*1(a1)
        LLO     t0, RS*1+RS-1(a1)
        LHI     t1, RS*2(a1)
        LLO     t1, RS*2+RS-1(a1)
        LHI     t2, RS*3(a1)
        LLO     t2, RS*3+RS-1(a1)
        S       v1, RS*0(a0)
        S       t0, RS*1(a0)
        S       t1, RS*2(a0)
        addu    a1, RS*4
        addu    a0, RS*4
        bne     a1, a3, 2b
        S       t2, -RS(a0)                 # keep back 1 store for the BDSLOT

1:      and     v1, a2, RS-1                # compute number of words left
        subu    a3, a2, v1
        beq     a3, zero, .smallcpy         # none?
        move    a2, v1                      # bytes remaining after word copy
        addu    a3, a1                      # compute ending address

2:      LHI     v1, 0(a1)                   # copy words a1 unaligned, a0 aligned
        LLO     v1, RS-1(a1)
        addu    a1, RS
        addu    a0, RS
        bne     a1, a3, 2b
        S       v1, -RS(a0)

        b       .smallcpy
        nop
```

```
.aligned:
    /* Both addresses have the same alignment: do initial bytes to align */
    beq     a3, zero, 1f
    subu    a2, a3                  # subtract from remaining count
    LHI     v1, 0(a1)               # copy 1, 2, or 3 bytes to align
    addu    a1,  a3
    SHI     v1, 0(a0)
    addu    a0, a3


    /* Try a 4X unrolled block copy */
1:  and     v1, a2, (RS*4)-1        # remaining size % blocksize
    subu    a3, a2, v1              # size of remaining blocks
    beq     a3, zero, 1f            # none?
    move    a2, v1                  # bytes remaining after block copy
    addu    a3, a1                  # compute ending address

2:  L       v1, RS*0(a1)
    L       t0, RS*1(a1)
    L       t1, RS*2(a1)
    L       t2, RS*3(a1)
    S       v1, RS*0(a0)
    S       t0, RS*1(a0)
    S       t1, RS*2(a0)
    addu    a1, RS*4
    addu    a0, RS*4
    bne     a1, a3, 2b
    S       t2, -RS(a0)


    /* Try a word at a time */
1:  and     v1, a2, RS-1            # remaining size % word size
    subu    a3, a2, v1              # size of remaining words
    beq     a3, zero, .smallcpy     # none?
    move    a2, v1                  # bytes remaining after word copy
    addu    a3, a1                  # compute ending address

2:  L       v1, 0(a1)               # copy words
    addu    a1, RS
    addu    a0, RS
    bne     a1, a3, 2b
    S       v1, -RS(a0)


.smallcpy:
    /* Last resort: byte at a time */
    beq     a2, zero, .ret
```

```
        addu    a3, a2, a1          # compute ending address

1:  lbu     v1, 0(a1)               # copy bytes
    addu    a1, 1
    addu    a0, 1
    bne     a1, a3, 1b
    sb      v1, -1(a0)

.ret: j       ra
    nop
    .set  reorder
END(memcpy)
```

Appendix

A

Instruction Timing and Optimization

MIPS CPUs are heavily pipelined, so the speed with which they can execute a piece of code depends on how well the pipeline works. In some cases, the correctness of the code depends on how the pipeline works—particularly with the CPU control coprocessor 0 instructions and registers.

Dependencies passing through explicitly used registers are fairly obvious, if messy; in addition, there are also occasional dependencies on implicitly used registers. For example, CPU control flags in the status register **SR** affect the operation of all instructions, and changes must be made very carefully.

The great majority of MIPS instructions need to obtain their operands for the end of the RD pipeline stage and need to produce their result at the end of the immediately following ALU stage, as illustrated in Figure A.1. If all instructions could always stick to these rules, any instruction sequence could be correctly run at maximum speed. The best trick in the MIPS architecture is that the vast majority of instructions can stick to these rules.

Where this can't be done, for some reason, then an instruction taking operands from the immediately preceding instruction can't run on time and correctly. This situation can be detected by the hardware and fixed by delaying the second instruction until the data is ready (an *interlock*) or it can be left to the programmer to avoid sequences of instructions that try to use data that isn't ready (a *pipeline hazard*).

A.1 Avoiding Hazards: Making Code Correct

Possible hazards include the following:

- *Load delay*: This was a hazard in early MIPS CPUs; the instruction immediately following a load could not reference the loaded data. That sometimes required the compiler/assembler to use a **nop** instruction

395

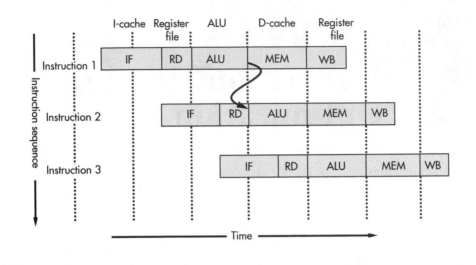

FIGURE A.1 Pipeline stages for two instructions with no delay needed

when nothing useful could be safely moved into the delay slot. But from the R4000 onward, MIPS CPUs have been interlocked so as to be free of hazards affecting ordinary user-level instructions.

- *Multiply unit hazards*: Results from the integer multiplier on MIPS CPUs are interlocked, so there's no delay slot from the **mflo** instruction that obtains the result. However, the independence of the integer multiply hardware produces its own problems; see Section A.3.

- *Coprocessor 0 hazards*: The coprocessor 0 control instructions often read or write registers with unusual timing, creating pipeline problems. Many of these are not interlocked. Detailed information must be sought in the user's manual for your particular CPU, but we'll look at what you have to do on an R4000 CPU (probably the most tricky of any MIPS CPU).

Note that the branch delay slot, although introduced to ease pipelining, is by definition part of the MIPS architecture and therefore not a hazard; it's just peculiar.

A.2   Avoiding Interlocks to Increase Performance

We lose performance with any interlock that happens when the CPU could, with cunning, have been doing useful work instead. We'd like to get the compiler (or for heavily used functions perhaps a dedicated human programmer) to reorganize code to run optimally.

Compilers—and humans—find this challenging. A program that is heavily optimized to avoid interlocks usually has several stages of computation pulled apart and then interleaved, and it gets very difficult to see what is going on. If code has only been moved from its natural sequential position by four or five instructions, it's usually possible to cope. Larger movements get more and more problematic.

In a single-pipeline machine (most MIPS CPUs to date), most instructions take one clock cycle, so we can expect to succeed at reorganizing instructions that take four to five clock cycles to complete and that can successfully overlap with other instructions. In MIPS CPUs, these criteria are a good fit only for floating-point instructions, so heroic scheduling improves FP performance but does little for integer code.[1] It's beyond the scope of this book to go into this in detail; if you want an excellent review of applicable compiler techniques look in Hennessy and Patterson, *Computer Architecture: A Quantitative Approach*. For detailed timing of individual CPUs, look in the specific user's manual.

On a smaller scale, there's an example of code optimized around load interlocks in Chapter 12 on page 388.

A.3   Multiply Unit Hazards: Early Modification of hi and lo

When a MIPS CPU takes an interrupt or other exception, most of the instructions in the pipeline are cancelled and the result write back is inhibited. But the integer multiply unit has few connections to the rest of the CPU and runs on, indifferent to an exception. This means that changes to the multiply unit result registers **lo** and **hi** cannot be prevented once multiply and divide instructions start.

An exception might occur just in time to prevent an **mfhi** or **mflo** from completing its write back but still might allow a subsequent multiply or divide instruction to start—and once the second operation gets launched the original data will be lost.

To avoid this, it's enough (on all MIPS CPUs) to ensure that at least two clock cycles separate an **mfhi** or **mflo** instruction from a following multiply or divide instruction. Good compilers and assemblers will police this for you, and you'll never know it's happening until you disassemble the code and find unexpected **nop**s.

---

1. That's one of the reasons why the Silicon Graphics compiler, while slightly worse than GNU C on integer code, is substantially faster—perhaps as much as 30%—on heavyweight floating-point programs.

A.4 Avoiding Coprocessor 0 Hazards: How Many nops?

The programmer's question is, how many instructions (perhaps **nop**s) do I need to put between a particular pair of instructions to make them work safely?

It would be possible, in principle, to produce an exhaustive list of pairs of instructions and how many clock cycles were required between them, but that would take a long time. But we can reduce the size of the job by noting that trouble occurs only when

- The instruction producing the data takes longer than the standard time (the standard time is the end of the ALU stage) and/or
- The instruction using the data requires it to be valid before the standard time (in this case, the standard time is the start of the ALU pipestage)

We don't need to document instructions that produce and use data at the standard time, only those that deviate from this righteous path. For each of those, we need to note when the result is produced and/or when the operand is needed.[1] Armed with that, we should be able to produce correct or efficient sequences for the most complicated cases.

Table A.1 shows the timing for an R4000/4400 CPU, essentially as found in Heinrich, *The R4000/R4400 User Manual* (see bibliography for Web address). This table gives the pipestage in which operands are used and in which results become available to succeeding instructions. The number of clock cycles

---

1. It would be enough—and simplest—to document the number of clock cycles by which the result is late or the operand early. But the MIPS-derived table uses pipeline stages.

TABLE A.1 Hazardous coprocessor 0 instructions and event timings for an R4000/R4400 CPU

Instruction/event	*Operands*		*Results*	
	What	*Pipestage*	*What*	*Pipestage*
`mtc0` `dmtc0`			CP reg	7
`mfc0` `dmfc0`	CP reg	4		
`tlbr`	Index, TLB	5–7	`PageMask`, `EntryHi` `EntryLo0`, `EntryLo1`	8
`tlbwi` `tlbwr`	Index/Random PageMask, EntryHi EntryLo0, EntryLo1	5–8	TLB	8

continued

TABLE A.1 *continued*

Instruction/event	Operands		Results	
	What	**Pipestage**	**What**	**Pipestage**
`tlbp`	PageMask, EntryHi	3–6	Index	7
`eret`	EPC/ErrorEPC TLB	4	SR[EXL,ERL]	4–8
	SR	3	LLbit	7
`cache xxHitxx`			SR[CH]	8
`cache`	cache line	x	cache line	x
`load/store`	EntryHi ASID SR[KSU,EXL,ERL,RE] Config[K0,DB] TLB	4		
	Config[SB]	7		
	WatchHi WatchLo	4–5		
`exception` `(load/store)`			EPC SR Cause BadVaddr Context, XContext	8
`exception` `(I-fetch)`			EPC SR	8
			Cause BadVaddr Context, XContext	4
`I-fetch`	EntryHi[ASID] SR[KSU,EXL,ERL,RE] Config[K0,IB]	0		
	Config[SB]	3		
	TLB	2		
`CP usable`	SR			
`Interrupt` `seen`	Cause[IP] SR[IM,IE,EXL,ERL]	3		

(typically **nop**s) required between a pair of dependent instructions is

$$ResultPipestage - OperandPipestage - 1$$

Why -1? A result produced in pipestage $n + 1$ and an operand needed in pipestage n produces ideal pipelining, so no **nop** is required. The -1 is an artifact of the way the pipestages are counted, really.

For most other MIPS CPUs you should find a similar table in the appropriate user's manual. We've used the R4000/4400 as an example here because its long pipeline (you'll see up to 8 pipestages in the table) and position as the head of the MIPS III CPU family mean that pretty much any sequence that runs on an R4000 will be safe (though perhaps not optimal) on any subsequent CPU.

Note that although the instruction **mfc0** delivers data late into its general-purpose register destination, the late result is not noted in the table because it's interlocked. This table only lists timings that can cause hazards.

A.5   Coprocessor 0 Instruction/Instruction Scheduling

We saw the following piece of code for a TLB miss handler on a 64-bit CPU (32-bit address space) in Chapter 6:

```
        .set    noreorder
        .set    noat
TLBmissR4K:
        dmfc0   k1,C0_CONTEXT
        nop                         # (1)
        lw      k0,0(k1)
        lw      k1,8(k1)
        mtc0    k0,C0_ENTRYLO0
        mtc0    k1,C0_ENTRYLO1
        nop                         # (2)
        tlbwr                       #
        nop                         # (3)
        eret                        # (4)
        nop                         # (5)
        .set    at
        .set    reorder
```

We're now in a position to account for the number of **nop**s placed in it:

(1) The R4000 CPU and most of its descendants are not capable of passing a coprocessor 0 register value through to the next instruction; the **dmfc0** instruction's timing is much like a load. The Heinrich R4000/R4400 User Manual gives hints that this operation may be fully interlocked in

an R4000, and certainly any delay greater than one clock cycle *is* inter-locked. But it's not made plain, and the **nop** here won't have any adverse effect on performance, so we'll leave it in.

(2) From Table A.1, **mtc0** writes the register **EntryLo1** in pipestage 7, and the **tlbwr** instruction needs that data set up for pipestage 5. So just one **nop** is needed (calculated as $7 - 5 - 1$). It may well not be required for some other CPU, but it's worth leaving in for portability reasons.

(3) The **tlbwr** has no obvious dependencies, but in fact it's important that all its side effects are completed before we return to user code. **tlbwr** does not finish writing the TLB until pipestage 8, and the fetch of a nor-mal instruction needs the TLB set up in pipestage 2; we must have a minimum of 5 instruction slots between the **tlbwr** and the exception return. The **eret** is followed by its branch delay slot—there's a **nop** at (5) in this case—and then (because of the R4000's long pipeline) by a two-clock-cycle delay while the pipeline refills after the branch. How-ever, that's still only four instructions; so we need an additional **nop** at (3), before the **eret**.

(4) Another dependency exists between **eret**, which resets the status reg-ister **SR(EXL)** field into its normal user state, and the first I-fetch of the user program. However, this timing is beyond the reach of the pro-grammer, so the machine is built so that the branch delay slot plus the two-cycle further branch delay is sufficient.

Armed with Table A.1, you should be able to work out anything!

A.6   Coprocessor 0 Flags and Instructions

As we saw previously, some of the CPU control registers (coprocessor 0) con-tain bitfield values or flags that have side effects on the operation of other in-structions. A usual rule of thumb is to assume that any such side effects will be unpredictable on the three instruction periods following the execution of an **mtc0**.

But the following are specifically noted:

■ *Enabling/disabling a group of coprocessor instructions*: If you enable a co-processor (making its particular instructions usable) by changing one of the **SR(CU)** bits, the **mtc0** instruction takes effect at pipestage 7 and the new value must be stable by pipestage 2 of a coprocessor instruction. So four intervening instruction issues are required in this case.

■ *Enabling/disabling interrupts*: If you change the interrupt state of the CPU by writing to **SR(IE)**, **SR(IM)**, or **SR(EXL)**, then Table A.1 says that that takes effect in pipestage 7. The interrupt signals are sampled for an instruction in pipestage 3, determining whether the instruction proceeds or is preempted by the interrupt. That means that three instructions (worked out as $7 - 3 - 1$) must be executed before the new interrupt state is safely installed.

During those three instruction times, an interrupt can be detected and can lead to an exception. But the status register was changed by an instruction that issued before the interrupted one, so the rules say the status register change will still occur.

Suppose then that you've disabled interrupts by setting the exception-level bit **SR(EXL)**. You will normally do this at only one place and that's at the end of an exception handler. An exception handler of any complexity saves the start-of-exception value of **SR** to be restored when control is about to be returned to the user program, and part of that start-of-exception value is that **SR(EXL)** is set.

If an interrupt occurs in one of the three instruction slots following the instruction that sets **SR(EXL)**, an interrupt exception will occur but with **SR(EXL)** already set; that causes very peculiar things to happen, including that the exception return address **EPC** is not recorded.[1] This would be unrecoverable, so it's vital to make sure that interrupts are already disabled when you set **SR(EXL)**; you can do this by making sure that you clear **SR(IE)** and/or **SR(IM)** at least three instruction times earlier.

■ *TLB changes and instruction fetches*: There is a five-instruction delay between a change to the TLB and when it can take effect on instruction translation. Additionally, there is a single-entry cache used for instruction translations (called the *micro-TLB*) that is implicitly flushed by loading **EntryHi**; this can also delay the effect.

You must obviously do TLB updates only in code running in an unmapped space. kseg0 is the usual choice.

---

1. See Section 6.7.2 for a discussion of why this bizarre behavior is a good idea.

Appendix

B Assembler Language Syntax

If you really want to figure out what can be in your assembler sources, read this appendix. The *compiler-dir* directives in the syntax are for use by compilers only, and they are not described in this book.

statement-list:
    statement
    statement statement-list

statement:
    stat **/n**
    stat **;**

stat:
    label
    label instruction
    label data
    instruction
    data
    symdef
    directive

label:
    identifier **:**
    decimal **:**

identifier:
    [A-Za-z.$_][A-Za-z0-9.$_]

403

instruction:
    op-code
    op-code operand
    op-code operand **,** operand
    op-code operand **,** operand **,** operand

op-code:
    add
    sub
    etc.

operand:
    register
    (register **)**
    addr-immed **(** register **)**
    addr-immed
    float-register
    float-const

register:
    $decimal

float-register:
    $fdecimal

addr-immed:
    label-expr
    label-expr **+** expr
    label-expr **-** expr
    expr

label-expr:
    label-ref
    label-ref **-** label-ref

label-ref:
    numeric-ref
    identifier
    .

numeric-ref:
    decimal**f**
    decimal**b**

data:

    data-mode data-list

    .ascii string

    .asciiz string

    .space expr

data-mode:

    .byte

    .half

    .word

    .float

    .double

data-list:

    data-expr

    data-list **,** data-expr

data-expr:

    expr

    float-const

    expr **:** repeat

    float-const **:** repeat

repeat:

    expr

symdef:

    constant-id **=** expr

constant-id:

    identifier

directive:

    set-dir

    segment-dir

    align-dir

    symbol-dir

    block-dir

    compiler-dir

set-dir:

    .set [no]volatile

    .set [no]reorder

    .set [no]at

    .set [no]macro

```
        .set [no]bopt
        .set [no]move
```

segment-dir:

```
    .text
    .data
    .rdata
    .sdata
```

align-dir:

```
    .align expr
```

symbol-dir:

```
    .globl identifier
    .extern identifier , constant
    .comm identifier , constant
    .lcomm identifier , constant
```

block-dir:

```
    .ent identifier
    .ent identifier , constant
    .aent identifier , constant
    .mask expr , expr
    .fmask expr , expr
    .frame register , expr , register
    .end identifier
    .end
```

compiler-dir:

```
    .alias register , register
    .bgnb expr
    .endb expr
    .file constant string
    .galive
    .gjaldef
    .gjrlive
    .lab identifier
    .livereg expr , expr
    .noalias register , register
    .option flag
    .verstamp constant constant
    .vreg expr , expr
```

expr:

```
    expr binary-op expr
    term
```

term:
    unary-operator term
    primary

primary:
    constant
    (expr)

binary-op: *one of the following*:
    * / %
    + -
    << >>
    &
    ^
    |

unary-operator: *one of the following*:
    + - ~ !

constant:
    decimal
    hexadecimal
    octal
    character-const
    constant-id

decimal:
    [1-9][0-9]+

hexadecimal:
    0x[0-9a-fA-F]+
    0X[0-9a-fA-F]+

octal:
    0[0-7]+

character-const:
    'x'

string:
    "xxxx"

float-const: *for example*:
    1.23 .23 0.23 1. 1.0 1.2e10 1.2e-15

C

Object Code

Object code is the unsavory gunk that becomes necessary so you can compile programs one module at a time and grows into the stuff that holds the many parts of a software development toolchain together.

To do its job properly, the object code must encapsulate the whole output of the compilation of a module, including the following:

- The code and initialized data.

- A symbol table relating shared names (functions, variables, etc.) to locations within the object module.

- Fixup records: These are recipes for how to reach and update address fields inside the code and data, as the module is linked with other modules and assigned a fixed set of program addresses.

- Debug information: A source-level debugger generally makes no attempt to interpret source code (C is easy enough to parse, but think of the difficulties involved when using conditional compilation). Instead, information such as the C source file and line number that gave rise to a problem piece of code and data is generated by the compiler and passed through the object module.

In an attempt to bring some order into this chaos, object files are split into chunks that are usually called *sections*: A section may contain code, a symbol table, or debug information, but all sections can be treated the same way for some purposes.

If object code were standardized, customers could mix and match tools from different vendors and have them cooperate seamlessly, and there would be a market in reusable software modules that could be distributed in object form. However, some source owners are unwilling to distribute source code because it can so easily be copied and disguised. The open-ended nature of

409

these aims, the need to evolve the object code as functions are added to tools anywhere within the toolchain, and the commitment to binary encoding have combined to make standardization difficult.

The problems have been further exacerbated by much-publicized standards efforts—notably common object file format (COFF), introduced by AT&T in the 80s—which fell far short of achieving interworking. COFF's successor executable and linking format (ELF), is better; however, the standards still tend to define the boxes in which information is kept, rather than the information inside them.

This appendix describes two object file formats that are often used in MIPS development systems: a COFF derivative called ECOFF, used and promoted by MIPS Corporation in its heyday, and a MIPS-specific variant of ELF.

The object files you meet can be classified as one of a few forms. A *relocatable object file* is the immediate output file generated by compiling a module, which is suitable for linking with other relocatable object files to create an executable object file, which holds a complete program, ready for direct execution by a CPU. A relocatable file includes fixup (relocation) information and symbol tables which allow the link editor to combine the individual modules and to patch instructions or data that depend on the program's final location in memory. Other parts of the file carry debug information, if the compiler was asked to provide it.

Although it's usual to link relocatable files into an executable file in a single step, it's not compulsory. You can just link relocatable files into another, larger file; some linkers give you ways to hide some symbols at this stage too, which can be useful if you're trying to glue together chunks of software that have name clashes (i.e., the same name used for two different functions).

An executable object file will not include relocation information and the program sections of it are accurate images of how the program should be in memory before you start it. The object file may add a simple header that tells the operating system or bootstrap loader where each part of the object file is to be located in memory and possibly where execution should start.

An *object code library* holds a collection of relocatable object files, with some kind of overall symbol table that allows a tool to pick out which file contains a definition for a particular named function or variable. Object code libraries provide a natural way to import into a program as much as is needed of a set of prebuilt software; they are an absolutely essential part of program development.

Unix-tradition libraries appear to have been shoehorned by accident into an existing mechanism designed to support multifile archives (for backup or transportation). The necessary symbol file was just glued on as another item in the archive. That's why unix-influenced systems call the library-generating tool ar and use a ". a" suffix for library files.

Your software development system will be equipped with tools to allow you to inspect the contents of an object file and tools to convert an executable file into alternative (possibly ASCII) formats that are acceptable to a PROM programmer or evaluation board. It's time we looked at what those are.

C.1 Tools

Figure C.1 shows you a typical compilation system. This figure shows the compiler generating an assembler intermediate file. This has the dual advantages of isolating the compiler from object code standards and ensuring that everything that the compiler can say to the linker has a textual (assembler) form. It would be more efficient for the compiler to generate object code directly, and some still do; however, as development platforms have become faster, that becomes less important.

To keep the picture fairly straightforward, we've left off a whole raft of tools that fiddle with object code, and we have ignored useful items like user-written libraries.

At the bottom of Figure C.1 you'll find the eventual consumers of object files: programs that interpret the file either to generate a runnable program in memory or debuggers that want to relate raw addresses in the program to symbols and line numbers in the code. With that in mind, we'll take a look inside a typical object file.

C.2 Sections and Segments

An object file consists of a number of separate *sections*: The biggest ones correspond to your program's instructions and data; additional sections hold information for linkers and debuggers. Each section has a name to identify it, such as `.text` or `.rdata`. A name starting with "." is one of those strange conventions that was probably intended to avoid conflict with any possible name of a function or variable. The standard program sections recognized by typical unix-influenced MIPS development systems are discussed in Section 9.5, and there's a bare list in Appendix B.

The object file needs to distinguish the program's code and data because the linker will eventually want to merge the different parts of your program that need to be located together in memory (e.g., a ROMmable program needs all code and read-only data in ROM, but writable data in RAM). When the link editor produces the final executable object file it concatenates all sections of the same name together and then further merges those sections that are located together in memory into a smaller number of contiguous *segments*. An object file header is prepended to identify the position of each segment in the file and its intended location in memory.

Of course, once we've invented separate sections to hold program data it's convenient to use the mechanisms for delimiting and naming sections to sepa-

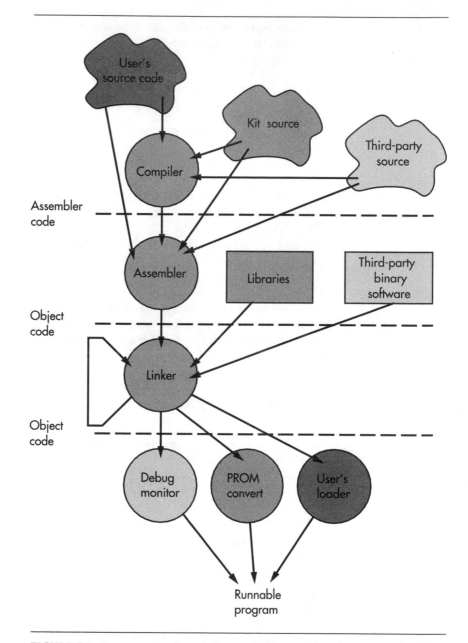

FIGURE C.1 Components of a typical cross-development toolkit: user-supplied files are dark, files that come with the toolkit are medium, and third-party files are light.

rate out other components of the module, such as symbol tables and relocation records. But we're now getting down toward individual flavors of object code.

C.3   ECOFF (RISC/OS)

The original MIPS Corporation compilers were UNIX-based and used the extended common object file format (ECOFF); this was eventually replaced in Silicon Graphics systems in about 1994. But development systems from other vendors often use or at least support interlinking with this format, in the interests of compatibility. ECOFF is based on an earlier format called common object file format (COFF), which first appeared in early versions of UNIX System V. COFF was a brave (and largely unsuccessful) attempt to define a flexible object code format that would be portable to a large number of processor architectures.

The MIPS engineers wanted the flexibility of COFF to support gp-relative addressing (Section 9.4.1), which would have been impossible with the restrictive format used on earlier UNIX systems. However, they decided to replace the COFF symbol table and debug data with a completely different design. The ECOFF symbol table format is certainly much more powerful and compact than the rather primitive COFF format, but it's complicated and proprietary—so much so that for several years its description was not generally available.

Fortunately, end users are unlikely to be concerned with the internal structure of the symbol tables: The most complex interface between the object code and user software is likely to be a run-time loader in your system, and helpful tool vendors should give you an example of such a loader as part of the software package. In any case, to load a fully resolved program you probably only need to recognize the COFF *file header* and optional *a.out* header, which are largely unchanged from the original COFF definitions.

C.3.1   *File Header*

The COFF file header consists of the 20 bytes at the start of the file listed in Table C.1 on page 414. Of this list, only the following fields are really important:

- *f_magic*: This must be one of the following values

Name	Value	Meaning
MIPSEBMAGIC	0x0160	Big-endian MIPS binary
MIPSELMAGIC	0x0162	Little-endian MIPS binary
SMIPSEBMAGIC	0x6001	Big-endian MIPS binary with little-endian headers
SMIPSELMAGIC	0x6201	Little-endian MIPS binary with big-endian headers

TABLE C.1 COFF file header

Offset	Type	Name	Purpose
0	unsigned short	f_magic	Magic number (see below)
2	unsigned short	f_nscns	Number of sections
4	long	f_timdat	Time and date stamp (unix-style)
8	long	f_symptr	File offset of symbol table
12	long	f_nsyms	Number of symbols
16	unsigned short	f_opthdr	Size of optional header
18	unsigned short	f_flags	Various flag bits

The endianness stuff looks worrisome, and it should be: You're looking at a naive bug retrospectively made into a feature. The COFF file is just a stream of bytes, and the way it represents longer integers (16-bit short and 32-bit long values) can be either big-endian (most-significant byte first) or little-endian (least-significant byte first). MIPS decided that the COFF file's convention would vary to match the endianness of the target for which this module was compiled. So long as the development host and target are the same sort of machine, the COFF format fits naturally onto the host.

But in cross-development the host and the target are different. It's quite possible to write endianness-safe object tools (you have to avoid the temptation to just lay C-defined data structures over raw file data); but MIPS didn't do that. So the SMIPSEBMAGIC and SMIPSELMAGIC magic numbers are what you see on object files where the host is of the wrong endianness for the target and the object code tools have been written naively.

Modern toolkits should only generate the first two file types, but tolerating the alternative forms might occasionally be useful.

- *f_nscns*: This is the number of section headers in the file. This is also needed to work out the program's offset.

- *f_opthdr*: This is the size in the file of the *a.out* header. You'll need this value to work out the program's offset in the file.

C.3.2 *Optional a.out Header*

The a.out header is a fossil from an earlier, simpler object code format, which has been shoehorned into COFF to make it easier to port loaders. It follows the COFF file header and does the job of coalescing the COFF sections into exactly three contiguous segments: text (instructions and read-only data); data (initialized, writable data); and BSS (uninitialized data, set to zero).

TABLE C.2 a.out header

Offset	Type	Name	Purpose
0	short	magic	Magic number
2	short	vstamp	Version stamp
4	long	tsize	Text size
8	long	dsize	Data size
12	long	bsize	BSS size
16	long	entry	Entry-point address
20	long	text_start	Text base address
24	long	data_start	Data base address
28	long	bss_start[a]	BSS base address
32	long	gprmask[a]	General registers used mask
36	long	cprmask[4][a]	Coprocessor registers used masks
52	long	gpvalue[a]	GP value for this file

a. New to ECOFF; not found in the original COFF definition.

The a.out header consists of the bytes listed in Table C.2.

The magic number in this structure does not specify the type of CPU, but instead describes the layout of the object file, as follows:

Name	Value	Meaning
OMAGIC	0x0107	Text segment is writable
NMAGIC	0x0108	Text segment is read-only
ZMAGIC	0x010b	File is demand-pageable (not for embedded use)

The following macro shows how to calculate the file offset of the text segment:

```
#define FILHSZ   sizeof(struct filehdr)
#define SCNHSZ   /*sizeof(struct scnhdr)*/ 40

#define N_TXTOFF(f, o) \
  ((a).magic == ZMAGIC ? 0 : ((a).vstamp < 23 ? \
    ((FILHSZ + (f).opthdr + (f).f_nscns * SCNHSZ + 7) & ~7) : \
    ((FILHSZ + (f).opthdr + (f).f_nscns * SCNHSZ + 15) & ~15) ) )
```

In words, and ignoring ZMAGIC files, it is found after the COFF file header, a.out header, and COFF section headers, rounded up to the next 8- or 16-byte boundary (depending on the compiler version).

C.3.3 *Example Loader*

The following code fragment, which returns the entry-point address of the program or zero on failure, draws together the above information to implement a very simple-minded ECOFF file loader, as might be found in a bootstrap PROM that can read files from disk or network:

```
unsigned long load_ecoff (int fd)
{
    struct filhdr fh;
    struct aouthdr ah;

    /* read file header and check */
    read (fd, &fh, sizeof (fh));
#ifdef MIPSEB
    if (fh.f_magic != MIPSEBMAGIC)
#else
    if (fh.f_magic != MIPSELMAGIC)
#endif
        return 0;

    /* read a.out header and check */
    read (fd, &ah, sizeof (ah));
    if (ah.magic != OMAGIC && ah.magic != NMAGIC)
        return 0;

    /* read text and data segments, and clear bss */
    lseek (fd, N_TXTOFF (fh, ah), SEEK_SET);
    read (fd, ah.text_start, ah.tsize);
    read (fd, ah.data_start, ah.dsize);
    memset (ah.bss_start, 0, ah.bsize);

    return ah.entry;
}
```

C.3.4 *Further Reading*

For more detailed information on the original COFF format, consult any programmer's guide for UNIX V.3. The ECOFF symbol table extensions are not documented, but the header files that define it (copyright MIPS Corporation, now MTI) are available for reuse and redistribution. You'll find copies with the rights documented in recent versions of GNU binary utilities.

TABLE C.3   ELF file header

Offset	Type	Name	Purpose
0	unsigned char	e_ident[16]	File format identification
16	unsigned short	e_type	Type of object file
18	unsigned short	e_machine	CPU type
20	unsigned long	e_version	File format
24	unsigned long	e_entry	Entry-point address
28	unsigned long	e_phoff	Program header file offset
32	unsigned long	e_shoff	Section header file offset
36	unsigned long	e_flags	CPU-specific flags
40	unsigned short	e_ehsize	File header size
42	unsigned short	e_phentsize	Program header entry size
44	unsigned short	e_phnum	Number of program header entries
46	unsigned short	e_shentsize	Section header entry size
48	unsigned short	e_shnum	Number of section header entries
50	unsigned short	e_shstrndx	Section header string table index

C.4   ELF (MIPS ABI)

Executable and linking format (ELF) is an attempt to improve on COFF and to define an object file format that supports a range of different processors while allowing vendor-specific extensions that do not break compatibility with other tools. It first appeared in UNIX System V Release 4 and is used by recent versions of MIPS Corporation compilers and some other development systems.

As in our examination of COFF/ECOFF, we will look only at the minimum amount of the structure necessary to load an executable file into memory.

C.4.1   *File Header*

The ELF file header consists of 52 bytes at the start of the file and provides the means to determine the location of all the other parts of the file, as listed in Table C.3. The following fields are relevant when loading an ELF file:

- e_ident: This contains machine-independent data to identify this as an ELF file and to describe its layout. The individual bytes within it are as follows:

Offset	Name	Expected value	Purpose
0	EI_MAG0	ELFMAG0=0x7f	Magic number identifying an ELF file
1	EI_MAG1	ELFMAG1='E'	
2	EI_MAG2	ELFMAG2='L'	
3	EI_MAG3	ELFMAG3='F'	
4	EI_CLASS	ELFCLASS32=1	Identifies file's word size
5	EI_DATA	ELFDATA2LSB=1	Indicates little-endian headers and program
		ELFDATA2MSB=2	Indicates big-endian headers and program
6	EI_VERSION	EV_CURRENT=1	Gives file format version number

- `e_machine`: This specifies the CPU type for which this file is intended, selected from among the following:

Name	Value	Meaning
EM_M32	1	AT&T WE32100
EM_SPARC	2	SPARC
EM_386	3	Intel 80386
EM_68K	4	Motorola 68000
EM_88K	5	Motorola 88000
EM_860	7	Intel 80860
EM_MIPS	8	MIPS R3000

Obviously, for this discussion the value should be EM_MIPS.

- `e_entry`: This is the entry-point address of the program.

- `e_phoff`: This is the file offset of the program header, which will be required to load the program.

- `e_phentsize`: This is the size (in bytes) of each program header entry.

- `e_phnum`: This is the number of entries in the program header.

C.4.2 *Program Header*

Having verified the ELF file header, you will require the program header. This part of the file contains a variable number of entries, each of which specifies a segment to be loaded into memory. Each entry is at least 32 bytes long and has the layout as noted in Table C.4. The relevant fields are as follows:

TABLE C.4   Program header

Offset	Type	Name	Purpose
0	unsigned long	p_type	Type of entry
4	unsigned long	p_offset	File offset of segment
8	unsigned long	p_vaddr	Virtual address of segment
12	unsigned long	p_paddr	Physical address of segment (unused)
16	unsigned long	p_filesz	Size of segment in file
20	unsigned long	p_memsz	Size of segment in memory
24	unsigned long	p_flags	Segment attribute flags
28	unsigned long	p_align	Segment alignment (power of 2)

- p_type: Only entries marked with a type of PT_LOAD (1) should be loaded; others can be safely ignored.

- p_offset: This holds the absolute offset in the file of the start of this segment.

- p_vaddr: This is the virtual address in memory at which the segment should be loaded.

- p_filesz: This is the size of the segment in the file; it may be zero.

- p_memsz: This is the size of the segment in memory. If it is greater than p_filesz, then the extra bytes should be cleared to zero.

- p_flags: This contains a bitmap giving read, write, and execute permissions for the segment:

Name	Value	Meaning
PF_X	0x1	Execute
PF_W	0x2	Write
PF_R	0x4	Read

It is largely irrelevant for embedded systems, but it does allow you to identify the code segment.

C.4.3   *Example Loader*

The following code fragment, which returns the entry-point address of the program or zero on failure, draws together the above information to implement a very simple-minded ELF file loader, as might be found in a bootstrap PROM that can read files from disk or network:

```
unsigned long load_elf (int fd)
{
    Elf32_Ehdr eh;
    Elf32_Phdr ph[16];
    int i;

    /* read file header and check */
    read (fd, &eh, sizeof (eh));

    /* check header validity */
    if (eh.e_ident[EI_MAG0] != ELFMAG0 ||
        eh.e_ident[EI_MAG1] != ELFMAG1 ||
        eh.e_ident[EI_MAG2] != ELFMAG2 ||
        eh.e_ident[EI_MAG3] != ELFMAG3 ||
        eh.e_ident[EI_CLASS] != ELFCLASS32 ||
#ifdef MIPSEB
        eh.e_ident[EI_DATA] != ELFDATA2MSB ||
#else
        eh.e_ident[EI_DATA] != ELFDATA2LSB ||
#endif
        eh.e_ident[EI_VERSION] != EV_CURRENT ||
        eh.e_machine != EM_MIPS)
      return 0;

    /* is there a program header of the right size? */
    if (eh.e_phoff == 0 || eh.e_phnum == 0 || eh.e_phnum > 16 ||
        eh.e_phentsize != sizeof(Elf32_Phdr))
        return 0;

    /* read program header */
    lseek (fd, eh.e_phoff, SEEK_SET);
    read (fd, ph, eh.e_phnum * eh.e_phentsize);

    /* load each program segment */
    for (i = 0; i < eh.e_phnum; i++) {
        if (ph[i].p_type == PT_LOAD) {
            if (ph->p_filesz) {
                lseek (fd, ph[i].p_offset, SEEK_SET);
                read (fd, ph[i].p_vaddr, ph[i].p_filesz);
            }
            if (ph[i].p_filesz < ph[i].p_memsz)
                memset (ph[i].p_vaddr + ph[i].p_filesz, 0,
                        ph[i].p_memsz - ph[i].p_filesz);
        }
    }
```

```
        return eh.eh_entry;
}
```

C.4.4   *Further Reading*

The ELF format, including MIPS-specific extensions, is extensively documented in the book *System Five ABI MIPS Processor Supplement* (Prentice Hall 1991).

C.5   Object Code Tools

Your software development system will be equipped with a number of tools for examining and manipulating object files. The following list assumes unix-type names, but systems with a different ancestry will have similar tools, even if the names are different.

Program name	Function
ar	This tool allows you to list object files and to add them to or remove them from a library. The name comes from archive, the historical UNIX name for the file type used to store libraries and later specialized for this purpose.
convert	Converts an executable object file from binary to some other format which can be downloaded to a PROM programmer or evaluation board.
ld	This is the linker/loader, which is used to glue object codes together and also to assign fixed target system addresses to sections (in some systems this would involve two separate programs, typically called link and locate).
nm	This lists the names in an object file's symbol table in alphabetic or numeric order.
objdump/odump	This displays the program data of the object file in various useful forms; in particular, it can usually disassemble the code sections.
ranlib	If present, this builds a global table of contents in a library, which makes it much faster for ld to read. On modern systems ar usually has an option to do this job, and ranlib may well just be an alias for that option.
size	This displays the size of each section in the object file.
strip	This removes everything from the object file that is not necessary to load the program, making it (much) smaller; it gets rid of symbol tables and debug information. Some people do this to make it harder to disassemble the program.

Appendix

D

Evolving MIPS

D.1   MIPS16

MIPS16 is an optional instruction set extension that can reduce the size of binary programs by 30–40%, and was launched to the world in mid-97. Its implementors hope that it will make the CPUs more attractive in contexts where code size is a major concern—which mostly means very low cost systems. While it will only be used in certain implementations, it is a multivendor standard: LSI, NEC, and Philips are all producing CPUs that support MIPS16.

We said back in Section 1.2 that what makes MIPS binaries larger than those for other architectures is not that MIPS instructions do less work, but that they are larger—each is 4 bytes in size, in contrast to a typical average of 3 bytes for some CISC architectures.

MIPS16 adds a mode in which the CPU decodes fixed-size 16-bit instructions. Most MIPS16 instructions expand to one regular MIPS III instruction, so it's clear that this will be a rather restricted subset of instructions. The trick is to make the subset sufficient to encode enough of the program efficiently to make a substantial impact on the overall program size.

Of course, 16-bit instructions don't make this a 16-bit instruction set; MIPS16 CPUs are real MIPS CPUs with either 32- or 64-bit registers and operations that work on the whole of those registers.

MIPS16 is far from a complete instruction set—there's neither CPU control nor floating-point instructions, for example.[1] But that's OK, because every MIPS16 CPU must also run a complete MIPS ISA. You can run a mixture of MIPS16 and regular MIPS code; every function call or jump-register instruction can change the mode.

---

1. MIPS did not invent the idea of providing an alternate half-size version of just part of the instruction set; Advanced RISC Machine's Thumb version of its ARM CPU was out first.

In MIPS16 it's convenient and effective to encode the mode as the least-significant bit of an instruction address. MIPS16 instructions have to be even byte aligned, so bit 0 has no role as part of the instruction pointer; instead, every jump to an odd address starts MIPS16 execution, and every jump to an even address returns to regular MIPS. The target address of the MIPS subroutine-call instruction **jal** is always word-aligned, so a new instruction **jalx** hides the mode change in the instruction.

To crush the instruction to half size we allocate only 3 bits to choose a register for most instructions, allowing free access to only eight general-purpose registers; also, the 16-bit constant field found in many MIPS instructions gets squeezed, often to 5 bits. Many MIPS16 instructions only specify two registers, not three; in addition, there are some special encodings described in the next section.

D.1.1   *Special Encodings and Instructions in MIPS16*

The squashed general-purpose instructions are OK, but there are two particular weaknesses that will add size back to the program; the 5-bit immediate field is inadequate to build constants, and there's not enough address range on load/store operations. Three new kinds of instruction and one extra convention help out.

extend is a special MIPS16 instruction consisting of a 5-bit code and an 11-bit field that is concatenated with the immediate field in the following instruction, to allow an instruction pair to encode a 16-bit immediate. It appears as an instruction prefix in assembly language.

Loading constants takes extra instructions even in regular MIPS and would be a huge burden in MIPS16; it's quicker to put the constants into memory and load them. MIPS16 adds support for loads relative to the instruction's own location (PC-relative loads), allowing constants to be embedded in the code segment (typically, just before the start of a function). These are the only MIPS16 instructions that don't correspond exactly to a normal MIPS instruction—MIPS has no PC-relative data operations.

Many MIPS load/stores are directed at the stack frame and **$29/sp** is probably the most popular base register. MIPS16 defines a group of instructions that implicitly use **sp**, allowing us to encode a function's stack frame references without needing a separate register field.

MIPS load instructions always generate a full 32-bit address. Since load word instructions are only valid for an address that is a multiple of four, the two least-significant bits are wasted. MIPS16 loads are scaled: The address offset is shifted left according to the size of the object being loaded/stored, increasing the address range available from the instruction.

As an additional escape mechanism, MIPS16 defines instructions that allow it to do an arbitrary move between one of the eight MIPS16-accessible registers and any of the 32 MIPS general registers.

D.1.2 *MIPS16 Evaluated*

MIPS16 is not a suitable language for assembly coding, and we're not going to document it here. It's intended for compilers. Most programs compiled with MIPS16 seem to shrink to 60–70% of their MIPS size, which is more compact than 32-bit CISC architectures, similar to ARM's Thumb and reasonably competitive with pure 16-bit CPUs.

There's no such thing as a free lunch however; a MIPS16 program will probably compile into 40–50% more instructions than would be required for MIPS. That means that running a program through the CPU core will take 40–50% more clock cycles. However, low-end CPUs are usually largely memory limited, not core limited, and the smaller MIPS16 program requires less bandwidth to fetch and will promote lower cache miss rates. Where the caches are small and program memory is narrow, MIPS16 will close the gap on and possibly overhaul regular MIPS code.

Because of the performance loss, MIPS16 code is not attractive in computers with large memory resources and wide buses. That's why it's an optional extension.

At the upper end of its range, MIPS16 will find itself in competition with software compression techniques. A regular MIPS program compressed into ROM storage with a general-purpose file compression algorithm will be smaller than the unencoded MIPS16 equivalent and little larger than the compressed MIPS16 equivalent;[1] if your system has enough volatile memory to be able to use ROM as a file system and to decompress code into RAM for execution, software decompression of a full ISA will most likely give you better overall performance.

There's also a clear trend toward writing systems that make extensive use of code written in a byte-coded interpreted language (Java or its successors) for the bulk of code that is not time critical. That kind of intermediate code is very small, much more efficient than any machine binary; if only the interpreter and a few performance-critical routines are left in the native machine ISA, a tighter instruction set encoding will only affect a small part of the program. Of course, interpreters (particularly for Java) may themselves be quite large, but the inexorable increase in application complexity should soon cause that to dwindle in importance.

I expect to see MIPS16 applied to a small range of low-power, size-, and cost-constrained systems between 1998–2003. It was worth inventing, because some of these systems—such as "intelligent" mobile phones—are likely to be produced in huge volumes.

---

1. Tighter encodings have less redundancy for a compression algorithm to exploit.

D.2   MIPS V/MDMX

MIPS V and MDMX were announced together in early 1997, and both were slated for introduction in a new MIPS/SGI CPU in 1998. But that CPU was cancelled, and there is some doubt about their future.

Both are aimed at overcoming the perceived deficiencies of conventional instruction sets when the ISAs are confronted by multimedia applications. Jobs like encoding/decoding audio for soft modem or streaming applications or image/video compression/decompression use mathematically based algorithms that were once seen as the preserve of special-purpose digital signal processors. At the computational level, multimedia tasks like this often involve the repeated application of the same operation to large vectors or arrays of data.

Inside a register-based machine, the solution commonly adopted is to pack multiple data items into a single machine register and then to perform a register-to-register instruction that does the same job on each field of each of its registers. This is a very explicit form of parallel processing called single instruction, multiple data (SIMD).

This idea was first seen in a microprocessor in Intel's now-vanished i860 CPU (circa 1988); it resurfaced much more visibly as the MMX extension to Intel's x86 instruction set, launched in 1996.

MDMX provides for manipulation of 8×8-bit integers within a 64-bit register, with a set of operations that do the same thing to all eight slices. The instructions include normal arithmetic (add, subtract, multiply), but there are also multiply-accumulate instructions that collect their results in a giant accumulator with enough precision to prevent overflow.

Since these instructions are used in contexts where the special data types are fairly clearly separated from normal program variables, it makes sense for the MDMX instruction set to work with the floating-point registers. Recycling existing registers in this way means that existing operating systems need not be changed (they already save and restore floating-point registers on task switches).

Like MDMX, Intel's MMX provides "octibyte" eight-way instructions for 8×8-bit numbers that are packed into one 64-bit register. The MIPS MDMX also defines 4×16-bit (quad-short) and 2×32-bit (paired-word) formats, but the early signs are that some MDMX implementations may decide that the octibyte formats and instructions are enough.

When arithmetic works on only 8-bit numbers, results frequently underflow and overflow. Multimedia application performance would not be enhanced if we had to program in lots of overflow test conditions, and it's often more helpful for the machine operations to quietly truncate overflowed and underflowed results to the largest and smallest representable numbers (255 and 0 for unsigned 8-bit), a process called *saturating* arithmetic. MDMX has that ability.

That brings us to MIPS V. Although named as if it intends to be an incremental instruction set like MIPS I through IV, MIPS V is a direct analog of MDMX in the floating-point domain, providing paired-single operations that do twin FP functions on pairs of single-precision numbers that are packed into 64-bit floating-point registers.

MIPS V is less weird than MDMX; MIPS IV includes a fairly comprehensive set of floating-point operations and it is straightforward to provide paired-single versions of most of them; even paired-compare can be done, since MIPS IV CPUs already have multiple floating-point condition bits to receive results. However, MIPS V does not provide paired versions of complex multicycle functions that would have required extensive new resources (no square root or divide, for example).

D.2.1   *Can Compilers Use Multimedia Instructions?*

The argument that led to the introduction of SIMD multimedia instructions parallels the argument that led to the provision of vector processing units in supercomputers from the late 70s onward. It's fairly easy to build a handcrafted matrix-arithmetic package for a vector processor. It's significantly harder to compile a program written in a high-level language to make use of vector operations, but supercomputer vendors made some progress with that, too. Often they were focusing on Fortran; the semantic weakness that makes Fortran a poor language for general programming does make it an easier language to optimize, because side effects are pretty explicit.

The consensus view seemed to be that a vectorizing Fortran compiler did not work well on old programs ("dusty decks," a charming piece of Fortran slang). Such a compiler required the programmer to write or adapt loops to make them optimizer friendly before it could deliver significant benefits. That may be a good division of labor: The loops may be stylized but can still be understood by programmers as sequential code when the resulting explicitly parallel code is hard to fathom. The term "optimizer friendly" is vague: A parallel processing theoretician would define it as the absence of specific kinds of side effects whereas a practical compiler may be looking for a loop that adheres to some much more rigid conventions so that a dumb pattern matcher can recognize it as safe to vectorize.

Vectorizing C is more difficult, because the memory and pointer-based model it uses implicitly for any array access can make it very hard to eliminate all side effects in anything but the simplest loops. It hasn't been done much in production.

Given this history, what prospect is there of developing C and C++ compilers that successfully optimize programs to exploit multimedia SIMD instructions? My guess is that prospects are poor in the immediate future. Intel's MMX is the most widely used modern SIMD instruction set and is currently being marketed to assembler language users only.[1] I don't expect to see compilers using x86 MMX. If large-scale successful use is made of MMX and is dependent on assembler subroutines, its effect would be to tie those applications into the x86 architecture; this would hardly be something that Intel would be in a hurry to change.

It's widely speculated, however, that in 1998 or 1999 Intel will introduce a further ISA extension that will add more data formats to a "son of MMX," including paired single-precision floating point. If this more capable instruction set gets compiler support, then that might create a pool of software that could also be applied to MIPS V.

D.2.2 *Applications for MDMX*

Like x86 MMX, MDMX should be useful for 3D graphics and video applications where the CPU pushes pixel values about and for the kind of relatively low-precision signal processing needed for a software modem.

Unfortunately, near-display 3D rendering depends for its performance on careful integration of video memory. CPUs, even well-equipped ones, can't compete with cheap PC-world accelerators which have glueless interfaces to wide video memory.[2] Image and video retouching applications do run programs that access pixels on this level, but they're desktop PC applications.

Software modems could be useful for low-end consumer devices that want to use telephony. They're in competition with cheap integrated modem devices, and on a wider scale they're in competition with a shift toward digital telephony delivered to the home.

It looks to me as if MDMX's best opportunity would be in a games console, in conjunction with a tightly integrated CPU/video system.

D.2.3 *Applications for MIPS V*

The paired-single floating-point instructions and formats aim to increase bandwidth on the kind of repetitive floating-point calculations found in applications for high-end graphics and multimedia. Although that looks like the Silicon Graphics market, increasing use of 3D graphics everywhere may make this kind of capability useful in a wider sphere.

Limited compiler support for MIPS V is also more plausible than for MDMX. While the paired operations look as if they are an alternative to dual-

---

1. A cynic would say that MMX has served its purpose by becoming required by any x86 clone and that whether it is actually used is quite beside the point. And such games and graphics applications as are likely to benefit are written by programmers who take a perverse delight in writing assembler.

2. Perhaps they could compete if anyone built CPUs with glueless interfaces to wide memory and integrated video refresh data channels. But I don't see much sign of MIPS products of that kind.

issue instructions in a superscalar CPU, they are actually complementary. The parallelism exploited by SIMD instructions comes from a higher level in the compiler, and the low-level scheduler may still find opportunities for dual-issuing a paired floating-point instruction with some integer or housekeeping operations.

D.2.4   *Likely Success of MDMX/MIPS V*

SGI's 1997 decision to abandon development of its H1 high-end processor project left both instruction sets without an announced vehicle. But I believe there will be at least one CPU aimed at the embedded market that supports MDMX. It will be interesting to see what happens.

So far MIPS V is without a CPU; however, it has a longer shelf life than MDMX and would still be a useful adjunct to a CPU launched in 1999.

MIPS Glossary

$f0–$f31 registers: The 32 general-purpose 32-bit floating-point registers. In MIPS I (32-bit) CPUs, only even-numbered registers can be used for arithmetic (the odd-numbered registers hold the low-order bits of 64-bit, double-precision numbers).

$nn register: One of the CPU's 32 general-purpose registers.

a0–a3 register: Aliases for CPU registers **$4–$7**, conventionally used for passing the first four words of the arguments to a function.

ABI (application binary interface): A particular standard for building program binaries that in turn is supposed to guarantee correct execution on a conforming environment. Note, in particular, MIPS/ABI which is an ABI for 32-bit MIPS programs available on computers from Silicon Graphics, Siemens/Nixdorf, and some other manufacturers.

Acrobat: Trade name for an online document-viewing program distributed (free, to date) by Adobe Systems. Often abused to mean the file format acceptable to the viewer, which Adobe calls PDF (Portable Document Format). PDF is a compressed, indexed, and obfuscated relative of PostScript.

address regions: Refers to the division of the MIPS program address space into regions called kuseg, kseg0, kseg1, and kseg2. See under individual region names.

address space: The whole range of addresses as seen by the application program. Programs running under a protected OS have their addresses checked for validity and translated since such an OS can run many applications concurrently, there are many address spaces.

Algorithmics: The UK company, specializing in MIPS technology and tools, of which the author is a partner.

alignment: Positioning of data in a memory with respect to byte-address boundaries. Data items are called *naturally aligned* if they start on an address that is zero modulo their own size. MIPS CPUs require that their machine-supported data objects are naturally aligned; hence words (4 bytes) must be on 4-byte boundaries, and a floating-point `double` datum must be on an 8-byte boundary.

alloca: C library function returning a memory area that will be implicitly freed on return from the function where the call is made from.

Alpha: The range of RISC CPUs made by Digital Semiconductor; it is the nearest relative to MIPS.

ALU (arithmetic/logic unit): A term applied to the part of the CPU that does computational functions

analyzer: See *logic analyzer*.

Apache group (SVR4.2): An industry group of suppliers of MIPS-architecture UNIX systems who are cooperating on a standard version of Univel's System V Release 4.2 operating system and the *MIPS ABI standard*.

architecture: See *instruction set architecture*.

archive: Alternative name for an *object code library*.

argument: In C terminology, a value passed to a function. Often called a parameter in other languages. C arguments are parameters passed by value, if that helps.

ASCII: Used very loosely for the character encoding used by the C language.

ASIC (Application-Specific Integrated Circuit): A chip specially designed or adapted for use in a particular circuit.

ASIC-core CPU: A microprocessor designed to be built in as one component of an ASIC, making what is sometimes called a "system on a chip." MIPS CPUs are increasingly being used as cores.

ASID: The address space ID maintained in the CPU register `EntryHi`. Used to select a particular set of address translations: Only those translations whose own ASID field matches the current value will produce valid physical addresses.

assembler, assembly code: Assembler code (sometimes called assembly code or assembly language) is the human-writable form of a computer's machine instructions. The assembler is the program that reads assembly language and translates it to an executable program, probably through an interim *object code*.

associative store: A memory that can be looked up by presenting part of the stored data. It requires a separate comparator for each data field, so large associative stores use up prodigious amounts of logic. The MIPS TLB, if fitted, uses a fully associative memory with between 32 and 64 entries.

associativity: See *cache, set-associativity*.

ATMizer: A component made by LSI Logic for ATM network interfacing, which has an internal MIPS CPU as just one component inside.

atomic, atomically, atomicity: In computer science jargon, a group of operations is atomic when either all of them happen or none of them do.

backtrace: See *stack backtrace*.

BadVaddr register: CPU control register that holds the value of an address that just caused a trap for some reason (misaligned, inaccessible, TLB miss, etc.).

bcopy: C library function to copy the contents of a chunk of memory.

benchmark: A program that can be run on many different computers, with a view to finding something about their relative performance. Benchmarks have evolved from fragments of code intended to measure the speed at some very specific task to large suites that should give some guidance as to the speed at which a system handles common applications.

BEV (boot exception vectors): A bit in the CPU status register that causes traps to go through a pair of alternate vectors located in uncached (kseg1) memory. The locations are close to the reset-time start point so that they can both conveniently be mapped to the same read-only memory.

bias: See *floating-point bias*.

BiCMOS: A particular technology for building chips, mixing dense and cool CMOS transistors for internal logic with faster and electrically quieter bipolar transistors for interface. It had a vogue for CPUs in the late 80s, but nobody used it successfully until Intel, who built some early Pentiums this way.

big-endian: Describes an architecture where the most-significant part of a multibyte integer is stored at the lowest byte address; see Section 11.6.

bitfield: A part of a word that is interpreted as a collection of individual bits.

blocksize: See *cache line size*.

bootstrap: A program or program fragment that is responsible for starting up from a condition where the state of the CPU or system is uncertain.

branch: In the MIPS instruction set, a PC-relative jump.

branch and link: A PC-relative subroutine call.

branch delay slot: The position in the memory-stored instruction sequence immediately following a jump/branch instruction. The instruction in the branch delay slot is always executed before the instruction that is the target of the branch. It is sometimes necessary to fill the branch delay slot with a "**nop**" instruction.

branch optimization: The process (carried out by the compiler, assembler, or programmer) of adjusting the memory sequence of instructions so as to make the best use of branch delay slots.

branch penalty: Many CPUs pause momentarily after taking a branch, because they have fetched instructions beyond the branch into their pipeline and must backtrack and refill the pipeline. This delay (in clock cycles) is called the branch penalty. It's zero on short-pipeline MIPS chips, but the two-clock-cycle branch penalty on the long-pipeline R4000 was a significant factor in reducing its efficiency.

BrCond3-0: CPU inputs that are directly tested by the coprocessor conditional branch instructions.

breakpoint: When debugging a program, a breakpoint is an instruction position where the debugger will take a trap and return control to the user. Implemented by pasting a break instruction into the instruction sequence under test.

BSS: In a compiled C program, that chunk of memory that holds variables declared but not explicitly initialized. Corresponds to a segment of object code. Nobody seems to be able to remember what BSS ever stood for!

bss: Most C compilation systems use this strange name for the data area to which are assigned global variables that have not been explicitly initialized.

burst read cycles: MIPS CPUs (except for some very early parts) refill their caches by fetching more than one word at a time from memory (4 words is common) in a burst read cycle.

busctrl register: CPU register, implemented only on IDT's R3041 CPU, that allows the programmer to set up some options for how bus accesses are carried out.

byte: An 8-bit datum.

byte order: Used to emphasize the ordering of items in memory by byte address. This seems obvious, but it can get confusing when considering the constituent parts of words and halfwords.

byte-swap: The action of reversing the order of the constituent bytes within a word. This may be required when adapting data acquire from a machine of nonmatching endianness.

C preprocessor: A program typically run as the first pass of the C compiler, which is responsible for textual substitutions and omissions. It processes comments and the useful directives that start with a "#", like #define, #include, and #ifdef. Despite its pairing with C, it is in fact a general-purpose macro language that can be, and often is, used with other languages. In this book, its important non-C application is to preprocess assembly language programs.

C++: A compiled language retaining much of the syntax and appearance of C, but offering a range of object-oriented extensions.

cache: A small auxiliary memory located close to the CPU, which holds copies of some data recently read from memory. MIPS caches are covered extensively in Chapter 4.

cache, direct-mapped: A direct-mapped cache has, for any particular location in memory, only one slot where it can store the contents of that location. Direct-mapped caches are particularly liable to become inefficient if a program happens to make frequent use of two variables in different parts of memory that happen to require the same cache slot; however, direct-mapped caches are simple, so they can run at high clock rates.

MIPS CPUs prior to some of the later members of the R4x00 family were direct mapped for speed. However, since about 1994 on-chip caches seem to have had little trouble keeping up with the CPU pipeline, and cache miss rates have become extremely important in performance. Most new CPU introductions from the mid-90s on feature more complicated caches.

cache, duplicate tags: In cache-coherent multiprocessors, the bus interface controller must often look at the CPU's cache—specifically, at the cache tags—to check whether a particular bus transaction should interact with the data currently in the cache. Such accesses are costly, either in delays to the CPU if the bus interface time-slices the tags with the CPU or in hardware and interlocks if the tags are dual ported. It's often cheaper to keep a second copy of the cache information the bus interface is interested in, which is updated in parallel with the main cache—the events that cause either to change are bus-visible anyway. The duplicate tags don't need to be perfect to be useful; if they allow the bus interface to avoid accessing the CPU's tags in a high proportion of cases, they'll still make the system more efficient.

cache, physical-addressed: A cache that is accessed entirely by using physical (translated) addresses. Early MIPS CPU caches, and all MIPS secondary caches, are like this.

cache, set-associative: A cache where there is more than one place in the cache where data from a particular memory location may be stored. You'll commonly see two-way set associative caches, which means there are two cache slots available for any particular memory data. In effect there are two caches searched simultaneously, so the system can cope with a situation where two frequently accessed items are sitting at the same cache index.

A set-associative cache requires wider buses than a direct-mapped cache and cannot run quite as fast. Early RISCs used direct-mapped caches to save pins on the external cache. Although the wide buses are not much of a problem for on-chip caches, some early integrated CPUs still had direct-mapped caches to boost the clock frequency. These days, set-associative on-chip caches are usually preferred for their lower miss rate.

cache, snooping: In a cache, snooping is the action of monitoring the bus activity of some other device (another CPU or DMA master) to look for references to data that are held in the cache. Originally, the term "snooping" was used for caches that could *intervene*, offering their own version of the data where it was more up to date than the memory data that would otherwise be obtained by the other master; the word has come to be used for any cache that monitors bus traffic.

cache, split: A cache that has separate caches for instruction fetches and for data references.

cache, write-back: A D-cache where CPU write data is kept in the cache but not (for the time being) sent to main memory. The cache line is marked as "dirty." The data gets written back to main memory either when that line in the cache is needed for data from some other location or when the line is deliberately targeted by a write-back operation.

cache, write-through: A D-cache where every write operation is made both to the cache (if the access hits a cached location) and simultaneously to memory. The advantage is that the cache never contains data that is not already in memory, so cache lines can be freely discarded.

Usually, the data bound for memory can be stored in a *write buffer* while the memory system's (relatively slow) write cycle runs, so the CPU does not have to wait for the memory write to finish.

Write-through caches work very well as long as the memory cycles fast enough to absorb writes at something a little higher than the CPU's average write rate.

cache aliases: In a memory-mapped OS you can sometimes have the same data mapped at different locations. This can happen with data shared between two tasks' distinct address spaces or with data for which there is a separate application and kernel view.

Now, many MIPS CPUs use program (virtual) addresses to index the cache—it saves time to be able to start the cache search in parallel with translating the address. But if different program addresses can access the same data, we could end up with the same data in the cache at two locations—a cache alias. If we then start writing the locations, that's going to go horribly wrong.

Cache aliases turn out to be avoidable. The paged address translation used in MIPS CPUs means that at least 12 low-order addresses are unchanged by translation, and it turns out that you only use about 15 low-order address bits to index the biggest likely cache. Kernel software needs to be careful when generating multiple different addresses for a page that the pages are allocated to program addresses where bits 12–15 are the same.

cache coherency: The name for that state of grace where the contents of your cache will always deliver precisely what your program and the rest of the system has stored into the cache/memory combination. Many complex techniques and hardware tricks are deployed in the search for coherency; MIPS CPUs like the R4000SC and R10000 have clever features in the cache for this. But such technology is not much used outside the world of large server computers, as yet.

cache flush: A somewhat ambiguous term, which we think is worth avoiding. It is never quite clear whether it means write back or invalidate or both.

cache hit: What happens when you look in the cache and find what you were looking for.

cache index: All practical caches are either direct mapped, consisting of a single memory array, or n-way set associative for some small n; in an n-way set-associative cache each set behaves like a direct-mapped cache. The cache index is that part of the address that is used to select the cache location in each set.

cache invalidation: Marks a line of cache data as no longer to be used. There's always some kind of valid bit in the control bits of the cache line for this purpose. It is an essential part of initialization for a MIPS CPU.

cache isolation: The basic mechanism for D-cache maintenance on pre-R4000 MIPS CPUs, described in Section 4.9. It puts the CPU into a mode where data loads/stores occur only to the cache and not to memory. In this mode partial-word stores cause the cache line to be invalidated.

cache line size: Each cache slot can hold one or more words of data, and the chunk of data marked with a single address tag is called a line. Big lines save tag space and can make for more efficient refill; but big lines waste space by loading more data you don't need.

The best line size tends to increase as you get further from the CPU and for big cache miss penalties. MIPS I CPUs always had 1-word data cache lines, but later CPUs tend to favor 4 or 8 words.

cache miss: What happens when you look in the cache and don't find what you are looking for.

cache miss penalty: The time the CPU spends stalled when it misses in the cache, which depends on the system's memory response time.

cache profiling: Measuring the cache traffic generated when a particular program runs, with a view to rearranging the program in memory to minimize the number of cache misses. It is not clear how practicable this is except for very small programs or sections of program.

cache refill: The memory read that is used to obtain a cache line of data after a cache miss. This is first read into the cache, and the CPU then restarts execution, this time "hitting" in the cache.

cache set: One chunk of a set-associative cache.

cache simulator: A software tool used for cache profiling.

cache tag: The information held with the cache line that identifies the main memory location of the data.

cache write back: The process that takes the contents of a cache line and copies them back into the appropriate block of main memory. It's usually performed conditionally, because cache lines have a "dirty" flag that remembers when they've been written since being fetched from memory.

cacheable: Used of an address region or a page defined by the memory translation system.

CacheERR register: CPU control (coprocessor 0) register in R4000 CPUs and descendants, full of information for analyzing and fixing cache parity/ECC errors.

cacheop: A CPU control instruction found in R4000 and later CPUs that provides all kinds of cache line maintenance operations.

callee: In a function call, the function that is called.

caller: In a function call, the function where the call instruction is found and where control is returned to afterward.

Cause register: CPU control register that, following a trap, tells you what kind of trap it was. **Cause** also shows you which external interrupt signals are active.

ceiling: A floating-point-to-integer conversion, rounded to the nearest integer that is as least as positive. Implemented by the MIPS instruction **ceil**.

char: C name for a small quantity used to hold character codes. In MIPS CPUs (and practically always, nowadays) this is a single byte.

CISC: An acronym used to refer to non-RISC architectures. In this book, we mean architectures like the DEC VAX, Motorola 680x0, and Intel x86 (32-bit version). All these instruction sets were invented before the great RISC discovery and all are much harder than a RISC CPU to execute fast.

clock cycle: The period of the CPU's clock signal. For a RISC CPU, this is the rate at which successive pipeline stages run.

CMOS: The transistor technology used to make all practical MIPS CPUs. CMOS chips are denser and use less power per transistor than any other kind, so they are favored for leading-edge integration. With CPUs the ability to put a lot of circuitry into a small space has proven to be the key performance factor, so all fast CPUs are now CMOS.

COFF: A standard object file format, which turned out to be far too loosely specified to let tools interoperate.

coherency: See *cache coherency*.

Compare register: CPU control register provided on CPUs for implementing a timer (all MIPS III CPUs do this, as do some MIPS I CPUs such as IDT's R3041).

Config register: CPU control register for configuring basic CPU behavior. It is standard on MIPS III and also found in some MIPS I derivatives.

console: The putative I/O channel on which messages can be sent for the user and user input can be read.

const: C data declaration attribute, implying that the data is read-only. It will often then be packed together with the instructions.

Context register: CPU control register seen only on CPU types with a TLB. Provides a fast way to process TLB misses on systems using a certain arrangement of page tables.

context switch: The job of changing the software environment from one task to another in a multitasking OS.

coprocessor: Some part of the CPU, or some other closely coupled machine part, that executes some particular set of reserved instruction encodings. This is a MIPS architecture concept that has succeeded in separating off optional or implementation-dependent parts of the instruction set and thus reducing the changes to the mainstream instruction set. It's been fairly successful, but the nomenclature has caused a lot of confusion.

coprocessor condition: Every coprocessor subset of special instructions in the MIPS architecture gets a single bit for communicating status to the integer CPU, tested by a **bcxt/bcxf** instruction. See Chapter 3.

coprocessor conditional branches: *The instructions* such as **bc0t** *label* branch according to the sense of coprocessor conditions which are usually CPU input signals; these can be useful sometimes. If there is a floating-point unit on-chip, coprocessor condition bit 1 is hardwired to the FP condition code.

coprocessor 0: The (rather fuzzily defined) bits of CPU function that are connected with the privileged control instructions for memory mapping, exception handling, and such like.

core CPU: See *ASIC-core CPU.*

Count register: Continuously running timer register, available in R4000-like CPUs and some earlier ones.

CPCOND: See *coprocessor conditional branches.*

cpp: The C preprocessor program.

CSE (common subexpression elimination): The most fundamental optimization step for an optimizing compiler (see Section 10.12).

cycle: Clock cycle.

D-cache: Data cache (MIPS CPUs always have separate instruction and data caches).

D-TLB: Some MIPS processors have tiny separate translation caches fed from the main TLB to avoid a resource conflict when translating both instruction and data addresses; a D-TLB is specifically for data and is found on the R4600 CPU and its successors. Its operation is invisible to software, other than an occasional extra clock spent fetching main TLB entries.

data dependencies: The relationship between an instruction that produces a value in a register and a subsequent instruction that wants to use that value.

data path swapper: See *byte-swap*.

data/instruction cache coherency: The job of keeping the I-cache and D-cache coherent. No MIPS CPU does this for you; it is vital to invalidate I-cache locations whenever you write or modify an instruction stream. See *cache coherency*.

debugger: A software tool for controlling and interrogating a running program.

DECstation: Digital Equipment Corporation's trade name for the MIPS-architecture workstations they produced between 1990 and 1993.

delayed branches: See *branch delay slot*.

delayed loads: See *load delay slot*.

demand paging: A process by which a program is loaded incrementally. It relies on an OS and underlying hardware that can implement virtual memory—references to thus-far-unloaded parts of the program are caught by the OS, which reads in the relevant data, maps it so that the program will see it in the right place, and then returns to the program, re-executing the reference that failed. It's called paging because the unit of memory translation and loading is a fixed-size block called a page.

denormalized: A floating-point number is denormalized when it is holding a value too small to be represented with the usual precision. The way the IEEE754 standard is defined means that it is quite hard for hardware to cope directly with denormalized representations, so MIPS CPUs always trap when presented with them or asked to compute them.

dereferencing: A fancy term for following a pointer and obtaining the memory data it points at.

direct mapped: See *cache, direct-mapped*.

directive: One of the terms used for the pieces of an assembler program that don't generate machine instructions but that tell the assembler what to do; for example, `.globl`. They're also called "pseudo-ops."

dirty: In a virtual memory system, this describes the state of a page of memory that has been written to since it was last fetched from or written back to secondary storage. Dirty pages must not be lost.

disassembler: A program that takes a binary instruction sequence in memory and produces a readable listing in assembler mnemonics.

DMA (direct memory access): An external device transferring data to or from memory without CPU intervention.

double: C and assembler language name for a double-precision (64-bit) floating-point number.

doubleword: The preferred term for a 64-bit data item (not used for floating point) in MIPS architecture descriptions.

download: The act of transferring data from host to target (in case of doubt, host tends to mean the machine to which the user is connected).

DRAM: Used sloppily to refer to large memory systems (which are usually built from DRAM components). Sometimes used less sloppily to discuss the typical attributes of memories built from DRAMs.

DSP (digital signal processor): A particular style of microprocessor aimed at applications that process a stream of data derived from an analog-to-digital convertor. DSPs focus on speed at certain popular analog algorithms, such as FFT, and are good at multiplying. Compared to a general-purpose processor they often lack precision, easy programming in high-level language, and the facilities to build basic OS facilities. But the definition of DSP is not much more firm than that of RISC.

duplicate tags: See *cache, duplicate tags.*

dword: The MIPS assembler name for a 64-bit integer datum, or doubleword.

dynamic linking: A term for the process by which an application finds a library subroutine at run time, immortalized by Microsoft as DLLs. Run-time linking with shared library functions is part of the MIPS/ABI standard and is used in every modern desktop and server OS; it is not yet relevant to embedded systems.

dynamic variables: An old-fashioned programmer's term for variables (like those defined inside C functions) that are really or notionally kept on the stack.

ECC (error correcting code): Stored data is accompanied by check bits that are not only effective in diagnosing corruption but permit errors (supposed to affect only a small number of bits) to be rectified. Some MIPS R4x00 CPUs use an ECC that adds 8 check bits to each 64-bit doubleword for data both in the caches and on the memory bus (and probably in memory too, though that's a system design decision).

ECL (emitter-coupled logic): An electrical standard for deciding whether a signal represents a one or a zero. ECL allows faster transitions and less noise susceptibility than the more common standard TTL, but with a penalty in higher power consumption. It's now pretty much obsolete. The name describes the transistor implementation originally used in this sort of chip.

ECOFF (extended common object file format): An object code format, particularly used by MIPS Corporation and Silicon Graphics, extensively evolved from Unix Systems Laboratories' COFF (common object file format).

ELF (executable and linking format): An object code format defined by Univel for UNIX SVR4.2, and which is mandated by the MIPS ABI standard.

emacs: The Swiss Army knife of text editors and the essential tool for real programmers, emacs runs the Lisp program of your choice every time you hit a key. It is indescribably customizable, so with any job you do you get small and valuable contributions from numerous people who went before you. This book was written with it.

embedded: Describes a computer system that is part of a larger object that is not (primarily) seen as a computer. Describes everything from video games to glass furnace controllers.

emulator: See *in-circuit emulator; software instruction emulators.*

endianness: Whether a machine is big-endian or little-endian. See Chapter 11.

endif: The end of a piece of code conditionally included by the magic of cpp. See also `ifdef, ifndef`.

EntryHi/EntryLo register: CPU control registers implemented only in CPUs with a TLB. Used to stage data to and from TLB entries.

EPC (exception program counter) register: CPU control register telling you where to restart the CPU after an exception.

epilogue: See *function epilogue.*

EPROM (erasable programmable read-only memory): The device most commonly used to provide read-only code for system bootstrap; used sloppily here to mean the location of that read-only code.

errno: The name of the global variable used for reporting I/O errors in most C libraries.

ErrorEPC register: R4x00 and later CPUs detect cache errors, and to allow them to do so even if the CPU is halfway through some critical (but regular) exception handler the cache-error system has its own separate register for remembering where to return to. See section 4.10.1.

ExcCode: The bitfield in the `Cause` register that contains a code showing what type of exception just occurred.

exception: In the MIPS architecture, an exception is any interrupt or trap that causes control to be diverted to one of the two trap entry points.

exception, IEEE: See *floating-point (IEEE) exception*. Alas, this is a different animal from a MIPS exception.

exception victim: On an exception, the victim is the first instruction in sequence *not* to be run (yet) as a result of the exception. For exceptions that are caused by the CPU's own activity, the victim is also the instruction that led to the exception. It's also normally the point to which control returns after the exception; but not always, because of the effect of branch delays.

Executable: Describes a file of object code that is ready to run.

exponent: Part of a floating-point number. See Chapter 7.

extended floating point: Not provided by the MIPS hardware, this usually refers to a floating-point format that uses more than 64 bits of storage (80 bits is popular).

extern: C data attribute for a variable that is defined in another module.

fault, faulting: See *page fault*.

FCC (Floating-point unit condition code): MIPS I through MIPS III CPUs have only one; higher-numbered ISAs have eight.

FCR31 register: Another name for `fpcsr` (floating-point control/status register). See Chapter 7.

FIFO (First-in, first-out): A queue that temporarily holds data, where the items have to come out in the same order they went in.

fixup: In object code, this is the action of a linker/locator program when it adjusts addresses in the instruction or data segments to match the location at which the program will eventually execute.

flag: Used here (and often in computer books) to mean a single-bit field in a control register.

floating-point accelerator (FPA): The name for the part of the MIPS CPU that does floating-point math. Historically, it was a separate chip.

floating-point bias: An offset added to the exponent of a floating-point number held in IEEE format to make sure that the exponent is positive for all legitimate values.

floating-point condition code/flag: A single bit set by FP compare instructions, which is communicated back to the main part of the CPU and tested by `bc1t` and `bc1f` instructions.

floating-point emulation trap: A trap taken by the CPU when it cannot implement a floating-point (coprocessor 1) operation. A software trap handler can be built that mimics the action of the FPA and returns control, so that application software need not know whether FPA hardware is installed or not. The software routine is likely to be 50–300 times slower.

floating-point (IEEE) exception: The IEEE754 standard for floating-point computation considers the possibility that the result can be "exceptional"—a catch-all term for various kinds of result that some users may not be happy with. The standard requires that conforming CPUs allow each type of exception to be caught—and then it gets confusing, because the MIPS mechanism for catching events in general is also called exception.

foo: The ubiquitous name for a junk or worthless file.

Fortran: Early computer language favored for scientific and numerical uses, where its reasonable portability outweighed its appalling flaws.

FP: Floating point.

fp (frame pointer) register: A CPU general-purpose register (`$30`) sometimes used conventionally to mark the base address of a *stack frame*.

FPA: Floating-point accelerator.

fpcond: Another name for the FP condition bit (also known as coprocessor 1 condition bit).

fpcsr register: The MIPS FPA's control/status register. See Chapter 7.

fraction, fractional part: Part of a floating-point value. (Also called the *mantissa*.) See Chapter 7.

frame, framesize: See *stack frame*.

Free Software Foundation: The Lone Rangers of free software and the (loose) organization that keeps the copyright of GNU software.

fully associative: See *associative store*.

function: The C language name for a subroutine, which we use through most of this book.

function epilogue: In assembler code, the stereotyped sequence of instructions and directives found at the end of a function and concerned with returning control to the caller.

function inlining: An optimization offered by advanced compilers, where a function call is replaced by an interpolated copy of the complete instruction sequence of the called function. In many architectures this is a big win (for very small functions) because it eliminates the function-call overhead. In the MIPS architecture the function-call overhead is negligible, but inlining is still sometimes valuable because it allows the optimizer to work on the function in context.

function prologue: In assembler language, a stereotyped set of instructions and directives that start a function, saving registers and setting up the stack frame.

gcc: The usual name for the *GNU C compiler*.

gdb: The GNU debugger, partner to GNU C.

global: Old-fashioned programmer's name for a data item whose name is known and whose value may be accessed across a whole program. Sloppily extended to any named data item that is awarded its own storage location—and that should properly be called static.

global pointer: The MIPS **gp** register, used in some MIPS programs to provide efficient access to those C data items defined as static or extern that live at a fixed program address. See Section 2.2.1.

globl: Assembler declaration attribute for data items or code entry points that are to be visible from outside the module.

GNU: The name of the Free Software Foundation's project to provide freely redistributable versions for all the components of a unix-like OS (with the possible exception of the kernel itself).

GNU C compiler: Free product of an extraordinary interaction between maverick programmer and Free Software Foundation leading light Richard Stallman and a diverse collection of volunteers from all over the world. GNU C is the best compiler for MIPS targets unless you're using a Silicon Graphics workstation.

GOT (global offset table): An essential part of the dynamic linking mechanism underlying MIPS/ABI applications.

gp register: CPU register **$28**, often used as a pointer to program data. Program data that can be linked within ±32K of the pointer value can be loaded with a single instruction. Not all toolchains, nor all run-time environments, support this.

halfword: MIPS architecture name for a 16-bit data type.

hazard: See *pipeline hazard*.

heap: Program data space allocated at runtime.

Heinrich, Joe: Esteemed author of the definitive *MIPS User's Manual*, from which almost all official MIPS ISA manuals are derived.

Hennessy, John: MIPS's intellectual father and founding parent, Professor Hennessy led the original MIPS research project at Stanford University.

hit, cache: See *cache hit*.

I-cache: Instruction cache (MIPS CPUs always have separate instruction and data caches). The I-cache is called upon when the CPU reads instructions.

ICU: Interrupt control unit.

idempotent: A mathematician's term for an operation that has the same effect when done twice as done once (and hence also the same effect when done nine times or 99). Stirring your coffee is an idempotent operation, but adding sugar isn't.

When a pipelined CPU takes an exception, and subsequently returns to the interrupted task, it's difficult to make sure that everything gets done exactly once; if you can make some of the operations idempotent, the system can survive a spuriously duplicated operation. All MIPS branch instructions, for example, are idempotent.

IDT: Integrated Device Technology Corporation.

IEEE: An acronym for the Institute of Electrical and Electronics Engineers. This professional body has done a lot to promulgate standards in computing. Their work is often more practicable, sensible, and constructive than that of other standards bodies.

IEEE754 floating-point standard: An industry standard for the representation of arithmetic values. This standard mandates the precise behavior of a group of basic functions, providing a stable base for the development of portable numeric algorithms.

`ifdef,ifndef:` `#ifdef` and `#endif` bracket conditionally compiled code in the C language. This feature is actually affected by the *C preprocessor* and so can be used in other languages too.

immediate: In instruction set descriptions, an immediate value is a constant that is embedded in the code sequence. In assembler language, it is any constant value.

implementation: Used in opposition to "architecture." In this book it most often means we're talking about how something is done in some particular CPU.

in-circuit emulator (ICE): A device that replaces a CPU chip with a module that, as well as being able to exactly imitate the behavior of the CPU, provides some means to control execution and examine CPU internals. Microprocessor ICE units are inevitably based on a version of the microprocessor chip (often a higher-speed grade).

It is often possible to do development without an ICE—and they are expensive and can prove troublesome.

index register: CPU control register used to define which TLB entry's contents will be read into or written from **EntryHi/EntryLo**.

index, cache: See *cache index.*

Indy: A popular Silicon Graphics workstation, powered by a MIPS CPU.

inexact: Describes a floating-point calculation that has lost precision. Note that this happens very frequently on the most everyday calculations; for example, the number 1/3 has no exact representation. IEEE754 compliance requires that MIPS CPUs can trap on an inexact result, but nobody ever turns that trap on.

infinity: A floating-point data value standing in for any value too big (or too negative) to represent. IEEE754 defines how computations with positive and negative versions of infinity should behave.

inline, inlined, inlining: See *function inlining.*

instruction scheduling: The process of moving instructions around to exploit the CPU's pipelining for maximum performance. On a simple pipelined MIPS CPU, that usually comes down to making the best use of delay slots. This is done by the compiler and (sometimes) by the assembler.

instruction set architecture (ISA): The functional description of the CPU, which defines exactly what it does with any legitimate instruction stream (but does not have to define how it is implemented).

instruction synthesis by assembler: The MIPS instruction set omits many useful and familiar operations (such as an instruction to load a constant outside the range ±32K). Most assemblers for the MIPS architecture will accept instructions (sometimes called macro-instructions) that they implement with a short sequence of machine instructions.

int: The C name for an integer data type. The language doesn't define how many bits are used to implement an int, and this freedom is intended to allow compilers to choose something that is efficient on the target machine.

interlock: A hardware feature where the execution of one instruction is delayed until something is ready. There are few interlocks in the MIPS architecture.

interrupt: An external signal that can cause an exception (if not masked).

interrupt mask: A bit-per-interrupt mask, held in the CPU status register, that determines which interrupt inputs are allowed to cause an interrupt at any given time.

interrupt priority: In many architectures the interrupt inputs have built-in priority; an interrupt will not take effect during the execution of an interrupt handler at equal or higher priority. The MIPS hardware doesn't do this, but the system software often imposes a conventional priority on the interrupt inputs.

interruptible: Generally used of a piece of program where an interrupt can be tolerated (and where the programmer has therefore allowed interrupts to occur).

invalidation: See *cache invalidation*.

IPL (interrupt priority level): A concept used in designing and describing operating systems. See Section 5.8.

Irix: The operating system on the Silicon Graphics workstations/servers.

ISA: Instruction set architecture.

isolate cache: See *cache isolation*.

issue, instruction: When talking about computer implementations, issue is the point where some CPU resources get used to begin doing the operations associated with some instruction.

I-TLB: A tiny hardware table duplicating information from the *TLB* that is used for translating instruction addresses without having to fight the hardware that is translating data addresses. Called the "micro-TLB" in early MIPS CPUs. It is not visible to software, unless you're counting time so carefully that you notice the one-clock pause in execution when an I-fetch has to access the main TLB.

JPEG: A standard for compressing image data.

JTAG: A standard for connecting electronic components to implement test functions. The JTAG signals are intended to be daisy chained through all the active components in a design, allowing one single point of access for everything. It's never been successful enough to do that, but it remains a popular and useful way of connecting up on-chip test functions.

jump and link (jal) instruction: MIPS instruction set name for a function call, which puts the return address (the link) into `ra`.

k0 and k1 registers: Two general-purpose registers that are reserved, by convention, for the use of trap handlers. It is difficult to contrive a trap handler that does not trash at least one register.

kernel: The smallest separately compiled unit of an operating system that contains task scheduling functions. Some OSs (like UNIX) are monolithic with big kernels that do a lot; some are modular with small kernels surrounded by helper tasks.

kernel privilege: For a protected CPU, a state where it's allowed to do anything. That's usually how it boots up; and in small systems or simple operating systems, that's how it stays.

Kernighan, Brian: Co-author (with Denis Richie) of the *C Programming Handbook*, and generally held responsible for systematizing the C language. No programmer should ever read another book about C.

kludge: An engineer's derogatory expression for a quick and dirty fix.

kseg0, kseg1: The unmapped address spaces (actually, they are mapped in the sense that the resulting physical addresses are in the low 512MB). kseg0 is for cached references and kseg1 for uncached references. Standalone programs, or programs using simple OSs, are likely to run wholly in kseg0/kseg1.

KSU, KU: The kernel/user privilege field in the status register (described in Section 3.3.)

kuseg: The low half of the MIPS program address space, which is accessible by programs running with user privileges and always translated (in CPUs equipped with a TLB). See Figure 2.1.

latency: The delay attributable to some unit or other. Memory read latency is the time taken for memory to deliver some data and is generally a much more important (and more neglected) parameter than bandwidth.

leaf function: A function that itself contains no other function call. This kind of function can return directly to the **ra** register and typically uses no stack space.

level sensitive: An attribute of a signal (particularly an interrupt signal). MIPS interrupt inputs are level sensitive; they will cause an interrupt any time they are active and unmasked.

library: See *object code library*.

line size: See *cache line size*.

linker: A program that joins together separately compiled object code modules, resolving external references.

little-endian: An architecture where the least-significant part of a multibyte integer is stored at the lowest byte address; see Section 11.6.

LLAddr register: A CPU control (coprocessor 0) register in R4000 and later CPUs, with no discernible software use outside diagnostics. It holds an address from a previous load-linked (**11**) instruction.

lo, hi registers: Dedicated output registers of the integer multiply/divide unit. These registers are interlocked—an attempt to copy data from them into a general-purpose register will be stalled until the multiply/divide can complete.

load delay: See *load delay slot*.

load delay slot: The position in the instruction sequence immediately following a load. An instruction in the load delay slot cannot use the value just loaded (the results would be unpredictable). The compiler, assembler, or programmer may move code around to try to make best use of load delay slots, but sometimes you just have to put a "**nop**" there.

load/store architecture: Describes an ISA like MIPS, where memory data can be accessed only by explicit load and store instructions. Many other architectures define instructions (e.g., "push" or arithmetic on a memory variable) that implicitly access memory.

loader: A program that takes an object code module and assigns fixed program addresses to instructions and data, in order to make an executable file.

local variable: A named data item accessible only within the module currently being compiled/assembled.

locality of reference: The tendency of programs to focus a large number of memory references on a small subset of memory locations (at least in the short term). It's what makes caches useful.

logic analyzer: A piece of test equipment that simultaneously monitors the logic level (i.e., as 1 or 0) of many signals. It is often used to keep a list of the addresses of accesses made by a microprocessor.

`long`: C extra-precision integer; it is 32 bits on MIPS (same as an `int`).

loop unrolling: An optimization used by advanced compilers. Program loops are compiled to code that can implement several iterations of the loop without branching out of line. This can be particularly advantageous on architectures (unlike MIPS) where a long pipeline and instruction prefetching makes taken branches costly. Even on the MIPS architecture, however, it can help by allowing intermingling of code from different loop iterations.

LSI: LSI Logic Corporation, which makes MIPS CPUs—these days, mostly as ASIC core components to be integrated by their customers into systems on a chip.

MAC (multiply/accumulate): An instruction that both does multiplications and keeps a running total of the results. Several 90s MIPS CPUs implement such instructions in the integer multiplier, accumulating in the multiply unit's own **hi/lo** output register. However, these instructions tend to be called **mad**.

macro: A "word" in a computer language that will be replaced by some predefined textual substitution before compilation/assembly. More specifically, it's something defined in a C preprocessor `#define` statement.

MAD, MADD: See *multiply-add*.

mantissa: Part of the representation of a floating-point number. (Also called *fraction* or *fractional part*.) See Chapter 7.

mapped: Term used to describe a range of addresses generated by a program that will be translated in some nontrivial way before appearing as physical addresses.

mask: A bitfield used to select part of a data structure with a bitwise logical "and" operation.

MDMX: A MIPS-proposed extension to the MIPS IV ISA that uses the FP registers to represent small arrays of integers (of length 8 or 16 bits) and provides arithmetic- and graphics-oriented operations that do the same thing simultaneously to all the integers in the array. This is similar to the MMX to the x86 architecture defined by Intel and available in their Pentium-MMX CPUs.

This kind of operation is thought to be useful for accelerating common tasks in audio and video processing (multimedia).

`memcpy()`: A function from the standard C library for copying blocks of data.

micro-TLB: The MIPS TLB is dedicated to translating data addresses. Use of the TLB to translate addresses for I-fetch would lead to resource conflict and would slow the CPU. The micro TLB remembers the last used I-fetch program page and physical page and saves a reference to the real TLB until execution crosses a page boundary. When this happens, a one-clock-cycle stall occurs while the micro-TLB is refilled from the data TLB.

microcode: Many CPUs consist of a low-level core (the micro-engine) programmed with a wide, obscure machine language (microcode). Instructions from the official ISA are implemented by microcode subroutines.

During the 70s microcode was the favored way of managing the complexity of a CPU design. As better design tools were developed in the 80s, particularly better circuit simulators, it became possible to go back to implementing ISA operations directly in hardware. But many CPUs (particularly CISCs) still use microcode for complicated or obscure instructions.

MiniRISC: An LSI Logic trade name for a series of MIPS CPU cores optimized for small size.

MIPS: We use this as the name of the architecture.

MIPS/ABI: The latest standard for MIPS applications, supported by all UNIX system vendors using the MIPS architecture in big-endian form.

MIPS Corporation: The organization that commercialized and promoted the MIPS architecture. Sometimes sloppily used to include its successor, the MIPS Technologies group within Silicon Graphics.

MIPS silicon vendor: Any company building and selling MIPS CPUs or components containing MIPS CPUs. The roll call includes LSI Logic, IDT, Performance Semiconductor, NEC, Siemens, Toshiba, NKK, Philips Semiconductor, QED, and Sony.

MIPS System VR3, RISC/OS, and Irix: These are all ways of referring to the same basic operating system, a derivative of UNIX System V Release 3. This OS supports RISCware applications.

MIPS UMIPS 4.3BSD: MIPS Corporation's first operating system was a derivative of Berkeley's BSD4.3 version of UNIX.

MIPSEB, MIPSEL: These are the words you use to request big-endian and little-endian output (respectively) from most MIPS compiler toolchains.

misaligned: Unaligned.

MMU (memory management unit): The only memory management hardware provided in the MIPS architecture is the *TLB*, which can translate program addresses from any of up to 64 pages into physical addresses.

Modula-2: Pascal programming language with a standardized separate-compilation extension. Mostly used in European computer science education.

MPEG: Standard for the efficient (compressed) digital representation of moving video images.

MTI (MIPS Technologies, Inc.): Subsidiary of Silicon Graphics and inheritor of the MIPS architecture.

multiply-add: A single instruction that multiplies two numbers together and then performs an addition sum. Multiply-add instructions are often a powerful and effective way of encoding numerical algorithms, particularly for floating point. MIPS IV and higher CPUs have an FP instruction called `madd`, and Toshiba's R3900 and its descendants have a genuine integer multiply-add.

Several other variant CPUs of the 90s have integer instructions called MAD or something like it, but they are strictly multiply-accumulate instructions, where the addend and results must both use a fixed register.

multiprocessor: A system with multiple processing elements; in practice we'll use it only when there are multiple similar processing elements dynamically scheduled to run a common pool of programs.

multitasking: A CPU operating system that supports multiple threads of control. At the most mundane level, a thread is characterized by a stack and a next-instruction address. There needs to be some scheduler in the OS that picks which task to run next and makes sure that all tasks make progress.

NaN (not a number): A special floating-point value defined by IEEE754 as the value to be returned from operations presented with illegal operands.

naturally aligned: A datum of length n is naturally aligned if its base address is zero mod n. A word is naturally aligned if it is on a 4-byte boundary; a halfword is naturally aligned if it is on a 2-byte boundary; see also *alignment*.

NEC: Electronic component manufacturer and leading supplier of MIPS CPU chips.

nested exception/interrupt: What happens when you get a MIPS exception while still executing the exception handler from the last one. This is sometimes OK.

nibble: A 4-bit quantity.

NKK: The semiconductor division of a large Japanese trading company. NKK started selling MIPS CPUs about 1994, in a generally low-key way, with second sources of lDT R46xx products.

NMI (nonmaskable interrupt): Available (both as an input signal and as an event) on R4000 and subsequent components. On MIPS CPUs, it's not quite clear whether it's a nonmaskable interrupt or a very soft reset; there's no real difference.

noalias, noat, nobopt, nomacro, noreorder, novolatile: Assembler language controls, which turn off various aspects of the way the assembler works. See Section 9.5.6 for details.

nonleaf function: A function that somewhere calls another function. Normally the compiler will translate them with a function prologue that saves the return address (and possibly other register values) on a stack and a function epilogue that restores these values.

nonvolatile memory: Applied to any memory technology that retains data with the system power off.

nop, no-op: No operation. On MIPS this is actually an alias for `sllv zero, zero, zero`, which doesn't have much effect; its binary code is all zeroes.

normalize: The action of converting a floating-point value to the normalized form by shifting the mantissa and modifying the exponent. The IEEE standard for all except very small numbers is a normalized representation.

NT: Windows/NT.

nullified: Applied to an instruction that although it has been started in the pipeline, will not be allowed to have any effect—its write back is suppressed and it's not allowed to cause an exception. In general, instructions never have any effect until at least the MEM pipestage. In 32-bit MIPS CPUs, instructions are only nullified when an exception occurs before they have committed to the MEM stage, but from MIPS II onward this technique is used more widely, for example to implement the "likely" variants of branch instructions.

NVRAM: Nonvolatile RAM, used rather generically to refer to any writable storage that is preserved while the system is powered down.

objdump: Typical name for a utility program that decodes and prints information from an object file.

object code: A special file format containing compiled program source and data, in a form that can be quickly and easily converted to executable format.

object code library: A file holding several (separately compiled) modules of object code, together with an index showing what public function or variable names are exported by each module. Sometimes called an archive. The system linker can accept libraries as well as object modules and will link only those modules from the library that are required to satisfy external references from the supplied modules.

octal: Base 8 notation for binary numbers, traditionally written with a leading zero. In fact, an integer written with a leading zero will most likely be interpreted as octal by the assembler.

offset: The name commonly used for the signed 16-bit integer field used in many MIPS instruction types.

op-code: The field of the binary representation of an instruction that is constant for a given instruction mnemonic, excluding register selectors, embedded constants, and so on.

operand: A value used by an operation.

optimizer: The part of a compiler that transforms one correct representation of a program into a different equivalent representation that (it is to be hoped) is either smaller or likely to run faster.

OS: Operating system.

overflow: When the result of an operation is too big to be represented in the output format.

padding: Spaces left in memory data structures and representations that are caused by the compiler's need to align data to the boundaries the hardware prefers.

page: A chunk of memory, a power-of-two bytes in size and naturally aligned, that is the unit of memory handled by the address translation system. Most MIPS operating systems deal in 4KB fixed-size pages, but the hardware is sometimes capable of mixing translations with a number of different page sizes.

page fault: An OS term meaning an event where a program accesses a location in a page for which there is no valid physical page translation assigned; in such an OS a page fault is resolved by fetching the appropriate contents, allocating physical memory, setting up the translation, and restarting the program at the offending instruction.

page mode memory: A way of using a DRAM memory array. In DRAMs it is much faster to make repeated access to a single region of memory where the row address presented to the DRAM component is common. Some memory controllers use this to optimize accesses where the CPU repeatedly reads/writes a particular area of memory.

page table: A possible implementation of the TLB miss exception is to keep a large number of page translations in a table indexed by the high-order virtual address; such a structure is called a page table.

paged: A memory management system (such as MIPS) where fixed-size pages (in MIPS they are 4KB in size) are mapped; high bits are translated while the low bits (11 bits for MIPS) are passed through unchanged.

PageMask register: Register used in the MIPS memory management system, see Chapter 6.

parameter: When talking about subroutines, some programmers talk about passing parameters to subroutines and some (following the C programming manual) talk about passing arguments to functions. They're talking about the same thing.

parity: The simplest error check. A redundant bit is added to a byte or other multibit datum and set so that the total number of 1 bits (including the parity bit) is made odd (odd parity) or even (even parity).

partial word: A piece of data less than a whole word but that the hardware can transfer as a unit. In the MIPS architecture this can be 1, 2, or 3 bytes.

Pascal: Computing language invented by Niklaus Wirth in the 70s as a simplified block-structured language suitable for teaching. There was a time during the 80s when Pascal was seriously canvassed as an alternative to C, but with no consensus on the desperately needed extensions it didn't succeed.

Patterson, David: From the MIPS point of view, he is Professor Hennessy's sidekick and co-author (see Hennessy and Patterson). Outside the MIPS field, David Patterson is probably just as famous, having led the Berkeley RISC project from which the Sparc descended.

PC (program counter): Shorthand for the address of the instruction currently being executed by a CPU.

PC relative: An instruction is PC relative if it uses an address that is encoded as an offset from the instruction's own location. PC-relative branches within modules are convenient because they need no fixing when the entire module is shifted in memory; this is a step toward *position-independent code*.

PCI: I/O bus invented for PCs about 1993 and now a universal way of gluing I/O controllers to computers.

PDP-11: The world's favorite minicomputer in the 70s, made by DEC. It was vastly influential, because good design decisions and superb documentation made it the best thing for programmers to play with.

peephole optimization: A form of optimization that recognizes particular patterns of instruction sequence and replaces them by shorter, simpler patterns. Peephole optimizations are not terribly important for RISCs, but they are very important to CISCs, where they provide the only mechanism by which compilers can exploit complex instructions.

PFN (physical frame number): The high-order part of the physical address, which is the output of the paged MMU.

Philips: A chip company that makes MIPS chips, mostly as cores.

physical address: The address that appears on the outer pins of your CPU and that is passed on to main memory and the I/O system. Not the same as the program address (virtual address).

physical cache: Short for "cache that is physically indexed and physically tagged," meaning that the physical (translated) address is used for both these functions.

PIC: See *position-independent code.*

pinout: For a chip, the allocation of signals to physical pins (and perhaps the list of interface signals required).

pipeline: The critical architectural feature by which several instructions are executed at once; see Section 1.1.

pipeline concealment by assembler: MIPS assembler language does not usually require the programmer to take account of the pipeline, even though the machine language does. The assembler moves code around, or inserts **nop**s, to prevent unwanted behavior.

pipeline hazard: A case where an instruction sequence won't work due to pipeline problems. Hazards affecting user-level programs are described in Section 1.5.5, and those resulting from CPU control instructions are discussed in Section A.4.

pipeline stall: See *stall.*

pipestage: One of the five phases of the MIPS pipeline.

pixie, pixprof: *Profiling* tools. pixie is a special tool provided by MIPS Corporation that can be used to measure the instruction-by-instruction behavior of programs at high speed. It works by translating the original program binary into a version that includes metering instructions that count the number of times each basic block is executed (a basic block is a section of code delimited by branches and/or branch targets).

pixprof takes the huge undigestible array of counts produced by a pixie run and munches them down into useful statistics. One day, perhaps, these tools or similar ones will be available with other toolkits.

PlayStation: Sony's 1995 games machine, driven by a 32-bit MIPS microprocessor.

porting/portability/portable: Adapting a program designed to work on one computer to work on another. A readily ported program is portable, and you can rate programs according to their portability.

PortSize register: CPU control register provided on IDT's R3041 CPU variant and used to define the bus transfer width used for accesses in various regions.

position-independent code (PIC): Code that can execute correctly regardless of where it is positioned in program address space. PIC is usually produced by making sure all references are *PC relative*. PIC is an essential part of the MIPS ABI standard, where sharable library code must be compiled to be position independent. Unfortunately, the MIPS architecture is poorly adapted for PIC.

POSIX: A still-evolving IEEE standard for the programming interface provided by a compliant operating system.

PostScript: A computing language as well as a digital way of representing a printed page. A truly brilliant idea, originally from Xerox Parc, which failed to take over the world mostly because Adobe Systems, Inc. thought it would make more money by keeping it out of the mass market.

pragma: The C compiler #pragma directive is used to select compiler options from within the source code.

precise exception: Following an exception, all instructions earlier in instruction sequence than the instruction referenced by **EPC** are completed whereas all instructions later in instruction sequence appear never to have happened. The MIPS architecture offers precise exceptions.

precision of data type: The number of bits available for data representation.

preprocessor: See *C preprocessor*.

PRId register: CPU control register (read-only) that tells you the type and revision number of your CPU. You shouldn't rely on it for much.

primary cache: In a system with more than one level of cache, this is the cache closest to the CPU.

privilege level: CPUs capable of running a secure OS must be able to operate at different privilege levels. The MIPS CPU can operate at just two: kernel and user. This is sufficient. User-privilege programs are not allowed to interfere with each other or with the privileged kernel programs; the privileged programs have got to work.

privilege violation: A program trying to do what it's not allowed to, which will cause an exception. The OS must then decide what punishment to mete out.

process: A unix word for that chunk of computation that corresponds to a word on the command line; it consists of a thread of control, a program to run, and an address space in which it can run safely.

profiling: Running a program with some kind of instrumentation to derive information about its resource usage and running.

program address: The software engineer's view of addresses, as generated by the program. Also known as virtual address.

prologue: The mysterious bit at the beginning of a function which is standardized by the needs of the toolchain, OS, or architecture.

PROM (programmable read-only memory): Used sloppily to mean any read-only program memory.

protected OS: An operating system that runs tasks at a low privilege level, where they can be prevented from doing destructive things.

PTEBase: Part of the MIPS `Context` or `XContext` registers and typically loaded with a pointer to an in-memory page table of translations ready to be loaded into the TLB.

QED: Quantum Effect Devices, Inc., the most prolific MIPS CPU design group of the 90s.

quad-precision (128-bit) floating point: Not supported by MIPS hardware, but referred to in some documentation.

R2000, R3000: The original implementations of the MIPS ISA, packaged to use external static RAMs as cache.

`ra` register: CPU register `$31`, conventionally used for the return address from subroutines. This use is supported by the ISA, in that it is used by the `jal` instruction (whose 26-bit target address field leaves it no room to specify which register should receive the return address value).

RAM (random access memory): Computer memory that can be both read and written. See *ROM*.

`Random` register: A CPU control register present only if there is a TLB. It increments continually and autonomously and is used for pseudorandom replacement of TLB entries.

ranlib: A program used to maintain object-code libraries: It makes indexes.

read priority: Because of the write buffer, the CPU package may simultaneously want to do a read and a (delayed) write. It is possible, and can boost performance, to do the read first. If the CPU is always waiting for the read data, the condition is called read priority. But it causes coherency problems when the location being read is affected by a pending write, so few MIPS CPUs tried it (LSI's LR33000 was an exception).

register renaming: A technique for implementing high-performance computers that permits instructions to be executed out of their normal sequence, without this sequence being visible to the programmer. Used (heroically) in the MIPS R10000.

relocatable object module: A chunk of object code that still contains the necessary information and records for a program to be able to find and alter all the offsets and hidden addresses that tie the module to a particular location in memory.

relocation: The process of patching binary object code to make it runnable at a different location in memory.

renormalization: After a floating-point calculation, the number is probably no longer *normalized*. Renormalization is the process of making it so again.

reset: Used in this manual for the event that happens when you activate the Reset input to the CPU; this happens at power-on or system re-initialization.

RISC (reduced instruction set computer): Generic term used in this book for a class of CPU architectures designed for easy pipelining. They were introduced in the second half of the 80s.

RISCware: A long-forgotten standard for interchange of binary programs between different unix-style OSs on MIPS CPUs.

RMW (read-modify-write): A frequently encountered sequence of actions on a storage location of any kind.

ROM (read-only memory): A storage device that can't be written. (More often these days, it means it can't be written in normal operation—there's often some off-line or exceptional means by which it can be reprogrammed.)

rounding mode: Defines the exact behavior of floating-point operations. Configurable through the floating-point status/control register (see Chapter 7).

s0–s9 registers: A collection of CPU general-purpose registers ($16–$23 and $30) conventionally used for variables of function scope. They must be saved by any function that modifies them.

S-cache: See *secondary cache*.

sandbox: A safely fenced off set of resources (disk, filespace, memory, CPU time) within which untrusted programs can be safely run. One of the Internet's best pieces of jargon.

scalar: A simple variable (as distinct from an array or data structure). By analogy, a CPU that operates on single chunks of data at a time is called scalar. This term was originally used to distinguish such a CPU from a vector processor, which can operate on a whole chunk at a time.

scheduler: In a multitasking system, the scheduler is the program that decides what task to run next.

SDE-MIPS: The Algorithmics toolkit for developing programs for MIPS targets, built around GNU C.

SDRAM (synchronous DRAM): Bulk memory chips with a supercharged interface that provide much bigger transfer rates than their predecessor (regular DRAM).

secondary cache: In a system with more than one level of cache, this is the cache second closest to the CPU.

section: The name for the chunks used to separate out the code, various kinds of data, debug information, and so on from a program and to carry them through the object code. Eventually, you get to decide where in memory each section ends up.

segment: See *kseg0,kseg1*.

segmentation: An obsolete approach to memory translation and protection, where program addresses are modified by being added to a base address. It was used in the x86, but it hasn't been needed since the 386.

semaphore: A powerful organizing concept for designing robustly cooperating multitasking or multiprocessing systems; see Section 5.8.4.

set, cache: See *cache set*.

set associative: See *cache, set associative*.

SGI: Silicon Graphics, Inc., dominant supplier of MIPS-powered computers and guardians of the MIPS architecture.

short: In C, the name for an integer data type at least as big as a `char` and no larger than an `int`. In 32- and 64-bit architectures, a `short` seems always to be a 16-bit integer.

signal: A kind of primitive interrupt that is fed to regular programs in a unix-type OS. Improved in Berkeley UNIX, and codified by the POSIX working group to represent a reasonably clean and simple way of communicating simple events in a multitasking system.

silicon vendor: In the MIPS world, one of the companies making and selling MIPS CPUs.

SIMM (single in-line memory module): A way of packaging memory on tiny plug-in circuit boards so you can fit it to PCs just prior to sale or even upgrade them in the field. Like a lot of PC hardware, this has taken over everywhere and is now the most popular way of attaching memory chips.

snooping, snoopy: See *cache, snooping*.

soft reset: In digital electronics, reset is that ubiquitous signal that is asserted to get everything back to a starting condition. For a CPU, it represents an instant roll of the karmic wheel—death and resurrection in a few milliseconds. Sometimes you'd rather reset your CPU in a way that allows it to remember something of its past life—that's a "soft reset." See Section 5.9.

software instruction emulators: A program that emulates the operation of a CPU/memory system. It can be used to check out software too low level to be compatible with a debugger.

software interrupts: Interrupts invoked by setting bits in the **Cause** register and that happen when those bits are unmasked. See Section 5.8.

Sony: Consumer electronics company that used MIPS chips in its PlayStations.

source-level debugger: A debugger that interprets current program state in terms of the source program (instruction lines, variable names, data structures). Source-level debuggers need access to source code, so when working with embedded system software the debugger must run on the host and obtains its information about the program state from a simple debug monitor running on the target.

sp register/stack pointer: CPU register **$29**, used by convention as a stack pointer.

SPARC: The Sun Microsystem RISC architecture, which has sold more desktop systems than any other. Derived fairly directly from the University of California at Berkeley RISC project, whereas MIPS came out of Stanford University. Stanford (on the San Francisco peninsula) is private and somewhat conservative; Berkeley (across the bay) is public and radical. There's a lot of social history in microprocessor design.

sparse address space: Some OS tactics (notably, using an object's address as a long-term handle) work only if you have a much larger address space than you really need, so you can afford to spread things out thinly and allocate space recklessly as a sparse address space. No sparse-address OS has been commercially successful yet.

speculative execution: A CPU implementation technique where the CPU runs instructions before it really knows it should (most commonly, while it's still figuring out whether or not a conditional branch should have happened). Used in the MIPS R10000.

SR register: CPU status register, one of the privileged control registers. Contains control bits for any modes the CPU respects. See Section 3.3 for details.

SRAM (Static RAM): Writable random-access memory that does not require periodic refresh and that has faster initial access time.

SRBrCond: See *BRCOND=0*.

stack: The last in, first out data structure used to record the execution state of CPUs that are running the most interesting languages.

stack argument structure: A conceptual data structure used in Section 10.1 to explain how arguments are passed to functions according to the MIPS convention.

stack backtrace: A debugger function that interprets the state of the program stack to show the nest of function calls that has got to the current position. Depends wholly on strict stack usage conventions, which assembler programs must notate with standard directives.

stack frame: A fancy phrase for the piece of stack used by a particular function.

stack underrun: An error that occurs when you try to pop more off a stack than was ever put on it.

stale data: Term used for data lying about that has been superseded by a more recent write. It could be data in memory where a CPU's cached copy has been updated but has not yet been written back; it could be data in a cache where the memory contents have been replaced by a DMA device and the cache has not yet been invalidated. Using stale data is a bug.

stall: Condition in which the pipeline is frozen (no instruction state is advanced) while the CPU waits for some resource to do its thing.

standalone software: Software operating without the benefit of any kind of operating system or standard run-time environment.

Stanford: The San Francisco-area university where the MIPS academic project was run by Professor Hennessy, and from where the MIPS company was born.

static variable: C terminology for a data item that has a compile-time fixed place in memory.

status register: The MIPS register **SR**. In an older CPU it would have been the control/status register and in fact there are far more control functions than status-reading functions provided through **SR**.

`stdarg`: ANSI-approved C macro package that hides the implementation-dependent details of how to provide for functions with a variable number of arguments or arguments whose type can only be determined at run time (or both).

`strcmp`: C library function that compares two (null-terminated) strings.

`strcpy`: C library function that copies a (null-terminated) string.

strength reduction: Optimization technique in which an "expensive" operation is replaced, where possible, by one or a short sequence of "cheaper" operations. For example, multiply by a constant may be more efficiently replaced by a sequence of shift and add operations.

supercomputer: Colloquially, a computer built for performance essentially without regard for cost. Computer architecture people tend to be referring to processors with vector floating-point instructions.

superpipelined CPU: If pipelining is a good thing, perhaps it can be made better by cranking up the clock rate and breaking down execution stages into smaller pieces, each of which can fit into the shrunken clock cycle. The MIPS R4000 CPU was slightly superpipelined, breaking each of the I-fetch and D-cache access stages into two and removing half clock cycles to get an eight-stage pipeline. In doing so, the R4000 established that over a wide range of RISC-like architectures, five stages is just about optimal.

superscalar: A CPU implementation that attempts to start more than one instruction at the same time. This ugly word comes from an attempt to define a third alternative to supercomputers or superpipelined CPUs.

supervisor privilege level: Intermediate privilege level between kernel and user; see Section 3.3.2.

swap caches: To temporarily reverse the roles of the I- and D-caches, so that the cache maintenance functions can operate on the I-cache. Controlled by a status register bit.

swapper: See *byte-swapper*.

Sweazey, Paul: Lead author of the "FutureBus" paper, which first described the approach to cache coherence used by modern multiprocessors.

sync, synchronization barrier: An instruction that allows a programmer to indicate where the order of reads and writes in a program really matters. Any read or write preceding the **sync** instruction in program order must be carried out before any read or write following the **sync**.

synthesized instructions: See *instruction synthesis by assembler*.

syscall (system call): An instruction that produces a trap. It has a spare field, uninterpreted by the hardware, that software can use to encode different system call types.

t0–t9 register/temporaries: CPU registers **$8–$15**, **$24–$25**, conventionally used as temporaries; any function can use these registers. The downside is that the values can't be guaranteed to survive any function call.

TagHi, TagLo registers: Coprocessor 0 registers in R4000-style MIPS CPUs, which are staging posts for cache tag contents. See Section 4.10.

temporary register: See **t0**.

thrashing: Collapse of a heuristic optimization characterized by a repeated cycle of failure. Cache thrashing is a specific case where two locations in frequent use by a program compete for the same cache storage, repeatedly displacing each other and making the cache ineffective.

timer: As a facility for CPUs, a constant-rate counter with some mechanism to cause an interrupt when the counter reaches some specified value.

TLB (translation lookaside buffer): The associative store that translates program to physical page numbers. When the TLB doesn't contain the translation entry you need, the CPU takes an exception and it is up to system software to load an appropriate entry before returning to re-execute the faulting reference. See Chapter 6.

TLB, wired entries: The first eight TLB entries are conventionally reserved for statically configured entries and are not randomly replaced.

TLB Invalid exception: The exception taken when a TLB entry matches the address but is marked as not valid.

TLB miss: The exception taken when no TLB entry matches the program address.

TLB Modified exception: The exception taken when a TLB entry matches a store address but that entry is not flagged as writable.

TLB Probe: An instruction used to submit a program address to the TLB to see what translations are currently in force.

TLB refill: The process of adding a new entry to the TLB following a miss.

toolchain, toolkit: The complete set of tools required to produce runnable programs starting from source code (compiler, assembler, linker, librarian, etc.).

Toshiba: Japanese chip maker and MIPS licensee. Toshiba has not been prominent as a supplier of CPU components but is more visible in the core CPU market, where their R3900 design has been influential.

translated address or address region: A MIPS program (virtual) address that is destined to be translated through the TLB (or to cause an error). This includes the kuseg region where all user-privilege software must run as well as the mapped kernel-privilege region kseg2. The 64-bit CPUs have more translated regions.

translation lookaside buffer: *See TLB.*

trap: An exception caused by some internal event affecting a particular instruction.

tribyte: A load/store that carries 3 bytes of data. Produced only by the special instructions **lwl/lwr**, as described in Section 2.5.2.

trunc: The floating-point instruction **trunc** rounds a floating-point number to the next integer toward zero.

TTL: An acronym for transistor-transistor logic, this is a signalling convention that enables you to decide whether an electrical signal represents 1, 0, or something in between and undefined. TTL is based on the habits of some early 5V logic families. TTL signalling has commonly been used in all microprocessor systems at least up to the late 90s; its most likely replacement is a slight modification to fit in with 3.3V power supplies.

two-way set associative: See *cache, set-associative.*

UART (universal asynchronous receiver/transmitter): A serial port controller.

Ultrix: DEC's trade name for their BSD-family operating system running on MIPS-based DECstation computers. Note that Ultrix, unlike practically all other MIPS unix-like systems, runs in little-endian mode and thus is completely software incompatible with MIPS ABI or RISCware.

UMIPS: MIPS Corporation's first unix port, a version of 4.3BSD.

unaligned access exception: Trap caused by a memory reference (load/store word or halfword) at a misaligned address.

unaligned data: Data stored in memory but not guaranteed to be on the proper alignment boundary. Unaligned data can only be accessed reliably by special code sequences.

uncacheable: Memory areas where CPU reads and writes never search through or affect the cache. True of the region kseg1 or translated address regions where the TLB entry is flagged as uncached.

uncached: A CPU read/write that doesn't search through or write to the cache.

underflow: What happens when a floating-point operation should produce a result that is too small to represent properly. See also *denormalized.*

unified cache: A cache that is searched and updated for all CPU cycles, regardless of whether they are instruction fetches or data references. By contrast, most MIPS caches are split into I- and D-cache.

unimplemented instruction exception: Exception taken when the CPU does not recognize the instruction code; it is also used when it cannot successfully complete a floating-point instruction and wants the software emulator to take over.

union: A C declaration of an item of data that is going to have alternative interpretations with different data types. If you store data of one type and read it back as the other type, the result is highly unportable, in an interesting sort of way.

uniprocessor: A CPU that doesn't share its memory with another.

Unisoft V.4 (Uniplus+): Another version of Unix SVR4, this one MIPS ABI compliant.

unix-type: When lowercase, means a system something of the manner of real UNIX, but without any implication as to ownership or regulation. Includes freeware like Linux and OSs from the various OpenBSD and FreeBSD groups and commercial OSs like Sun's Solaris or SGI's Irix.

unmapped: The *kseg0,kseg1* address spaces.

unrolled loop: A loop in a program, transformed by arranging that (most of the time) the work of more than one iteration of the loop is done between jumps. It can often make programs go faster; it's sometimes done automatically by clever compilers.

user-privilege level: The lowest privilege state for a MIPS CPU, where only the regular instruction set is usable and program addresses must stay inside kuseg. An operating system can prevent user-privilege programs from interfering with each other or the OS.

user space: The space of user-privilege-accessible addresses (kuseg).

utlbmiss exception: An exception caused by a user-privilege address for which no mapping is present in the TLB. A utlbmiss exception is vectored to a unique, second exception entry point. This was done because this is by far the most common trap in a hardworking operating system, and it saves time to avoid the code that must work out what kind of trap has occurred. Strictly speaking, the name only applies to the R3000; R4000-style CPUs send all TLB misses through the special entry point.

v0–v1 registers: CPU registers `$2`–`$3`, conventionally used to hold values being returned by functions.

`varargs`: An old but now deprecated version of `stdarg`.

VAX: DEC's groundbreaking 32-bit minicomputer architecture, definitely not a RISC. The first minicomputer to support virtual memory (hence the "V").

vector, vector processor: A processor that has instructions that perform the same operation on a whole collection of data at a time, mostly floating-point operations. This is an example of parallel processing characterized as single instruction, multiple data (SIMD); it was the first kind of parallel processing to be useful. Number-crunching supercomputers depend on vector processing for their speed.

virtual address: See *program address*.

virtual memory (VM): A way of running an application without actually giving it all the memory it thinks it needs, but in such a way that it doesn't know the difference. You do this by arranging that an attempt to access something that isn't really there causes the operating system to be called in. The OS finds the required memory (be it code or data), changes the mapping so the application will find it, and then restarts the application at the instruction that led to the bad access. Bigger OSs (unix-like or modern Windows) always use virtual memory.

VMS: The operating system DEC developed for the VAX minicomputer.

void: A data type used to tidy up C programs, indicating that no value is available.

volatile: An attribute of declared data in either C or assembler. A volatile variable is one that may not simply behave like memory (i.e., does not simply return the value last stored in it). In the absence of this attribute, optimizers may assume that it is unnecessary to reread a value; and if the variable represents a memory-mapped I/O location you are polling, this will be a mistake.

VPN (virtual page number): The part of a program (virtual) address that gets translated. The low-order bits of the program address (which are the address within a page, usually a 4KB page) pass unchanged through to the physical address.

VxWorks: A real-time OS used in embedded applications, written and sold by Wind River Systems, Inc.

WatchHi, WatchLo register: Coprocessor 0 registers that implement a data watchpoint, available in some R4000-style CPUs.

watchpoint: A debugger feature that will cause the running program to be suspended and control passed back to the user whenever an access is made to the specified address. NEC's Vr4300 CPU has one of these.

wbflush: A standard name for the routine/macro that ensures that the write buffer is empty.

wbflush(): The MIPS-convention name for a function that returns only after all the CPU's pending writes are completed on the CPU bus interface.

Whitechapel: A briefly flowering UK-based unix workstation company that shipped the first MIPS desktop computers.

workstation: Used here to mean a desktop computer running a unix-like OS.

wraparound: Some memory systems (including the MIPS cache when isolated) have the property that accesses beyond the memory array size simply wrap around and start accessing the memory again at the beginning.

write buffer: A FIFO store that keeps both the address and data of a CPU write cycle (usually up to four of each). The CPU can continue execution while the writes are carried out as fast as the memory system will manage. A write buffer is particularly effective when used with a write-through cache.

write-back cache: See *cache, write-back*.

write-through cache: See *cache, write-through*.

XContext register: Coprocessor 0 register associated with the TLB (memory management hardware). Provides a fast way to process TLB misses on systems using a certain arrangement of page tables for 64-bit-addressed virtual memory regions.

zero register: CPU register $0, which is very special: Regardless of what is written to it, it always returns the value zero.

References

Books and Papers

Cohen, D. "On Holy Wars and a Plea for Peace." *USC/ISI IEN 137*, April 1, 1980.

Farquhar, E., and Bunce, P. *The MIPS Programmer's Handbook.* San Francisco: Morgan Kaufmann, 1994.

A readable introduction to the practice of programming MIPS at the low level. A strength is the use of lots of examples. A weakness is that the book left out some big pieces of the architecture (such as memory management, floating point, and advanced caches) because they didn't feature in the LSI embedded products that the book was meant to partner.

Heinrich, J. *MIPS R4000 User's Manual.* Englewood Cliffs, NJ: Prentice Hall, 1993.

The bible of the MIPS architecture; lots of details, but sometimes hard to find. It also takes a rather rigid view of what is implementation specific and can thus be left out. You can probably find a version of this to download from SGI's technical library.

Hennessy, J., and Patterson, D. *Computer Architecture: A Quantitative Approach.* San Francisco: Morgan Kaufmann, 1996.

Outside the MIPS-specific field, this is the only book worth having on modern computer architecture. Its sole defect is its size, but in this case it's worth it.

Kernighan, B., and Richie, D. *The C Programming Language*, 2nd edition. Englewood Cliffs, NJ: Prentice Hall, 1988.

This is the book to have if you want to learn more about C. You should probably get the updated ANSI edition now, although regrettably it is somewhat fatter.

Sweazey, P., and Smith, A. J. "A Class of Compatible Cache-Consistency Protocols and Their Support by the IEEE Future Bus." *Proceedings of the 13th International Symposium on Computer Architecture*, 1986.

On-Line Resources

Algorithmics: On the web at `http://www.algor.co.uk/`. This gives additional information about the author's more commercial activities and MIPS support operations.

IDT: IDT is on the web at `http://www.idt.com/`. This site gives a fair amount of on-line data.

MIPS Technologies: The current guardians of the MIPS architecture are a wholly owned subsidiary of Silicon Graphics and are on the web at `http://www.mips.com`. You'll find numerous links to other companies involved in MIPS.

NEC: NEC is not so used to being on-line. You can find some data starting at `http://www.nec.com/`.

QED: QED is the newest MIPS silicon vendor. QED keeps data sheets on-line and can be found at `http://www.qedinc.com/`.

R4000/R4400 User Manual: The second edition of Joe Heinrich's book is available on-line at `http://www.sgi.com/MIPS/products/r4400/UMan/`. You can view a web (HTML) version or download PostScript or Acrobat files.

SGI's FTP server: This is at `ftp://sgigate.sgi.com/pub/doc/`. It has some older documents.

SGI's technical document library: This is at `http://techpubs.sgi.com/`. Although it is focused on information for SGI workstation users, it seems to have documents available that are not to be found elsewhere. You'll find an assembler language manual under the Irix headings, and ISA manuals for the MIPS CPUs that are in current SGI products in the Hardware section.

As with any printed information about the world wide web, these pointers are likely to change. Fortunately, there are lots of ways of finding where they went.

Index